*Slavery
in the Great Lakes Region
of East Africa*

EASTERN AFRICAN STUDIES

Revealing Prophets
Edited by DAVID M. ANDERSON
& DOUGLAS H. JOHNSON

*East African Expressions
of Christianity*
Edited by THOMAS SPEAR
& ISARIA N. KIMAMBO

The Poor Are Not Us
Edited by DAVID M. ANDERSON
& VIGDIS BROCH-DUE

Potent Brews
JUSTIN WILLIS

Swahili Origins
JAMES DE VERE ALLEN

Being Maasai
Edited by THOMAS SPEAR
& RICHARD WALLER

Jua Kali Kenya
KENNETH KING

Control & Crisis in Colonial Kenya
BRUCE BERMAN

Unhappy Valley
Book One: State & Class
Book Two: Violence
& Ethnicity
BRUCE BERMAN
& JOHN LONSDALE

Mau Mau from Below
GREET KERSHAW

*The Mau Mau War
in Perspective*
FRANK FUREDI

*Squatters & the Roots
of Mau Mau* 1905-63
TABITHA KANOGO

*Economic & Social Origins
of Mau Mau* 1945-53
DAVID W. THROUP

Multi-Party Politics in Kenya
DAVID W. THROUP
& CHARLES HORNSBY

Empire State-Building
JOANNA LEWIS

*Decolonization & Independence
in Kenya* 1940-93
Edited by B.A. OGOT
& WILLIAM R. OCHIENG'

Eroding the Commons
DAVID ANDERSON

Penetration & Protest in Tanzania
ISARIA N. KIMAMBO

Custodians of the Land
Edited by GREGORY MADDOX, JAMES
L. GIBLIN & ISARIA N. KIMAMBO

*Education in the Development
of Tanzania* 1919-1990
LENE BUCHERT

The Second Economy in Tanzania
T.L. MALIYAMKONO
& M.S.D. BAGACHWA

*Ecology Control & Economic Development
in East African History*
HELGE KJEKSHUS

Siaya
DAVID WILLIAM COHEN
& E.S. ATIENO ODHIAMBO

*Uganda Now • Changing Uganda
Developing Uganda • From Chaos to Order
Religion & Politics in East Africa*
Edited by HOLGER BERNT HANSEN
& MICHAEL TWADDLE

*Kakungulu & the Creation
of Uganda* 1868-1928
MICHAEL TWADDLE

Controlling Anger
SUZETTE HEALD

Kampala Women Getting By
SANDRA WALLMAN

Political Power in Pre-Colonial Buganda
RICHARD J. REID

Alice Lakwena & the Holy Spirits
HEIKE BEHREND

Slaves, Spices & Ivory in Zanzibar
ABDUL SHERIFF

Zanzibar Under Colonial Rule
Edited by ABDUL SHERIFF &
ED FERGUSON

*The History & Conservation of Zanzibar
Stone Town*
Edited by ABDUL SHERIFF

Pastimes & Politics
LAURA FAIR

*Ethnicity & Conflict in
the Horn of Africa*
Edited by KATSUYOSHI FUKUI
& JOHN MARKAKIS

*Conflict, Age & Power in
North East Africa*
Edited by EISEI KURIMOTO
& SIMON SIMONSE

*Property Rights & Political
Development in Ethiopia & Eritrea*
SANDRA FULLERTON JOIREMAN

Revolution & Religion in Ethiopia
ØYVIND M. EIDE

Brothers at War
TEKESTE NEGASH &
KJETIL TRONVOLL

From Guerrillas to Government
DAVID POOL

Mau Mau & Nationhood
Edited by E.S. ATIENO ODHIAMBO
& JOHN LONSDALE

*A History of Modern Ethiopia,
1855-1991*
(2nd edn) BAHRU ZEWDE

Pioneers of Change in Ethiopia
BAHRU ZEWDE

Remapping Ethiopia
Edited by W. JAMES, D. DONHAM,
E. KURIMOTO & A. TRIULZI

Southern Marches of Imperial Ethiopia
Edited by DONALD L. DONHAM
& WENDY JAMES

A Modern History of the Somali
(4th edn)
I.M. LEWIS

*Islands of Intensive Agriculture in
East Africa*
Edited by MATS WIDGREN
& JOHN E.G. SUTTON

Leaf of Allah
EZEKIEL GEBISSA

*Dhows & the Colonial Economy
of Zanzibar* 1860-1970
ERIK GILBERT

African Womanhood in Colonial Kenya
TABITHA KANOGO

African Underclass
ANDREW BURTON

In Search of a Nation
Edited by GREGORY H. MADDOX
& JAMES L. GIBLIN

A History of the Excluded
JAMES L. GIBLIN

Black Poachers, White Hunters
EDWARD I. STEINHART

Ethnic Federalism
DAVID TURTON

Crisis & Decline in Bunyoro
SHANE DOYLE

*Emancipation without Abolition in
German East Africa*
JAN-GEORG DEUTSCH

*Women, Work & Domestic
Virtue in Uganda* 1900-2003
GRACE BANTEBYA KYOMUHENDO &
MARJORIE KENISTON McINTOSH

Cultivating Success in Uganda
GRACE CARSWELL

*War in Pre-Colonial
Eastern Africa*
RICHARD REID

*Slavery in the Great Lakes Region
of East Africa*
Edited by HENRI MÉDARD &
SHANE DOYLE

* forthcoming

Slavery in the Great Lakes Region of East Africa

Edited by

HENRI MÉDARD
Lecturer in History, University of Paris I
Panthéon Sorbonne & Cemaf

&

SHANE DOYLE
Lecturer in History, University of Leeds

James Currey
OXFORD

Fountain Publishers
KAMPALA

EAEP
NAIROBI

Ohio University Press
ATHENS

James Currey Ltd
73 Botley Road
Oxford OX2 0BS

Fountain Publishers
PO Box 488
Kampala

East African Educational Publishers
PO Box 45314
Nairobi

Ohio University Press
19 Circle Drive, The Ridges
Athens, Ohio 45701

© James Currey Ltd 2007
First published 2007

1 2 3 4 5 11 10 09 08 07

British Library Cataloguing in Publication Data
Slavery in the Great Lakes Region of East Africa. - (East
    African studies)
    1. Slavery - Great Lakes Region (Africa) - History - 19th
    century 2. Slavery - Great Lakes Region (Africa) - History
    - 20th century
    I. Medard, Henri II. Doyle, Shane (Shane Declan)
    306.3'62'09676

ISBN 978-1-84701-602-7 (James Currey Cloth)
ISBN 978-1-84701-603-4 (James Currey Paper)
ISBN 978-9970-02-727-9 (Fountain Publishers Paper)

**Library of Congress Cataloging-in-Publication Data
available on request**

ISBN-10 0-8214-1792-4 (Ohio University Press Cloth)
ISBN-13 978-0-8214-1792-8 (Ohio University Press Cloth)
ISBN-10 0-8214-1793-2 (Ohio University Press Paper)
ISBN-13 978-0-8214-1793-5 (Ohio University Press Paper)

Typeset in 10/11 pt Baskerville
by Longhouse Publishing Services, Cumbria, UK

To François Renault

Contents

List of Maps & Tables	ix
Notes on Contributors	x
Introduction HENRI MÉDARD	1

1
Violence, Marginality, Scorn & Honour
Language evidence of slavery to the eighteenth century — 38
DAVID SCHOENBRUN

2
Notes on the Rise of Slavery & Social Change in Unyamwezi
c. 1860–1900 — 76
JAN-GEORG DEUTSCH

3
Slavery & Forced Labour in the Eastern Congo
1850–1910 — 111
DAVID NORTHRUP

4
Legacies of Slavery in North West Uganda
The story of the 'One-Elevens' — 124
MARK LEOPOLD

5
Human Booty in Buganda
Some observations on the seizure of people in war
c.1700–1890 — 145
RICHARD REID

6
Stolen People & Autonomous Chiefs
in Nineteenth-Century Buganda
The social consequences of non-free followers — 161
HOLLY HANSON

Contents

7
Women's Experiences of Enslavement & Slavery
in Late Nineteenth & Early Twentieth-Century Uganda   174
MICHAEL W. TUCK

8
Slavery & Other Forms of Social Oppression
in Ankole
1890–1940   189
EDWARD I. STEINHART

9
The Slave Trade in Burundi & Rwanda
at the Beginning of German Colonisation
1890–1906   210
JEAN-PIERRE CHRÉTIEN

10
Bunyoro & the Demography
of Slavery Debate   231
Fertility, kinship & assimilation
SHANE DOYLE

References   252
Index   269

List of Maps & Tables

Maps

1	The Great Lakes Region of East Africa on the eve of colonial conquest	xiv
2	The East African slave trade routes in the nineteenth century	9
3	Buganda's expansion (c.1640–1900)	146
4	Bunyoro, Nkore and the Sudanese (1870–1900)	190
5	Missions and trading places in Burundi and Rwanda (c.1895–1905)	211

Tables

7.1	How women became slaves	176
7.2	Prices of women/girls sold into slavery	178
9.1	Emancipated slaves at Usumbura, 1899–1901	216

Notes on Contributors

Jean-Pierre Chrétien first taught history at l'École Normale Supérieure of Burundi before moving to the University of Lille III. He is a former director of the African Studies Centre of the University of Paris I (now included in Cemaf (Centre d'Études des Mondes Africains), and is now a researcher at CNRS (Centre National de Recherche Scientifique). He has published widely on East Africa: *Burundi. L'histoire retrouvée* (1993); *Rwanda, les médias du génocide* (1995); *The Great Lakes of Africa* (2003 [French edition, 2000]). He has also contributed to the *Unesco General History of Africa* and has been the editor of several collective books dealing with ethnicity and the relations between memory and history in Africa. His current research focuses on the history of the Great Lakes Region of East Africa in the nineteenth and twentieth centuries.

Jan-Georg Deutsch studied at the University of Hanover and the School of Oriental and African Studies before completing his Habilitation at Humboldt University in Berlin. He is currently a University Lecturer in Commonwealth History at the University of Oxford. His research on the social and economic history of West and East Africa in the nineteenth and twentieth centuries has recently focused on the end of slavery. He is currently working on the history of Zanzibar. He has published two monographs, *Educating the Middlemen. A Political and Economic History of Statutory Cocoa Marketing in Nigeria, 1936–1947* (1995) and *Emancipation without Abolition in German East Africa c.1884–1914* (2006), and co-edited *Geschichte in Afrika. Einführung in Probleme und Debatten* (1997), *African Modernities. Entangled Meanings in Current Debate* (2002) and *Space on the Move. Transformations of the Indian Ocean Seascape in the Nineteenth and Twentieth Centuries* (2002).

Shane Doyle is a Lecturer in History at the University of Leeds. He is the author of several articles on the history of western Uganda and has

Notes on Contributors

recently published *Crisis and Decline in Bunyoro: Population and Environment in Western Uganda, 1860–1955* (2006). His current research focuses on the history of demographic change, sexual behaviour and the family in East Africa.

Holly Hanson is Associate Professor in History at Mount Holyoke College. She has a variety of research interests, including agrarian change in Africa, social history of the Buganda kingdom, pre-colonial African political culture, and globalisation as a historical process. These interests recently culminated in the publication of *Landed Obligation: The Practice of Power in Buganda* (2003). She has also published numerous articles on a variety of topics, from Ganda women to global inequality.

Mark Leopold is a Lecturer in Social Anthropology at the University of Sussex. He is the author of *Inside West Nile: Violence, History and Representation on an African Frontier* (2005), based on archival research and ethnographic fieldwork in North West Uganda, by the borders with Sudan and the Democratic Republic of Congo. He is currently working on Idi Amin as an icon of evil, and on the prospects for peace in southern Sudan.

Henri Médard is a Lecturer in African History at the University of Paris I Panthéon Sorbonne and Cemaf (Centre d'Études des Mondes Africains). He is the author of several articles on the history of Buganda and of *Le royaume du Buganda au XIX siècle. Mutations politiques et religieuses d'un grand État d'Afrique de l'Est* (2007).

David Northrup is Professor of African History at Boston College and immediate past president of the World History Association. He is the author of *Trade without Rulers: Pre-colonial Economic Development in Eastern Nigeria* (1978); *Beyond the Bend in the River: African Labor in Eastern Zaire, 1865–1940* (1988); *Indentured Labor in the Age of Imperialism, 1834–1922* (1995); *Africa's Discovery of Europe, 1450–1850* (2002). His classroom-directed works include *The Earth and Its Peoples: A Global History* (3rd ed., 2004), *The Atlantic Slave Trade* (2nd ed., 2002), and *Cross-currents in the Black Atlantic, 1770–1965* (2007). He is currently working on a history of how English became the global language.

Richard Reid is a Lecturer in History at the University of Durham. He works on African and Imperial history, focusing recently on the nature of warfare in pre-colonial Eastern Africa, the modern political history of Eritrea and the origins of recent conflict in the Horn of Africa. In addition to a large number of articles he has published *Political Power in Pre-Colonial Buganda: Economy, Society and Warfare in the Nineteenth Century* (2002).

David Schoenbrun is Associate Professor of History at Northwestern University. His first book, *A Green Place, A Good Place: Agrarian Change, Gender, and*

Notes on Contributors

Social Organization between the Great Lakes to the 15th Century (1998) was named a 1999 Choice Outstanding Academic Title. He has published articles in the *Uganda Journal, Journal of African History, African Archaeological Review, History and Theory, History Compass*, and the *American Historical Review*. He is working on a book on violence between the Great Lakes over the last millennium.

Edward Steinhart is Professor of African History at Texas Tech University. His early work on state formation and the colonial encounter in western Uganda produced numerous articles and *Conflict and Collaboration: The Kingdoms of Western Uganda, 1890–1907* (1977). Recent research on the history of hunting in Kenya has resulted in a number of publications, including *Black Poachers, White Hunters* (2006). Other projects include a history of slavery in East Africa, and the evolution of modern religious movements in Uganda.

Michael W. Tuck is currently Associate Professor of History at Northeastern Illinois University in Chicago. His research on the social history of nineteenth- and twentieth-century Uganda has appeared in *The International Journal of African Historical Studies, History in Africa*, and in edited volumes from Routledge and Cambridge. His latest research project is a comparative examination of the integration of rural communities into Atlantic trade. Using case studies from The Gambia, Tanzania, Angola and the United States, it examines the trade in beeswax from the fifteenth through the twentieth centuries.

Acknowledgement

The editors and publishers gratefully acknowledge
the financial contribution of CEMAF, Centre d'études des
mondes africains (CNRS, Université de Paris 1, Université de
Provence, EPHE) towards the publication of this book.

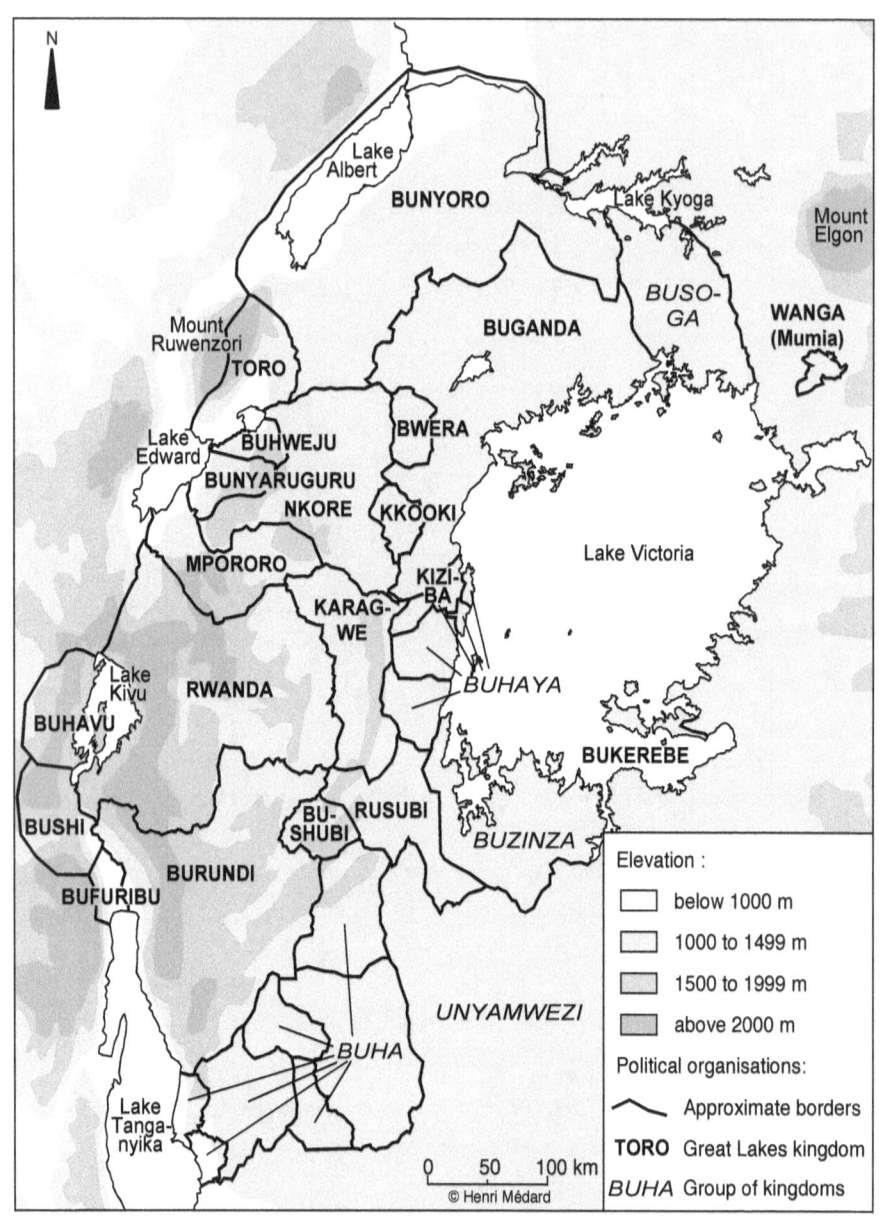

Map 1 The Great Lakes Region of East Africa on the eve of colonial conquest

Introduction

HENRI MÉDARD

While there is an extensive literature on the history and anthropology of the Great Lakes or interlacustrine region of East Africa (see Map 1), there are few works which focus on slavery. This constitutes a striking contrast with the historiography of the rest of the African continent in which slavery and the slave trade are some of the most prominent themes. Until recently authors working on the Great Lakes region considered that the institution was never a feature of Great Lakes societies or that it existed for only a very short time during the late nineteenth century and even then was of marginal significance, so they did not write about it.[1] In the late 1980s Michael Twaddle re-opened the debate by demonstrating the importance and longevity of slavery in Buganda, but little new work was done in response to this. Indeed, the idea for this book came when Michael Twaddle examined Henri Médard's 2001 dissertation on the nineteenth-century history of Buganda and commented on how little attention had been paid to slavery in it.[2] This led in turn to a conference held in Paris on 16–17 December 2002, hosted by the Centre de Recherches Africaines (University of Paris I/Centre National de la Recherche Scientifique) at which most of the contributors to this book were present.

The starting point of the project, then, was the need to answer very basic questions. Did slavery exist in that region? How old was it? Was the institution marginal or central to these societies? The aim of this book is to demonstrate the diversity of slave institutions across the region and to open up the subject to future and more specific research.[3]

The debate originally concerned Buganda and Bunyoro, two kingdoms in present-day Uganda with intertwined histories. Why enlarge the subject to the Great Lakes region of East Africa? Why not a wider area, say Africa or East Africa? The primary reason is that the Great Lakes region has a distinctive cultural unity. It is a fairly coherent area, socially, religiously and politically (the region is dominated by the interlacustrine kingdoms). Many similar institutions can be found across the region, some of which should have been structured around slavery. Furthermore, by choosing the Great Lakes region of East Africa we have tried to avoid thinking about the area's precolonial past within the framework of the colonial and postcolonial borders, and also to overcome the conceptual biases/distortions that result from the geographical organisation of colonial archives. This geographical separation is aggravated by contemporary language barriers that divide the region into Francophone Burundi, Rwanda and the Democratic Republic of the Congo, the former Belgian colonies, and Anglophone Uganda, Tanganyika, Zanzibar, Kenya and Sudan, the former British colonies. The picture is further complicated by the existence of the written sources relating to the pre-1918 colony of German East Africa (which consisted of Tanganyika, Burundi and Rwanda) and others relating to the Egyptian Sudan from the nineteenth and twentieth centuries written mostly in Turkish, Arabic, French and English.

In physical terms the Great Lakes region of East Africa extends from Lakes Albert and Kyoga in the north to Lake Victoria in the east, Lake Tanganyika in the south and Lakes Edward and Kivu in the west. In other words, with today's borders, it includes southern and western Uganda, north-western Tanzania, Burundi, Rwanda and the eastern fringes of the Democratic Republic of the Congo. Its two or three sub-regions have long maintained intensive contact with each other (in the form of, for example, origin myths, migrations, trade and competition). Linguistically, languages spoken in this region belong to the Great Lakes Bantu family.

This collection of essays shows, firstly, that slavery was much more important in this region than has usually been assumed and, secondly, that the role of non-coastal Africans in the slave trade was more complex and important than has hitherto been recognised. These conclusions indicate that slavery and the slave trade in the Great Lakes region were not so different from the rest of Africa. In particular, these essays largely reinforce Edward Alpers' emphasis on the importance of African initiative in the East African slave trade.[4] But the inhabitants of the Great Lakes region were much more autonomous of the intercontinental market than Africans further south, whose trade was largely focused on Kilwa and the Indian Ocean slave network beyond. The role of local demand was even more important around Lake Victoria than in the Ruvuma and Zambezi valleys.

These concepts will be explored further in this Introduction. We have chosen to illustrate the arguments made in this introductory chapter mostly with references to Buganda. This is not to privilege Buganda over the rest of the region, but instead reflects the imbalance of sources and knowledge. Much more is known about slavery in Buganda than in any other part of the region.

Introduction

The Nature of the Sources

European sources relating to slavery in the Great Lakes region also tended to be distorted by the alternating imperatives of concealment or propaganda. In general, where slavery persisted, it was an embarrassment to colonial officials, though in the Great Lakes region this was more true for British and Belgian officials than for German officers. References to slavery are almost absent from colonial archival documents after 1900 in Uganda (at any rate those concerning Buganda, Nkore (Ankole) and Bunyoro). From the colonial records it would be impossible to guess that these societies had been structured around slavery only a few decades previously. The absence of post-conquest colonial references to slavery in Uganda may be indicative of a desire to avoid discussing the subject.[5] Yet the ending of the slave trade had previously been used and over-used as a justification for the colonial takeover, not only by British, German and Belgian imperialists, but by most of the Christian missions as well (see David Northrup's and Jean-Pierre Chrétien's chapters). For example, the annihilation of Bunyoro in the 1890s was justified by the necessity of fighting the Arab slave trade, even though the Baganda and the Sudanese troops used by the imperial forces were as much involved in the slave trade as the Banyoro (see Shane Doyle's chapter). The same can be said of the wars against the Baganda Muslims between 1888 and 1893 and of the Baganda rebellion and Sudanese mutiny of 1897–9.

    In the absence of reliable colonial sources, Africanist historians have tended to turn to oral or written African sources instead. Documents that were written by Africans from the Great Lakes region in the late nineteenth and early twentieth centuries mention slavery, but only briefly. Most of the authors were high in the chiefly hierarchy and so were not preoccupied with such lowly people. Slavery was a dangerous subject for them, better to be avoided or belittled (the major reason for Baganda chiefs to fall out of favour with the British administration in the 1890s was the accusation of slavery). The Ugandan authors were Christians, and so did not wish to appear too knowledgeable about slavery, just as too much knowledge about women suggested sin (to make matters worse, most slaves were women).

    Oral sources have seldom yielded much on the matter of slavery, for a very simple reason; early scholars, being unaware of or uninterested in the matter, did not ask about it. When they did, informants were not always eager to speak about such an embarrassing theme.[6] However, E.M.K. Mulira in the early 1950s managed to collect for Audrey Richards a limited but precious amount of information on slavery using oral sources.[7] Michele Wagner's paper on Buha given orally at the conference and Eugénie Mujawimana's undergraduate thesis on Rwanda show that the obstacles can be overcome. Jean-Pierre Chrétien, Shane Doyle and

Edward Steinhart have also relied on interviews collected at different times during their fieldwork. It is our hope that this book will encourage future collections of oral data on this theme.

Early ethnographic work such as that of the missionary John Roscoe, who lived in Uganda off and on between the 1890s and the 1920s, mentions slavery, among many other things, but in the descriptive and unhistorical way of the time.[8] The anthropologist Lucy Mair also offered rich insights, but she was interested in the Uganda of the 1930s, when slavery was no longer functioning.[9] Quite logically many of the scholars in the 1950s and 1960s felt awkward about the exaggeration of slavery in colonial propaganda and literature.[10] They strove to show newer, more positive and more contemporary aspects of the societies they were studying.[11]

The 1970s did produce a handful of significant works, but these did not have the impact that might have been expected. In 1974 Roger Botte published the first article wholly devoted to unfree labour in the region, about the '*abashumba*' in Burundi.[12] Their status was extremely close to slavery, and some of them could be and were called slaves (*umuja*), though others had kin and were free to change masters (see Jean-Pierre Chrétien's chapter, as well as Edward Steinhart's discussion of the related institution of '*abashumba*' in Nkore and David Schoenbrun's analysis of the root word -súmba). Though Botte's article has been famous in some circles, this was more because of the contemporary Marxist preoccupations about social classes than the careful nature of his use of oral and written sources on unfree labour. It has been mostly unnoticed by scholars interested in slavery. A year later the same Marxist preoccupation about social classes led Walter Rusch to emphasise the role of slavery in Buganda.[13] The Marxist approach has been very important in focusing attention on slavery, but its influence has declined as its theoretical aspect has fallen out of fashion. The best example of this phenomenon is in France where the formerly famous anthropologist, Claude Meillassoux, had in less than fifteen years fallen into total oblivion even among his former disciples and students, although his recent death revived interest in his work (he had, however, continued to be used in the English-speaking world). In the case of Walter Rusch, the language barrier (the book is in German) and his reliance on a limited range of sources (only published texts available in Europe) have made sure his book had a very limited impact.

One exception is worth noting, though. Rusch's work helped John Iliffe in 1987 to write his brief but illuminating pages about the condition of slaves in Buganda. Iliffe's focus on poverty and hunger gives an original view on slavery, illuminating other aspects of slave life than the usual labour, exploitation, violence and domination issues.[14] Hartwig's original work on Bukerebe (Ukerewe) has been widely read. However, the specialists of the more cattle-obsessed and land-based kingdoms further west detected few similarities between the societies they studied and this small island kingdom on Lake Victoria.[15] Augustin Nzanze also mentions

Introduction

slavery very briefly in his work, but his concern is to imply that the exploitation of the Hutu by the Tutsi in the nineteenth and twentieth centuries was as harsh and shameful as slavery.[16]

The slave trade and its impact have received more attention than slavery as an institution, mainly thanks to the work of François Renault, Jacques Marissal and Eugénie Mujawimana.[17] One important early work was John Milner Gray's 1949 biography of a Muganda slave, Majwara. Gray showed how Majwara's father, Namujulirwa, a very important chief of Kings Suuna and Muteesa, head of the large province of Buddu in southern Buganda, fell from grace and was executed. His family, including the young Majwara, were sold into slavery. Most of the article deals with the later life of this former slave after he was bought in 1871 from a Swahili trader in Tabora by the explorer, Henry Morton Stanley. Majwara accompanied Stanley, then the missionary David Livingstone, and then Stanley again across the whole of Africa.[18] A number of other publications deal with the Indian Ocean or Sudanese trade, which taken together do contribute towards a global understanding of the slave trade. But these are essentially local studies, mainly focusing on other sub-regions outside the Great Lakes: Southern Sudan, the Nuba mountains, the Swahili coast, today's border lands between Tanzania, Mozambique, and Zambia, or the Congo forest.[19] Because of the organisation of the sources and because of the links the authors are trying to build between pre-colonial history and national history, the geographical focus can be slightly artificial.[20]

These then are the sources most used by the anthropologists and historians working on the Great Lakes of East Africa. Three factors have drawn historians towards the study of slavery anew. The first is that teaching African history courses (which most of us do) compels historians specialised in this region to know a minimal amount about the general literature on slavery in Africa. This leads to new questions and new approaches to the region's history. During the last thirty years knowledge on slavery in Africa has advanced so much that it has allowed regional specialists to look at their local sources anew. Pier Larson is the foremost example of this; he has used this huge general literature to enable him to construct a vivid image of slavery in Madagascar before the nineteenth century, despite the very scanty sources.[21]

The second reason is the systematic use by David Schoenbrun of historical linguistics as a source on slavery. The third reason is the use of neglected European sources, particularly the records of the French White Fathers mission. These sources provide especially rich insights into the history of slavery in the Great Lakes region of East Africa. Before the 1980s the written sources that had been most heavily used were those written in English (those of Protestant missionaries and colonial officers) concerning the period before the First World War, and those in both English and French (for Burundi and Rwanda) after that period. For obvious reasons, with the decline of slavery, sources related to our subject are mostly found in older documents dating from before 1914. The Catholic missionaries, many of whom were French, are particularly interesting because they actually bought and owned many slaves. The Church Missionary Society (CMS), the main Protestant mission (Anglophone and well-studied) in the area, rejected the policy of redeeming slaves, and so what they have to say on slavery is quite marginal.

It is not surprising that the first major breakthrough on slavery in the region was made in 1983 by Eugénie Mujawimana who was supervised by Father Roger Heremans, a White Father teaching history at the University of Rwanda. Unfortunately this dissertation is hard to come by, and has remained unpublished. It therefore has had little impact on the scholarly community. It seems, moreover, that Michael Twaddle's pioneering work on slavery in Buganda[22] came only after he had access to the White Fathers Archives, decades after he had first seen the CMS and colonial archives and conducted interviews in Uganda. But even with the Catholic White Fathers and Mill Hill Fathers, the amount of information collected on slavery is not large compared with other places. The White Fathers in Buganda bought only a couple of hundred slaves, whereas the White Fathers on Lake Tanganyika, just outside our zone of interest, during the same timespan bought ten times as many. This obviously had an impact on the frequency of references to slavery in the sources. Slavery in the White Fathers mission on Lake Tanganyika is much better documented. The same contrast can be found with other missions in Eastern Africa or Sudan. The Verona Fathers in Sudan, the London Missionary Society and Berlin Mission Society in south-west Tanzania, and the Holy Ghost Fathers on the Indian Ocean coast have deposited much more information on slavery than the missions in the area we are interested in here.[23]

The explanation is simple. The Catholic missionaries in Buganda and surrounding areas had little need to buy converts because of their dramatic evangelical success among the free population. Most of the energy and the hopes of the missionaries were focused on these free converts, not on redeemed slaves. It is not surprising therefore that some of the richest documents containing life histories of Ganda slaves were collected not in Buganda, but on the southern side of Lake Victoria where the White Fathers were less successful among the free population and had more time to spare on their redeemed slaves.[24] In Buganda itself most information on slavery is to be found in documents dating from 1879 to 1883 before the number of free converts became overwhelming.[25] After 1883, only during the inquiry into the potential canonisation of the Uganda Martyrs of 1886, some of whom were former slaves, did missionaries pay particular attention to slavery.[26]

After this point missionaries only tended to discuss Ganda slavery when it touched on a particular theological issue. Thus, for example, Michael Twaddle (at the White Fathers archives in Rome)[27] and Michael Tuck (at the Mill Hill Fathers archives in Jinja) (see his chapter) have studied documents dating from the early twentieth century concerning 'Marriage

Cases'. These were compiled when missionaries interviewed parishioners in order to make sure they did not baptise polygamists. A large part of these life histories refer to the period before slavery was abolished and before what Frederick Cooper has described as 'the removal of its coercive and exploitative dimensions'. Such sources avoid the danger of reducing slavery to what was left, its residual 'social dimension'.[28]

The other important neglected sources on slavery are in German (see Jan-Georg Deutsch and Jean-Pierre Chrétien's chapters). The standard colonial approach to slavery in Africa was that adopted by the British, French and Belgian governments, officially banning the institution but choosing to ignore continuing slaving practices. The behaviour of the German colonial authorities in Tanganyika varied significantly from this norm. The Germans kept slavery (but not the slave trade) legal and chose to control it openly (see Jan-Georg Deutsch's chapter). For example, in Unyamwezi colonial law stated that slaves who had misbehaved could be caned but the actual execution of the sentence had to be carried out by representatives of the German authorities. The frankness of the German authorities on issues of slavery permits new insights into the nature of slavery both before and during the era of abolition.

The Impact of the Slave Trade

The use of these new sources in this book transforms our understanding of slavery in the Great Lakes region of East Africa. Many historians thought slavery and the slave trade appeared in the Great Lakes region only with the growth of the Swahili trade from the Indian Ocean coast during the nineteenth century. It is now quite obvious that this is not so. David Schoenbrun's chapter using historical linguistics shows that slavery (or very similar institutions) was long established in this region, probably as old as the societies themselves. Michael Twaddle had an intuition of this point, acquired from more traditional sources, in his 1988 paper.[29] At first glance these papers go against the so-called 'transformation theory', which is best illustrated in Paul Lovejoy's book *Transformations in Slavery*. This theory emphasises the leading role of the slave trade in the rise of slavery in Africa.[30] Instead, they would appear to support John Thornton's theory that the slave trade grew rapidly in Africa because slavery was already well established.[31] François Renault had made this point concerning the East African slave trade as early as 1971.[32]

To say that slavery was ancient, however, does not mean that the institution never evolved. In other words slavery was subject to historical change. Gerald Hartwig showed this clearly in his work on Bukerebe in 1977. Slavery appeared (or new forms of the institution were established) in the seventeenth century, but was then modified in the nineteenth century through the impact of the Swahili trade.[33] Did the nineteenth-century slave trade transform these societies from societies in which slavery was incidental to their structure to societies where slavery was central? It is hard to detect a common pattern. Unyamwezi, according to Jan-Georg Deutsch, did follow this trajectory. But according to Holly Hanson's chapter, slavery became a fundamental part of Buganda's social structure in the eighteenth century if not before, prior to the kingdom's connection to the Indian Ocean and Sudanese slave trade networks. In societies such as Burundi, meanwhile, it is still doubtful whether slavery had become central even as late as 1900. Most of the chapters in this book confirm that a major modification of slavery took place in reaction to the slave trade, but whether or not such change made slavery central is still a matter of debate.

It is obvious that African slavery cannot be studied independently from the slave trade. For example, in Rwanda one-third to one-fifth of the slaves were said by informants to be retained by the inhabitants of the major slave transit and trading points.[34] Nor can the international slave trade in East Africa and Sudan be separated from that of ivory. Even if one product seems to dominate, without the other the trade would have collapsed due to the combination of a lack of profit, transport or currency. Ivory and slaves were exchanged for a variety of imports from the wider world and facilitated the merging of the new long-distance trade with long-standing networks of African trade (in copper from Katanga or in less specialised products such as food, goats, salt or hoes.)

In the nineteenth century the Great Lakes region of East Africa found itself at the confluence of three trade networks of very unequal importance, stemming from the Indian Ocean, the Nile Valley and the Ethiopian Highlands. As Thomas Vernet pointed out at the conference in 2002,[35] the East African coast has a long history of slave trading dating from antiquity. This does not, of course, mean that this coastal trade never evolved. In the eighteenth century massive exportation towards the islands of La Réunion and Mauritius supplemented the older trade with the Arab world. The growth of the slave trade continued into the nineteenth century in spite of the progressive suppression of coastal exports. Overseas markets were replaced by demand from expanding plantation agriculture relying on slave labour in the Zanzibari Empire, the most famous product of this agriculture being cloves.

Before the nineteenth century most of the coastal settlements of present-day Kenya and Tanzania are thought to have not extended their contacts deep into the interior because of geographical obstacles. According to Andrew Roberts, the East African interior possessed a number of regional trade networks based on local production of, for example, salt or iron, or on ecological complementarities.[36] These networks were interconnected and goods from the coast, changing hands many times, would have meandered towards the Great Lakes region of East Africa (this is how François Renault understood the central slave trade in the nineteenth century, with a surplus of slaves flowing eastwards).[37] This explains the presence of glass beads, in very limited amounts, found in pre-

Introduction

Map 2 *The East African slave trade routes in the nineteenth century*

eighteenth-century archaeological sites in Uganda and Rwanda. The interconnections may also account for the increase of epidemics linked to the growing contact between the coast and the interior which appears to date from the end of the eighteenth century. According to Sheriff, it was the constant rise of international ivory prices that enabled the unification of these regional trade systems into one single network during the nineteenth century.[38] But East Africa's integration into the globalising economy was not solely driven by coastal initiatives. The presence at the coast of the inland groups that were most prominent in long-distance trade across the region, the Kamba (from eastern Kenya) and the Nyamwezi (from central Tanzania),[39] was mentioned for the first time in the seventeenth and eighteenth centuries respectively. It was only in 1825 that the first traders from the coast reached Unyamwezi. In c.1830 Lake Tanganyika was attained and about ten years later the lake was crossed. To the north, Buganda was reached during the 1840s via Karagwe.[40] Swahili were already present in Bunyoro when Speke reached the kingdom in the early 1860s.[41]

The main route into the interior left the coast near Zanzibar from harbours like Bagamayo and proceeded through what is today central Tanzania to Unyamwezi where it branched off to either Lake Tanganyika or Lake Victoria (see map 2). Other routes, such as that through Maasailand are not as well known, though it was via this latter route that the earliest reports concerning Bukerebe reached the coast in around 1811.[42] Insecurity and logistical problems seem to have caused this route to decline by the 1850s, before European interest in the interior of East Africa picked up. It linked the ports of Tanga, Pangani and Mombasa to Kilimanjaro and then went through Maasailand to Bukerebe and the east coast of Lake Victoria. It is unfortunate that we know so little about what is probably the oldest direct link between the Great Lakes region of East Africa and the Indian Ocean coast. We also know very little about the important Swahili community resident in what is today western Kenya, and their relations with Busoga and what is today eastern Uganda. At the end of the nineteenth century, though, the sources do indicate that the areas around Mount Elgon were hit hard by the slave and ivory trades coming from Buganda and Mumia.[43]

The impact of long-distance trade through the Sudan, Congo and Abyssinia was much less significant than that of the Indian Ocean coast. Mark Leopold deals briefly with the Sudanese trade in his chapter. The chronology here is easier to establish. In 1841 the great flooded plains of the Nile (the Sudd) in what is today Southern Sudan were crossed for the first time by Egyptian boats. Before that no contact across the marshes can be safely assumed. The rare trade goods found among the Bari and the Pari came from Abyssinia and via Bunyoro.[44] The latter was reached by Sudanese traders in the 1860s, around the same time as the Swahili traders. Sudanese goods, however, were not competitive with items imported from the Indian Ocean. Instead the Sudanese interacted mostly

Introduction

through the use of force or political interference. Their relations with the indigenous rulers were characterised by conflict and violence. The successful resistance of Bunyoro and Buganda limited Sudanese influence to Bunyoro's borderlands and the shores of Lake Albert. The highhanded behaviour of the Sudanese was very different from the submissive coastal Swahili behaviour in kingdoms like Karagwe, Buganda and Bunyoro. On the other hand, there was not much difference between Sudanese and Swahili behaviour in other areas, in the Congo forest, for example. It is telling that Swahili and Manyema who reached Burundi, Rwanda, Nkore (see Edward Steinhart's chapter) or Bunyoro from the west behaved in a similarly brutal way to the Sudanese who came directly from the Nile. The Swahili and Manyema had adopted predatory habits in the Congo, because the longer distance their goods had to travel from the Indian Ocean meant that their prices could not compete with those of goods that had followed a more direct route. These raiders, however, were not as militarily organised as the formidable Sudanese, lacking the necessary physical might to overcome kingdoms like Nkore, Bunyoro, Burundi or Rwanda.[45] The antagonistic relations that resulted help explain the limited impact these Manyema slave raiders had on the Great Lakes region before the general free-for-all of the 1890s. As for Abyssinian traders, very little is known about them. They may have reached the area east of Bunyoro in the 1890s. At the end of the century ivory from Bunyoro may have been sold in Brava on the Somali coast.[46] The scarce sources found at the Uganda National Archives are full of potential lies and exaggerations, because the Abyssinian advance was used to impose restrictions on the movement of the local Ugandan population and to compel the British government to act against Abyssinian infiltration.

Coastal or Sudanese traders are easier to identify than local African traders in the contemporary sources because of their appearance (dress, language and religion) and the scale of their business. They have therefore attracted more attention from historians. It is nonetheless likely that traders from the interior, such as Banyamwezi,[47] Bahaya, Banyambo (from Karagwe), Basubi, Banyoro and Bakerebe did control much of the slave trade, though they usually operated on a smaller scale (one to ten slaves). These local traders were almost invisible to European commentators, and were such a normal sight that they were not mentioned by African sources. Despite these difficulties Eugénie Mujawimana has provided a detailed description of the different categories of Rwandese slave dealers between the end of the nineteenth and the beginning of the twentieth century. She describes large-scale and small-scale professional slave caravan leaders, and also occasional traders, some of them chiefs or bandits. She also mentions, but in much less detail, numerous traders from outside Rwanda, the two main groups being Basumbwa (who are sometimes considered a sub-group of the Banyamwezi) and Basubi (who are sometimes considered a sub-group of the Bazinza). Bahaya and in particular Baziba traders are also mentioned but to a lesser extent. Mujawimana unfortunately says little about the few Swahili traders. Comparing her analysis with the sources on which it is based, it is clear that she treated the Swahili more like a stereotype than an actual actor in the slave trade inside Rwanda. Rather than documenting the actual actions of the Swahili traders, she makes assumptions about them, just as her European sources assumed that their enemies, the 'Arab slave traders', were the key actors in the slave trade even if they were in fact absent or very few in number.[48]

In 1971 François Renault wrote that in the nineteenth century 'the [slave] trade was therefore mostly in the interior, finding its own market on the spot. What reached the coast was only a small portion.'[49] Just before, in 1970, Andrew Roberts had reached similar conclusions.[50] According to François Renault, two distinct but connected markets existed in East Africa, one around Unyamwezi and the Great Lakes, the other on the Indian Ocean coast.[51] Jan-Georg Deutsch's chapter reinforces this argument about the primacy of the internal trade, but the detail of his research requires a major change in the understanding of the East African slave trade. Deutsch tells us that the major slave market in this area of East Africa was Unyamwezi, not Zanzibar. This may also help explain why Kilwa harbour dominated the Indian Ocean slave trade to such an extent. The towns of the Mrima coast, opposite Zanzibar Island, faced too much competition for slaves in the interior. What is today central Tanzania constituted not only an important staging post for caravans travelling from the coast to the interior or vice versa. Unyamwezi was also a massive importer of slaves, with the demand coming not only from the export-oriented Swahili settlements at Tabora or Ujiji, but mostly from the Nyamwezi themselves for internal consumption. Part of the inflow of slaves into Unyamwezi came from Swahili traders who gave large numbers of them to local leaders, just as Hartwig has shown in Bukerebe.[52] The study of the slave trade can therefore no longer be limited to the Swahili and Sudanese traders and markets. Other African buyers and traders must also be taken into account.

Poverty and the lack of food were major factors that led to the rise of slavery and the slave trade. Hartwig has shown how famines greatly increased the supply of slaves in Bukerebe. Using oral interviews and the local White Fathers archives, Mujawimana found similar processes occurring in Rwanda (see also Jean-Pierre Chrétien's chapter). The slave trade became particularly important in Rwanda during famines, not only because of the breakdown of social relations but also because of the rise of insecurity and kidnapping. It is worth mentioning that enslavers in Rwanda and Burundi captured both Hutu and Tutsi indiscriminately, unconcerned by the distinctions between these identities.[53] Even in Buganda, with its reputation for precolonial food security, periods of hunger brought a surge of slaves to market.[54] In Burundi poverty was the main reason why people were compelled to become *bashumba* (servants or day labourers).[55] David Schoenbrun in his chapter notes, for example, that 'the word -*muhuuku* (Nkore and Kiga) or -*mupfûku* (Hunde)' meant 'servant,

Introduction

bondsman, or slave'. The source for this noun appears to have been a verb, *-kupuuka* 'to get thinner, lose weight; to fail'. Poverty and hunger influenced the origins as well as the experience of enslavement.[56]

The antiquity of slavery in the Great Lakes region, which is emphasised throughout this book, has an impact on our understanding of the slave trade. Holly Hanson's chapter, and also her recent book, (and Richard Reid's chapter to a lesser extent), show a significant growth of slavery during the eighteenth century in Buganda.[57] This eighteenth-century crisis is fascinating. According to existing assumptions it seems too early to be linked to the Swahili or Sudanese trades. We have already noted that it is unlikely that a regular trade could have crossed the Nile marshes in the eighteenth century. It is more conceivable that the date at which significant contact was made between the interior and the Swahili coast may have been earlier than has commonly been assumed, as the technical and geographical obstacles here could have been overcome more easily than in the Nile Valley. David Schoenbrun's chapter provides some linguistic evidence in this direction. It is interesting to note that Thomas Vernet's recent work in the Portuguese archives has pushed the evidence of the presence of Kamba traders in Mombasa much further into the past (from 1829 to before 1689). As far as is known, the Kamba networks were not connected to the Great Lakes region, but this may be a sign that historians have underestimated the antiquity of relations between the coast and the interior.[58]

The rise of slavery in the eighteenth century opens new perspectives not only on civil war and changes in the economic and political organisation of production in Buganda (see Holly Hanson's chapter),[59] but also on the wider regional crisis associated with the breakdown of Bunyoro's regional hegemony. During the eighteenth century Nyoro forays are recorded all over the region, in Rwanda, Buhaya, Buganda, Nkore and Busoga. The eighteenth-century explosion of Nyoro raiding was closely followed by the breakdown of Nyoro hegemony and the rise of a militarised Buganda, in a pattern which is similar to the evolutions of other regions across Africa in response to the slave trade. It is possible that the transformation of Bukerebe society may have been linked to this eighteenth-century crisis. Hartwig linked the emergence of slavery on this island to a series of invasions from Buhaya and the consequent establishment of institutions of kingship, which he believes occurred in the seventeenth century. It is likely, however, that a historian today, looking at his sources anew, might interpret the oral traditions differently. Developments in historiography would suggest that traditions which explain the establishment of kingship in terms of conquest should be treated with some scepticism, and that the antiquity of these new institutions may have been exaggerated in the oral sources.[60] Perhaps when Buhaya's early history is finally written, Bukerebe's history, and indeed that of the entire region, will become much clearer.

The existence of slavery in the eighteenth century raises new issues.

Where did the captives go? Was there a trade? What were they used for? All these questions need further investigation on a regional scale. Wrigley and Vansina were the first to mention the desire for captives as an important element in warfare in pre-nineteenth-century Buganda and Rwanda.[61] But they deal with this issue extremely briefly. Vansina seems to regard the importance of slave kidnapping during warfare as so obvious that he does not feel compelled to demonstrate its existence. He seems simply to rely mostly on the derivation of the word *umuja* (female slave), whose origins have been analysed in a recent study by David Schoenbrun.[62] Wrigley has the same assumptions and tools as Vansina but he can at least rely on a wider range of sources, since written accounts indicate that Buganda was a provider of slaves for Bunyoro in a far away mythical past.[63] What made slavery suddenly attractive in the eighteenth century? Could it be that Unyamwezi created a regional slave trade a century earlier than has previously been assumed, or were there internal innovations in some of the kingdoms that suddenly made slavery more appealing or possible on a much larger scale? Michael Tuck's and David Schoenbrun's conclusions definitely suggest that the initiative came from an internal evolution within the Great Lakes region.

This issue of the internal evolution of slavery and the slave trade is extremely relevant to the transformation debate, which has hinged on the question of whether Africa played a major role in the international slave trade because slavery already existed there, or whether slavery became common in Africa as a result of the slave trade. In the Great Lakes, Bukerebe, Buganda, Bunyoro, Toro, Ussuwi, Buhaya and Busoga appear to have played the major regional role in the nineteenth-century slave trade because slavery within these societies was already considerable, whereas the early slave trade bypassed those areas such as Burundi and Nkore which had very few slaves. Certainly in the 1880s and 1890s, the role of domestic slavery in the development of the slave trade in Rwanda was very obvious.[64]

The varying significance of domestic slavery helps explain the very unequal integration of Great Lakes societies into the nineteenth-century Indian Ocean trade. Areas in which slavery was already considerable participated willingly in the Nyamwezi and Swahili trade, whereas the others first refused contact, then either subsequently accepted it reluctantly and subject to restrictions or had it imposed on them by force. As a whole, therefore, the region was being dragged by external forces into new forms of slavery and the slave trade. The pre-existing pattern of slavery gave shape to the new slave trade, but once involved in the intercontinental slave trade, local slavery or dependence underwent noteworthy changes (see Richard Reid and Michael Tuck's chapters). This is in concordance with Manning's, Miers's, and Willis's arguments that the 'expansion of slave holding' tended to 'corrupt and subvert and otherwise transform kinship systems' and in this case other aspects of the 'social order' as well.[65] Thus the experience of the Great Lakes region does not fully support

Introduction

either side of the transformation debate (see David Schoenbrun's chapter). Moderate proponents of the transformation theory, like Paul Lovejoy, who do not exclude autonomous inventions of slavery in Africa, are quite right to emphasise the impact of the intercontinental slave trade on local African slavery, but John Thornton is also correct in insisting on the key role of African slavery in the making of Africa as a major slave market.[66]

The nineteenth-century slave trade had a strong impact on slavery. One must take into account that the long-distance slave trade in the Great Lakes region had a rather short lifespan compared with societies on Africa's Atlantic coast. It is possible that the full impact of the new slave trade did not have time to develop fully in East Africa. If one considers Buzinza, Burundi, Rwanda and Nkore, it seems possible to detect an increasing involvement in slavery. For example, towards the end of the nineteenth century, Rujumbura, a small kingdom that was later incorporated into colonial Kigezi, organised itself for predation (see Edward Steinhart's chapter). Nkore during the 1890s became more and more involved in the slave trade, emerging as a major market for slaves captured in Buganda civil wars, most notably between 1897 and 1899, and allowing Nyamwezi, Haya and Swahili traders to cross its territory regularly. In Rwanda at the end of the nineteenth century, during the reign of Rwabugiri, indirect relations with long-distance commercial networks linked up its indigenous war economy with the slave trade.[67]

Hartwig's pioneering work on Bukerebe showed that the growing trade in people in the nineteenth century resulted in the marketisation of social relations, bringing about new, harsher, commercial forms of slavery. Institutions akin to adoption, fostering and pawning were transformed into chattel slavery.[68] Jonathon Glassman has defined the commodification of social relations on the Mrima coast of the Indian Ocean as '[t]he uneven process by which an increasing amount of social interaction is mediated through market relations'.[69] Several chapters in this book confirm this evolution (those of Jean-Pierre Chrétien, Jan-Georg Deutsch and David Northrup), supporting Marcia Wright's and Edward Alpers' evidence that, through commodification, vulnerable individuals such as widows, orphans, the poor, concubines, rivals and isolated people without connections became very vulnerable to enslavement.[70] Ties of clientship or kinship were perverted and used to enslave people. Free servants and dependants were sold. Michael Tuck in his chapter describes how slavery became a web which entrapped the defenceless, with slave women in Buganda being repeatedly re-enslaved (through inheritance, trade, capture and so on). Fugitive women or children might change their masters, but not their status.

More globally there was a process of subjugation in these societies, with the transformation of poor and vulnerable people into slaves being just the tip of the iceberg.[71] Nineteenth-century kings of Buganda called all their subjects their slaves, even the highest ranking chiefs.[72] In Buganda, as was very common in the rest of the region, words describing status were relative, dependent on the context. To be called a slave of the king did not mean that at all times one was a slave. As Richard Reid has written, such terminology could be the expression of royal ideology more than actual status.[73] The confusion was made worse by the indiscriminate use of the word 'slave' in contemporary European sources. An oppressed free person was often described as a slave in such sources, while a slave who enjoyed significant privileges would not be defined as unfree in these commentators' minds. Europeans frequently misinterpreted the exchange of bridewealth which characterised the marriage of a free woman and the emancipation of a female slave as the selling of women. Claudia Mattalucci made this clear in her conference presentation on Buhaya. The White Fathers typically used the word *Bazaana* to describe women prevented by their families or masters from becoming Christians rather than to refer to actual slaves. The use of a term which implied enslavement was in fact used to try to compel the German authorities to defend these women's freedom of worship.

For the Baganda the opposite of slave was *musenze* (client/freeman). The main difference between these statuses was that a client could change patrons, whereas a slave could not (see Richard Reid's and Shane Doyle's chapters).[74] During the second half of the nineteenth century the punishment for fleeing Buganda or changing allegiance to another king was death. Mwanga went so far as to send an expedition to Tabora expressly to have all Baganda refugees who could be found executed.[75] In the sense that they were not allowed to leave their kings, the Baganda *were* the slaves of their rulers in the nineteenth century. Of course, Buganda was an extreme case, but during the nineteenth century the exercise of power became more and more autocratic and one-sided across the region (see Shane Doyle's chapter). This, as David Northrup indicates in his chapter, blurred the limits between slavery and freedom.[76]

The relationship between slavery and patron-client relations needs to be further studied. For a long time, in spite of the example of ancient Rome, it seemed to scholars of Great Lakes societies that clientship was so widespread that it had made slavery redundant in the region.[77] Michael Twaddle in 1988 suggested that slavery and clientship were not exclusive choices for a society.[78] Recently Paul Lovejoy has shown how slavery affected clientage in West Africa.[79] Insecurity and the threat of being enslaved forced independent communities to seek protection against slavery through patronage. It is very tempting to draw parallels with the eighteenth-century Great Lakes region where both clientage and slavery changed enormously in scale. Holly Hanson and Michael Tuck's work adds further complexity to our understanding of the relationship between clientship and slavery in Buganda. Hanson's chapter emphasises the important role that slavery played in the institution that has symbolised clientship in Buganda's historiography, (the *Butongole*). She has also examined the fascinating growth in female tenancy in post-emancipation, early colonial Buganda, which transformed the gender relations of clientship.[80] Before the twentieth century, women (other than princesses and ritualists) could not achieve such relative autonomy, as they could only access land through men and could not live independently from their male protectors (kin, husband or master). Michael Tuck's chapter shows that women, and especially slave women, were key to the smooth functioning of patron-client relations in Buganda. This research on slavery has shown the huge amount of work that is still left to be done on the nature of dependence and citizenship in the Great Lakes region of East Africa.

In some societies, such as Bukerebe,[81] another important change in social relations that seems to have accompanied involvement in the Indian Ocean slave trade was a rise in witchcraft accusations. This development is a common occurrence in the literature on African slavery.[82] However, it does not appear that such a change occurred in the better-studied areas (Burundi, Rwanda, Bunyoro, Toro, Buganda) of this region. It may be that, as in the case of slavery, witchcraft has simply not hitherto attracted the attention of researchers, but this is unlikely. Of course, fear of witchcraft did exist to some extent in this region, but it cannot be compared with the intensity of such fear in, for example, Cameroon or Ivory Coast.[83] This can perhaps be explained by the protection that the kings of the Great Lakes region gave to their subjects. The rise of witchcraft which Hartwig observed followed Bukerebe's monarchs' loss of control over the life and death of their subjects. This was an innovation specific to Bukerebe and did not apply to the rest of the region (though the study of other small kingdoms from the region could reveal some surprises.)

The impact of slavery and the slave trade on the state is better studied. Kingdoms like Buganda, Rwanda, Bunyoro and Ussuwi became increasingly warlike and predatory. The impact of Ganda raids is studied in detail in Henri Médard's thesis. Ganda support enabled some neighbouring kings to extend their territory and exploit their subjects. Bukooli in Busoga, for example, expanded thanks to Ganda support. The cost of this support, the large number of slaves that were given in tribute to the king of Buganda, was high. Often, as in Karagwe after 1878, the cost proved too heavy for the societies to bear and the polities imploded. Resistance to Ganda hegemony could also lead to depopulated, destroyed and fragmented polities. Some territories experienced both processes, one followed by the other. Bunyoro, for instance, was in the process of being dismantled up to 1870, but then expanded with Ganda support between 1870 and 1884. Rwoma's Kingdom in Buzinza was almost destroyed by the Ganda army and navy in 1884, but in 1887-8 Buganda almost made Rwoma king of a unified Buzinza.

Buganda provides the clearest evidence of the consequences of slavery and the slave trade for Great Lakes societies (although slavery was, of course, only one of many factors leading to the changes described below). It is important to note that the expansion of slavery (and clientship) and the growth of the state are parallel processes in the eighteenth and nineteenth centuries. According to Holly Hanson, a key institution during the nineteenth century, the *Butongole* chieftainship, was invented in the eighteenth century to accommodate the growing number of slaves.[84] It was the leaders of these *Butongole* chieftainships who converted to Islam and Christianity in the late nineteenth century and then took over power in Buganda after 1888.

The early history of Buganda was dominated by the conquest of land and the incorporation of its resident populations. But after the first decades of the nineteenth century, Buganda stopped expanding. Due to its growing appetite for slaves, Buganda lost its integrative capacities and became incapable of assimilating large parts of Busoga and Buhaya.[85] It evolved instead through a balance between plunder and predation abroad and a more ancient policy of wealth in land and people within its borders. The slaving frontier moved further and further away until the complex logistics of the Ganda war machine reached its limits in the 1880s. The multiple contradictions of the slave trade prevented the Baganda from building stable trade routes and allies, across Busoga for example, and from efficiently waging war further afield in Bukedi.[86] As in many other kingdoms that became involved in the slave trade, Buganda's leaders started plundering and exporting their own people.[87] A dual process developed, in which leaders lost their legitimacy and followers lost value. These contradictions wore away at Buganda's social contract, which eventually collapsed during the 1880s, with both land and people losing their importance. Chaos and civil war erupted in 1888; warlords (often former *Batongole* chiefs) started multiplying. Warbands, usually closely knit around new religions and a pretender to the throne with little or no territory, fought each other and plundered the population indiscriminately. Many of the women mentioned in Michael Tuck's chapter were captured at this time. Between 1888 and 1890 various warbands ravaged the country and the people of Buganda, assisted by all its neighbours.

After two years of war, with Buganda in ruins and famine looming, the system of looting had exhausted itself, a degree of peace returned and King Mwanga was restored. Mwanga managed, with the support of allies in Buhaya, Kooki, Nkore, Busoga and among the foreign missionaries, to unite the Ganda masses, the Christian warlords and the traditionalists around an anti-slavery policy (or more accurately a policy of old-fashioned, non-commercial slavery, good governance and stability).[88] Defeated, hated by the common people but still powerful, the Muslims chose another option, that of roaming warbands as adopted by many other slaving groups across the continent (as with, for example, Rabah or Samori). Ganda Muslim warbands preferred following the slave frontier rather than losing access to it. To a great extent they abandoned territorial control and the 'reciprocal obligation pledged in land', to use Holly Hanson's phrase,[89] for the freedom to plunder those who used to be their subjects and brothers and now became their prey and potential slaves.

Introduction

According to Muslim sources, 20,000 Ganda captives were sold to the Banyoro for food, guns and cloth between 1889 and 1892![90] The change of scale is considerable. Slave exports ten years earlier were estimated by Protestant missionary sources at 1,000 or 2,000 persons a year, few of whom were Baganda.

The arrival of the imperial powers eventually destroyed the Muslim slaving war economy and ultimately stabilised the moderate option chosen by Mwanga, but not without initially using slavery (despite their denials) as a tool of conquest to reward Sudanese and Swahili mercenaries as well as Baganda warlords and levies.[91] Mwanga's revolt and the Sudanese mutiny (1897–9), together with the Nyoro wars (1894–9), was the last and fiercest episode of the history of slaving. This was a general regional upheaval. It spread over Buganda, Bunyoro, Kooki, Busoga, Toro, Nkore, Acholi and Lango. Anti-British guerrillas lived off the country, selling captives often to Banyamwezi, Bahaya and Swahili traders. Britain's allies did the same, but their captives fed their own local demand. This early colonial apotheosis of slavery reached even higher peaks in the Congo Free State (described in David Northrup's chapter).

The colonial conquest wars had contradictory effects on slavery. They helped some allies of the British (such as the Baganda and Sudanese) to capture many slaves, whereas in a place like Bunyoro which resisted British conquest very few slaves remained with their masters by 1900. War not only provided the opportunity to run away but compelled many slaves to flee for their lives and abandon their masters (see Shane Doyle's chapter). In Rwanda the most active involvement in the slave trade occurred just before the German takeover and during the German occupation. The Germans were not partcularly active in fighting slavery. Partly this was because they were very few in number and relied mostly on indirect rule. Moreover, when a series of famines afflicted Rwanda during the first decades of the twentieth century, the German authorities were reluctant to prosecute starving people who sold others simply to stay alive (see Jean-Pierre Chrétien's chapter). During the First World War famine and chaos led to a renewal of slave trading, but this ended in the 1920s when the new Belgian authorities actively suppressed slavery, partly for propaganda reasons, to contrast favourably with the Germans, and partly because it was part of their international mandate from the League of Nations.[92]

The End of Slavery and its Aftermath

Jan-Georg Deutsch's chapter helps us to understand how slavery progressively died out during the first decades of colonial rule. Legal bans, first of the slave trade, then of slavery itself, were applied across the region during the 1890s. However, the regular renewal of the bans suggests that they had a limited impact.[93] As elsewhere, it is likely that what really was efficient in destroying this institution was the difficulty owners experienced in replacing old slaves with new ones. Colonial taxes, wages and compulsory labour also played an important part. But one should be cautious before making any systematic generalisation about the nature of the ending of slavery. The Sudanese former slave soldiers had an unusual experience. They did not merge into an older society; instead they formed a new ethnic group (see Mark Leopold's chapter). In Buganda migrant workers, as in parts of Senegal and Mozambique, soon occupied the place left empty by the disappearing slaves.[94] To many Africans of the Great Lakes region, the massive abuses and endless hunger for manpower of colonialism seemed similar to a massive enslavement of the population (see David Northrup's and Edward Steinhart's chapters).[95]

Great differences existed from one area of the Great Lakes region to another. Christian Thibon in his oral presentation at the conference in 2002 had noticed an apparent correlation between the depth of involvement in the slave trade and the degree of demographic problems during the colonial period. Michael Tuck's findings in Buganda, showing very low birth rates, imply the same thing. Through a variety of means, slavery has often had a strong negative effect on a society's ability to reproduce itself; the Bobangi on the Zaïre River were one out of many staggering examples of this.[96] However, current work being done by Shane Doyle on the contrasts in population densities in today's Great Lakes region, shows that there was a much more complex evolution where slavery was only one contributory factor in subsequent patterns. In his chapter, Doyle, following recent studies on the American South, goes against the standard thesis about the systematic relationship between slavery and underpopulation. On the contrary, in Bunyoro he suggests that slave women were more fertile than local women. Eugénie Mujawimana's sources report a similar idea. Rwandese slaves were popular among the Bazinza and the Bahaya because they had higher fertility than the local women.[97] This debate is not settled in this book, and more research will be needed to overcome these contradictions if the sources will allow it. These apparent contradictions may simply be a sign of much more varied and complex demographic change in the Great Lakes region than might superficially be assumed.

The Significance and the Legacy of Slavery across the Region

It is clear that a corridor of slavery existed in the nineteenth century starting at Lake Albert in Bunyoro and Toro going though Buganda, then branching east to Busoga and south to Karagwe, Buhaya, Buzinza and Bukerebe. In this corridor slaves were numerous and circulated along established routes of trade and plunder. The cases of Bukerebe and

Introduction

Buganda[98] are now fairly well known. Karagwe, Buhaya and Ussuwi played a major role in the regional slave trade, but they are under-researched areas and it is difficult to be sure what precisely was going on there. The Buvuma islands must have been a major actor in the slave trade. The existence of the largest war fleet on Lake Victoria cannot be explained solely by the need for defence against Ganda aggression; it must have been put to use also in a more offensive way along the Busoga coast and the eastern shore of the lake. Some of the captives were probably traded back into Buganda, Busoga and Buhaya. The number of Luo slaves found in Bukerebe cannot solely be explained by the presence of one Swahili trader on the lake, as Hartwig has suggested. The more likely explanation is that they were bought from the Bavuma, as Buvuma and Bukerebe had direct commercial contacts in the nineteenth century.[99] Unfortunately we know so little about these islands that one can only conjecture. The major sources of slaves for Buganda were Toro, Bunyoro and Busoga. Bunyoro is interesting as it evolved from being a hunting ground for Ganda and Sudanese raiders in the middle decades of the nineteenth century to becoming a slave hunter in the 1880s and then hunted again in the 1890s.

As mentioned above, slavery does not seem to have been as widespread in Burundi, Rwanda and Nkore.[100] Vansina believes that women and children were captured by the Rwandese army as early as the seventeenth century.[101] Perhaps the prevalence of cattle theft in these societies concealed the capture of slaves from the eyes of historians. Certainly Burundi seems to have been the society least involved in slavery in the entire region (see Jean-Pierre Chrétien's chapter). However, the sheer size of the population of Rwanda and Burundi (each possessed around 1,500,000 inhabitants around 1900) meant that even a very limited slave trade would have involved many more slaves than the major involvement of a kingdom like Bukerebe with a population of c.40,000 inhabitants. This would explain why Oscar Baumann, while describing slaves originating from 'between the lakes' as being few in number in Zanzibar, nonetheless mentioned Baganda and Barundi as featuring among the slaves encountered on that island. Possibly, though, on Zanzibar Basoga might have been lumped in with Baganda and Banyarwanda called Barundi.[102] Moreover, in Burundi and Rwanda major differences in the scale of activity in the slave trade may have existed from one district to the other. For example, in Burundi the trade was certainly more developed on the shores of Lake Tanganyika than in the interior of the kingdom.[103] Did the restrictions on the entry of coastal slave dealers into their territories by Burundi, Rwanda and Nkore actually stop the slave trade as much as has been assumed? The importance of African actors at all stages in this trade can no longer be doubted. These western kingdoms allowed a significant level of trade to be carried out by their own subjects or by Baha, Bahaya and Banyamwezi itinerant traders in various commodities, including slaves. Further research will be needed to clarify this point, but according to Mujawimana several thousand slaves were exported from and imported into Rwanda each year between c.1890 and 1918, without much involvement of coastal traders.[104]

The diversity in experience that existed across the region can be seen most clearly on the southern shore of Lake Victoria. The White Fathers had a mission in Bukumbi (on the lake shore in Usukuma) from 1883.[105] They were eager to redeem slaves, yet very few slaves could be bought from Buzinza and Usukuma even though the White Fathers had many contacts who were eager to trade with them. Buzinza (excluding Ussuwi further to the west) was not a major trader in slaves even though by the 1890s it had been devastated by civil wars and Ganda and Ngoni invasions. Many slaves bought by the Catholic missionaries in that region had been imported by Swahili traders. Another important slave dealer that the White Fathers could approach was the king of Bukerebe. However, as he had murdered O'Neil and Smith, two CMS missionaries, Sungura Tarib, an important Swahili trader, and many of their followers in 1877, both Europeans and Swahili were reluctant to visit him. The other major purveyors of slaves to the White Fathers in Bukumbi were the Baganda. Slaves were either bought by fellow missionaries in Buganda, where slaves were cheap and numerous, and sent south, or they could be bought directly from Ganda fleets or passing Ganda armies. The Baganda and the Swahili were by far the major purveyors of slaves even of Bazinza or Basukuma origins.

Quantifying the relative importance of the total slave population in each society is another major question, but one that is very difficult to answer. The only existing estimate from the region is that slaves made up less than 15 per cent of the population in Bukerebe around 1900. This is a useful benchmark, as this kingdom was one of the places in which we can assume slaves were most numerous.[106] Bukerebe, Buganda and Bunyoro definitely had more slaves than Nkore and Rwanda, while Rwanda had more than Burundi, but it is hard to be more precise. It seems that slavery was not particularly common in this region, especially as one of the leading specialists on slavery in Africa, Ralph Austen, did not find slavery significant enough to mention in his first major work, a study of northwestern Tanzania. Humphrey Fisher, in his book *Slavery in the History of Muslim Black Africa*, has recently observed that a travel book written by a mid-nineteenth-century German traveller, *Sahara and the Sudan*, 'is a treasure-trove of slavery data, not because Nachtigal [the author] went as "independent counsel" looking for this specifically, but because slavery confronted him at every turn'.[107] Equivalent travellers in the Great Lakes region did not notice slavery so often. The most logical explanation is that slavery was not as common there. This impression was reinforced by reading through comparable sources, the White Fathers Archives for the Great Lakes region and the Comboniani's archives in Sudan, where it quickly became obvious that slavery was mentioned much more frequently in the latter than in the former. It is therefore unlikely that the Great Lakes

Introduction

region had comparable numbers of slaves to those found in, for example, West Africa or the Swahili coast (where slaves comprised perhaps half of the population at Kano or Zaria and maybe two-thirds of the population on Pemba Island).

The question of the legacy of slavery remains to be answered. Before now, as scholars of the region considered slavery non-existent or marginal, no legacy was worth noting. The slave trade was another matter, but the guilt was transferred to Swahili or Arab traders and Muslims more generally. The overuse by Christians of the memory of the slave trade as a weapon against Muslim communities during the colonial period brought a backlash in the 1960s and 1970s. It has now lost much of its emotional and mobilising power. While religious tension has at times been quite high in the region, Muslims, except in the nineteenth century, have been marginal actors in the conflicts. Only the sectarian animosity between the two Christian heavyweights, the Protestants and the Roman Catholics, has really mattered. In any case the major conflicts during the twentieth century have been ethnic, between Baganda and non-Baganda, Tutsi and Hutu, or Hima and Iru. The tension between Baganda and non-Baganda in Uganda could be understood as a legacy of Baganda slave raiding, but in reality it was mostly inherited from the favoured position of the Baganda during the colonial period. The second major confrontation (between Tutsi-Hutu and Hima-Bairu) should not be interpreted simplistically as a purely ethnic conflict. In any case it erased or camouflaged much of the legacy of both the slave trade and slavery (see Edward Steinhart's chapter).

The most visible legacy of slavery was the Nubi community in Uganda and Kenya, which grew in importance when Idi Amin, one of its members, gained power (see Mark Leopold's chapter). These former slave soldiers from the Egyptian Sudan, recruited by the British (and to a lesser extent by the Germans) in the 1890s, subsequently played a major role in the East African armed forces. It is fascinating how they were transformed from slave soldiers to Muslims and then into an ethnic group. It would be wrong to see this community purely as victims of the nineteenth-century system of slavery, as these soldiers from the 1870s–1890s were heavily involved in capturing and enslaving people in the Sudan, northern Uganda and eastern Congo even after they came under British command. British officers dealt with this problem inconsistently, either covering up their troops' slaving practice or stopping it when they needed to impose their own power.

This brings us to another legacy of the slave trade that will be familiar to readers of the Ugandan press today. The wars in northern Uganda and the Congo bring back memories of the nineteenth century with armed bands kidnapping women and children, boys being forcibly drafted into guerrilla armies and women being un-free 'wives' of the soldiers, passing from one 'husband' to another with a frightful regularity. The sense of continuity is heightened by the way in which the Lord's Resistance Army is held together by a form of syncretic Christianity, just as Islam unified the Egyptians' slave soldiers.

Definitions

The definition of what constituted slavery in the past is so important because it influenced the visibility, and therefore the reporting, of the institution in the nineteenth and early twentieth centuries. For many Europeans, real slavery was American-style plantation slavery. Slavery imbedded in Islamic traditions (as in West Africa or Zanzibar) was also familiar to them, to some extent. African slavery often differed so significantly from the American form that it seemed to Europeans to hardly count as slavery at all. The moment when African slaves looked like slaves to European eyes was when they were being traded. This explains, among other things, why the slave trade was rooted up much more vigorously than slavery by the colonial authorities. The institution often appeared too insignificant to be mentioned, and indeed often went unnoticed by foreign commentators. Where slavery in Africa was reported, it was depicted as 'domestic slavery', almost an extreme form of clientage.[108] But Cooper has clearly shown that 'violence was part of paternalism', and that a culture of violence in African slave-based societies explained 'the coexistence of obedience and resistance on the part of the slaves, and kindness and brutality on the part of the master'. There was no such thing as benign or endemic slavery, only a 'continual testing' and stretching of customs by both sides.[109]

In the past therefore many African terms were not translated as part of a vocabulary of slavery. Often categories such as dependant, servant, wife or child were employed instead. The translation of African terms as 'slavery' is still a complicated matter today. Moses Finley accused Suzanne Miers and Igor Kopytoff of defining as slavery African realities that had nothing to do with slavery.[110] Hartwig did not use the word 'slave' in his discussion of Bukerebe. No one can deny the truth of the Italian saying *traduttore traditore* (translator traitor). However, to communicate one needs common words and concepts (Moses Finley does accept this).[111] The now huge amount of comparative material on slavery reveals the great variety of forms which slavery has taken and how unique each situation was; but also that slavery has a logic, is coherent and repeats itself in similar ways across the world. I believe a careful use of the word 'slavery' accompanied by references to local words is justified. One must, however, keep in mind the continuum of meaning concerning slavery, kinship and patronage. There are many borderline cases as many of the chapters assembled here show. The boundaries between freedom and slavery are not clear-cut. Semantic meanings, moreover, change with time (the most famous example is from *servus*, slave in Latin, to serf). However, though the distinctions may seem very slight to an outsider, the actors did consider

Introduction

them important. Poor and vulnerable dependants would resist, if they could, being made into slaves by their superiors. Jan-Georg Deutsch, influenced by Frederick Cooper,[112] notes in his chapter: 'As far as Unyamwezi is concerned, but arguably also in general terms, kinship and patronage relations should thus not merely be seen as a continuum comprising a variety of different social relations. They are also fields of social conflict whose substance and meaning were constantly reworked, particularly when the social, political and economic conditions by which they were shaped underwent significant change.'[113]

No definition of slavery was imposed on the authors, but a classic definition of African slavery emerged on its own.[114] The slave is a 'kinless outsider'[115] and an un-free dependant. And as Steinhart puts it in his chapter, 'The status of slaves as distinct from other forms of dependent labour in pre-colonial society was far more a matter of the alienation of honour rather than the alienation of labour.'[116] The nature of slavery can vary significantly from one place to another. As Alain Testart says: 'The slave is a joker card whose use depends on the strategies […] of the society. The existence of slavery does not define a type of society; it's the society that defines the type of slavery. In other words, there are as many types of slavery as societies practising slavery.'[117] This is why Victor Uchendu's idea of defining African slavery through the image of a 'bundle of traits' is so interesting.[118] It allows consideration of other less universal but often important features of slavery (questions of property and commodification, unpaid compulsory labour, control of tools of production and reproduction, violence, domination, loss of identity, absence of fundamental rights, exploitation, low status, shame, inheritance and so on).[119] For example, slaves were often mutilated or scarified.[120] Even in Buganda where free people were too often victims of such indignities to allow disfigurement to be a characteristic of slavery, slaves were still much more likely than anybody else to suffer such a common and pitiful fate.

Modern definitions also often liken slaves to foreigners. Schoenbrun's chapter in this volume uses linguistic evidence to show that slavery can usefully be understood in that way in the Great Lakes region. It is important to remember, however, that not all foreign migrants in the Great Lakes region were slaves. Many Banyoro and Basoga technicians (such as religious specialists, potters and cattle herders) are known to have migrated to Buganda as both captives and free migrants. Free migrants in the Great Lakes region were numerous, welcomed and well integrated, the best examples being Bamogera (from the area east of Busoga) and Bahima (from Nkore and Bunyoro) within Buganda, Bakedi in Bunyoro, and Bajita in Bukerebe.[121] Buganda was particularly renowned for assimilating foreigners easily.[122] These examples of integration support the distinction Moses Finley has made between enslaving a person and subjecting a community.[123]

Equally, foreigners who were incorporated into host societies through conquest should not be confused with slaves. Banabuddu (the people of

Buddu, an area conquered by Buganda from Bunyoro at the end of the eighteenth century) were not slaves, even though their name has the same root as 'baddu' (slaves). They remained on their own land and were fully integrated in kinship networks. Conquered people, though, were particularly vulnerable to enslavement. In the 1890s Banyoro living in the 'lost counties' were often kidnapped by their new Baganda overlords. This, however, was an individual process even though it may have concerned many people. A slightly different example was the servile relationship through which communities of Lendu became dependent on the Sudanese soldiers known as the Nubi. In the 1890s these Sudanese soldiers of the defunct Egyptian empire were transferred by the British from their garrisons among the Lendu on the western shore of Lake Albert to Buganda, and a considerable group of Lendu followed the Sudanese as a distinct but subordinate community. These Lendu may have been subordinate to the Sudanese as a group but their status was different from the individual slaves owned by the members of the Nubi community.

For decades authors have noted that the opposition between free and un-free is a difficult concept to use in the African context. Jan-Georg Deutsch in his chapter writes:

> Kopytoff has argued that there is no substantive meaning to the term 'free', as slavery as much as kinship is embedded into a 'continuum of dependency'. Arguably, there are different kinds of dependency, for instance, only some forms of kinship in nineteenth-century East Africa allowed a person to become a 'commodity'. Thus, the term 'free' is used here primarily to denote a person's status that precluded his or her outright sale under 'normal' circumstances.

In the nineteenth century slaves in this region were un-free, in the sense that they were not at liberty to change masters, or at least this freedom was strongly limited. The opposite of slave in Luganda was *musenze*, which can be translated as 'freeman' but also means 'tenant' or 'client'.[124] Would we, in the twenty-first century, define somebody as dependent as a *musenze* as 'free'?

What does the use of the concept 'freedom' mean in relation to the extremely autocratic, hierarchical and violent regime of Buganda in the mid-nineteenth century? Ironically it may have meant more freedom than in other societies in Africa where individual rights were crushed by collective rights. By forcibly limiting the clans' influence, the bloody autocrats of Buganda largely freed individual Baganda from their elders' control. One of the most significant outcomes of this decline in the role of kinship was that it made room for individual choice outside the clan structure, thus enabling the dramatic conversions to world religions in the late nineteenth century for which Buganda is so famous. Alain Testart suggests that despotism is as much in competition with slavery as it is with clanship. Despots' claim to absolute power over their subjects, including slaves, was in conflict with the theoretically absolute or near absolute rights of masters over their slaves.[125] It is likely that, even though slavery was becoming harsher because of the slave trade, the integration of male slaves accelerated in the nineteenth century in very despotic states such as Buganda and Bunyoro where clans' political role was in decline (see Shane Doyle's chapter).

Freedom can be understood as the respect of specific privileges of a group or of individuals. In the Great Lakes region these were in large part inherited, through gender, occupation, or especially family, lineage and clan. As Suzanne Miers and Igor Kopytoff have written, Africans' 'full citizenship derived from belonging to a kin group, usually corporate, which was the fundamental social, legal, political and ritual protective unit'.[126] Privileges could more rarely also be acquired, through, for example, royal favour. The relative importance of inherited versus achieved rights was varied over space and time in the Great Lakes region.[127] There was no unity on the regional scale.

Cutting an individual off from his or her kinship group removed that person's rights of citizenship. The absence of a kin-group put slaves at the margin of society. This is why kinship is the most distinctive feature in the definition of slavery in Africa.[128] Since we have defined slavery through the kinship structure, the role of clans in society must be considered a key element in the evolution of the status of slaves. The history of clans since the seventeenth century must be better understood if we are to reach a better understanding of slavery. Regional studies show, as is very often the case in Africa, that clans owe less to filiation than their ideology implies. Studies of Rwanda, and to a lesser extent Buganda and Buhweju (a principality that became part of Ankole during the colonial period), show the importance of kingship in moulding this institution.[129] A great reorganisation and mutation of clans seems to have occurred in the eighteenth century at the same time as the rise of slavery on a regional scale. The relationship between these institutions is just starting to be investigated (see Holly Hanson's chapter). These changes led to a great heterogeneity in the clan structure at the regional level. Theoretically, that would in turn lead to an equivalent heterogeneity in the nature of slavery across the region.

Buganda is again a useful case study, partly because of the richness of its documentary sources. Buganda is famous for the decline in the power of its clans that began in the eighteenth century. Clans had not become anachronistic relics by the nineteenth century, but their role and function changed from being competing political units to becoming structures that maintained the unity of a kingdom divided by political feuds. Nonetheless, many of the usual prerogatives of clans and lineage leaders (such as control over marriage and land) were transferred to or shared with patron-client networks between the eighteenth and nineteenth centuries. Clans were also used to make connections across political borders and affiliations were constructed between clans from different countries, most clearly between Bunyoro and Buganda. This gave Nyoro slaves in Buganda an intermediate position between totally foreign slaves and Buganda-born slaves, thus helping their assimilation.[130]

The specific structure and history of clans in Buganda explains in great part the nature of slavery in Buganda. Part of the reason for this is that in Buganda, Burundi, Rwanda and Bunyoro, as in many other parts of Africa, women and children were preferred as slaves to men (see Jan-Georg Deutsch's chapter). In Rwanda, out of 445 slaves whose gender Eugénie Mujawimana could determine, only 18 were male, the rest being women and girls. She could not even identify a Kinyarwanda word for an adult male slave.[131]

In most African societies slaves were 'legal minors', even if they were male adults. Even when freed from their masters, male former slaves remained kinless, and so were still socially similar to slaves.[132] In Buganda, however, the typical slave was a minor in a literal as well as a figurative sense. As male slaves grew up they melted into the patronage and clan structure of the kingdom. In nineteenth-century Buganda clan identity was not very important in everyday life.[133] Free Ganda often changed clans and names, so for freed slaves an adopted clan identity could convince people that they had been free at birth. It was therefore not so unusual for former slaves to achieve high ascribed positions in Ganda society.[134] On the other hand, though, when faced with the threat of a fine, persecution or human sacrifice, the absence of good clan connections was sorely felt. Moreover, former slaves were rarely chosen to be heirs, with important exceptions.[135] The most important inheritance one could receive in Buganda was the position of clan head or *Mutaka* (pl. *Bataka*). Access to a position of this type, though formally decided within the clan, in reality required the king's agreement. Often chiefs (including *Bataka*) sent one of their slaves to serve at the royal palace, pretending that this slave was in fact one of the chief's sons. The motivation for this deception was that chiefs wanted to protect their children from the dangers of court life and to avoid presenting the king with a hostage. Naturally *Bataka* only sent slaves who possessed the ability to excel, confident that a successful slave would be obliged to repay his benefactor in the future. But some slaves did so well at court that the king decided to appoint them to succeed their 'fathers' as clan heads. What member of the clan would dare bring on himself (and on his clan since it would be held collectively responsible) the king's wrath by admitting publicly that the king had been deliberately lied to? Therefore even a slave could inherit the highest clan positions in the kingdom.[136]

There were practical reasons why in Buganda it was relatively easy for slaves to improve their situation through their own actions. One factor was that Buganda's thirty or so clans were very large, by the standards of the region, so the process of confirming a man's true identity was so tedious and expensive that it was used only in exceptional circumstances such as political slander and conflict over inheritance. One case where this did occur was when the Prime Minister Apolo Kaggwa in 1904 was accused of being a Musoga (which implied slave origin).[137] Buganda, moreover, was large enough to allow mobility; a boy kidnapped in Busoga and sold in Buganda would have no difficulty, as a freed adult in another part of the kingdom, in disguising himself as a native of Buganda. Mobility enabled a former male slave to reinvent his origins.[138] Had the Ganda state made more of an effort to prevent the flight of slaves, its occurrence doubtless would have diminished. The Ganda state was a fairly efficient one by nineteenth-century African standards. But little energy was spent on locating and returning fugitive slaves. This was because large-scale government action against runaway slaves would have interfered with other more vital priorities. Instead, the owner himself had to find where the slave had taken refuge and take the fugitive and his new protector to court (not always a wise thing to do if the new patron was powerful or well-connected).[139]

Mobility was structurally encouraged by the political system. A chief could expect to be moved around the kingdom about ten times on average during his lifetime to fill different positions. This prevented chiefs from acquiring a regional footing and made patron-client relations unstable. When a chief was transferred some of his clients followed him, but others decided to stay and make a new arrangement with the chief's successor. The hunger for men during the second half of the nineteenth century, as a result of demographic decline, guaranteed that a potential client would be welcomed reasonably easily and land would be found for him. In these circumstances, though the deterrent of extraordinary violence was real, flight must have been particularly easy for male slaves (the White Fathers had an extraordinarily large number of slaves running away from them, though they were hardly typical Ganda masters).[140] Therefore, to avoid flight, masters had to grant male adult slaves very similar conditions to those enjoyed by freemen, and adopting their master's clan identity was made relatively easy.

Another way for slaves to obtain protection and assimilation was through blood brotherhood.[141] Tefiro Mulamba Kulugi, a former chief of Muteesa, recorded that

> if a man e.g. Mamba clan makes blood-brotherhood with a man of another clan or Munyoro, that man does not become a member of the Mamba clan, but if the Mamba man dies, and the relations did not know that the man who made blood brotherhood with him was not his relation, he may be regarded as a member, this usually happened when a child was captured from Unyoro, grew up in the clan, makes blood-brotherhood when he grows up with member of the clan.[142]

Slaves in Buganda could also trap their masters into granting them freedom by entering into a blood-brotherhood relationship with one of their young children. This practice was described by Tefiro Mulamba Kulugi in 1906:

We had slaves in Uganda in the old days, we captured our slaves in war, slaves made blood brotherhood with young boys on the quiet, so as to get their masters' protection by catching hold of a child and performing the ceremony, and then telling the child to tell his parents. He does not become one of the clan but no harm comes to him, he would not have his eyes taken out or ears cut, his master's clan have to pay fines incurred by him and see he comes to no harm. If he were a good slave to his master the latter would help him without this, but even if he were bad, if there were the ceremony, the master would have to help him. A slave could be given or buy his freedom by giving his master another slave or cow which he captured in war, he could be free and settle where he liked but he could not enter a clan.[143]

More generally blood brotherhood could be used by runaways or former slaves to acquire a new clan identity in a discreet manner. Baganda slaves could also redeem themselves. It is likely that, as in Bukerebe where the prices were similar, this would have taken three to four years of work as a slave.[144] Warfare, where according to Richard Reid slaves played a key role, also offered the opportunity to obtain freedom by capturing another, substitute, slave.[145]

It was the conjunction of all these elements that made slave status impermanent for boys in Buganda, as it melted away with adulthood. The conditions of male slaves in Rwanda, Burundi and Bunyoro were probably not so different from those in Buganda (see Shane Doyle's and Jean-Pierre Chrétien's chapters).

As has now been well established for the rest of Africa, the experience of female slaves differed markedly from that of their male counterparts.[146] The ability of a handful of men to achieve relatively speedy manumission and assimilation in Buganda obscured the fact that the overwhelming majority of slaves, women, found it much harder to escape slave status. Michael Tuck's chapter shows that women who ran away[147] typically remained slaves, though in the service of new masters. Why was this? Partly it was because many of them were captured as adults and could not easily pass for Baganda. The famous mobility of Ganda society did not apply to women. To some extent free adult women remained minors throughout their lives, with marriage transferring most of the authority over them from their fathers or brothers to their husbands. Buganda was a strongly patriarchal society, a characteristic that was strengthened by the growth of slavery and of kingship (the king being the father, the husband and the owner of the Baganda).[148] The decline in women's status which accompanied slavery may have been even more pronounced in Bunyoro, according to Shane Doyle's chapter. The trend was the same all over East Africa; the status of women generally declined with the development of the nineteenth-century slave trade (see Jan-Georg Deutsch's chapter).[149]

Gender in late nineteenth-century Buganda was partially defined by power. A woman with power, a princess for example, was a 'man', whereas a man with no power, a slave for instance, was by contrast considered a

Introduction

'woman'.[150] Another obstacle to the emancipation of female slaves was to be found in the role of clans in marriage customs. Bridewealth, as has been shown in many parts of Africa, was a very important status marker for married women. Being kinless, a slave woman was less likely to be married with a high brideprice, thus being regarded more as a concubine than a wife. More importantly, the woman's family was her protection in marriage; without that protection she was like a slave to her husband (even if she was technically free). Therefore, even if a woman obtained manumission through childbirth, even if a woman could move upwards within the domestic hierarchy (from unfree servant to wife to senior wife),[151] she retained the powerlessness of a slave. This explains why former slaves were so often chosen as wives by Baganda Christian chiefs eager to have their authority uncontested in their home, as Michael Twaddle has observed.[152]

As suggested earlier, though this needs more research for confirmation, the integration of slaves varied greatly in the Great Lakes region, matching the great diversity of clan structures. Though the varying evolution of relations between clans and kings was the main reason for this heterogeneity, kingship did have a homogenising effect in some ways. Structurally speaking, kings in the region tended to ally themselves with young people, which to some extent meant not only people young in age but also those young in status. Kings regularly raised cadets against their fathers, favouring achievement over ascription.

Chapter Outline

The order we have chosen in this book follows a more or less geographical outline. The first chapter, written by David Schoenbrun, deals with the linguistics of the whole region and with the earliest manifestations of slavery. Then the chapters of Jan-Georg Deutsch (Chapter 2), David Northrup (Chapter 3) and Mark Leopold (Chapter 4), deal with, respectively, the southern, western and northern peripheries of the region, as well as discussing the major long-distance slave trading groups, the Nyamwezi, Swahili, Manyema and Sudanese. Then the focus turns to the best documented area: Buganda. First Richard Reid (Chapter 5) discusses the relationship between war and slavery, then Holly Hanson (Chapter 6) examines the integration of the growing number of slaves in Buganda from the eighteenth century, while Michael Tuck (Chapter 7) concentrates on issues of gender and female slavery. Lastly we finish with the western kingdoms, Nkore, Rwanda, Burundi and Bunyoro. Edward Steinhart (Chapter 8) gives a general presentation of slavery before and after colonialism in Nkore. Jean-Pierre Chrétien (Chapter 9) analyses the conflicts between the German authorities and the Catholic White Fathers missionaries concerning slavery and the slave trade, and discusses how this dispute can increase our understanding of slavery. Finally Shane Doyle (Chapter 10) deals with the demographic history of slavery in Bunyoro.

Conclusion

This collection of essays re-evaluates the role of slavery in the Great Lakes region of East Africa. It shows that slavery was far from being insignificant in nineteenth-century interlacustrine kingdoms. Not only that, but slavery had a deep history, much older than the classical nineteenth-century Sudanese and Swahili slave trades. Lovejoy's and Thornton's competing theories both seem to be right in this case. The international slave trade grew at first because slavery was already widespread in the region but Great Lakes slavery experienced an important transformation as social relations became increasingly commodified in response to the slave trade in the nineteenth century. The role of Swahili or Sudanese slave traders was far from being insignificant but Africans from the interior were the main actors in the slave trade. Not only did they control and conduct most of the trade but most enslaved people were kept in the interior of East Africa. Only a trickle reached the Indian Ocean coast. Local demand for slaves was greatest in Unyamwezi, but in many other areas such as Bunyoro and Bukerebe slaves were highly valued.

The Great Lakes region of East Africa is known for a number of specific features: kingship, the importance of clientage, social divisions such as Hutu/Tutsi and Iru/Hima, the high density of population and intensive agricultural systems. Slavery interacted with these specific characteristics. For example, slavery did not operate in opposition to clientage as some have thought, but instead appears to have been complementary to it, female subordinates frequently being slaves while male dependants were more likely to be clients. The impact of Hutu-Tutsi and Iru-Hima categories on slavery seems to have been marginal apart from the logical conclusion that rich people had more slaves than the poor.

The density of the population was already very high by African standards in the nineteenth century. But the arrival of the international slave trade coincided with a terrible demographic crisis across the region. This crisis cannot only be blamed on slavery. The slave trade was just one aspect of the opening up of Africa. The general acceleration of communication in the nineteenth century and colonial conquest were equally responsible for spreading new diseases and increasing people's vulnerability to infection. Dense populations and powerful governments to some extent protected the inhabitants of the region from the worst attacks by foreign slave raiding parties. Burundi was able to repulse the Congo-based raiders of Rumaliza the Swahili warlord; Bunyoro and Buganda contained, though with difficulty, the Sudanese coming up the Nile. On the other hand, the militarised kingdoms of the Great Lakes region of East Africa actively participated in the slave trade as enslavers as well as consumers or exporters. It seems clear that the rise of powerful centralised states accompanied the rise of slavery in these societies from the eighteenth century, if not before.

Introduction

Identifying unique features of slavery in the Great Lakes region is difficult since its experience of the international slave trade was so much briefer than that of societies involved in the Atlantic Ocean trade. Sometimes developments such as political crises that seem to have taken centuries to emerge elsewhere materialised within decades in the Great Lakes region. In others the Great Lakes experience was very different. For example, slavery here did not leave a lasting social stigma, but we cannot be sure whether this was because the Great Lakes societies had particularly resisted this development or whether it was simply that the slave trade did not have time to take full effect. Overall the impact of the slave trade on the interlacustrine kingdoms appears very similar to its impact in other parts of Africa. This fits with the wider evolution of Great Lakes historiography which has shifted from overemphasising the uniqueness of its peoples to showing that this region of East Africa should not be considered distinct from the rest of the continent.

Notes

1. For example, J. Beattie, *The Nyoro State* (Oxford, 1971); L.A. Fallers, *Bantu Bureaucracy* (Chicago, 1956); J.J. Maquet, *The Premise of Inequality in Ruanda* (London, 1970).
2. H. Médard, 'Croissance et crises de la royauté du Buganda au XIXe siècle' (unpublished PhD dissertation, Université Paris-I, 2001), published as H. Médard, *Le royaume du Buganda au XIXe siècle: mutations politiques et religieuses d'un grand état d'Afrique de l'est* (Paris, 2007); S.D. Doyle, 'An environmental history of the kingdom of Bunyoro in Western Uganda, from c.1860 to 1940' (unpublished PhD dissertation, Cambridge, 1998).
3. Several participants (Christian Thibon, Michael Twaddle, Claudia Mattalucci and Michele Wagner) did not contribute papers to this volume. Thomas Vernet (as planned) published his paper in 2003 (T. Vernet, 'Le commerce des esclaves sur la côte swahili, 1500–1750', *Azania*, 38 (2003), pp.69–97). Since they contributed significantly to the conference, I wish to thank them and use their oral interventions in this introduction.
4. E.A. Alpers, *Ivory and Slaves* (Berkeley, CA, 1975).
5. Pers. comm. Shane Doyle.
6. G.N. Uzoigwe, 'Precolonial Markets in Bunyoro Kitara', *Comparative Studies in Society and History*, 14 (1972), pp.446–7; E. Mujawimana, 'Le Commerce des esclaves au Rwanda' (unpublished BA thesis, Université Nationale du Rwanda, Ruhengeri, 1983), pp.8–9, 37, 40–1.
7. A.I. Richards, *Economic Development and Tribal Change* (Cambridge, 1954), pp.170–3.
8. J. Roscoe, *The Baganda* (London, 1911).
9. L.P. Mair, *An African People in the Twentieth Century* (London, 1934), pp.32–3, 62, 183–4.
10. M. Leopold, 'Slavery in Sudan, past and present', *African Affairs*, 102 (2003) p.654.
11. M. Twaddle, 'The ending of slavery in Buganda', in S. Miers and R. Roberts (eds), *The End of Slavery in Africa* (Madison, WI, 1988), p.144; F. Cooper, 'The problem of slavery in African studies', *Journal of African History* 20, 1 (1979), p.103.
12. R. Botte. 'Processus de formation d'une classe sociale dans une société africaine précapitaliste', *Cahiers d'études africaines*, 14, 4 (1974), pp.605–26.
13. W. Rusch, *Klassen und Staat in Buganda vor der Kolonialzeit* (Berlin, 1975).
14. J. Iliffe, *The African Poor* (Cambridge, 1987), pp.59–64.
15. G.W. Hartwig, 'Changing forms of servitude among the Kerebe of Tanzania', in S.

	Miers and I. Kopytoff (eds), *Slavery in Africa* (Madison, WI, 1977), pp.261–85.
16	A. Nsanze's book, *Le Burundi ancien*. *L'économie du pouvoir de 1875–1920* (Paris, 2001) should not be judged by his use of the word 'slavery', a very marginal aspect of his work.
17	F. Renault, *Lavigerie, l'esclavage africain et l'Europe* (Paris, 1971); J. Marissal, 'Le commerce zanzibarite dans l'Afrique des Grands Lacs au XIXe siècle', *Revue Française d'Histoire d'Outre-Mer*, 65, 239 (1978), pp.212–55; Mujawimana, 'Le Commerce'.
18	J.M. Gray, 'Livingstone's Muganda Servant', *Uganda Journal*, 13, 2 (Sept. 1949), pp.119–29.
19	A. Sheriff, *Slaves, Spices and Ivory in Zanzibar* (London, 1987); J. Glassman, *Feasts and Riot* (Portsmouth, NH, 1995); M. Wright, *Strategies of Slaves and Women* (New York, 1993); J.J. Ewald, *Soldiers, Traders and Slaves* (Madison, WI, 1990); R. Gray, *A History of Southern Sudan 1839-1889* (London, 1961); S. Feierman, 'A century of ironies in East Africa (c.1780-1890)', in P. Curtin, S. Feierman, L. Thompson and J. Vansina (eds), *African History* (London, 1978), pp.391–418; Alpers, *Ivory*; E.A. Alpers, 'The Story of Swema', in C.C. Robertson and M.A. Klein (eds), *Women and Slavery in Africa* (Portsmouth, NH, 1997), pp.185–219; Leopold, 'Slavery'; F. Cooper, *Plantation Slavery on the East Coast of Africa* (New Haven, CT, 1977); F. Cooper, *From Slaves to Squatters* (New Haven, CT, 1980); D. Northrup, *Beyond the Bend in the River* (Athens, OH, 1988).
20	J. Iliffe, *A Modern History of Tanganyika* (Cambridge, 1979); J. Koponen, *People and Production in Late Precolonial Tanzania* (Uppsala, 1988).
21	P. Larson, *History and Memory in the Age of Enslavement* (Portsmouth, NH, 2000).
22	M. Twaddle, 'Slaves and peasants in Buganda', in L. Archer (ed.), *Slavery and Other Forms of Unfree Labour* (London, 1988), pp.118–29; Twaddle, 'The ending'.
23	Wright, *Strategies*; Alpers, 'The story of Swema'.
24	White Fathers Archives (Rome), c14-417, R.P. Couilaud, 'Rapport sur l'orphelinat de Notre Dame de Kamoga', 25 Oct. 1890–10 Oct. 1891.
25	For example, White Fathers Archives (Rome), Levesque à confrère, Rubaga, 19 Nov. 1881.
26	V. Vannutelli, *Beatificationis seu declarationis martyrii ven. servorum dei Caroli Lwanga, Matthiae Mulumba et sociorum vulgo 'de Ouganda'* (Rome, 1918).
27	Twaddle, 'Slaves'; Twaddle, 'The ending'.
28	Cooper, 'The problem', p.111.
29	Twaddle, 'Slaves'.
30	P. Lovejoy, *Transformations in Slavery* (Cambridge, 2000).
31	J.K. Thornton, *Africa and Africans in the Making of the Atlantic World, 1400-1800* (Cambridge, 1998).
32	Renault, *Lavigerie*, pp.12, 28.
33	Hartwig, 'Changing forms', pp.272–83.
34	Mujawimana, 'Le Commerce', pp.202, 204–205.
35	Vernet, 'Le commerce'.
36	A.D. Roberts, 'Nyamwezi Trade', in R. Gray and D. Birmingham (eds), *Precolonial African Trade* (London, 1970), pp.43–9; Sheriff, *Slaves*, p.155.
37	Renault, *Lavigerie*, pp.95–6, 288.
38	Sheriff, *Slaves*, p.75.
39	T. Vernet, 'Les Cités-états swahili de l'archipel de Lamu, 1585–1810' (unpublished PhD dissertation, Université Paris I, 2005), pp.365–67.
40	Marissal, 'Le commerce', pp.216–217.
41	J.M. Gray, 'Arabs on Lake Victoria', *Uganda Journal*, 22, 1 (March 1958), p.76.
42	Marissal, 'Le commerce', pp.220–1.
43	J. Thomson, *Through Masai Land* (London, 1885), pp.298–99; G.A. Fischer, 'Am Ostufer des Victoria-Njanza', *Petermanns Mittheilungen*, 41 (1895) pp.45, 67, 69.
44	Gray, *A History*, p.38.
45	Renault, *Lavigerie*, pp.326–27.
46	Sheriff, *Slaves*, p.165.
47	F. Stuhlmann, *Mit Emin Pasha in Herz von Africa* (Berlin, 1894), p.186.

Introduction

48 Mujawimana, 'Le Commerce', pp.153–80.
49 Renault, *Lavigerie*, p.89.
50 Roberts, 'Nyamwezi', pp.59–60.
51 Renault, *Lavigerie*, pp.88–9, 95–6; Cooper, *Plantation*, p.125.
52 Hartwig, 'Changing forms', p.280.
53 Mujawimana, 'Le Commerce', pp.130–3; I. Linden, *Christianisme et pouvoir au Rwanda 1900–1990* (Paris, 1999), pp.43, 90.
54 R. Reid, *Political Power in Pre-colonial Buganda* (Oxford, 2002), pp.118–19; Uzoigwe, 'Precolonial markets', p.447.
55 Botte, 'Processus'.
56 Iliffe, *African Poor*, pp.59–64.
57 H.E. Hanson, *Landed Obligation* (Portsmouth, NH, 2003), pp.59–92.
58 Vernet, 'Cités-états', pp.365–67.
59 Hanson, *Landed Obligation*, pp.59–126.
60 Hartwig, 'Changing', p.265.
61 C. Wrigley, *Kingship and State, the Buganda Dynasty* (Cambridge, 1996), pp.236, 240–41; J. Vansina, *Le Rwanda ancien* (Paris, 2001), pp.40, 46, 75, 102, 125.
62 D.L. Schoenbrun, *The Historical Reconstruction of Great Lakes Bantu Cultural Vocabulary* (Köln, 1997).
63 R.H. Fisher, *Twiglight Tales of the Black Baganda* (London, 1912), pp.121–3; H. Johnston, *The Uganda Protectorate* (London, 1902), p.679.
64 Mujawimana, 'Le Commerce'.
65 J. Willis and S. Miers, 'Becoming a child of the house', *Journal of African History*, 38, 3 (1997), pp.481, 494–5; P. Manning, *Slavery and African Life* (Cambridge, 1990), pp.118–20.
66 Thornton, *Africa*; Lovejoy, *Transformations*.
67 Vansina, *Le Rwanda*, pp.199–200, 220–27; Mujawimana, 'Le Commerce'.
68 Hartwig, 'Changing forms'.
69 Glassman, *Feasts*, p.36.
70 Wright, *Strategies*; Alpers, 'The story of Swema'.
71 Twaddle, 'Slaves', p.137; Reid, *Political Power*, p.129.
72 Reid, *Political Power*, p.123
73 *Ibid.*, pp.119–20.
74 Roscoe, *The Baganda*, pp.246, 426; White Fathers Archives (Rome), Levesque à confrère, Rubaga, 19 Nov. 1881.
75 'St. Joseph de Kipalapala', *Chronique trimestrielle*, 35 (July 1887) pp.433–5; White Fathers Archives (Rome), Diary of Kipalapala, 19–25 Sept. 1886.
76 Rusch, *Klassen*, pp.108–10, 380–2.
77 H. Meyer, *Les Barundi* (Paris, 1984), pp.129–130; Iliffe, *African Poor*, p.61.
78 Twaddle, 'The ending', pp.123–4.
79 Lovejoy, *Transformations*, pp.119–20.
80 Hanson, *Landed Obligation*, pp.177–82.
81 Hartwig, 'Changing'.
82 For example: R. Shaw, 'The production of witchcraft, witchcraft as production', *American Ethnologist*, 24, 4 (1997), pp.856–76.
83 Claudine Vidal suggested this idea to me in a conversation during the mid-1990s.
84 Hanson, *Landed Obligation*, pp.82–9.
85 Médard, *Croissance*, pp.206–335.
86 For a detailed account see Médard, 'Croissance', pp.37–64, 129, 206–335.
87 Renault, *Lavigerie*, pp.173, 347. See also Iliffe, *A Modern History*, pp.52–66; Feierman, 'A century'.
88 Twaddle, 'The ending', p.127; Médard, 'Croissance', pp.202–4, 491–508.
89 Hanson, *Landed Obligation*, p.3.
90 White Fathers Archives (Rome), Diaire de Rubaga, 28 May 1892. Buganda had approximately 1,000,000 inhabitants at this time.
91 Twaddle, 'Slaves', pp.133–6.

92 Mujawimana, 'Le Commerce', pp.217–43.
93 See also Médard, 'Croissance', p.202; Stuhlmann, *Mit Emin Pasha*, p.186.
94 Richards, *Economic Development*; Hanson, *Landed Obligation*, pp.177–8; S. Miers and I. Kopytoff (eds), *Slavery in Africa* (Madison, WI, 1977) p.76.
95 Twaddle, 'The ending', pp.135–6, 142–4; Hanson, *Landed Obligation*, pp.221–2; J. Gahama, *Le Burundi sous l'administration Belge* (Paris, 2001), p.377; Northrup, *Beyond the Bend*.
96 R. Harms, 'Sustaining the system: trading towns along Middle Zaire', in C. Robertson and M. Klein (eds), *Women and Slavery in Africa* (Madison, WI, 1983) pp.95–110.
97 Mujawimana, 'Le Commerce', pp.189–90.
98 Stuhlmann, *Mit Emin Pasha*, pp.186, 223.
99 Hartwig, 'Changing', p. 280; White Fathers Archives (Rome), Diary of Rubaga, 10 June 1886, Hirth to Livinhac, Kasozi, 25 Aug. 1891, c14-495 525; Uganda National Archives (Entebbe), Williams, 'Memo on Busoga', 1 Mar. 1893, A2 1.
100 Renault, *Lavigerie*, pp.44–5.
101 Vansina, *Le Rwanda*, pp.40, 47, 75, 102, 125.
102 O. Baumann, *Der Sansibar-Archipel* (Leipzig, 1897), p.21.
103 Renault, *Lavigerie*, pp.48, 188-189, 326, 346.
104 Mujawimana, 'Le Commerce'; Linden, *Christianisme*, p.43.
105 White Fathers Archives (Rome), Girault to RP, Kamoga, 31 Dec. 1883, c14-257; Diary of Bukumbi, 11–17 Feb. 1885.
106 Hartwig, 'Changing forms', p.264.
107 H.J. Fisher. *Slavery in the History of Muslim Black Africa* (London, 2001), p.xx.
108 Miers and Kopitoff, *Slavery*, pp.6-7; C. Meillassoux, *L'esclavage en Afrique precoloniale* (Paris, 1975), pp.11–14; M.I. Finley, *Esclavage antique et idéologie moderne* (Paris, 1981).
109 Cooper, *Plantation*, pp.154–56, 169–70, 208.
110 Finley, *Esclavage*, p.90; Miers and Kopitoff, *Slavery*.
111 Cooper, 'The problem', p.105.
112 Cooper, *Plantation*, p.155; Cooper, 'The problem'.
113 See also David Schoenbrun's chapter in this volume.
114 Cooper, *Plantation*, pp.1–2, 15–17; A. Testart, *L'esclave, la dette et le pouvoir* (Paris, 2001), pp.19–25, 115.
115 J.C. Miller, 'Imbangala lineage slavery (Angola)', in Miers and Kopitoff (eds), *Slavery*, p.205.
116 O. Patterson, *Slavery and Social Death* (Cambridge, MA, 1982), pp.77–101. Of course as John Iliffe notes, it was not because slaves were deprived of honour by the dominant ideology that they accepted this situation; nor was it the case that honour did not exist among slaves. J. Iliffe, *Honour in African History* (Cambridge, 2005), pp.119–39.
117 Testart, *L'esclave*, pp.26–7.
118 Miers and Kopitoff, *Slavery*, pp.5, 122–3.
119 Miers and Kopitoff, *Slavery*; Testart, *L'esclave*; Meillassoux, *Anthropologie*; A. Tuden and L. Plotnicov, *Social Stratification in Africa* (New York, 1970), pp.11–12; Renault, *Lavigerie*, pp.204–5; Fisher, *Slavery*, pp.40–97.
120 See Edward Steinhart's and Mark Leopold's chapters in this volume; for Western Rwanda, see Mujawimana, 'Le Commerce', p.151.
121 Hartwig, 'Changing', pp.263–64, 276.
122 Reid, *Political Power*, p.115; White Fathers Archives (Rome), Diary of Rubaga, 20 Mar. 1881 (Algiers version).
123 Finley, *Esclavage*, p.93.
124 Roscoe, *The Baganda*, pp.246, 426.
125 Testart, *L'esclave*, pp.26, 42–3, 66. For Burundi see Botte, 'Processus', pp.610–11.
126 Miers and Kopitoff, *Slavery*, p.17.
127 Fallers, *Bantu*; L.A. Fallers, *The King's Men* (London, 1964).
128 Miers and Kopitoff, *Slavery*, pp.24, 35; Testart, *L'esclave*, p.23.
129 D.S. Newbury, 'The clans of Rwanda', *Africa*, 50, 4 (1980), pp.389–403; J. Willis, 'Clan and history in Western Uganda', *The International Journal of African Historical Studies*, 30, 3

Introduction

(1997), pp.583–600; J. Jensen, 'Die Erweiterung des Lungenfischs-clan in Buganda (Uganda) durch den Anschluss von Bavuma Gruppen', *Sociologus*, 19, 2 (1969), pp.153–66.

130 J. Roscoe and A. Kagwa, *Enquiry into Native Land Tenure in the Uganda Protectorat* (1906), Rhodes House (Oxford), MSS Afr.s.17, p.36 (Tefiro Mulamba Kulugi), p.93 (Isaiah Kunsa).

131 Mujawimana, 'Le Commerce', p.191; White Fathers Archives (Rome), Story told by Fortunat Kwatoti, a redeemed slave aged c.11 years old and future White Fathers Brother, 'Tous les hommes et les enfants plus grands que moi sont tués à coups de lances et tous ceux qui ne peuvent pas bien marcher quand il pleuvait étaient assommés à coups de bâtons'; Levesque to confrère, Rubaga, 10 May 1882, C14-325. Bukerebe seems to have been an exception to this rule. See Hartwig, 'Changing', p.270.

132 Miers and Kopitoff, *Slavery*, pp.24–5.

133 Roscoe and Kagwa, *Enquiry*, p.42 (Tefiro Mulamba Kulugi); Richards, *Economic Development*, pp.184, 192.

134 Richards, *Economic Development*, pp.171, 179.

135 Mair, *An African*, p.33; J. Roscoe, J. and A. Kagwa, *Enquiry into Native Land Tenure in the Uganda Protectorat* (1906), Rhodes House (Oxford) MSS Afr.s.17, p.48 (Tefiro Mulamba Kulugi), p.93 (Isaiah Kunsa).

136 M.L. Perlman, 'The traditional systems of stratification among the Ganda and Nyoro of Uganda', in A. Tuden and L. Plotnicov (eds), *Social Stratification in Africa* (New York, 1970) p.140; Fallers, *The Kings*, p.176; Richards, *Economic Development*, pp.171, 179–80.

137 C. Obbo, 'Village strangers in Buganda society', in W.A. Shack and E.P. Skinner (eds), *Strangers in African Societies* (Berkeley, CA, 1979), p.232.

138 Richards, *Economic Development*, pp.166–7, 171–3, 175–6, 184.

139 White Fathers Archives (Rome), Diary of Rubaga, 9 Apr. 1881 (Rubaga version); Reid, *Political Power*, p.129.

140 *Ibid.*, p.127.

141 Obbo, 'Village', pp.229–31; Roscoe and Kagwa, *Enquiry*, pp.1, 71 (Apolo Kagwa), 43, 48–9, 112 (Tefiro Mulamba Kulugi), 73 (Stanislas Mugwanya).

142 *Ibid.*, p.112 (Tefiro Mulamba Kulugi).

143 *Ibid.*, p.43 (Tefiro Mulamba Kulugi).

144 Mair, *An African*, pp.183–4; Roscoe and Kagwa, *Enquiry*, p.43 (Tefiro Mulamba Kulugi); Hartwig, 'Changing', p.271.

145 Reid, *Political Power*, p.116.

146 Robertson and Klein, *Women*.

147 Reid, *Political Power*, p.123.

148 S. Nannyonga-Tamusuza, 'The Ngalabi and Mbuutu: Man and woman drums of the Baganda people of Uganda', Paper presented at Torino University, 22 Oct. 2003.

149 Wrigley, *Kingship*, pp.446–7; Wright, *Strategies*.

150 'I am not going to list the task which the slaves had to do since I have related those of the women, for they were the same or worse': H. Mukasa, *Simuda Nyuma part III*, microfilm shown at the Center for Research Libraries (University of Chicago), pp.2–7.

151 See also Reid, *Political Power*, p.123.

152 Twaddle, 'Slaves', p.140.

One

Violence, Marginality, Scorn & Honour
Language evidence of slavery to the eighteenth century

DAVID SCHOENBRUN*

Introduction

How did words for slaves, captives, dependants, and enslavement used by Bantu-speaking communities in the Great Lakes region of East Africa change and endure in the centuries before 1800? Which of the earlier kinds of violence and ideologies of hierarchy underpinned enslavement and commercial slavery in the nineteenth century? This essay will explore these questions by focusing on two types of language evidence: new words with relatively new meanings for forms of slavery, and new meanings related to slavery that Great Lakes Bantu-speakers attached to words whose earlier meanings had no clear connection to the commercialised forms of marginality that were so prominent in the nineteenth century (see Appendix).[1] The shifts in meanings revealed in the analysis of these words' semantic variability open up ideas about honour, scorn and hierarchy that distinguish the elite from the common people, the insider from the outsider, and shed light on notions of authority and legal practices that enforced those divides. The shifts in meaning also touch on theories of gender and generation that assigned significant weight to types of work as defining features of individuals and appropriately distinct capacities of different generations. Approaching a history of slaveries in Africa in this manner sidesteps stubborn, recent and highly politicised dichotomies between malignant and benign, open and closed, forms of slavery because it analyses the inventions and extensions of meaning in specific historical contexts. The antiquity of thinking about forms of social marginalisation and experiences of violence must first be assessed as significant historical conclusions in their own right, before exploring how they might have shaped more recent meanings of slavery and enslavement.[2]

The slaveries mentioned in the nineteenth- and twentieth-century documentary records have very different historical depths, with the great majority reaching no further than the eighteenth century. They emphasised degrees of immobility and social marginalisation in a commercial context. The common concern with fixing slaves inside or outside a particular social nexus, an exclusionist impulse in Great Lakes and coastal East African cultural habits, is much older than the eighteenth century and is linked to broader historical processes than a study of terms for slavery alone can reveal.[3] Not every form of social violence with deep historical roots turned into the forms and conditions of 'enslavement' familiar from the long nineteenth century. Their histories unfolded in other, sometimes older, contexts. However, within the narrow compass of the slaveries described in the recent, documentary record, the master's concern to define the nature of the 'social death' imposed on slaves comes across clearly. The language evidence in these sources speaks to these claims of the dominant far more than it reveals a slave's concern to define the nature of her humanity inside and against a master's social responsibility.[4] The etymologies of words for slavery and enslavement in the Great Lakes region reveal a consistent obsession with claiming a slave's marginality, but they also reveal much about the differing historical contexts that generated slaves and the contexts in which the enslaved could work against the sometimes greatly exaggerated rumours of their social deaths.

Those contexts included an agricultural intensification in the region which unfolded around bananas in wetter zones nearer to Lake Victoria, and around cattle and grain in the drier zones to the west of the lake. Larger-scale environmental and climatic shifts, well under way by the opening of the second millennium CE, conditioned these agricultural changes.[5] Intensified farming and herding created new pressures on land and labour, pressures that supported the growth of centralised political cultures after the sixteenth century, strong militarisms from the seventeenth century, and eventually the growth of commodification, late in the eighteenth century. These more recent developments shaped the social histories of slavery and enslavement outlined in this essay. Widespread social and political hierarchies, especially after the sixteenth century, knitted together by various forms of reciprocity and coercion, constituted the specific contexts for socially marginal persons to think about and pursue their aspirations.[6] The outlines of agrarian change and the development of centralised political cultures have been developed elsewhere and will only be alluded to in this essay. Other threads – like the social and technological study of violence – have yet to receive careful historical treatment for early periods and have received virtually no study for the eras before the sixteenth century C.E.[7] The outlines of these stories can only be touched on here. Still, the genealogies of the regional and local meanings given to words for what we might gloss as 'slavery' and enslavement, presented in this essay, constitute a first step in that larger project on the social and intellectual history of violence, vulnerability, and authority in Greater Eastern Africa.[8]

We can know rather more about the nature and sources of slavery, enslavement and inequality in the Great Lakes region than one might surmise, given the slight volume of work focused solely on this complex topic.[9] Studies of the nineteenth century consistently touch on what Europeans perceived as slavery – and some take considerable pains to translate local vocabulary related to these perceptions – but we have very little sustained scholarly inquiry into the intellectual, social, and military genealogies of domination and dependence in the region before the eighteenth century.[10] We know very little about how Africans between the Great Lakes understood commercial slavery and enslavement, and how they managed the combined mercantile and military transformations for which the nineteenth century is infamous. Scholars – including African intellectuals writing throughout the colonial period – often claim that eighteenth-century militarism and its associated dislocations made enslavement common. But this insistence only serves as the baseline against which to measure the gradual commodification of economic life, including the buying and selling of persons and firearms, which engulfed the region after the 1840s. It does little to disentangle the many different sources of slavehood, most pressingly, the older from the newer. This state of affairs is perfectly understandable, given the other attractions the region and its histories have offered to intellectuals, local or otherwise. It is also understandable, given the fact that historical sources on the topic are notoriously recalcitrant for eras before the eighteenth century.

People between the Great Lakes shared a common discourse on the nature of hierarchy and dependence that sustained arguments about who could and could not belong to the different categories in the hierarchies. For much of the time period this essay covers, I cannot hope to reconstruct even a single instance of such arguing, but some of the semantic results of the arguments emerge as different shades of meaning attached to the words people commonly used to name different parts of the hierarchies. Tracing differences in meaning and examining the conditions under which they emerged suggest some of the contents of the arguments and struggles people had over what it meant to belong in the categories they valued and over how to move between them or how to avoid such movement.[11] Against these temporally deep and spatially broad currents of still recognisably distinct and, sometimes, frankly disjointed social and intellectual histories, we can begin to make greater sense of the more familiar nineteenth- and twentieth-century notions of equality and inequality. These are the questions that guide this essay even though I cannot hope to take up each one in wholly satisfying detail.

An earlier work argued that a host of social, intellectual, economic, agricultural and environmental changes informed the development of ideologies of patriarchal descent and inheritance, ideologies which could be used to exclude certain persons.[12] Changing ideologies of kinship between the Great Lakes shaped the contours of slavery, dependence and vulnerability before the eighteenth century because Great Lakes Bantu-speakers used kinship ideologies to promote some aspects of marginality and set others aside.[13] This approach to kinship highlights the insight of

Igor Kopytoff and Suzanne Miers that a continuum of social integration was central to the nature of 'slavery' in Africa, though neither insists on a single static form for that continuum nor downplays issues of struggle and power.[14] The marginality that made dependants vulnerable – and the vulnerability that marginalised people – were created in a variety of ways between the Great Lakes. People could be taken as war prisoners, kidnapped, sold (by relatives, patrons, to pay fines and debts), bought, inherited, and ejected from their communities by legal decision, as a gift to a chief or king or other social superior, or due to illness.[15] The sexually transmitted diseases that afflicted men and women in the region, with the advent of caravanning in the 1840s, may have disproportionately driven women into isolated, vulnerable positions.[16] The prevalence of one or another of these means to create slaves 'from within' changed dramatically over time.

Comparative linguistic evidence is well suited to tracing continuities and ruptures in a social formulation like 'slavery'. This is because the spatial distribution of words and the shapes of the semantic fields they mark reflect both inherited forms whose meaning had force and value across many generations and the innovation of new words or meanings with the emergence of novel conditions for masters and the enslaved. Moreover, studying sequences of change in the densities of terminologies for modes of marginalisation and dependence takes us into the realm of semantic history. When combined with what we know about other aspects of the social history of the Great Lakes region, historical linguistic evidence thus offers a compelling picture of violence and vulnerability which enables their impact on commercial slavery and enslavement in the region to begin to emerge. This history's most distinctive features include (i) the great antiquity of plunder and pillage; (ii) the emergence before the eighteenth century of generic and gendered social categories for 'the slave'; (iii) the florescence of different words for new and more commodified sorts of slaves, after the eighteenth century; (iv) the centrality of fear to the performance of honour; and (v) the entanglement of fear and honour with notions of scorn and struggles over the capacity to speak that lie at the heart of owners' efforts to define 'the slave'.

Linguistic Evidence and a Poetic of Labelling[17]

'There are always more meanings than words', the linguist Raimo Anttila has said, but language surprises us with 'its ability to adapt to such a semantic challenge'.[18] With the radical changes in the conditions of hierarchy and service that unfolded in the eighteenth and nineteenth century, Great Lakes Bantu languages were put to the test of their semantic creativity. '*Toute époque a ses idées propres, il faut aussi qu'elle ait les mots propres à ces idées,*' as Victor Hugo observed about the tendency for synonyms to proliferate around issues of great importance to a community.[19] The people who lived through those tumultuous centuries created a rich vocabulary concerning slavery and enslavement.

Scholars of semantics have long noted that high numbers of synonyms for particular things, actions and ideas reflect a high level of interest in those things, actions and ideas held by members of the speech community.[20] More or fewer synonyms for slavery in different subgroups of Great Lakes Bantu languages reveal the shifting importance of slavery over time and by region. Subgroups or individual languages with many terms for slavery needed them in order to make sense of eras in which recruiting outsiders was important to them.[21] Subgroups of related languages – or individual languages – with fewer or no terms for 'slavery' reflect eras in which slavery was of little or at least of lesser importance.

Despite the temptation to assume a monolithic, primordial slavery undergirding the Great Lakes region's investments in social hierarchy, we should begin instead to excavate its historical development in this manner. What speakers did with these words in the very distant past, we cannot know exactly. But the shades of meaning people made them express – and the sheer mass of terminology – speak volumes to us now about the past worlds they struggled to understand and manipulate through speech.[22] These sorts of lives – isolated, dependent, and vulnerable – are very old between the Lakes as, indeed, they are very old the world over.[23] The words people used to speak about them tell us a lot about how they gave those lives meaning, and the meanings they gave them took surprisingly similar forms across a very broad swath of Bantu-speaking Africa.

Pillage, Plunder, Prisoners and Captives

Inventing this vocabulary drew on earlier semantic resources in a number of ways. Some labellers drew on polysemy – the capacity for a single word to signify a broad range of meanings depending on the context – to craft new terms for long-standing social realities that were later connected with slavery. For example, the verb *-kuboha* 'to tie up, fasten' often underwent a natural extension of meaning to include 'to imprison, to capture'. The verb is distributed widely but discontinuously across Bantu-speaking Eastern Africa, suggesting that people fashioned this meaning extension nearly three millennia ago, when the Proto-Mashariki speech community existed.[24] In the Lakes region – as well as in other parts of the vast region in which daughter speech communities of Proto Mashariki lived – the innovators exploited the semantic vagueness of 'to tie up, to fasten' by including the meaning 'to imprison' within the signifying field of *-kubóha*. Among other meanings linked to physical restraint, speakers made a noun in order to refer to a 'prisoner' or a 'captive'. Capturing people and the physical coercion involved therefore seems to have been a long-standing part of the social reality of Bantu-speaking communities, even if confinement is far more difficult to perceive for periods before the eighteenth century, from the available evidence. But in late precolonial and colonial documents, people do not use this noun to refer to those then considered a 'slave'. Though capture may have been the first step into slavery for some, this word for 'captive' or 'prisoner' only rarely and recently worked as a synonym for slavery (Appendix nos. 14.2, 14.6, and probably 14.4). Immobility and confinement helped define slavery in the nineteenth century,[25] but persons other than slaves were also immobile.

The sheer number of verbs and nouns describing capture and pillage reveals that these were widespread and perhaps long-standing activities between the Great Lakes (Appendix nos. 1, 7, 8, 12.1, 12.2, 13, 14.1-14.6). Many of the nouns in this list were derived from verbs for these actions, verbs which may be reconstructed as parts of the lexicon in speech communities ancestral to Great Lakes Bantu. The distribution of cognate vocabulary for coercive 'captivity' occurs in contemporary languages descended from this group, whose ancestral speech community, it has been argued elsewhere, existed between 2500 and 3500 years ago.[26] These durable verbs named violent raiding for forms of property, including persons, but the fuller significance and meaning of these ancient practices cannot be understood solely through the lens of slaveries, however important raiding for people was to the trajectories of violence in the eighteenth and nineteenth centuries.[27] They must be considered in light of the growth of contemporaneous categories of dependence and of the semantic histories of words for forms of dependence, a task this essay can only begin to address.

Creating Generic, Gendered Slaves as Outsiders

Two terms for a generic and gendered status of dependence (Appendix nos. 10 and 18) – #*mwiru* and #*muzaana* – emerged sometime after the fourteenth or fifteenth centuries, when the North Nyanzan and Rutaran speech communities had begun to diverge into their daughter languages. In the nineteenth century, these terms often named the broadest, most inclusive category of male and female slaves, respectively. In the second half of the twentieth century, the terms either dropped from use or took on different generic meanings, most often related to material poverty. From the fourteenth century, locals saw the #*mwiru* and the #*muzaana* as social outsiders, newcomers, even refugees.

A few widely separated attestations for #*mwiru* include the non-gender-specific meaning 'peasant' or 'farmer' – a relict distribution of this less dependency-oriented referent that might reflect the earliest contexts for the invention of the noun. At the turn of the first millennium CE, archaeological, linguistic and ecological evidence all suggest that grain farmers and livestock-keepers formed communities much larger and much more widespread than previously, and moved into the drier zones between Lake Victoria and the eastern massifs of the Kivu Rift.[28] Specialised pastoralism and grain farming divided the micro-environments within this zone, revolutionising patron-client relations over the following several hundred years and ushering in a new set of social and ethnic hierarchies built around these occupational specialisations, which foregrounded competitive firstcomer-newcomer distinctions. This may well have been the period when the binaries Bahíma-Bairu and Batuutsi-Bahutu emerged. At this point, #*bairu* most likely were newcomers whose sedentary farming lifestyle required permanent settlement, a permanence that intruded on cyclical pastoralist usage of their lands and exposed them and their fields to the risks of an uncertain climate. Small or localised effects of climatic uncertainty drew farmers and herders into mutually beneficial social networks. But large-scale or pronounced oscillations in the timing and intensity of rainfall could create enormous asymmetries of economic advantage in those ties. It seems likely that these material realities underlay, in part, the growth of these occupational-cum-ethnic groups.[29]

The gendered meanings 'male dependant, client or servant' (all of which were clearly very common in the nineteenth century) are the most widespread meanings for #*mwiru*. They show a clear block distribution across the entire territory, from Unyamwezi to Bunyole, in which the term existed until the colonial period. This uniformity suggests strongly that these meanings emerged no earlier than 1200, by which time new dialect clusters had begun to form in North Nyanzan and Rutaran speech communities, signalling the beginning of their breaking up. These meanings may have been first used much more recently than that, however, given that they did not displace the older meaning 'farmer'. This vast period since 1200 includes the development of centralised political power in the core of this territory, and it seems likely that the intensification of social hierarchy that accompanied and constituted such centralisation drew on these forms of subordinated masculinity.[30]

The root #-*zaana* consistently refers to a female servant or slave and thus appears to have been gendered from the beginning of its existence. Unlike the meaning 'farmer' for *mwiru, a more widespread relict distribution of additional meaning cannot be expressed by #*muzaana*. Everywhere the term is in evidence, it is best glossed by the English meanings 'female servant, female slave'. Its block distribution and uniformly gendered meanings suggest strongly that the term was probably developed no earlier than the sixteenth century. That was when the breakup of Rutara, which was the centre of this word's distribution, was complete. Thus, #*muzaana* may have emerged in the same period that #*mwiru* took on meanings of dependence, clientship or servitude and marked a gendered contrast to it. And this was the period in which the leaders of politically centralised states such as Bunyoro and the ranked nodes of authority visible in the archaeological and oral historical records for places like Mubende, Munsa, Ntusi, Kibengo and Kisengwe may have begun the practice of exchanging persons, especially females, who lacked social standing.[31]

The etymology of this term is unclear. People may have derived it from a verb #-*kuijaaana* meaning 'to come with', an associative form of #-*kuija* 'to come'.[32] But the outcomes of the substantive form are irregular in many of the Rutaran languages, in Rwenzori and in Rwanda. This suggests that the word was invented in one or more places and spread rapidly from there, as gifts and persons moved around.³³ Though the absence of a clear etymology makes it difficult to date the invention and dispersal of this term, the meanings it has carried over the last century tell us that the #*muzaana* was someone who entered a community as the extension of another person, either the giver, the captor or a master of some sort. A #*muzaana*'s identity was a function of her captor's or her master's. It could therefore have worked as part of an ideological claim that foregrounded a newcomer, outsider, even refugee standing for female slaves at the same time that it highlighted the composite strength of a high-status person's standing.

Another name for slave – common in nineteenth-century accounts from the region – was also generic but was not gendered. The etymology of this term, *muja [Appendix no. 11], is also exceedingly difficult to sort out. The term may have been an innovation from a verb that no longer exists, but looked like #-*dįa*.³⁴ It may simply be a stand-alone substantive innovation, not tied to any verbal form.³⁵ In any case, *muja is very broadly distributed in Western Lakes languages. The *muja was a 'dependant, servant, slave, or refugee' and was also familiar to people who spoke Bemba, Luba and Ila in Central Africa, and the Sabaki languages of the Indian Ocean coastal region.³⁶ At first glance, this vast distribution might suggest a great antiquity for this form of slavery. But at the coast, in Proto Sabaki, the noun meant 'newcomer or refugee' and its gendered form, *-*mujakazi*, meant 'female slave'. Only meanings connected explicitly to slavery, including the exclusively female form referred to by *-*mujakazi*, turn up in Forest and West Highlands languages. And the distribution is a block, connecting the interior speech communities with the coast. These facts strongly suggest a history where these terms spread to inland speech communities from the Sabaki-speaking communities living in the coastal lands between the Sabaki and Rufiji rivers. The regular sound correspondences between attestations of this word in each of the speech communities in the interior is best accounted for by arguing that the term was in use before those intermediate language groups began to break up. Given that these roots have been reconstructed for the Proto Sabaki lexicon, they could have moved repeatedly into the interior any time over the last fourteen centuries or so since Proto-Sabaki was spoken.³⁷ The *muja and specifically the *mujakazi may well have been the earliest sorts of 'newcomers' (in Sabaki-speaking societies) or 'refugees' (in the interior) to enter the coastwise trade and Sabaki-speaking society as female dependants, perhaps well before the famous caravan phase was under way in the early nineteenth century.

The notion of the newcomer is the most widespread one that Lakes people used to name a slave. Firstcomers claimed that a newcomer was a social infant, without the rights and responsibilities of an adult insider. But the idea that newcomers could expect lower social standing than others in a community is a long-standing commonplace in ideologies of hierarchy between the Great Lakes and at the Indian Ocean coast. It did not first come into existence around the experiences of slavery; the reverse is more likely to have been true. Political hierarchies that relied on an ideology of firstcomer standing rested on notions of the newcomer for their force. When people argued that slaves were newcomers – an argument suggested by the range of meanings carried by terms such as *-*muja*, *-*mwiru*, and *-*muzaana* – they put established principles of acceptable status and authority to work in marginalising slaves. They also drew on forms of social control beyond the taxonomies of hierarchy in order to define a slave. The distinctive power and sting of such marginalisation revolved around notions of honour and of the force of scornful speech.

Scorn and Honour: New Names for Slaves from the 1700s to 1850s

The ubiquitous metaphor of the slave-as-newcomer (or 'refugee') between the Great Lakes was supplemented by a metaphor that connected slaves with scorn and disdain. In the Lakes region, many different nouns that signified 'slave' in the nineteenth century were derived from verbs that meant 'to scorn, disdain or backbite' (Appendix nos. 2 and 5).[38] One of these terms, '*mugaya*' worked virtually as an ethnic slur in southeast Lake Victoria. Kerewe-speakers claim that Jita- and Kwaya-speaking raiders hurled this term at Luo-speakers who were most often the objects of their raids. This metaphorical extension from 'a scorned person' to 'a slave' to a generically enslaveable people played on the social reality between the Great Lakes that a person's capacity to act with social consequence flowed in no small part from their capacity to speak with force, authority and respect in whatever settings were appropriate to their standing. Powerful speech was authoritative speech if its audience conferred legitimacy on the speech through approbation or respectful assent. It was also powerful if a speaker could marshal the necessary persons to support and defend him/her should s/he be attacked by another powerful speaker. By using this metaphor, people argued that the scornable slave could not do this because her outsider status meant she had no social network that could counter her enemy's scorn; she was too vulnerable to such talk. She might even have been 'seen' by others as the embodiment of scorn itself.[39] In this way Great Lakes Bantu-speaking societies could 'add' a newcomer to their community while simultaneously restraining that person from becoming an insider.[40] It is not yet possible to argue this with the conviction of an exhaustive comparative search in regional oral and ethnographic sources, but these metaphorical extensions occurred in discrete parts of the region and flowed from different verbal forms. The distribution of the 'slave-as-newcomer' metaphor – expressed in the terms #*muzaana*, #*muja* and #*mujakazi* – takes the shape of a continuous, discrete block. The notion that slaves could be scorned and backbitten was far more widespread and could be expressed using any of several terms for varying aspects of this condition. A slave between the Great Lakes was fixed as an outsider, with no family or friends to speak of upon arrival in a new community.

Violence, Marginality, Scorn & Honour

In the late nineteenth century, in Buganda, the noun *nvuma* named a 'female chattel slave'. It was derived from a widespread verb, *kuvuma*, meaning 'to speak ill of, to scorn'. Such a person had little prospect of bettering their circumstances, according to historian Michael Twaddle.[41] Other substantive derivations, *ikivumé* in Kinyarwanda, for example, clearly point out that a person burdened by scorn and disdain was not a supportable person; she or he could not be part of society. The importance of reputation and the rumour and gossip that made or broke reputations were very much at issue in defining slavehood in nineteenth-century Buganda and in Rwanda. If clients and patrons enjoyed a measure of reciprocal obligation, slaves were tainted by bad talk and their backtalk could be ignored. That was both a sign of their weak position and a cause of that weakness.

With *ikivume* and *nvumu*, a speaker could raise ontological questions about the labelled person's status as an articulate, sentient being. People made these words for slaves by using the class 7 or class 9 noun prefix which put them into noun classes largely populated with inanimate things, some sorts of animals and insects, and strange, unusual people.[42] Whoever uttered these names, then, raised issues of a slave's outsider standing; they claimed that slaves were, in effect, not 'normal' people. They claimed that a slave did not have to be listened to. Obviously, in actual speech, the word could work either as part of a strategy to contest that status or to insist on it.[43] But the general absence of such a semantic poetics from the earlier, generic names for outsiders or dependants perhaps reflects a time before the intensification of marginalising slaves, a time before their value lay in being a 'liquid' form of social capital whose gendered labour might or might not have immediate utility but whose persons their 'masters' could easily dispose of.[44] When it became far more common for her exchange value to constitute at least part of what made a slave valuable to her labellers, this dehumanising naming strategy grew more prominent. The more recent commodification of people intensified discursive efforts to keep slaves from social incorporation.

Social incorporation is a cold abstraction with a vast number of potential glosses. One of the richest revolved around notions of honour and how it is produced and circulated. Honour is important, its historians tell us, because it is a subjective desire that requires public recognition in order to come into existence.[45] For this reason, getting at historical contexts for changing practices and understandings of honour is fraught with difficulties. If honour is interactional at heart, as some of its finest students have reminded us,[46] how can the socially 'flat' evidence of historical linguistics open this up? Between the Great Lakes, the derivational processes of one of the most common terms for 'honour, respect, dignity, pomp, majesty, authority' and so forth tells us much [Roots 16.1, 16.2, 16.3, and 16.4]. The term is *ekitíibwa* (in North Nyanza), *ekitíinwa* or *kutíina* (in Rutara), and *kutíinya* (in West Highlands). Each speech community derived these different forms from the same underlying verb, *kutîia*, which means 'to fear'.[47] Different derivational processes suggest that different speech communities connected fear and honour at separate times, in separate historical circumstances, and by drawing on different phenomenological claims.[48]

Following Orlando Patterson's work on slavery and social death, the historian John Iliffe has argued that masters in Africa 'did commonly deny honour to their slaves'.[49] For Great Lakes Bantu-speakers, the subjectivity of the fear that produced and constituted the recognition of honour differed from other, embodied and potentially mortal fears. They used different terms to name the latter sort of fears, terms not connected to questions of honour and respect. For example, very early in the twentieth century, the sorts of fear that drove the body to tremble were called *ensisi*, in Luganda, whereas the sort of fear that underpinned honour was called *entîisa*, in Luganda. Luganda-speakers made that noun from the verb *okutîisa*, a causative of the verb *kutya*, a transitive form meaning 'to fear, hold in reverence'. Some centuries earlier, before North Nyanza had broken up into its constituent daughter languages, Ganda- and Soga-speakers drew on the transitivity of the verb *kutya*, added a passive suffix (-*bwa*) and derived the noun *ekitîibwa* [Appendix nos. 16.1 and 16.2] which carries many closely related meanings in English concerning honour: prestige, pomp, majesty, authority, dignity, respect and so on. With a poetic efficiency, this derivation described fear and honour as two sides of a coin. But the passive formulation makes clear that fear was a principal manifestation of honour. It also reveals that, whereas fear was an action, at least as early as the later nineteenth century, honour was thing-like, an attribute of action, an aspiration which had to have a concrete form as well as a subjective home. And, once acquired, honour had the capacity to transform its possessor into a special sort of person, the *ekitîibwa*, whose name belonged in an entirely different class of nouns.

Though a full exploration lies beyond the scope of this essay, connections between honour and the fear that generated it and that drove people to seek it, clearly shaped and constituted gendered aspirations for manhood and womanhood, in important social ways, around notions of and strategies for gaining honour.[50] West Highlands-speakers named the practice of seclusion for young wives with the same verb (°-*tînya*) that they used to describe the fear and honour of the respected person (°-*tînywa*).[51] Though it might seem paradoxical, the absence of the secluded woman from public life was a clear statement about the standing of her marriage, the capacity for her sisters and other members of her natal lineage to support her, not to mention a time of relaxation and pleasure for her. These forms of seeking and keeping honour took shape vertically, across and in relation to different stations in a regional social hierarchy, from the small-scale hierarchy of the homestead to the larger public space of a royal court or ritual.[52] And people shaped them horizontally, within particular social groups such as young men and women, wives, hunters, etc. Forms of honour were highly motivating and multivalent framing factors for social action, including the social action of owners toward slaves and of slaves toward owners and each other.[53]

If the subjective desire for honour required public recognition in order to be transformed into a social force, then it seems likely that scorn – as the public refusal of a person's honour – was an important part of an owner's or a community's effort to create and maintain social hierarchy in gendered ways.[54] The logics of competition and aspiration for honour among the elite relied on productive and reproductive labour to underwrite them – the symbolic capital embodied by a chief's following also took the form of gifts and tribute, including women – but the poetics of the semantic histories of some of the terms – such as the *muja and the *muzaana – that Great Lakes Bantu-speakers used to talk about the social hierarchies they formed foreground sources of honour other than productive labour.

It seems quite likely that the logic of scorn lay at the heart of denials of honour, at least to the extent that masters and others successfully used scorn to publicly refuse a slave's own sense of her honour.[55] It seems equally likely that owners could use this equation with meaner results as state-sponsored violence grew in the eighteenth century, and as the volume and velocity of the coastwise trade increased in the nineteenth century. Both of these trajectories led to larger groups of slaves living further from their original homes than had been the case previously, when territorial alienation was probably rare or of limited scope. None of this, however, speaks to a slave's own sense of refusing such conditions of her standing and, in the absence of evidence to the contrary, it is preferable to assume that the well-documented techniques of slave resistance – in other historical settings – were in play between the Great Lakes during these centuries of intensified violence. At this point, however, these speculations await careful work in the rich oral traditions from the region's monarchies.

A slave's honour must be reckoned as something different from the honour of a client if only because her negotiating leverage did not normally include changing masters, whereas clients famously – and according to their own calculus – could seek other patrons.[56] However, the central 'paradox of slavery', in which an owner exerted dominance – and a slave might accept that dominance – only in exchange for respecting particular concessions to her created openings a slave might exploit in improving her circumstances according to her own, albeit severely limited, calculus.[57] Historians of this dimension of slavery tell us that the particular form these concessions took resulted from struggles between owners and slaves, especially struggles over labour and property.[58]

Work, War and Exchange:
Genealogies for the Worlding of Slavery and Enslavement in the Nineteenth Century
Between the Great Lakes, before the 1870s, only a few of the labels analysed in this essay were derived from the forms of work their bearers carried out. Their distributions suggest strongly that work-related

terminology for marking people's status emerged largely in the wake of the growth of waged labour, early in the twentieth century.[59] The exception to this claim must surely be the forms of indentured labour associated with livestock-keeping, most clearly conveyed through the history of the label °-*súmba* which meant in Proto West Nyanza 'someone who looks after someone else's cattle', conveying a general sense of being a dependent male (Appendix nos. 15.1 and 15.2).[60] The term is widely distributed from the Great Lakes region to the Swahili coast, but across this broad region it was used to name very different features of work and lower social standing. In the Lakes region, the meanings 'herder' or 'hired shepherd' were derived from a far more widespread verb #-*sumba* 'to look after, care for', a meaning that also supported semantic extensions to include 'youth; groom' in Kaskazi languages.[61] These meaning chains refer elegantly to the overlapping realities for young men of the salience of elders' control over resources that could drive the young men into service in pursuit of the material wealth they might need in order to marry or to escape from bad economic circumstances. In North Rutara societies, a °-*musumba* was someone who might be at one and the same time a 'herder', a 'slave' or a 'bondservant'. In West Highlands societies, the term could refer to a 'client', a 'slave', or a 'servant'. In the absence of corroborating evidence from comparative oral traditions, the narrow distribution of this particular polysemy makes dating its creation impossible, but it was clearly in play across the twentieth century.

When James Augustus Grant described the sort of person reckoned most valuable as a slave in Unyanyembe in 1861, his observations constituted a short-hand for the stereotypes of slavery in Africa that fired the moral imaginations of missionaries and colonials. It also captured something of the intensified associations between labour and slavery and an implicit equation of female reproductive power with slavery.

> Slaves from the northern kingdoms of Uganda, &c., were considered the most valuable, just in the same way as many persons consider a country girl the best servant. They were held to be more trustworthy than men from the coast, made excellent servants, and were famous at killing or capturing wild animals. The most esteemed women were of the Wahumah tribe from Karague; they resembled the Abyssinians.[62]

Grant's characterisations of skill and phenotype emphasised gendered divisions of labour, referred obliquely to racialised categories, and suggested the importance of sexuality to the consumption of slaves south of Lake Victoria.

In another passage, Grant also described a slave hierarchy in Buzinza, with a gang of male slaves in irons working as rice gleaners – thrashing the grain heads with their feet and toes and winnowing the thrashed grain by throwing it up into the wind – while women used small hand knives to reap the ripe heads of rice in Buzinza.[63] Yet a little further on in his account, Grant opined that 'the slaves of the Wezees' [Banyamwezi] enjoyed a status very different from slaves at Zanzibar being 'very well dressed, and treated with great kindness, never doing but what they choose'.[64] Though Grant lumps all slaves together under that seemingly straightforward rubric, it is clear enough that the 'very well dressed' persons who could do what they wanted belonged to a social standing in which privation and constraint were not defining features.[65]

The semantic distance between military captive and slave was not often bridged in Great Lakes Bantu languages; they were rarely synonyms.[66] Though plundering property, including people, is a practice with deep roots in this region and beyond, it is important to notice that virtually none of the large nineteenth-century lexicon for forms of slavery was derived from verbs which described plunder and pillage. In the few instances where this particular semantic extension from 'captive' to 'slave' did occur (Appendix nos. 1, 14.2, 14.4, 14.6), we find echoes of the claim that 'acts of disruption and bodily alienation … are at the beginning of every slave's story'.[67] Even though captivity, among all the other circumstances that produced enslavement, clearly became prominent in the Lakes region only in the eighteenth century, it is still surprising that such alienation was suppressed by the general refusal to name slaves with nouns derived from verbs for acts of capture, raiding, or pillage and plunder.

Labellers used metonymy to locate slavery alongside familiar forms of social life. In the later 1950s, the word °-*muhuuku* (Nkore and Kiga) or °-*mupfuku* (Hunde) meant 'servant, bondsman or slave'. The phonological structure of these two words corresponds regularly. Hunde-speakers pronounce the consonant /p/ as a voiced labial fricative /pf/ when it is surrounded by the vowel /u/. Nkore and Kiga-speakers pronounce /p/ as an /h/ in the same vowel environment. Given these regularities, it is unlikely that the word and its meanings were transferred between these three languages. Yet, the distribution has a block shape that overruns the boundaries of established subgroups of Great Lakes Bantu. According to lexicostatistical analyses and a set of shared innovations, Hunde belongs in the Forest group, while Nkore and Kiga belong in the Rutara group.[68] So the phonological and distributional evidence combine to suggest that the term was invented separately in Hunde and in Nkore and Kiga. These linguistic neighbours experienced similar circumstances and drew on similar parts of speech in reacting to and interpreting those circumstances. The source for this noun appears to have been a verb, °-*kupuuka* 'to get thinner, lose weight; to fail'. The poetics of naming a slave or a servant by using a verb for physical privation took place between the seventeenth and nineteenth centuries, when the three languages had clearly diverged. The very chain of meanings that the word had accumulated by the twentieth century included unwaged work and seemed to fold slavehood into servitude.

The semantics of labelling slave statuses, service relationships and social hierarchy in Great Lakes Bantu languages can be seen in the light of Kopytoff and Miers' sense of institutionalised marginality in African slaveries.[69] In the Lakes region, many people created and sustained a distinction between slaves produced by warfare and those who slipped from clientship to pawnship into slavehood, a continuum echoed by the meanings attached to the word °-*muhuuku*/°-*mupfûku*. Military captives had far fewer options[70] to mitigate their vulnerability compared with slaves who had been pawns or even former clients who could at least hope to draw various members of their lineage or clan or their former village or workgroup, and so on, into the work of redeeming them. In the course of the nineteenth century, as the circuits in which slaves might move came more often to include disappearance to the coast, a new sense of urgency must have entered such negotiations. One side of the distinction between captive and pawn appears in the common practice of stretching the semantic field around some old and widespread terms for domestic or noble servitude (Appendix 4.1, 4.2, 4.3) – which often, though not exclusively, were recruited into forms of pawnship – to include notions of unwaged domestic work in the twentieth century.

This essay has taken seriously the scholarly commonplace of locating in the nineteenth century the beginnings of the commodification of social relationships as a feature of the intensification of coastwise trade. And terms related to purchasing slaves lend strong support to the timing of this transition, even if they also support a claim for considerable variation in its local and regional lexical forms and, hence, historical experiences. Ganda, Masaaβa, Hanga, North Rutara and West Highlands-speakers each separately derived a word naming a slave gotten by purchase or exchange from a verb #-*gùla* which means 'to buy' (Appendix nos. 6.1, 6.2, 6.3). The derivation tells us nothing about what sorts of people – captives, pawns, criminals, 'witches' and so on – might have become purchased people or moved through purchase.

Regional and local differences in the derivational processes people used to create these labels reveal some of the contexts that shaped these innovations. West Highlands-speakers added an associative suffix and thereby underscored the importance of exchange at the heart of the purchase (Appendix no. 6.1). When they invented their noun for a purchased slave (Appendix no. 6.2), North Rutara-speakers added a passive infix in order to mark a purchased slave's lack of agency. Ganda-speakers used phrases, and a simple agentive noun, that emphasised the act of buying and the agency of the buyer (Appendix no. 6.3). Hanga-speakers simply added the appropriate noun class marker to the stem, without the agentive. Masaaβa-speakers used the passive infix, like Nyoro, Nkore and Kiga-speakers. For all this diversity in perception and in deriving these names, they all share the notion that some sort of involuntary transfer created the enslaved person. This most commonly referred to the act of purchasing an enslaved person, but was not restricted to this meaning. That fact suggests that the invention of words for 'purchased slave' drew on older patterns of exchanging people, even if the context for that innovation was the violently commodifying world of the nineteenth century in which commercial exchange involved less permanent connections between buyers and sellers.

Language evidence suggests that roots for these transitions run deeper than the nineteenth century. The most interesting example comes from thinking about the historical semantics of the verb #-*gùla*, 'to buy'. In one of the few large-scale studies of innovations in Savannah Bantu, Christopher Ehret argues that this root is an inherited feature in Great Lakes – having undergone a semantic shift during the earlier East Savanna era.[71] The innovation lay in East Savannah-speaking people having begun to use the verb to mean 'to buy' instead of 'to sell', its purportedly older meaning for Proto Bantu-speakers. The strength of Ehret's claim rests entirely on distributional evidence: the new meaning attached to #-*gùla* occurs in select, non-contiguous branches of Eastern Savanna Bantu, while the older meaning occurs in select, non-contiguous branches of Forest Bantu. Assuming Ehret is correct, what contexts might explain this semantic shift, an apparent reversal of perspective from donor to recipient?

The practice of using one verbal form to refer to 'buying' and another to refer to 'selling' emerged in social settings where new financial arrangements – perhaps based on currency forms – and impersonal forms of exchange (even if carried out in markets) split up what had earlier been a single conceptual field of 'exchange'. This semantic splitting developed and spread in the contexts of newly commodified trade relations, where 'buying' and 'selling' were undertaken by respectively specialised producers and consumers and could mark the standing of debtor and creditor. This could be connected with the growth of complex networks of trade in rare goods, like kaolin or iron, or with trade in exotic goods, like glass beads, cloth and foreign metalwork, or with trade and exchange in foodstuffs, persons and firearms.[72] Abundant evidence exists for these specialisations by the eighteenth century, at the very latest, and we suspect them to be much older.[73] In each case, the argument that inventing a word for 'selling' also meant inventing a word for 'buying' implies that both came into existence from a single, unified concept involving things and social relationships, a conceptualisation that might be rather poetically glossed as 'to connect socially through the movement of things'. Though difficult to date from language evidence alone, the semantic shift does make sense in the light of any of the well-known periods in the history of commodification in Africa.[74]

Consider this somewhat tortured suggestion in the light of Christopher Ehret's argument concerning the semantic history of Eastern Savannah's #-*gùla*, 'to buy'. The larger claim for the antiquity of commodified people, people who were 'bought and sold', is supported by the semantic history of another root, °-*suumba* or °-*somba* 'slave'. This term might just be a deverbative of the verb, °-*cúmba*, 'to buy' (Appendix no. 15.2), replaced in Eastern Savannah times by #-*gùla*. Transfers of persons – outside of pawning and marriage – between households or institutional settings such as shrines may well be extremely ancient; certainly they are at least as old as the sorts of violence and ill-health that could produce exchangeable, socially dislocated, persons.

The linguistic evidence discussed so far could be read as confirming the observation, made by the historian John Iliffe, that 'the assimilative capacity of tropical African societies created a hierarchy among slaves'.[75] But they were actually plural hierarchies, depending on the period and region under consideration. And relations between the levels also differed according to the same contextual factors, even while some aspects of slave hierarchies appear to be quite ancient. Eighteenth-century militarisms increased the volume of displaced persons, even if the distance they had travelled seems comparatively small in relation to the growth of coastwise trade in the nineteenth century. In the sixteenth and seventeenth centuries, statuses such as page and court slave included both pawned persons and 'placed' persons with noble standing or noble pretensions. Dynastic oral traditions and other historical tales take for granted such social distinctions – they recognise some court followers as menials and others as clients on a continuum – and do not confuse such persons with captives and criminals whose fate a royal court may decide.

Gender and hierarchies mutually constituted each other, as well. One of the most important ways in which this worked revolved around the forms of honour and respect which slaves at different levels of a hierarchy could hope to accumulate and use to improve the concessions they could win from superiors. For female dependants and slaves, this was most often – and over the longer term – tied to their reproductive powers. The core meaning of the *muzaana* as an auxiliary, infantilised person captures the ambiguous nature of this power. It reminds us of the fuzzy, changing relationships between hegemonic notions – fantasies, really, shaped in key ways by gender, generation, and status – of social hierarchy and the everyday realities of social life in a hierarchical world.

Conclusions and Future Research

The linguistic evidence reviewed here confirms the commonplaces of enslavement. Over the last millennium, between the Great Lakes, people became slaves by capture, by purchase and by debt-pawning.[76] By itself, language evidence is a dangerous foundation for offering calendar dates, but the evidence presented here can be read inside already well-established chronologies for regional social history to suggest that violent capture and pillage have long histories, reaching well into the first millennium CE.[77] It is quite likely that pawning has been around just as long, but it seems clearly to have grown in prominence in the seventeenth and eighteenth centuries, with the rise of politically centralised states with territorial ambitions, and increasing levels of pressure and insecurity in highly specialised food systems.[78] One of the more important responsibilities of leaders in these states lay in providing refuge at court to struggling followers and their families. Transfers of persons through markets seem a more recent development, probably no older than the eighteenth century, but gaining in velocity and volume throughout the nineteenth century.[79]

Different labels for slaves often referred to the different realities they faced, as historians have determined for the Mrima coast, Unguja and Buganda in the second half of the nineteenth century.[80] Some of those who were initially labelled in the fashions just discussed, could find themselves living later in life under a different designation altogether. The connections between newcomers and persons lacking the social capital to sustain responses to scornful and backbiting talk are clear enough. They describe a slave's extremely vulnerable condition, having been removed from her or his community and made a stranger elsewhere. But the connection underscores the reality of a common conceptual framework – the framework of social hierarchy – inside which different sorts of people could strategically work their way up the ladder from enslaved newcomer or refugee to affiliated insider.

People could achieve this social integration if they could initiate and sever patron-client relationships according to their own calculus, within the precepts of the system. The latitude to give service, support or children to one another formed a fundament of social life between the Great Lakes. Persons who entered a community as an outsider, as a slave, had the least capacity to prosecute such ties. Yet, as Jonathon Glassman has shown us for central coastal towns such as Bagamoyo, Pangani, and Sadani, such slaves could use the patriarchal and paternalist logics of mutual obligation to create roles for themselves as patrons of others still more recently arrived. Women possessed skills and capacities which put them at an advantage over men in negotiating modes of obligated social ties. The loss of mobility in the social system – a mobility most often realised through their successful movement through socially sanctioned phases in a life course – faced by women who had been stolen in raids and removed from their affinal and sanguineous networks of support limited their capacity to move through generational phases in a socially recognised fashion. The chance to use brideprice, motherhood and formal marriage arrangements to create a new place, a relational standing for themselves – just as has been documented so compellingly for southern Tanzania by Marcia Wright – was their most effective tool to combat the marginalisation and indignity of recent transfer.[81]

The labels discussed in this essay are remarkable for another reason. Many of them are unique to different parts of the Great Lakes region rather than constituting local extensions of much farther-flung networks of notions of slaving.[82] More than any other argument presented here, this distinctive quality of the language evidence points to regional social historical forces as central to shaping the development of slavehoods and slaving between the Great Lakes. However, other forms of semantic extension point to the antiquity of the practice of capture and raiding or the antiquity of discourses of the socially marginal person as a newcomer.

These data for the early history of slavery and enslavement between the Great Lakes only touch the surface of these issues.[83] And their treatment in this essay might give the misleading impression that a historian can use the well-known features of nineteenth-century slavery as transhistorical criteria for isolating earlier forms.[84] Nothing could be further from the truth, and this is why future studies must develop further the interests of states, the various forms and scales of violence, and numerous aspects of vulnerability and dependence. These contextual factors shaped the experience of slavery in earlier centuries very differently from the way commodification did in the nineteenth century. Just considering state interests will require a full accounting of the nature and significance of building archly patriarchal ideologies designed to control male access to fertile women, extending the monarch's claims to have absolute control over the power to take life, and providing nobles and military personnel (sometimes the same persons) with new sources of 'followers'.[85] As the late historian Gerald Hartwig argued more than 25 years ago for Bukerebe, slavery came along 'when a centralised system of government was introduced and a stratified society developed'.[86] But we know now that social stratification had been configured and reconfigured many times over before anything resembling political centralisation appeared in the Great Lakes region. In that sense, the roots of inequality and dependence run deep in the region. Yet the genealogies of slavery, inequality and dependence are highly diverse there.[87] Exploring their particular forms and interrelations in the region's larger states – by re-reading dynastic and other oral traditions – should reveal much of interest.

Paul Lovejoy, a leading historian of slavery in Africa and of commerce in slaves in and out of Africa, has argued famously that slavery in Africa was transformed in a complex dynamic by overseas demand during the centuries of the transatlantic slave trade. For Lovejoy, this transformation involved slavery becoming central to production in particular African societies, especially as enslavement became integrated into a slave system and markets for slaves shaped local situations in discernible and powerful ways.[88] Histories of slavery in the Great Lakes region cannot easily be fitted into Paul Lovejoy's transformation thesis. For one thing, dependency and hierarchy and militarism – which together were key elements of the engines of the transformation – are each and together older than the market and the cultural forces driving coastwise demand for slaves, a mode of demand to which he attributes new and harsher forms of enslavement.[89] On the other hand, the importance of militarism to eighteenth-century state-building between the Great Lakes seems likely to have increased internal dislocations of dependent persons but not as a function of markets. Markets for slaves grew, and supplies and demand increased in volume and velocity in the nineteenth century, when something like Lovejoy's transformation thesis can be seen in parts of East Africa, including Buganda.[90]

Another leading scholar of slavery in Africa, John Thornton, has characterised it as widespread in the continent after 1680.[91] But disentangling the many forms of slavery – from Lovejoy's violent alienations of labour to Miers' and Kopytoff's kin-incorporation continuum – and distinguishing the forces that shaped each particular form during this recent period from their deeper roots is fraught with teleological pitfalls. Some aspects of the coastwise trade in slaves, so well documented from late in the eighteenth century, may well have been the 'outgrowth of this internal slavery', and, thus, the opposite of the essentially external causation of Lovejoy and Thornton. But teleology may lurk in such an analytical approach, in the form of a transhistorical importance assigned to dislocation. We must take seriously how radically different were the conditions of a slave's vulnerability in the early sixteenth and the later eighteenth centuries. Then, in order for a modified form of Lovejoy's thesis, applicable in the region beginning perhaps as early as the seventeenth century and clearly in evidence by the second half of the nineteenth century, to help us understand the historical forces that 'ejected' persons into the coastwise trade, we will need to cast our net much wider than the fairly narrow category of 'the slave' in the long nineteenth century to include the broad, local notions of social differentiation within the region.

Deeper social histories of violence, vulnerability and authority will provide the historical contexts for thinking about dependence, marginality and slavery between the Great Lakes. Though this essay has offered meaningful generalisations about these broader pools of experience and their intellectual output, it is clear from the semantic histories of the names for slaves most commonly recorded in the 1860s and 1870s that isolating the slave from kinship systems and from social networks that might generate honour and respect was a key means to establish private, corporate and state ownership of a slave's labour and person. Thornton has argued that 'private ownership of labour...provided the African entrepreneur with secure and reproducing wealth.'[92] Establishing and maintaining a slave's solitude was central to the master's 'security'.

The most exciting aspect of future work in the history of slavery in the Lakes region will be the ways in which it opens up questions of the distinctive roots of African histories of individuality, of hierarchy and obligation, of honour and shame, and of a militarised commerce in property, including persons as property. Such histories will project outward from Africa a complex series of engagements, constructions and various contributions to cosmopolitan diasporic modernities well beyond the scope of this essay.[93] Details of these humanistic themes in African histories of slavery and enslavement will emerge more clearly in studies of the needs and aspirations of embodied individuals, of atomised collectivities, and of the shifting boundaries among them. The nature of slavery and freedom, inequality and hierarchy, is not fixed but in flux, and that means that we can only understand the futility of definitions if we begin by claiming them and then working to demolish them.

In the centuries before 1600, Great Lakes Bantu-speakers, like others around the globe, had no way to speak of 'freedom' as a condition of an atomised personal independence. The ideal – if not the idea – of individually embodied independence was untenable in a political economy of reciprocity, obligation, hierarchy, assumed inequalities, separate spheres of gendered activity and theories of composite corporeal power. As an ideal to be aspired to by state and society, this notion would have seemed absurd to people living between the Great Lakes before the seventeenth century. However, with the birth of organised state-sponsored violence in which large numbers of captives were moved fairly long distances from their networks of support and aspiration, 'freedom' might well have come to mean the absence of such depredations.[94] By the nineteenth century, captives, criminals, 'sorcerers' and outcasts of every stripe had to consider that their fate might take them even farther away from 'home' – to 'the coast', for example. This new reality, together with the increasingly frequent and non-centralised raiding, might have intensified the notions of 'freedom' as the absence of removal.

Even if a social hierarchy that required clear if debatable lines between insiders and outsiders has been developing for more than a millennium between the Lakes, it is not at all clear that it is helpful to use the term 'slave' to refer to those at the bottom of that hierarchy at any given point in time before the seventeenth century. In the centuries before states, agrarian societies did not possess mechanisms to enforce the creation of class relations over the long term. However, as the territorial boundaries between increasingly aggressive states took firmer shape, beginning in the seventeenth century and clearly in place in the eighteenth century, something like Claude Meillassoux's 'womb of iron' may have begun to grow as violence dislodged persons whose labour was central to continuing warfare.[95] In the second half of the eighteenth century, and throughout the course of the nineteenth century, Meillassoux's 'womb of gold' swelled and the exchange of commodified persons drove a calculus of individual male and royal female accumulation as a central feature of wealth that underwrote state aggrandisement.[96]

The language evidence discussed in this essay suggests that the intellectual tool kit of eighteenth- and nineteenth-century Great Lakes Africans could not have confused notions of the individual as a free person embodying elements of stand-alone choice and will with notions of social justice and/or capacities to achieve satisfaction, health and peace. Indeed, people argued most passionately about who could occupy (or invent) which stations in a complex network of hierarchical positions tied together by obligations designed to provide flows of mutual aid and material support.[97] And they argued about the moral conditions that ensured that those obligations would remain reciprocal, a set of moral conditions whose roots ran equally to intellectual habits and to material circumstance.[98] They argued about these issues, in part, by appealing to other notions of cultural superiority and inferiority which had largely local and subregional scope. In the mid-nineteenth century, well before Europeans 'arrived' in the region, Ganda and Nyoro, Rwanda and Shi opinions of their own and of each other's cultural power exemplified one form of this.[99] Hima and Iru or Tuutsi and Hutu attitudes toward each other's cultural, material and political power exemplified another.[100] All of them in common appealed to glorious past conquests, to notions of common descent and the exclusions made possible by that metaphor, and to steadfast rankings of these inalterable – because past – 'facts' and allegedly inherent 'traits'. Other oppositional binaries could be adduced. Participation and exclusion, articulation and silence, as couplets, formed key intellectual and substantive contexts for these arguments.

Their richness notwithstanding, these data cannot tell us how vulnerable people understood and talked about their own lives. We have no access to slave discourse through reconstructed lexical material. We can only glimpse some of the effects of this discourse on the development of the lexis by considering carefully the conceits and explicit judgments contained in semantic histories. Metaphor, metonymy and synonymy are not value-free tools; they reflect choices, and choices express the interests of the chooser. In order to suggest what interests might say about who did the choosing, we can draw on what we already know about historical shifts and continuities in the social logic of obligation and hierarchy between the Great Lakes to the eighteenth century. In this way, we can infer the nature of the interests that motivated different acts of metaphorical extension, metonymic joining and the maintenance of a rich environment of synonymy during different periods in the past. And we can suggest who might have offered those 'moves' and why they might have been accepted by the speaking and audible public and taken into speech so that they remained alive to turn up in the accounts – oral and written and mixtures of the two – generated in the nineteenth century, or to appear in the twentieth- and twenty-first-century work of the philologists and linguists of the region's tongues.

A Brief Note on Historical Linguistic Method

Historical linguistic work in the relevant Bantu languages in the Great Lakes region and in coastal Eastern Africa is highly advanced.[101] It involves the comparative study of words and meanings in historically related sub-groups of contemporary Bantu languages. By discovering words with similar meanings and regularly corresponding sounds, scholars can reconstruct their earlier forms.[102] The reconstructed vocabulary discussed in this essay and presented in the following Appendix, is inferred from the regularities in sound correspondence and in patterns of semantic range observed in a set of contemporary Bantu languages. It constitutes part of a 'proto' language ancestral to the contemporary languages. It reflects the historical persistence of a community of speakers using those words and meanings. As people invented new terms or added new meanings to existing terms, increased linguistic difference is recognisable in distinctive sets of reconstructed words and meanings shared by different groups of contemporary languages. The denser the webs of reconstructed vocabulary and of contrasting meanings carried by different words in each proto language, the more such contrasts reveal about the normative values used by East Africans to make moral, phenomenological and political distinctions at different times in the past.[103]

Appendix: Reconstructed Vocabulary[104]

1. °-*bóhe* 1/2, 9 'captive, prisoner'; °-*bóha* 1/2, 14 'prisoner, captivity'; °-*bóhwa* 1/2 'prisoner, enslaved person'.

Nyoro, Nkore, Kiga, Haya, Ziba, Rwanda, Rundi, Ha; Nande, Kuria, Masaaβa, Hanga; Rundi, Nyoro, Nkore, Kiga, Nande.

Derived from the Proto Eastern Savannah verb #-*βópa* 'to tie up, bind up'. The variety of forms suggests separate innovations, in the last five centuries, after the Proto Rutara- and Proto West Highlands- and Proto Central Luhyia-speech communities had broken up.

2. °–*vuma* 9, 1/2; °-*vumo* 1/2 'slave, chattel slave; royal employee'.

Ganda, Kerewe.

Derived from Proto Eastern Savannah #-*βyma* 'talk bad about, scorn, curse'. Gwere attest *kivuma* 'item of tribute'. The association of a bad talk and social inferiority seems to date at least from Proto West Nyanza, but is probably much older. The specific meaning in Ganda could have emerged any time after the sixteenth century, by which time Proto North Nyanza had fully broken up.

4.1. °-*garagú* 1/2 'male servant, client (someone who has received gifts)'.

Shi, Haavu, Goyi; Rwanda, Rundi; Kiga.

One of three related forms with areal distributions. This one has Lake Kivu at its epicentre and its spread – likely from multiple centres – reflects the increasingly dense networks of obligation that accompanied the growth of royal power in Rwanda and Bushi during the eighteenth century. It probably derived from #-gàla 'to come back, go back' by reduplication.

4.2. °–*gàlágwa* 1/4 and 14 'royal's servant; service to a king'.

Kiga, Nyoro, Nkore, Haya.

During German colonial rule, the Haya noun named an uncivilised, poorly educated person. This may point to the uncertain circumstances that sometimes produced royal pages or pawns. A passive infix suggests a separate innovation in this zone, perhaps conserving the importance of the absence of agency at the moment a person entered this social condition. A North Rutaran innovation, from between the sixteenth century (when glottochronology suggests this subgroup had begun to break up) and the very recent past.

4.3.°-*galagala* 1/2 'young male courtier, sometimes with specific responsibilities'.

Ganda; Kooki, Nyoro; Koonzo.

In the 1980s, the Koonzo noun named someone who worked as a domestic for no wages, a condition considered slave-like. This shows how notions of service changed from the nineteenth to the twentieth centuries, as commodification and the thinning of networks of obligation created a deeper relief around the figure of the dependent individual. In the absence of detailed language evidence from Lugwere and Lusoga, it is dangerous to say much about the time depth of this innovation. It has been most carefully described in Ganda settings, descriptions that dominate any sense of the range of meanings the term could name. At the very least, its distribution further underscores the close relationship between Ganda and Nyoro royalty.

5. °–*gaya* 1/2 'servile, enslavable people'.

Jita, Kwaya; Kerewe.

According to Kerewe-speakers, this is a slur hurled at Luo people who suffered raids for slaves in the later nineteenth century led by Suguti-speaking peoples. It is derived from a Proto Bantu verb *-*gaya* 'despise', retained in Great Lakes Bantu.

6.1. –*gurano*, –*guranyi* 1/2 'purchase slave; an endangerer, slaver'.

Rwanda, Rundi.

As with the next two entries, this term was derived from #-*gùla* 'to buy'. The extremely narrow distribution points to the later nineteenth century, when Rundi and Rwandan monarchies were distinct. Its apparent absence in the Ha dialects should be checked. If this holds up, this term and its relatives, below, strongly point to the novelty of the coastwise exchange of slaves.

6.2. –*gúrwa* 1/2 'bondman, slave; bought person'.

Nyoro, Nkore, Kiga; Masaaßa.

Only the Masaaßa attestations specify a purchase slave. North Rutarans made the term work as a generic.

6.3. –*gule*, –*gula* 1/2 'purchase slave'

Ganda; Hanga; Gusii.

In the 1930s, this had become a generic term for 'slave' in Hanga. Both Gusii and Ganda specify the meaning 'purchase slave'. This distribution is quite strange. At first glance it might suggest a considerable antiquity for the term, especially since the Gusii attestation displays the vowel-lowering characteristic of North Mara languages. But since this is still active in Kuria, it cannot be used as a diagnostic sound change. Instead, the distribution might reflect a series of innovations for purchase slaves that emerged along the Mara slaving route/zone.

7. °–wáambi, °-hàmbè 1/2 'captor, prisoner of war, captive'; °–hambuzi 1/2 'captor'.

Ganda; Northern and Southern Gisu; Hanga; Nyoro, Nkore.

An agentive noun derived from the Proto Eastern Savannah verb #-pámba 'tie down, immobilise' which supported a widespread and naturalistic semantic extension to acts of seizure and plunder. The equation of captivity with plunder and internal displacements of people is clear. The skewing suggests separate innovations of these nouns, perhaps in the context of Gandan and Luhyia military traditions, increasingly prominent in the eighteenth century. The tonal differences between North Nyanza and North Luhyia seem regular.

8. °-aambuzi 1/2 'robber; destroyer, brigand, pillager', °-aamburo 7/8 'authorisation to pillage'.

Rwanda, Rundi.

This agentive noun was derived from the verb (in Rundi and Rwanda [with a long V_1]) kwambura 'to undress; to take by force,' which is the reversive form of the verb °-ambara 'to dress'. The derivation shows clearly that robbing and pillaging involved some fundamental violations of the public, dressed body, at least in the central West Highlands area. Shi has oomwaambali 1/2 'subject, servant', very likely from KiNgwana: mwambali 'from far away'. If this was a cognate form, we should expect oomwaambazi.

9. –huuku; -pfúku 1/2 'slave, servant, bondsman'.

Nkore, Kiga; Hunde.

The term omunyagahukú also appears in Hunde. It carries the following, literal meaning: omu-nya-gahukú, 'one who has been taken over by crushing circumstances'. The Hunde attestation corresponds regularly, by spirantisation. This suggests a separate innovation in Nkore and Kiga, on the one hand, and in Hunde, on the other hand. Confer Hunde ipfúka 'to fail, be beaten'.[105] That, in turn, suggests broadly similar circumstances across the three speech communities, rather than some sort of stimulus diffusion. Etymology is uncertain, but perhaps a deverbative from the stem *-huka 'get thinner, lose weight'. The derivation suggests links with hunger and vulnerability and perhaps refugees of famine.

10. –irù 1/2; 14 'dependant, servant, client, bondman, slave; servitude'.

Violence, Marginality, Scorn & Honour

Ganda, Gwere, Soga; Kerewe, Kiga, Nkore, Nyoro, Yóòza, Ziba; Nyole; Sumbwa, Nyamwezi

The glosses given to this term in the literature bear the traces of late precolonial- and colonial-era patrician efforts to promote their views on social hierarchies in the Great Lakes region. Royals and pastoralists had the most at stake in this regard. Early in the twentieth century, the noun in Haya stated this position explicitly: 'slave, farm labourer, servant; subject (original inhabitant, racially separate from *Muhííma*)'. It is therefore dangerous to rely solely on them as a guide to any earlier meanings the term might have carried. Nevertheless, for our purposes, it is clear enough that where the term referred to the status of client, this was the meaning that supported extensions into the realms of coerced work and the attempt to fix such persons at the bottom of a given social hierarchy. The Kiga meaning is 'peasant' and hints at an earlier period where formulating the occupation of the farmer as distinct from that of other, especially pastoralist activities had political and social traction. This seems plausible if only because Kigezi – where RuKiga is spoken – remained peripheral to the main currents of slaving, if not to those of precolonial state militarisms and colonial violence. By the 1970s, in South Rutara, the term meant 'poor person' and had lost connections with bonded labour. The operation of germination in Ganda and the distributional evidence strongly support a claim for Proto West Nyanza as the speech community in which this term first appeared. It is not hard to see a semantic history proceeding from the invention of a term for farmer as part of a politicisation of pastoralism and agriculture in general. This meaning quickly accumulated nuances associated with clientship, especially as clientship was embodied most commonly through the transfer of land and/or cattle, in the middle of the second millennium CE. Applying notions of coerced labour and political subjugation came last, as subordination became a vehicle to differentiation in these terms. Etymology is uncertain. One possibility is a verb #-*ida* (reflexive) 'come back, return', often replaced by #-*garuka* in Great Lakes Bantu, and thus shows the sort of relict distribution expected from a fairly old term. The semantic connection would seem to have been that dependants and clients should be dependable, reliable supporters.

11. *–ja* 1/2; 14 'dependant, servant, slave. Newcomer, refugee'.

In Great Lakes Bantu: Shi, Hunde, Haavu, Fuliru, Tembo, Goyi; Rwanda, Rundi, Ha, Vinza; Zu, Shashi

Beyond Great Lakes Bantu: Sumbwa, Nyamwezi (Tabora dialect); Luba-Katanga, Luba-Sanga; Nyika; Bemba, Nsenga; Ila; Lenje; Guha; Tabwa; Mambwe; Bisa; Lala-Lamba; Fipa; Pimbwe; Wungu. Proto Sabaki.

Peta (Johnston 1919, Vol. 1, 259) has *ntsākazi* 'female slave'; *Mang'anja* (Johnston 1919, Vol. 1, 243) has *mdzakazi*, in the same meaning. This is one of the very few terms for slavery in Great Lakes Bantu with a very broad, nearly block distribution that closely marks the territory of long-distance trade routes of any sort, let alone those which reached into and beyond the lands of both the Luba state and the Indian Ocean caravanning routes. Only a few from Swahili (*-*tumwa* ?) and one or two reaching westwards (*-*peka*?) have similarly vast distributions. In the Lakes region, it is concentrated in Forest and West Highlands, though it does turn up in two of the Mara languages (a branch of East Nyanza). It is often gendered female with the addition of #-*kazi* 'woman', with the male form unmarked. Shi attests the reverse. The etymology is unclear. Meeussen gives *-*dįa* [L] or *-*ja* 'slave'.[106] Nurse and Hinnebusch reconstruct Proto Sabaki *-*muja* 'newcomer'.[107]

12.1. °–*kwatwa* 1/2, 9/10; 'captive, prisoner'.

Nyoro, Nkore, Kerewe.

In the later 1980s, the verbal form in Hangaza meant 'to marry by abduction'. Together with the following entry, these two areal forms are deverbatives of the stem *-*kúát*- 'seize' (C.S. #1172 in Guthrie 1967–71, Vol. 3, 304) which is itself very likely derived from *Proto Bantu* (Meeussen 1980, 29) *-*gu*- 'fall' and showing Dahl's Law with the addition of the contactive suffix *-*at*-. *Rundi* (Rodegem 1970, 133) has *kugwata* 'to fall on and seize firmly, to seize, take, hold and squeeze'. This noun was made from a passive form of that verb. The gaps in the distribution support a claim that the noun was innovated in the Proto Rutara era, between 700 and 900 years ago by glottochronological dating. A more recent set of separate innovations cannot be ruled out, given the easy derivational process involved and the absence of distinctive sound changes.

12.2. °–*kwâsi* 1/2 'captor, catcher'.

Rundi; Ganda; Nyoro, Nkore, Kiga.

This noun was made from the foregoing stem by adding the agentive suffix *-*i*. It is not hard to see the block distribution as a reflection of repeated raiding between the four different language zones.

13. °-*fáté* 9/10; -*fatwa* 1/2 'captive, defendant; prisoner of war'.

Rwanda; Rundi, Ha.

This noun was made from the widespread stem *-*pát*- 'hold' (C.S. #1453 in Guthrie 1967-71, Vol. 4, 43). The restricted distribution, as well as the formal skewing, suggests the innovation developed no earlier than the eighteenth century, after Rwandan and Rundi polities had taken shape and begun to exert pressure on linguistic standardisation.

14.1. #-*nyagi̧* 1/2; 14 'captor, pillager; thief, robber; pillaging'.

Ganda; Haya, Nyoro, Nkore; Nande; Shi; Rundi, Rwanda, Ha.

Hanga has –*nyewa* 'to abuse'. The skewing suggests multiple, separate innovations either by internal derivations or by loaning. Together with the block distribution, the evidence points to an areal feature developed since the breakup of North Nyanza, Rutara, and Rwenzori. This was no longer ago than the oldest of these groups: North Nyanza at about 800 CE. Or not more recently than the breakup of the youngest of these groups: Rwenzori at about 1400 CE. Both dates come from glottochronology. The following narrowly distributed and broadly synonymous forms reveal a social world awash with plundered things and people. These nouns were made from the Proto Savannah verb #-*nyag*- 'pillage; repossess'.

14.2. °–*nyage* 1/2 'plunder slaves; captive (from a raid)'.

Ganda.

14.3. °-*nyagwa* 1/2 'captive'.

Nyoro, Nkore.

14.4. -*nyagáno* 1/2 'female captive; war captive'.

Haya; Rwanda.

14.5. °-*nyago* 3/4 'plunder, booty'.

Ganda; Nyoro, Nkore.

14.6. °-*nyewa*, °-*nyewo* 14 'bondage, captivity'; °-*nyegawa*, °-*nyewa* 1/2 'captive, slave'.

Nande.

The skewing of these substantives strongly suggests these are recent innovations, perhaps loanwords, in Nande.

15.1. °-*sumba* 'youth, unmarried man; groom, fiancé'.

Ha; Samia, Hanga; Sumbwa, Sukuma; Nyilamba; Swahili.

The distribution suggests this meaning – essentially 'dependent male' – was the source for the following term, although it is entirely possible, even likely, that the two semantic fields – 'herder' and 'dependent male' – emerged and grew together. Generational politics often meant that young men who desired to marry with bridewealth had to indenture themselves to richer families. And the term held a rich metaphor of low status: anyone who entered such labour relations acted like a young unmarried man. Jan Vansina has suggested (personal communication, 15 February 2005) a derivation from #-*cumb*- 'accumulate, be on top, surpass', showing links with compositional wealth in people. But another possibility exists and it may be connected to the foregoing. The term may be a deverbative of C.S. 414 *-*cúmb*- (-*cúúmb*-) 'buy'.[108] This verb was replaced in Eastern Savannah by #-*gùl*- 'buy'. For this proposed derivation to hold, the noun must be a retention from Proto-Savannah. In that era, that verbal meaning that touched on exchange could have informed the meaning of the noun – young unmarried man – in the context of the movement of men into matrifocal groups.

15.2

. °-*shúmba*, °-*shūmba* 1/2 'herdsman, hired shepherd'; °-*suumba*, °-*somba* 1/2 'slave, bondservant'.

Nyoro, Nkore, Kiga, Yóòza, Haya, Ziba; Haavu, Hunde; Rwanda, Rundi; Gusii; Samia, Hanga.

In Ha the noun means 'adopted child'. In Rundi, the word also means 'client, valet, or serf'. In Hangaza *inshumba* 9 names a sort of cattle loan. In Gikuyu *gĩthũmbi*; *i-* 7/8 is 'one who works for food instead of pay (e.g. a poor or disabled woman who helps in harvesting a crop and is given the rejects as her reward)'. In the 1970s, Gusii, Samia, and Hanga terms meant 'slave, bondservant', perhaps capturing the essence of life as a herdsman in archly pastoralist settings.

16.1 #-*tíî* (itr.) 'to fear'; #-*mutî* 1/2 'coward, timid person, fearful person'; #-*butî* 14 'fear, timidity, dread'.

Ganda, Gusii, Wanga, Masaba.

Ila, Totela, Bua, Yeyi, Mvita, Amu, Tikuu, Cewa, Teve, Subia, Mpongwe, Manyang' (Upper Cross River), Munshi (South Benue Basin).

Widespread in Bantoid and the source for much semantic innovation that connects notions of 'fear' to recognition of 'honour' in a much narrower set of speech communities. In Rutara, the substantive °-*tiini*, is derived from the associative form of the verb, °-*tiina*.

16.2. #-*tûbwa* 7/8 'fear, respect, honour'.

North Nyanza: Ganda, Soga, Gwere.

A deverbative innovation in North Nyanza from a passive form of the verb *-*tíî* (itr.) 'to fear'.

16.3. #-*tíinwa* 7/8 'honour'.

Rutara: Nyoro, Nkore, Kiga, Haya, Ziba, Kerewe, Zinza, Kyamtwara.

A deverbative innovation in Rutara from a passive form of the associative verb *-*tîina* 'to fear each other, be afraid, fear'.

16.4. #-*tîinya* 'to generate fear in; make afraid, cause to fear and respect'.

West Highlands: Rundi, Rwanda, Goyi.

A causative associative form of the verb *-*tíî* 'to fear'. Rutara used the causative associative form to derive the substantives #-*tíini* 14, 1 'fear; coward' and the verb *-*tíina* 'be afraid'.

17. *–tumwa* 'slave, male servant; messenger'.

Kuria; Regi; Bukusu; Luvale.

The meaning 'slave' seems likely to be a loan transfer from Swahili and Sabaki during the era of the caravan trade, even if the stem is much older and far more widespread. The derivation from the widespread verb #-*tumwa* (passive) 'be sent, be employed or used' is so common that firm conclusions are difficult in the absence of distinctive sound change. Bukusu attests both a Swahili form, which retains the initial /t/, and a North Luhyia form, in which the stem-initial /t/ has shifted to /r/ suggesting strongly that the meaning and not the stem was transferred from Swahili-speaking caravaners to Bukusu-speakers.

18. *–zaana* 1/2; *-zanakazi* 1/2 'servant; female slave, slave; slavery; maidservant, domestic, prostitute'.

Ganda; Kerewe, Zinza, Haya, Ziba, Nyoro, Nkore, Kiga; Nande, Koonzo; Rwanda.

A widespread, block distribution reflects recent innovation and subsequent direct diffusion of this term. It is nearly always gendered female and thus reflects the strong preference for female slaves both for local use and for the coastwise trade. The etymology is unclear, but the range of meanings carried by the term suggests that the *muzaana* was someone who came into a community setting as the extension of another person, presumably the captor or master, thereby subsuming the *muzaana*'s identity into that of her captor's. Meeussen gives *-*jij*- [L] 'to come',[109] surface forms of which take different shapes in Great Lakes languages.

Notes

* My thanks to Kate de Luna, Steven Feierman, Kathryn Geurts, Jonathon Glassman, Chris Hayden, Nancy Hunt, Neil Kodesh, Murray Last, Julie Livingston, Wyatt MacGaffey, Sinfree Makoni, Henri Médard, Joseph Miller, Godwin Murunga, Alphonse Otieno, Rhiannon Stephens, Lynn Thomas and Jan Vansina for salutary comments on earlier drafts. Feierman, MacGaffey, Miller and Vansina helped especially with framing the arguments and expanding and interpreting the evidentiary base.
1 In a linguist's parlance, both of these forms of evidence are 'innovations'. In the first instance, a new word and meaning are created together. In the second instance, people attach a new meaning to an existing word. In reality these two operations are not always as discrete as my description might imply. New words and meanings often come into existence through simple derivational operations – for example, making a verb into a noun – which any competent speaker of a language can manage. In this example, both the noun – a new word – and its new meaning are the inventions.
2 To the extent that these legacies inform talk of power, standing, and political culture in the very recent past – as in the commonplace opposition of freedom to slavery – they disrupt a conventional temporality in which slavery is understood to have been vanquished in and through the uneven victories of colonial and postcolonial practices of embodied, individual freedom. And they raise the possibility of understanding epochal

breaks like 'emancipation' and 'independence' as radical redefinitions of the terms on which we understand vulnerability, violence and authority, even though they clearly marked the death of a particular political economy of slavery, in the first instance, and of a political culture of disenfranchisement, in the second instance; cf. Frederick Cooper, *Colonialism in Question, Theory, Knowledge, History* (Berkeley and Los Angeles, 2005), pp.237-8.

3 See David Schoenbrun, *A Green Place, A Good Place, Agrarian Chance, Gender, and Social Identity in the Great Lakes Region to the 15th Century* (Portsmouth, NH, 1998), pp.100ff; Jeff Fleisher, 'Behind the Sultan of Kilwa's "rebellious conduct"', in Andrew M. Reid and Paul J. Lane (eds), *African Historical Archaeologies* (New York, 2004), pp.101-10.

4 For more on these issues, see Jonathon Glassman, 'No words of their own', *Slavery and Abolition*, 16, 1 (1995), pp.131-45.

5 Peter Robertshaw and David Taylor, 'Climate change and the rise of political complexity in Western Uganda', *Journal of African History*, 41, 1 (2000), pp.1-28.

6 For discussions of these structures see Schoenbrun, *A Green Place*, pp.144ff, 176ff, 223ff; Jean-Pierre Chrétien, *The Great Lakes of Africa, Two Thousand Years of History* (New York, 2003), pp.170-83; Holly Elisabeth Hanson, *Landed Obligation, The Practice of Power in Buganda* (Portsmouth, NH, 2003), pp.36-52; David Newbury, *Kings and Clans, Ijwi Island and the Lake Kivu Rift, 1780-1840* (Madison, WI, 1991), p.201ff; Jan Vansina, *Le Rwanda ancien, le royaume Nyiginya* (Paris, 2000), pp.98-127. Though Richard Reid claims that slaves inside such hierarchies in Buganda 'appear on the whole to have been resigned to their status' (*Political Power in Pre-Colonial Buganda* (Oxford, 2002), p.127) he nonetheless presents evidence which could be read against the grain to show how slaves used the social logics of these hierarchies to pursue their own aspirations; then see *ibid.*, pp.113ff. See also Hanson, *Landed Obligation*, pp.94-104, for a sense of how slave raiding destabilised the networks of reciprocal obligation in late-nineteenth-century Buganda; and Gerald W. Hartwig, 'The Victoria Nyanza as a trade route in the nineteenth century,' *Journal of African History*, 11, 4 (1970), pp.535-52.

7 But see suggestions in Bethwell A. Ogot (ed.), *War and Society in Africa* (London, 1972); and essays by Godfrey N. Uzoigwe, Warren Weinstein, and Dent Ocaya-Lakidi in Ali A. Mazrui (ed.), *The Warrior Tradition in Modern Africa* (Leiden, 1977); Robert S. Smith, *Warfare & Diplomacy in Pre-Colonial West Africa*, 2nd edn (London, 1989); John K. Thornton, *Warfare in Atlantic Africa, 1500-1800* (London, 1999); Wim van Binsbergen, '"Then give him to the crocodiles", violence, state formation, and cultural discontinuity in west central Zambia, 1600-2000', in Wim van Binsbergen (ed.), *The Dynamics of Power and the Rule of Law* (Leiden, 2003), pp.197-219; Jean Bazin and Emmanuel Terray (eds), *Guerres de lignages et guerres d'états en Afrique* (Paris, 1982); Jack Goody, *Technology, Tradition, and the State in Africa* (Cambridge, 1971), Chapters 2 and 3; Joseph Smalldone, *Warfare in the Sokoto Caliphate* (Cambridge, 1975); Emmanuel Terray, 'Contribution à une etude de l'armée asante', *Cahiers d'Études Africaines* 16, 1-2 (1976), pp.297-356; Stephen P. Reyna, *Wars Without End, The Political Economy of a Precolonial African State* (Hanover, NH, 1990).

8 The historical linguistic strands of this evidentiary appear in David Schoenbrun, *Comparative Vocabularies for Slavery, Vulnerability, Violence, and Social Standing in Great Lakes Bantu: Etymologies, Semantics, and Distributions* (Köln, in preparation).

9 With the publication of this volume, we have the first book-length study devoted to slavery in the Great Lakes region since early colonial days. For early academic treatments of the topic, see Michael Wright, *Buganda in the Heroic Age* (Nairobi, 1971), especially Chapter 6; John Rowe, 'Revolution in Buganda, 1856-1900, Part One: The Reign of Kabaka Mukabya Mutesa, 1856-1884' (Unpublished PhD Dissertation, University of Wisconsin, Madison, 1966), pp.2-44; Randall Packard, *Chiefship and Cosmology* (Bloomington, IN, 1981); Newbury, *Kings and Clans*.

10 On a short list, Christopher Wrigley, *Kingship and State* (Cambridge, 1996), p.224 and Chapter 11; Hanson, *Landed Obligation*, pp.94-104; Chrétien, *Great Lakes of Africa*, pp.170-3. Partly for thematic reasons and perhaps as a result of Michael Twaddle's influence, only Richard Reid has carried out a sustained study of slavery (and, then, only for Buganda most compellingly for the later nineteenth century). See his *Political*

Power, Chapter 6. Gerald Hartwig's considerable *oeuvre* on Bukerebe in East African history consistently brings slavery threads into his analysis; see his 'Changing forms of servitude among the Kerebe of Tanzania,' in Suzanne Miers and Igor Kopytoff (eds), *Slavery in Africa: Historical and Anthropological Perspectives* (Madison, WI, 1977), pp.261–85. The encyclopedic thesis of H. Médard, 'Croissances et crises de la royauté du Buganda au XIXe siècle' (Thèse de doctorat, Université Paris I, 2001), contains surprisingly little systematic consideration of slavery. By far the most sustained and integrated engagement with violence and militarism in the region appears in Jan Vansina's *Antecedents to Modern Rwanda: The Nyiginya Kingdom* (Madison, WI, 2004), pp.44–54, 68–79, 95–8.

11   See Schoenbrun, *Comparative Vocabularies*, Introduction.
12   David Schoenbrun, 'Gendered histories between the Great Lakes: varieties and limits,' *International Journal of African Historical Studies*, 29, 3 (1996), pp.461–92. The hurly burly of this dynamic is absent from the historical record until the denser, dynastic traditions of the seventeenth and eighteenth centuries. Before then, kinship ideologies and the aspirations of their users must be reconstructed by historical inference from the shapes of more recent examples.
13   Sandra E. Greene, *Gender, Ethnicity and Social Change on the Upper Slave Coast: A History of the Anlo-Ewe* (Portsmouth, NH, 1996).
14   It is important not to overplay the importance of lineage politics in social history because the apparent logic of genealogies which shape much political struggle between lineages tends to smuggle a functionalism into analysing them that belies the shifting nature of the overlapping networks of social obligation created by any number of social relationships other than those created by genealogical and generational issues. See Igor Kopytoff and Suzanne Miers, 'African "slavery" as an institution of marginality', in Miers and Kopytoff, *Slavery in Africa*, pp.3–81; Hanson, *Landed Obligation*, pp.28–36; and more recently, Wyatt MacGaffey, 'Changing representations in Central African history', *Journal of African History*, 46, 2 (2005), pp.195–201.
15   Israel Katoke, *The Karagwe Kingdom: A History of the Abanyambo of North-West Tanzania* (Nairobi, 1975), p.75ff; Hartwig, 'Changing forms', pp.269–70, 283–4; see also P.M. Larson, *History and Memory in the Age of Enslavement* (Portsmouth, NH, 2000), pp.6–23.
16   Hanson, *Landed Obligation*, p.180; Shane Doyle, 'An Environmental History of the Kingdom of Bunyoro in Western Uganda, from c. 1860 to 1940', (Unpublished Ph.D. Thesis, University of Cambridge, 1998).
17   The historical constitution and interrelationships between the various branches of Great Lakes Bantu, and of various other proto-language communities ancestral to Great Lakes Bantu form the basic analytical grid against which the historical reality of these language data may be argued. Detailed arguments concerning the integrity of these different classifications are not repeated here and may be found in the following sources: David Schoenbrun, 'Great Lakes Bantu: classification and settlement chronology', *Sprache und Geschichte in Afrika*, 15 (1994), pp.91–152; Christopher Ehret, 'Subclassifying Bantu: the evidence of stem morpheme innovation', in J-M. Hombert and Larry M. Hyman (eds), *Bantu Historical Linguistics: Theoretical and Empirical Perspectives* (Stanford, CA, 1999), pp.43–147; Derek Nurse, 'Towards an historical classification of East African Bantu languages', in Hombert and Hyman, *Bantu Historical Linguistics*, pp. 1–41; Catherine Cymone Fourshey, *Agriculture, Ecology, Kinship and Gender, A Social and Economic History of Tanzania's Corridor 500 BC to 1900 AD* (Ann Arbor, MI, 2002).
18   Raimo Anttila, *Historical and Comparative Linguistics* (Amsterdam, 1989), p.136.
19   From Hugo's 'Préface de Cromwell,' quoted in Stephen Ullman, *Semantics: An Introduction to the Science of Meaning* (New York, 1979), p.149.
20   Ullman, *Semantics*, pp.145–55. These few concepts do not exhaust the tools available to the historian in search of semantic histories; among many others, see Anttila, *Historical and Comparative Linguistics*, p.144, for a schematic sense of other processes of semantic change, such as folk etymology, loan translation and allomorphic alternation.
21   It might be noted that this logic renders the successful recruiters best positioned to leave a legacy, linguistic or otherwise, some of which historians then use as their evidence. And, given that the 'enslaved' were defined by an ideology of social isolation, it seems

unlikely or uncommon that their semantic contributions – as humour, as irony, as sarcasm – to the communal fund of language will have been systematically retained and transferred across the generations. For these reasons, I have the language of the dominant, the 'recruiters', as evidence. Thanks to Joe Miller, personal communication, for stimulating these thoughts.

22 Only a fraction of the language evidence is discussed here. Many names for slaves were phrases in which the identity of the slave subject was glossed by an adverbial compound. Thus, in Kerewe, a person who had become enslaved by being convicted of witchcraft was named *omuzana w'ilogo* (if a female) or *omwiru w'ilogo* (if male). See Hartwig, 'Changing forms', p.284.

23 Joseph Miller, personal communication, April 2004.

24 Proto-Mashariki is the speech community ancestral to such widely separated but demonstrably historically related eastern Bantu languages as Kiswahili, Gikuyu, Luganda, Nyakyusa, Chiyao, Kisukuma, Ruhehe, Chaga, Langi, Fipa, Chinyanja, Makua, Shona and Sotho. It has two clear clusters, in each of which the languages are more closely related to each other, roughly divided by the Ruvuma River. See Christopher Ehret, 'Bantu expansions, re-envisioning a central problem in early African history', *International Journal of African Historical Studies*, 34, 1 (2001), pp.5–40.

25 Among many others, see Reid, *Political Power*, p.113. Negative evidence is a notoriously unstable foundation for an argument, but I have looked widely in the sources. If this semantic boundary was breached, it was probably not done so with great regularity nor did speech communities welcome it.

26 Schoenbrun, 'Great Lakes Bantu', pp.105–7.

27 See, for example, David William Cohen's description of a Ganda plundering expedition in Busoga in his *Womunafu's Bunafu: A Study of Authority in a Nineteenth Century African Community* (Princeton, NJ, 1977), pp.73–80. I am now involved in exploring the various roots of violence – including capturing people – in Savannah Bantu-speaking societies. The language evidence for this study will appear in Schoenbrun, *Comparative Vocabularies*.

28 Andrew Reid and David Schoenbrun, 'The emergence of social formations and inequality in the Great Lakes Region,' *Archaeological Review from Cambridge*, 13,1 (1994), pp.51–60; Peter Robertshaw and David Taylor, 'Climate change and the rise of political complexity in Western Uganda,' *Journal of African History*, 41 (2000), pp.1–28; Peter Robertshaw, 'The age and function of earthworks sites in Western Uganda', *Uganda Journal*, 47 (2001), pp.20–33.

29 Renee Tantala, 'The Early History of Kitara in Western Uganda, Process Models of Religious and Political Change' (Unpublished Ph.D. Dissertation, University of Wisconsin, Madison, 1989), pp.477–87; Schoenbrun, *A Green Place*, pp.153–6, 219–26; Vansina, *Le Rwanda Ancien*, pp.34–44; Chrétien, *Great Lakes of Africa*, pp.142–7.

30 The etymology of this term does not explain why a gendered contrast developed with another term, #*muzaana*. Did these new meanings for #*mwiru* refer to new sorts of work or service that a male dependant or servant might provide for his patron? Did performing these sorts of labour form integral aspects of or preconditions for masculine forms of political action? Is this gendered aspect of these meanings a residual effect of a regional preference for male dependants – as objects of raiding and as auxiliaries in future raids – during the eighteenth century's ubiquitous militarism? Careful work in dynastic traditions that tell of war booty and patronage might produce some new leads; cf. Vansina, *Antecedents*, pp.73–90.

31 The practice is recorded from Bukerebe, Buganda, Rwanda and many of the Haya states. See Peter Robertshaw, 'Women, labour, and state formation in Western Uganda', in E. A. Baucus and L. J. Lucero (eds), *Complex Polities in the Ancient Tropical World* (Washington, DC, 1999), pp.55–8, 62; Vansina, *Antecedents*, pp.32, 232 fn 93. For an argument that combines agrarian change, militarism and the rise of sexually transmitted disease in creating sexual asymmetries in Ganda demographic health, see Wrigley, *Kingship and State*, pp.234–41.

32 But regular sound correspondences tell us that the reflex should be something like #-*mwija*.

33 Rather than having been innovated once, in Proto Rutara, and retained as cognate terms – which would show regular sound correspondences among them – in each daughter language.
34 This form would produce all the attested forms regularly. Indeed, A. E. Meeussen gives *-dįa* 1 'slave', see his *Bantu Lexical Reconstructions* (Tervuren, 1980), p.9.
35 As, indeed, Nurse and Hinnebusch suggest with their Proto-Sabaki (Indian Ocean coastal) form, *-muja* 'newcomer' and *mujakazi* 'female slave'. See Derek Nurse and Thomas Hinnebusch, *Swahili and Sabaki: A Linguistic History* (Berkeley and Los Angeles, 1993), p.616.
36 Thanks to Steven Feierman, personal communication, for suggesting 'refugee' as a more apt gloss, though I have not recorded such a gloss in the available sources.
37 Nurse and Hinnebusch, *Swahili and Sabaki*, pp.22–3; Thomas Spear, 'Early Swahili history reconsidered', *International Journal of African Historical Studies*, 33, 2 (2000), pp.279–83; Randall Pouwels, 'Eastern Africa and the Indian Ocean to 1800: reviewing relations in historical perspective', *International Journal of African Historical Studies*, 35, 2/3 (2002), pp.395–6, and citations therein to documents from the ninth century CE that refer to an export slave trade from the East African coast to other parts of the greater Indian Ocean world.
38 The metaphor occurs elsewhere, too. See Harry Johnston, *A Comparative Study of the Bantu and Semi-Bantu Languages*, Vol. 1 (Oxford, 1919), p.513, where Bisia and Soko languages spoken in the Ituri region of the Democratic Republic of Congo derived a noun for 'slave', *motuke* and *motuki*, respectively, from the Proto Bantu verb *-túka* 'to abuse'. In a personal communication, Joseph Miller noted that these metaphors reflect the situationality of social status and underscore the different aspects of the lives of people subject to particular forms of personal, physical and verbal manipulation.
39 See Reid, *Political Power*, pp.121–3. But, the difficulty of 'hearing' a slave's 'voice' in the sort of linguistic evidence discussed here should not be taken to mean that slaves uttered nothing or that no one heard their words.
40 A conundrum put well in Miers and Kopytoff, quoting Joseph Miller, 'African "slavery"', pp.15–16.
41 Michael Twaddle, 'Slaves and peasants in Buganda', in Léonie Archer (ed.), *Slavery and Other Forms of Unfree Labour* (London, 1988), p.121.
42 In Bantu languages, nouns may be classed together according to the prefix they take to mark singular and plural forms. Linguists refer to each pair of classes as a gender. The semantic coherence of noun classes varies greatly between languages. See Francis Katamba, 'Bantu nominal morphology,' in Derek Nurse and Gérard Philippson (eds), *The Bantu Languages* (London, 2003), pp.103–20.
43 Future work might focus on language and practice applied to slaves' bodies. How were they labelled? Were they handled any differently in life or after the departure of the life force? For example, the Luganda term *omusale* refers to a person who has had a bodily part cut off, as in the phrase *'omusale w'amatu'* which means 'one whose ears have been cut off'. See John D. Murphy, *Luganda-English Dictionary* (Washington, DC, 1972), p.378. The noun was created from the verb *okusala* 'to cut' but the term probably emerged in the contexts of the violence of making war and the violence of punishing criminal transgression.
44 Joseph Miller, personal communication.
45 John Iliffe, *Honour in African History* (Cambridge, 2005), p.4ff; Frank Henderson Stewart, *Honour* (Chicago, 1994), p.12ff.
46 Unni Wikan, 'Shame and honour, a contestable pair', *Man*, New Series 19 (1984), p.635.
47 In one case, people derived the substantive from a passive form of the verb; in another setting, people derived the substantive from a causative form of the verb. It takes little imagination to see subtle differences in the cognition of the relationship between fear and honour in these two derivational moves. Complete distributional and semantic evidence for these terms appears in Schoenbrun, *Comparative Vocabularies*, Chapter 4.
48 A preliminary survey of the distributions of these different derivational paths suggests

that the connections between fear and honour were most pronounced in societies with well-developed vertical differences in power and standing, most often where state forms had emerged. See Iliffe, *Honour*, pp.161–8. Further research should help explore the mutual influences of social stratification, state structures, and cultures of honour, scorn and vendetta. What is more, Rutara derives the noun from a passive reciprocal form of the verb, thus underscoring the dialogic basis for commuting honour from fear. It takes two or more to accomplish this transformation. North Nyanza derives the noun from a simple passive perhaps as a result of a more unidirectional transaction in which the feared are due honour as a matter of course. These observations, while stimulating, must be deepened with ethnographic and oral historical examples of the processes in action.

49 Iliffe, *Honour*, p.119.
50 Iliffe, *Honour*, p.3; Rhiannon Stephens, 'Historical linguistic approaches to a history of motherhood in West Nyanza, 500–1500 CE,' Seminar Paper, Northwestern University, pp.14-24; Schoenbrun, *A Green Place*, pp.151–6.
51 A class 9/10 noun – *intinyi* – has an even wider distribution (Rwanda and Haavu) and carries glosses describing a woman who does not like having sex with men. Considering that the great majority of informants for these dictionaries were men, one wonders what other meanings the word carried, especially for women.
52 Schoenbrun, *A Green Place*, pp.255–8; Newbury, *Kings and Clans*, pp.200–26; Vansina, *Antecedents*, pp.54–8.
53 Many Great Lakes Bantu languages distinguished acts of praising someone's practical knowledge *in absentia* from acts of conferring respect upon someone in person. See Pauline Fraas, *A Nande-English and English-Nande Dictionary* (Washington, DC, 1961), p.88. And I have said nothing about the capacity of things to generate and attract honour. The famous, mobile medicine horns – *jjembe* – used by healers, warriors, other leaders and malicious persons in North Nyanza society would be fine examples to study through these lenses.
54 Pierre Bourdieu, [Philip Sherrard, trans.] 'The sentiment of honour in Kabyle society', in John G. Peristiany (ed.), *Honour and Shame: The Values of Mediterranean Society* (London, 1965), pp.197–8. In a stimulating essay on grace, Julian Pitt-Rivers opens up an intriguing path towards understanding what might be called an 'excess' in the pursuit of honour; it points to the unique and extraordinary things a person does beyond what is expected. If the pursuit of honour is banal in its ubiquity, the achievement of honour might rely in part on an individual's capacity for the extraordinary, the graceful. Such a connection is clearly in evidence in notions of the material substance which exists inside the bodies of extraordinary persons – witches, successful politicians – and which embodies the unusual, the extraordinary, as a function of a discursive autopsy on a person's achievements. See Pitt-Rivers, 'Postscript: the place of grace in anthropology', in John G. Peristiany and Julian Pitt-Rivers (eds), *Honor and Grace in Anthropology* (Cambridge, 1992), pp.217, 220.
55 It will be important to scour the dynastic sources for evidence that enslaved war captives used flight and even suicide to refuse their condition; see Iliffe, *Honour*, p.131; Glassman, *Feasts and Riot*, pp.109–113, on the fugitive slave community of Makorora on the Mrima in 1873.
56 Schoenbrun, *A Green Place*, pp.183–4; Hanson, *Landed Obligation*, pp.61ff; Jean-Pierre Chrétien, 'Exchanges and hierarchies in the East African Interlacustrine kingdoms', *Research in Economic Anthropology* 4 (1981), pp.19–30.
57 Iliffe, *Honour*, p.137.
58 Dylan Penningroth, *The Claims of Kinfolk* (Chapel Hill, NC, 2003), Introduction; Frederick Cooper, *Plantation Slavery on the East Coast of Africa* (New Haven, CT, 1977), *passim*; Glassman, *Feasts and Riot*, pp.79–114; Reid, *Political Power*, pp.98–112, 124–30.
59 The vocabulary for forms of labour grows dramatically in number at the same time.
60 For some more detail on this condition in twentieth-century Nkore, see Steinhart's chapter in this volume.
61 This term refers to an areal cluster of intercommunicating speech communities in

existence before Proto Great Lakes and after Proto Mashariki.
62 James Augustus Grant, *A Walk Across Africa or Domestic Scenes from my Nile Journal* (Edinburgh and London, 1864), p.48.
63 *Ibid.*, p.61. Cohen, 'Food production', pp.13ff, emphasised the 'reorganization of work and labor' that must have driven and been driven by food systems specialised for trade and tribute.
64 Grant, *A Walk Across Africa*, p.78.
65 For examples from the Mrima and Zanzibar, see Glassman, *Feasts and Riot*, pp.85–96; Laura Fair, 'Dressing up: clothing, class and gender in post-abolition Zanzibar', *Journal of African History*, 39, 1 (1998), pp.67–74. And Grant's descriptions suggest that one's origin and standing rather than one's involvement in commerce were central to defining 'slavehood' in the eyes of the master.
66 The gloss 'slave' often covers a term for 'seized' or 'captured' person where warfare and enslavement have been widespread. Among many other possible examples, see Frederick Lamp, *The Art of the Baga: A Drama of Cultural Reinvention* (New York and Munich, 1996), p.44. Thanks to Edda Fields for bringing this to my attention. Of course, trickery, naiveté, and debt also framed this 'alienation'.
67 Wendy James, referring to Claude Meillassoux. See James, 'Perceptions from an African slaving frontier', in Archer, *Slavery and Other Forms of Unfree Labour*, p.139.
68 Schoenbrun, 'Great Lakes Bantu', pp.114, 116–17, 144, 149–51; Derek Nurse and Henry R. T. Muzale, 'Tense and aspect in Great Lakes Bantu languages', in Jean-Marie Hombert and Larry Hyman (eds), *Bantu Historical Linguistics: Theoretical and Empirical Perspectives* (Stanford, CA, 1999), pp.518–21.
69 Miers and Kopytoff, 'African "slavery"', pp.14–20.
70 Unless they were of noble status, in which case they might either be ransomed or take up powerful positions in exile, as was often the case in Rwanda and its neighbouring monarchies. See Vansina, *Antecedents*.
71 Ehret, 'Subclassifying Bantu', p.80.
72 Vansina, *Paths*, pp.93-4; Kairn Klieman, *'Pygmies Were our Compass': Bantu and Batwa in the History of West Central Africa, early times to c. 1900 C.E.* (Portsmouth, NH, 2003), pp.173–83; Pierre de Maret, 'L'évolution monétaire du Shaba Central entre le 7e et le 18e siècle', *African Economic History*, 10 (1981), pp.117–49.
73 David William Cohen, 'Food production and food exchange in the precolonial Lakes Plateau Region', in Robert I. Rotberg (ed.), *Imperialism, Colonialism, and Hunger in East and Central Africa* (Lexington, MA, 1983), p.10; David Newbury, 'Lake Kivu regional trade in the nineteenth century', *Journal des Africanistes*, 50, 2 (1980), pp.6–30; Michael G. Kenny, 'Pre-colonial trade in Eastern Lake Victoria', *Azania*, 14 (1979), pp.97–107; Gerald Hartwig, *The Art of Survival in East Africa: The Kerebe and Long-Distance Trade, 1800-1895* (New York, 1976), pp.62–83; Ephraim Kamuhangire, 'The pre-colonial economic and social history of East Africa, with special reference to south-western Uganda salt lakes region', *Hadith*, 5 (1976), pp.67–91; Kathryn Barrett-Gaines, 'Katwe Salt in the African Great Lakes Regional Economy, 1750s–1950s,' (PhD Dissertation, Stanford University, 2001) pp.43–8; Frederick Peter Batala-Nayenga, 'An Economic History of the Lacustrine States of Busoga, Uganda, 1750–1930,' (PhD Dissertation, University of Michigan, Ann Arbor, 1976).
74 Among very many, see Jane I. Guyer, *Marginal Gains: Monetary Transaction in Atlantic Africa* (Chicago, 2004), pp.27–50; Jane I. Guyer and Samuel M. Eno Belinga, 'Wealth in people as wealth in knowledge: accumulation and composition in Equatorial Africa', *Journal of African History*, 36, 1 (1995), pp.91–129.
75 Iliffe, *Honour*, p.136.
76 This essay has not considered evidence relating to enslavement by formal legal action or debt-pawning. However, legal precepts in Lakes societies almost certainly guided the fates of pawns and of political or social adversaries.
77 Twaddle, 'Slaves and peasants in Buganda', p.122.
78 Including royal exactions in the form of food, even if these adventures were 'conceived to fail' in order for rulers to dispose of a difficult adversary; see Cohen, 'Food

production', pp.2–3 and 5–6; and for violent resistance to such exactions, see Kenny, 'Pre-colonial trade', pp.97–107.
79   L. J. Wood and C. Ehret, 'The origins and diffusions of the market institution in East Africa', *Journal of African Studies*, 7 (1980), pp.1–17.
80   Glassman, *Feasts and Riot*, Chapter 3; Cooper, *Plantation Slavery*, *passim*; Twaddle, 'Slaves and peasants in Buganda', pp.118–29; Reid, *Political Power*, pp.124–30.
81   Marcia Wright, *Strategies of Slaves and Women* (New York, 1993), Introduction.
82   Reid, *Political Power*, pp.124–30, 132.
83   Wrigley, *Kingship and State*, pp.215–20; Hanson, *Landed Obligation*, pp.94–8; Hartwig, 'Changing forms', pp.265–7, 272–82.
84   But we can take elements of nineteenth-century slavery and trace them back to various notional points of origin.
85   Vansina, *Antecedents*, pp.67–125, does so for Rwanda. See also Hermann Rehse, *Land und Leute* (Stuttgart, 1910), Chapter 11, page 9, who makes it clear that female pawns were common in royal courts and that male slaves married women of their master's choosing, while female slaves married sons of the master's other slaves, if they were not taken as concubines by the male master. In short, the picture painted for the turn of the twentieth century is a familiar tableau of paternalist images with sometimes hard to see pieces – for example the casual remark (p.15 of Chapter 11) that male slaves could make formal legal complaints against their masters – of a mutually obligated system. See also the new work begun by Rhiannon Stephens, 'Motherhood in interlacustrine Africa, ca. 500–ca. 1500 CE, Infertility, adoption, gender and marriage,' Unpublished Seminar Paper, Northwestern University, 2003.
86   Hartwig, 'Changing forms', p.282.
87   Hanson, *Landed Obligation*, pp.94–104; Reid, *Political Power*, pp.222–6; Vansina, *Le Rwanda*, pp.227–46.
88   Paul Lovejoy, *Transformations in Slavery* (Cambridge, 2000), p.xxi.
89   *Ibid.*, p.19.
90   Hanson, *Landed Obligation*, pp.75–87; Reid, *Political Power*, pp.177–90; Vansina, *Antecedents*, pp.180ff.
91   John Thornton, *Africa and Africans in the Making of the Atlantic World: 1400–1800*, 2nd edn (Cambridge, 1998), p.74.
92   *Ibid.*, 85.
93   David Schoenbrun, 'Conjuring contemporary Africa, healing between the Great Lakes', Paper presented to First Annual Body/Antibody Collective, Falls River, MA, 2 November 2003, pp.52ff; MacGaffey, 'Changing representations', pp.189–208; Jeremy Prestholdt, 'On the global repercussions of East African consumerism', *American Historical Review*, 109, 3 (2004), pp.779–81.
94   Or freedom is the absence of slavery; see Steven Feierman, *Peasant Intellectuals: Anthropology and History in Tanzania* (Madison, WI, 1990), pp.226ff; Glassman, *Feasts and Riot*, Chapter 9.
95   Claude Meillassoux (Alide Dasnois, trans.), *The Anthropology of Slavery: The Womb of Iron and Gold* (Chicago, 1991), pp.144–56.
96   Vansina, *Antecedents*, Chapters 4 and 5; Hanson, *Landed Obligation*, pp.94-104; Reid, *Political Power*, pp.251-7.
97   Schoenbrun, *A Green Place*, *passim*; Mikael Karlström, 'Modernity and its aspirants: moral community and developmental eutopianism', *Current Anthropology*, 45, 5 (2005), pp.595–619.
98   Hanson, *Landed Obligation*, pp.25–57.
99   Reid, *Political Power*, pp.115, 117; David Newbury, '"Bunyabungo": the Western Rwandan frontier, 1750–1850', in Igor Kopytoff (ed.), *The Internal African Frontier: The Reproduction of Traditional African Societies* (Bloomington, IN, 1987), pp.164–92.
100 It is extremely difficult to capture the nuances of early conceptualisations of the individual using oral testimony collected over the last eighty years or more because the atomised person that constitutes the legal and practical ground of a wage-labour system and, later, of various modes of parliamentary democracy has become hegemonic. For

the complexity of such a transformation, see Hanson, *Landed Obligation*, pp.169–93, 233–41; and Vansina, *Antecedents*, pp.134–9.
101 David Schoenbrun, *The Historical Reconstruction of Great Lakes Bantu Cultural Vocabulary: Etymologies and Distributions* (Köln, 1997); C. Ehret, *An African Classical Age* (Charlottesville, VA, 1998); Nurse and Hinnebusch, *Swahili and Sabaki*.
102 Raimo Anttila, *Historical and Comparative Linguistics* (Amsterdam, 1989).
103 Wyatt MacGaffey, *Religion and Society in Central Africa* (Chicago, 1986), p.9.
104 This table presents only the bare essentials of the evidence. The first paragraph includes: a proposed lexical reconstruction, its grammatical standing, (numbers mark a noun's standing in a noun class), and an English gloss or glosses. Lexical reconstructions appear as stems, fronted by a dash and one of three possible symbols: the ° tags a word with an uncertain or regional distribution, suggesting a loanspread; the # tags a word that is an ancestral form in a given proto language other than Proto Bantu; the * tags a Proto Bantu item. A second paragraph includes the names of the languages with attestations of the proposed lexical reconstruction, listed serially. A third paragraph includes comments on derivation, etymology, and a proposed proto language for the reconstruction. Complete information on sources and a full treatment of these roots and of a far greater number of allied semantic materials will appear in Schoenbrun, *Comparative Vocabularies*.
105 Shigeki Kaji, *Vocabulaire Hunde* (Tokyo, 1992), p.142.
106 Albert E. Meeussen, *Bantu Lexical Reconstructions* (Tervuren, 1980), p.9.
107 Nurse and Hinnebusch, *Swahili and Sabaki*, p.616.
108 M. Guthrie, *Comparative Bantu* (Fairnborough, 1967–71), Vol. 3, p.121.
109 Meeussen, *Bantu Lexical Reconstructions*, p.8.

Two

Notes on the Rise of Slavery & Social Change in Unyamwezi
c. 1860–1900

JAN-GEORG DEUTSCH

Introduction

When German explorers and colonial officials arrived in Unyamwezi in the 1880s and 1890s, they recorded the presence of very large numbers of slaves residing in the area. Based on his visits to the town of Tabora in the mid-1880s, the traveller Reichard noted that about 75 per cent of the population in Unyamwezi were slaves.[1] The first person who actually calculated their total number was Hauptmann Puder, one of the earliest permanent administrative officers in Tabora district. Without giving an indication of whom he considered to be a slave or how he arrived at this particular estimate, he stated in an official report in 1890 that about two-thirds of Tabora district's total population of around 350,000, i.e. approximately 233,000 people, were locally regarded as slaves.[2] Both Reichard's and Puder's figures are likely to be on the high side,[3] but, even allowing for a wide margin of error, the numbers are still impressive, especially as they seem to have risen to that high level in a comparatively short period of time, probably in less than forty years.[4]

This essay endeavours to provide an historical account of the rise of slavery in Unyamwezi in the second half of the nineteenth century. It will be argued that this expansion is best understood as a dynamic social process, which altered Unyamwezi society as a whole. This requires us to show that, in the relevant period, the local economy (the forms of wealth production, especially the organisation of labour), social relationships (the means of acquiring status and honour, particularly local gender and kinship relations), and the political order (the forms of exercising chiefly power, both within local society and with regard to neighbouring polities), underwent significant and large-scale change.[5]

Slavery in Nineteenth-century Tanganyika

The social history of slavery and the slave trade in Tanganyika in the nineteenth century evolved around the interaction, tensions and contradictions of the social relations that defined personhood within a community (as *insiders*), and the commercial transactions that actually or potentially reduced people to mere objects of exchange and exploitation (as *outsiders*).[6] It was within these social extremes, which seem to represent opposing configurations of social relations, that slaves had to make their living. Yet, historically they overlapped: whether slaves or, for that matter, in some areas other marginalised groups such as women, were regarded as tradeable currency or as upright members of a household, extended family or local community, was often defined situationally and thus subject to sudden change, particularly in periods of social dislocation such as internal strife, war or famine. This 'radical uncertainty' was probably the most critical feature in the everyday life of slaves.[7]

Configurations of social relations are politically, culturally and economically circumscribed and, of course, subject to historical change. They also vary enormously between different societies and locations. Moreover, developments in one sphere necessarily influence others, not least because, as elsewhere, social actions in Africa are not perceived to be exclusively economic, political or cultural in nature. As far as the procurement and use of slaves on the East African mainland are concerned, perhaps the single most important development in the nineteenth century was the quantitative expansion and qualitative change of the caravan trade centred in Zanzibar, transforming not only local patterns of commodity production, distribution and consumption, but – as will be shown later – also those of political authority, public morality and social interaction.[8] In the late eighteenth and early nineteenth centuries, when the long-distance slave trade and commercial slavery gradually spread along the trade routes, 'attitudes to life and freedom were brutalised' all over East Africa.[9] This transformation has been aptly described as the *commodification of social relations*, that is, as an 'uneven process by which an increasing amount of social interaction [is] mediated through market relations'.[10] This process took place in localities showing a high degree of social, cultural and political diversity. Unyamwezi was one of these localities and the remainder of this chapter will focus on its social history.

Trade and Politics in Unyamwezi

In the early nineteenth century the area around Tabora acquired the name Unyamwezi and its inhabitants came to be called Nyamwezi.[11] This was an assigned name; at the time the 'Nyamwezi' preferred to identify themselves by the chiefdom in which they were born. The label Nyamwezi was coined from outside and indicated that the *Wanyamwezi* lived somewhere in the far west; one possible meaning of the word Nyamwezi is 'people of the new moon', a term coastal people associated with that particular direction.[12] For them, the label carried the derogatory connotation of being 'uncivilised' or 'rural'.[13] In the European literature the name Nyamwezi or a recognisable variant appears in various nineteenth-century exploration accounts of East Africa, but it is often uncertain precisely what area was being referred to.[14] Sometimes Unyamwezi merely denoted the immediate environs of Tabora, sometimes the powerful chiefdom of Unyanyembe, but equally often the entire area between Lake Tanganyika and Lake Victoria.[15] In this study the descriptive term Unyamwezi relates to a geographical area that was considered to be the heartland of Unyamwezi settlements by most contemporary observers. In German colonial times this area was called Tabora district.[16]

The local language was first recorded by missionaries in the second half of the nineteenth century.[17] As elsewhere, this process accentuated the linguistic differences with the languages spoken by neighbouring peoples, for instance by the Sukuma and Sumbwa in the north or the Kimbu in the south. Yet, cultural differences between these groups were not as pronounced as their ethnic or linguistic labels suggest. Due to intermarriage and large-scale migration in the eighteenth century, neighbouring peoples in this region were usually able to understand each other, especially in the border areas. However, communication problems did exist when longer distances were involved, as when people living in Ufipa on the south-eastern shores of Lake Tanganyika encountered people living in Uzinza on the southern shores of Lake Victoria.[18] The Nyamwezi were ruled by separate but historically often closely related headmen and chiefs of very different local making, involving various kinds of religious beliefs and local political traditions that included different forms of dynastic rules of succession. Thus, in terms of cultural identity, language and political organisation, Unyamwezi was neither a homogenous ethnic unit nor a clearly defined territorial entity, although many nineteenth-century observers believed that this was the case.[19]

In the mid-nineteenth century Unyamwezi was one of the most densely populated areas in what later became Tanganyika. This was due to its agricultural potential. The traveller Richard Burton, who visited Unyamwezi in the late 1850s, called it the 'Garden of Central Africa'.[20] In addition to tobacco, millet and sorghum, people produced large quantities of maize, rice and sweet potatoes, exotic crops that had been introduced into the area earlier in the century, probably in the 1830s or 1840s. Large herds of cattle were found especially in the northern parts of Unyamwezi, which were less infested by tsetse fly than the southern forest areas.[21] The size of these cattle herds increased considerably in the first half of the century. They were apparently not looked after by Nyamwezi pastoralists but by an ever-increasing number of immigrants, mainly 'Tutsis', as they are called in archival sources, who came from the north and north-west, that is, from present-day Kagera Region, Rwanda and Burundi.²² Agriculture was augmented by craft industries, particularly extensive iron-working and the making of cotton cloth, which only declined when the consumption of imported goods acquired social prestige in the second half of the century.²³

Another important source of wealth was trade. In the eighteenth century Nyamwezi traders appear to have already engaged in regional commercial transactions involving the exchange of salt, iron hoes, pottery and foodstuffs, including honey, dried fish and grain. Around 1800 Nyamwezi traders seem to have discovered the rewards of long-distance trade.²⁴ Using the wealth and experience generated in regional trade, they ventured further afield, exploring various routes to the coast and exchanging locally produced commodities including iron hoes, salt, cattle and, increasingly, ivory for imported goods such as beads, cotton cloth (in ki-Swahili *kaniki* or *merikani* according to their Indian or American origin), guns and metalware including brass and copper wire.²⁵ Moreover, Nyamwezi traders extended their regular commercial contacts towards the north-west (Buganda), the south-west (Ufipa), the north (Lake Victoria) and to Ujiji, a settlement on the shores of Lake Tanganyika.

During the first half of the nineteenth century Unyamwezi developed into an ivory trading centre where professional hunters (in ki-Nyamwezi *badandu*) from across the region brought their elephant tusks and hippopotamus teeth. Previously, ivory had had little commercial value in Unyamwezi, where, as elsewhere in Central Africa, it was probably used for decorative and ceremonial purposes only; indeed, elephants were largely hunted for their meat.²⁶ However, due to rising Indian and later European and American demand, East African ivory prices steadily improved. Having already been in commercial contact with the coast, it is likely that the prospects of obtaining foreign goods, especially cotton cloth, induced some Nyamwezi traders to export ivory from their home region on a more regular basis. Very early on they also seem to have been accompanied by slaves.²⁷ The caravans went to coastal settlements such as Pangani, Saadani and Mbwamaji, towns and villages situated opposite Zanzibar's twin islands of Unguja and Pemba, the chief East African ivory market at the time.²⁸

For security reasons, early nineteenth-century Nyamwezi caravans consisted of large numbers, sometimes thousands, of porters (in ki-Swahili *wapagazi*, sing. *pagazi*).²⁹ These caravans elected their own leaders who were called *viongozi* (sing. *kiongozi*) in ki-Swahili.³⁰ Many porters, usually accompanied by local headmen, made the arduous and dangerous 350-mile journey to the coast on their own or their families' account.³¹ In this period, the caravans probably consisted of young men seeking to escape control of the elders by acquiring the capital to start trading for themselves and by earning enough independently and rapidly to pay the often immense bridewealth expenses due in either goods, such as cattle, or personal services, should they wish to marry the elders' daughters.[32] In the first half of the century, trading and porterage seem to have developed at great speed into more than just a means of gaining (bride)wealth. It became an accepted way of life and a source of male prestige.[33] Nyamwezi men, it was said, were not allowed to marry until they had been to the coast and brought back a piece of cloth, beads or some metal wire.[34]

Participating in the caravan trade was not exclusively a male occupation.[35] Nyamwezi women also joined the caravans to make the long journey to the coast either independently or with their often temporary husbands. A number of these women even worked as porters alongside the men, carrying smaller parcels of merchandise or foodstuffs. Neither was porterage the occupation of 'free' Nyamwezi alone, since some local notables employed trusted slaves as carriers, or even agents. However, such cases were the exception. It was more common for enterprising slaves to leave their owners and join the caravans as 'free' porters, never to return to Unyamwezi again.[36]

Those who came back from the coast brought with them novel experiences and new ideas, particularly about religion. This was one of the main avenues by which Islamic beliefs and coastal manners of dress, speaking and behaviour found their way into the interior.[37] Conversely, however, Nyamwezi religion and culture, and in particular ki-Nyamwezi, acquired currency along the trade routes. By mid-century the language had not only developed into an important regional *lingua franca*, but was set to become one of the three most widespread languages in the whole of Tanganyika, its number of speakers probably even surpassing those who used ki-Swahili or ki-Yao as their main medium of communication in the nineteenth century.[38] The rapid expansion of Nyamwezi culture was further underpinned by the founding of semi-permanent Nyamwezi settlements not just on the coast, but also in the west near the copper belt area of Katanga in what later became the Belgian Congo, in the southwest around the southern end of Lake Tanganyika, especially Ufipa, and to the east in Ugogo, Irangi and Usandawe.[39] The most important settlement in the west was that of Chief Msiri in Katanga. He had moved there in the 1850s with a large group of Unyamwezi henchmen armed with guns, ousted the local ruler and established himself as an independent chief. His principal trade was in slaves, ivory and copper.[40]

The establishment of long-distance trade routes necessarily also affected the regional and local economies through which the caravans passed. On their journeys to the coast, Nyamwezi porters exchanged goods, including salt, cattle, iron hoes and tobacco, for foodstuffs and trade products. They also had to pay road tolls. Supplying the caravans stimulated the production of food and commercial crops, particularly in areas previously less important to translocal commercial transactions, such as Ugogo, Usangu and the Uluguru mountains in central and eastern Tanganyika.

Developments took a different turn from about mid-century onwards, however, as the independent Nyamwezi ivory trade began to decline.[41]

Caravans from the interior had probably outnumbered those originating from the coast up to the 1850s,[42] but from this point coastal traders appear to have gained the upper hand. This was due, first of all, to the Sultan of Zanzibar's new tax regime on the coast, which heavily favoured local ivory traders, particularly those based in Zanzibar. Some Nyamwezi traders still managed to sell their ivory directly in the Zanzibar market. They even had their own quarter in the town.[43] However, the majority of the Nyamwezi traders were induced, not least by the Zanzibari tax regime, to sell their ivory to local merchants, apparently at a very heavy discount.[44]

The second reason for the decline in Nyamwezi-controlled commerce was that the ivory frontier was rapidly advancing towards the west, moving out of the ambit of local Nyamwezi hunters and traders.[45] Between the 1850s and 1870s the number of elephant herds in Unyamwezi and the adjoining areas severely declined and local elephant hunters found it exceedingly difficult to track down their prey. Some Nyamwezi hunters and traders followed the ivory frontier but, due to lack of capital and military power, their success was limited, especially in the later period when they were faced with strong competition.

Thirdly, and perhaps most decisively, traders from the coast and from Zanzibar had already begun to settle in the interior in the early 1830s along the caravan routes, founding resting places such as Ujiji on the eastern shores of Lake Tanganyika. Coastal and Zanzibari traders then established the more permanent settlement of Kazeh in the early 1850s, near present-day Tabora in the heart of Unyamwezi.[46] Thereafter, coastal presence in the East African interior expanded rapidly.[47] By 1870 Tabora 'town' consisted of about 50 scattered homesteads (in ki-Swahili *tembe*). These were large square dwellings, accommodating in some cases several hundred people, with an inner courtyard, adjacent garden plots, storerooms, servants' quarters and out-houses for slaves.[48] Tabora was surrounded by dense clusters of Nyamwezi villages, from which the porters and soldiers were drawn for the caravans. At the time, the settlement was governed by an appointed representative of the Sultan of Zanzibar. Superseding the older Nyamwezi trade networks, Tabora developed into the centre of the 'coastal' trade routes, one radiating northwards to Mwanza on the southern shores of Lake Victoria, a second one passing north-west through Karagwe to the Kingdom of Buganda, a third running west towards Ujiji on Lake Tanganyika, and a fourth extending south-west to Ufipa.[49]

Thus, in the period between 1850 and 1870, coastal and Zanzibari traders, some of whom were financially or personally well-connected to Indian and Omani merchants in Zanzibar, were able to get the better of their Nyamwezi competitors, especially in long-distance, wholesale trade.[50] They had better access to long-term credit provided by Zanzibar moneylenders and could offer the commodities used for the exchange of ivory and slaves more cheaply. These entailed imported goods such as cotton cloth and arms as well as regional commodities like salt and copper wire.

After exhausting Unyamwezi ivory supplies, they had the financial and, above all, the military means – in contrast to their local Nyamwezi competitors – to extend the ivory frontier beyond Katanga and Kazembe on the south-western side of Lake Tanganyika towards the north into Manyema region, in present-day eastern Congo. In the 1870s, the most prominent of these ivory and slave traders, warlords like Rumaliza and Tippu Tip, were able to build up 'commercial empires' where ivory trading by local competitors was, to say the least, strictly limited.[51]

The retreat of the ivory frontier and the relative decline of the independent Unyamwezi-based ivory trade forced younger men to look for other sources of income. Some seem to have followed the westward movement of the ivory frontier,[52] while others engaged in commercial food production. However, the great majority appear to have sought employment in the growing long-distance caravan trade between Unyamwezi and the coast. Wage-labour employment was by no means unknown. In the early 1830s some Nyamwezi men had already been hired as carriers by Tabora and Ujiji merchants to carry goods to and from the coast or to accompany them on their trading journeys into the east for an agreed wage. Earlier on, merchants had used coastal slaves for this task but since so many of them tried to flee as soon as an opportunity arose, their employment costs were found to be too high. Consequently, the merchants turned more and more to local sources of labour when they became available.[53]

Porterage had become a significant source of income for many young Nyamwezi men by the 1850s and gained further importance as the century progressed. In the early 1880s tens of thousands of Nyamwezi porters arrived annually on the coast, particularly in Bagamoyo, where small semi-permanent Nyamwezi settlements emerged for those who preferred to work on the coast for a while, finding employment as labourers in the growing coastal economy or tending small garden plots of vegetables and cassava.[54] Those who stayed on the coast often became indebted to coastal traders, particularly those of Indian origin who had come to settle there in the second half of the nineteenth century. Indebtedness was probably chiefly responsible for the impoverishment of the Nyamwezi porters who were sold as slaves to work on the Pemba clove plantations in the 1870s.[55] After having stayed on the coast for some time, other Nyamwezi porters appear to have completely severed their family ties. They abandoned their non-coastal, 'non-Islamic' identity and tried to present themselves as *Waswahili*.[56]

By the 1890s up to a third of the adult male population in Unyamwezi were engaged as porters in the caravan trade each year.[57] Taking Tanganyika as a whole, Nyamwezi porters and traders were probably the single most important means of long-distance transport in the nineteenth century and also the key medium of cultural (ex)change. It was only in the early twentieth century that their numbers began to decline, primarily due to the construction of the central railway, which ran almost parallel to the old caravan route.

Slavery & Social Change in Unyamwezi, c. 1860–1900

In the nineteenth century, the increase in the number and size of the caravans passing through Unyamwezi, often resting and restocking for several weeks, especially in Tabora, was accompanied by the expansion of commercial food production.[58] In the early part of the century, Nyamwezi participation in the caravan trade had been largely a seasonal activity, pursued mainly in the months between May and November when the demand arising from agricultural pursuits was comparatively low.[59] Many Nyamwezi porters sought to return to their villages at the beginning of the rainy season around December. Food crops would then be harvested in the dry season, starting around May, before the majority of caravans left for the coast.[60] Initially, therefore, the expansion of the caravan trade had a comparatively low impact on agricultural food production. Over time, though, Nyamwezi men increasingly regarded long-distance trading and porterage as their full-time rather than seasonal occupation. Their absence necessarily affected local food production. Moreover, with some notable exceptions, neither the growing coastal communities in Ujiji and Tabora, which were thought to number several thousand people in the late 1870s,[61] nor their slaves engaged in agricultural market production, although the latter produced foodstuffs for their own and their owners' consumption.

In any case, the inhabitants of 'coastal' settlements like Tabora were unable to produce enough food crops to sustain the growing number of long-distance caravans passing through or resting in the area. Thus, these caravans purchased their provisions from Nyamwezi foodstuff traders instead, particularly in the regional markets of Tabora and Ujiji.[62] Here large quantities of grain, rice and sweet potatoes as well as meat, (dried) fish, beans, and bananas changed hands regularly. Given that by mid-century a sizeable proportion of Nyamwezi men were already engaged in porterage all year round, the task of producing these foodstuffs fell increasingly on immigrants from Buha and Burundi, Nyamwezi women and, probably of equal significance, on agricultural slaves who worked the farms in the absence of their owners.[63]

Nineteenth-century commercial expansion was, therefore, marked by a contradictory development. While more and more young Nyamwezi men engaged in various forms of wage labour elsewhere – a process one historian has described as 'proletarianisation'[64] – the use of slaves became more widespread at home because the demands of the local economy could not entirely be met by family or immigrant labour.[65] By the late 1830s a few Nyamwezi notables are said to have already owned several hundred slaves, and slave-holding increased throughout the century, especially in the southern more commercially developed parts of Unyamwezi, where even ordinary Nyamwezi seemed to have acquired slaves.[66] Most of these slaves lived with their owners' families, so that for the outside observer it was almost impossible to distinguish those regarded as 'free' from those who could be sold to a passing caravan or a neighbour when the need arose.[67]

This development was aided unintentionally by the partial blockade of the ocean-going slave trade carried out by the British naval squadron from mid-century onwards. In the first half of the nineteenth century Zanzibar had developed into one of the main slave ports of East Africa, satisfying not only the demand of the local clove plantation owners for cheap labour but also supplying slaves to more distant coastal markets in the north (as discussed later). The blockade aimed at limiting the clandestine overseas maritime slave trade to India, Arabia and the Americas. Subsequent to the 1873 anti-slave trade treaty between Britain and Zanzibar, suppression of the illegal importation of slaves to the islands of Unguja and Pemba became the squadron's main task. Initially, the long-distance supply of slaves continued unabated, but as shipment to Zanzibar became more difficult, slave prices dropped, probably first on the coast and subsequently in the interior. Slave traders were thus encouraged to look for new customers. They not only found them on the coast, but also in areas adjacent to the long-distance caravan routes, principally in southern Unyamwezi, the most prosperous area of the region.[68] Due to long and intense involvement in the caravan trade, there was a particular demand for labour in this area and many of its inhabitants had the means to buy slaves, especially female slaves. As slave prices dropped, local residents felt encouraged to employ more and more slaves.

Unyamwezi was a slave importing rather than exporting region.[69] As far as slaves of Nyamwezi origin were concerned, export slave trading took place only on a minor scale, as Tabora-based coastal slave traders did not consider Unyamwezi to be a slave hunting ground. The reason for this is unclear, but these traders probably felt that local slave raiding in Unyamwezi would seriously disturb their precarious political relations with the local chiefs.[70] With the notable exception of Chief Mirambo, these chiefs also appear to have largely abstained from local slave raiding for export.[71] Nyamwezi transit slave trading, however, was extensive. The first slave caravans from Unyamwezi probably reached the coast in the early 1810s.[72] The trade seems to have grown from then on, especially in the second half of the century. According to Burton, while the 'Wanyamwezi rarely sell one another',[73] they

> will sell their criminals and captives; when want drives, they part with their wives, their children and even their parents. For economy, they import their serviles from Ujiji and the adjoining regions; from the people living towards the south-east angle of the Tanganyika Lake, as the Wafipa, the Wapoka, and the Wagara; and from the Nyanza [sic] races and the northern kingdoms of Karakwah [sic], Uganda and Unyoro.[74]

Some, however, came from much further afield, especially from Katanga and the southern Manyema region in the eastern Congo where Nyamwezi slave traders and raiders were particularly active from the 1860s.[75] According to a later observer, these raiding expeditions were carried out with traders from Zanzibar and the coast. They 'consisted of the leaders – rich men who provided muzzle loaders and gunpowder – and the *ruga-ruga* who carried and used the firearms and a number of porters'.[76] Like everywhere else in East Africa, those who were kidnapped, bought or judicially enslaved were the most vulnerable in local society: women and children unprotected by their families, victims of famine and local wars, and the unfortunate who fell prey to their autocratic chiefs.[77]

In addition to selling slaves directly to the coast, Nyamwezi slave traders supplied large numbers of slaves internally, especially to Zanzibari slave traders and local notables who were their main customers.[78] More importantly, they used imported slaves as a medium of exchange to obtain the ivory they subsequently carried to the coast. This was particularly the case in areas such as Ugogo that were rich in ivory and where the inhabitants had little demand for foreign goods.[79]

Apart from facilitating bridewealth payments and the acquisition of imported commodities, the proceeds from the slave and ivory trade seem to have been of great help to some chiefs and Nyamwezi men in acquiring guns and ammunition from about mid-century onwards. The weapons were primarily used for defence purposes, but also to expand hunting activities and as a means of kidnapping more slaves. The slave, arms and ivory trades fed on each other in rapidly widening cycles of violence, as Nolan noted: 'The introduction of firearms and the appreciating value of prisoners of war in the slave trade, seems to have changed the nature of war, people replacing cattle as a prime object of plunder.'[80] Whereas Burton found few firearms in the hands of Nyamwezi notables or chiefs in the late 1850s,[81] by the late 1870s even 'ordinary' Nyamwezi porters sometimes received their wages in firearms.[82] Probably overstating the extent of their use, missionaries working in the area claimed that by the 1890s every adult man in Unyamwezi was carrying a gun, even if it was only an old musket.[83]

The 'militarisation' of Nyamwezi society was also reflected in changing settlement patterns.[84] In the early part of the nineteenth century, Unyamwezi was cluttered with small settlements and hamlets (in ki-Nyamwezi *makayas*, sing. *kaya*) of about 20–100 people who were ruled by a headman, usually the founder of the village (in ki-Nyamwezi *muzenga kaya*).[85] In the third quarter of the century, these settlements appear to have given way to a much smaller number of large stockaded villages (in ki-Nyamwezi *limbuda*), as the use of firearms became more widespread in the region. Armed men were in a far better position to defend stockaded villages against raiders, especially against groups such as the dreaded Ngoni who, from the 1850s on, regularly invaded Unyamwezi from the south and south-west looking for cattle and women.[86] Thus, in the second half of the nineteenth century, some observers compared Unyamwezi to a sea in which isolated villages provided a safe harbour for the intrepid traveller passing through the area.[87]

Along with social and economic transformation, Unyamwezi also underwent considerable political change in the nineteenth century. While central political authority had never been particularly strong in this part of Tanganyika, especially in northern Unyamwezi, the second half of the nineteenth century saw the rise of powerful chiefs.[88] Some *batemi* (sing. *butemi* or *mtemi*), as they were called in ki-Nyamwezi, such as Chief Fundikira in the 1840s and 1850s or Chief Mirambo and Chief Sike in the 1870s and 1880s, had large numbers of personal followers. This strength in numbers enabled them to challenge militarily not only their immediate neighbours, whom they raided for cattle, ivory stores and, increasingly, slaves, but also the coastal merchants of Tabora whom they constantly pressed for tribute when they were not actually at war or in partial alliance with them.[89] The third quarter of the nineteenth century was a particularly troubled time, when local wars forced people to move away from their predatory neighbours or relocate to the stockaded defence villages of strong headmen and chiefs.[90] At that time, local circumstances and the power of the chiefs were strong enough to prevent subjects from relocating their residence from one stockaded village to another if they were dissatisfied with the local ruler.[91]

The centralisation of power in the hands of a few chiefs was accompanied by a change in the nature of their political authority. Their main instruments for the attainment of wider territorial recognition in the early part of the century were translocal marriages and the installing of family members in outlying, newly-conquered sub-chiefdoms. Religious authority, in particular rainmaking magic, was still one of the main pillars of the chiefs' political power. Authority was only rarely absolute but was based, at least to some extent, on the consent of other local notables such as competing members of the ruling family. The caravan trade changed that balance.[92] Local hunters were required to hand over part of the ivory they had collected – one tusk, as a rule – to the local chief. This rule was probably not observed regularly in remote areas where chiefs were of little consequence, but in the more centrally organised chiefdoms, it was rigidly enforced.[93] The growing ivory trade enabled some chiefs to amass considerable wealth. In addition, these chiefs levied passing caravans with a sometimes heavy toll (in ki-Swahili *mahongo*, sing. *hongo*), the payment of which allowed members of the caravan to purchase foodstuffs from the chiefs' subjects.[94]

As nineteenth-century trade increased, so, too, did the revenue Nyamwezi chiefs derived from this source. This provided ambitious chiefs with an extra income to create networks, which bound people, especially headmen, by rewarding their personal loyalty with a share in the spoils of trade. It also provided the means for building standing armies, often consisting of unruly and brutal bands of young unmarried men (in ki-Swahili *ruga-ruga*).[95] These bands consisted largely of slaves, many of whom regarded themselves as personal followers of the chief, having been bought as children from passing caravans in exchange for ivory. These young men were rewarded for their services by the chiefs with part of the loot they had collected on their raids, especially with slaves. The latter were sold for them to local or coastal traders by the chiefs, if and when the need arose.[96] These bands were mostly led by members of the ruling chief's family, but also by elevated slaves who had shown military aptitude. Thus, chiefs became less and less reliant on their subjects as they could now use slaves to expand the numbers of their followers.[97] Consequently, at the end of the nineteenth century, prestige was no longer measured in terms of charismatic virtues, but rather in the possession of material wealth, that is, of cattle, women and slaves.[98]

The most important and perhaps best known of these new chiefs was Mirambo who lived north-west of Tabora in the 1860s and 1870s.[99] He came from a Nyamwezi noble family and was a well-known rainmaker, but, above all, a highly feared warlord who successfully subdued smaller, less powerful neighbouring chiefdoms. His *ruga-ruga* bands raided deep into Sukuma territory in the north, returning with cattle and slaves, particularly female slaves. His persistent attempts to gain control over the caravan routes running to Lake Tanganyika and Lake Victoria brought him into constant conflict with the coastal merchants of Tabora, an issue that was only settled after his death in 1884.[100] He was well known for his involvement in the slave trade, exporting war captives to the coast.[101]

Yet, while commercial expansion created opportunities for chiefs, ultimately they were unable to monopolise long-distance trade. Some of their local subjects, particularly headmen living far from the chief's main residence, gained the means to become more independent of them.[102] In the early part of the century some of these headmen had already become free-trading, long-distance merchants (in ki-Nyamwezi *wandewa* or *vbandevba*) who led their own caravans to the coast.[103] Contrary to the wishes of their chiefs, the headmen often traded on their own account, exchanging slaves, ivory and arms, and forging their own political alliances, for instance, with coastal merchants in Tabora with whom they had much in common. Thus, while commercial expansion had strengthened some leading chiefs, enabling them to build up sizeable empires which only the German occupation force was finally able to destroy, as in the case of Chief Sike, for instance, it also strengthened their local rivals, the ambitious and commercially-minded headmen.[104] Much of the political history of nineteenth-century Unyamwezi, therefore, centred around the competition, conflicts and alliances between local power holders, chiefs and headmen whose authority and personal fortune came increasingly to rest on their successful participation in trade and their possession of arms and, above all, slaves.

Slavery and the slave trade thus played an important, if not crucial, role in nineteenth-century Nyamwezi politics. Both commercial expansion and the development of militarised chiefdoms depended on the importation and social control of slaves. Commercial expansion, however, had different effects on different groups of people within society. It enabled some people, especially those who had already enjoyed privileged access to local resources, like chiefs and merchant headmen, to advance their interests further, while it dispossessed others, especially those who were already vulnerable and living on the margins of their society. In short, the growth of slavery and the slave trade in the nineteenth century not only exaggerated already existing political divisions, but furthermore, and perhaps more decisively, it changed the social relationship between social groups.

The Making of Slaves

In the second half of the nineteenth century there were four major modes of enslavement: the application of brute force and coercion, judicial processes, the power of adverse circumstances such as famine and indebtedness, and birth.[105] As will be shown, all these modes occurred in principle in Unyamwezi, although not to the same degree.

The majority of people were enslaved through acts of physical violence.[106] Large-scale organised slave-raiding operations as well as more opportunistic small-scale kidnapping activities both took place in areas neighbouring Unyamwezi. From the sources available it is impossible to determine categorically whether small-scale kidnapping occurred more frequently than large-scale raiding, but from circumstantial evidence, such as biographical accounts and descriptive sources, it does appear that on the whole small-scale kidnapping was probably more prevalent.[107]

Violence was used primarily during the initial capturing of slaves. Apart from the indiscriminate killings that frequently occurred during slave raids, captives who resisted were often beaten into compliance.[108] After being captured, adults were usually bound individually or chained together in groups of ten or more people, at least for the first few days.[109] The dreaded slave stick (in ki-Swahili *kongwa*, pl. *makongwa*) was sometimes applied to particularly disobedient captives.[110] Children, however, were usually left unconstrained, since they had little choice but to accompany their enslaved relatives after the devastation of their home villages.

The violence of enslavement was also experienced in the aftermath of local wars and civil strife in the areas which bordered Unyamwezi, particularly to the west. Sometimes the slave traders actively participated in these wars, since they were rewarded with captives for the military services they and their followers had rendered to the victorious side. The involvement of slave traders in local wars very likely increased as the possession of firearms became more and more important in these conflicts. Slave traders had more access to imported arms and ammunition than local chiefs and headmen, so that their support was often crucial in local conflicts and, consequently, much sought after. In turn, they hired out the services of their followers, often slaves, to whoever offered the right kind of inducement, usually the prospect of acquiring large amounts of ivory or of slaves.[111]

During local wars and slave raids, women and children were captured, while men were frequently killed.[112] It was thought that, if left alive, these men would seek retribution. It was also believed that they would show resistance or attempt flight, especially in the first few days after their capture while still in the vicinity of their home areas. This does not mean that women were acquiescent to their fate. Importantly, though, there was a strong belief in Unyamwezi that adult men did not make 'good', that is docile, slaves.[113]

According to one observer, Paul Reichard, who visited East Africa in the mid-1880s, the violence of enslavement came to an end after capture. Having forcefully broken their resistance, commercial slave raiders and traders had little interest in wilfully maltreating slaves, as this would only diminish their exchange value.[114] Reichard states that according to his own observation 'only' very few, perhaps less than 5 per cent of the captives, were killed in the days following a raid. However, he apparently did not reflect upon the possible effect of his presence on the behaviour of the slave traders he observed, nor was he too concerned about those who were killed. His account nevertheless contradicts one of the most enduring stereotypes in missionary and early colonial descriptions of the East African slave trade, according to which the brutality of slave raiders and traders was the reason why the majority of those captured never reached the first point of sale.[115] Moreover, according to Reichard's observations, between a quarter and a half of those captured usually escaped in the first few days after the raid, and most of the actual deaths on the march could be attributed to illness and disease.[116]

The second means, by which people in Unyamwezi in the second half of the nineteenth century became slaves, was by a judicial process involving punishment for such crimes as adultery and 'witchcraft'.[117] Furthermore, supposedly 'free' persons[118] were transferred between families[119] as compensation for criminal offences perpetrated by a member of one family against another. Typical offences included theft, grievous bodily harm and homicide. Those handed over as compensation were regarded as slaves and could be sold freely.[120] Finally, local chiefs and headmen in Unyamwezi enslaved an unknown number of 'free' people, most of them women, in order to exchange them for goodwill from distrustful traders or hostile neighbours.[121]

Thirdly, debt settlements could lead to enslavement, especially when a member of the family had already been given away as security for a loan. These pawns were frequently younger women. Although they could not be sold immediately, the creditor could enjoy the fruits of their labour until the debt was paid. In the event that the debtor or his family eventually failed to honour the debt, the creditor had the right to recoup the loan by enslavement and subsequent sale of the pawn.[122]

Furthermore, people were pawned into slavery by their relatives, often the male head of the household, in periods of ecological crisis such as famines, caused by drought, plant disease or epizootic.[123] As one acute observer noted, these famines were often distinctly local affairs, pointing out that 'until the smallness of the resources of the people and the difficulties of transport have been considered, the sharpness of the boundary between want and plenty is amazing.'[124] Pawning a family member was done with the greatest reluctance in the majority of cases, and only then, if such a measure appeared to assure the physical survival of the family.[125] Pawning was presumably accompanied by a promise that relatives would eventually ransom the person in question, but since only a minority of the enslaved actually remained within reach of their home areas, such promises were more likely to be broken than honoured.[126] In effect, pawning was often a means of disguising the outright sale of a person by his or her family since the latter was regarded as an exceedingly dishonourable act.[127] Local chiefs and headmen in Unyamwezi acquired these slaves in order to swell the number of their followers and dependants.

Finally, there was a group of people who were treated as slaves because their parents or, in the case of the coast, their grandparents or even great-grandparents had been enslaved and they had inherited that status. More detail on slaves of this kind will be provided below.

Slaves were traded regularly at slave auctions held in local markets in Unyamwezi.[128] At these auctions slaves were publicly displayed and their bodies closely investigated.[129] The traveller Cameron described an auction he had observed in Tabora in the early 1870s. He noted:

> In two large rooms were assembled nearly a hundred and fifty traders – Arabs, Wasuahili [sic] and Wamerima [sic] – and three auctioneers. The first part of the sale consisted of household utensils...the second was devoted to the sale of slaves. They were led around, made to show their teeth, to cough, run, and lift weights, and in some instances to exhibit their dexterity in handling a musket. All the slaves were semi-domestics and fetched high prices; one woman who was reputed to be a good cook going for $MT 200, and many of the men reached eighty dollars.[130]

Slaves intermittently changed hands, often several times, in private transactions between individual buyers and sellers before reaching their final place of residence.[131] They were also offered to passing caravans, either near the coast or up-country in the hinterland.[132] How slave transactions were actually conducted is largely unknown, for instance whether the buying and selling of slaves always involved lengthy negotiations about the price of the 'commodity' in question, as was the case with the purchase of ivory. There is, however, one description of such a sale by Wilhelm Blohm, a Moravian missionary. He cites an extract from an interview with a Nyamwezi convert conducted before the outbreak of World War I. The convert in question is reported to have said:

> If a man wants to buy a boy, he will stay there over night. When the principals [*Herren*] have come to an agreement about the purchase, then the one who owns the boy will say: 'I want thirty pieces of cloth'. But the one who has the cloth will say: 'I will give you twenty'. If the slave owner agrees [on that price], the purchase [contract] is sealed. Then, the owner of the cloth gives [the slave owner] something, perhaps one or two lengths of cloth or a

hoe. This piece [of cloth] is called *tja lufupi* or *tja luywili* 'the thing which has to be spat on' (with sacrificial porridge). When the *tja lufupi* has been handed over, the slave owner takes some flour and water and prepares the sacrificial porridge. He then spits on the slave boy whom he had just sold and says: 'Go and have many children and acquire wealth for your master'. When he has done that, the one who had the cloth [the buyer] takes the boy he has bought....

When he [the new owner] comes back to his village, his wife will take some sacrificial porridge and spit on the person he [her husband] has bought. After that she returns to the house. She cooks some food for her husband and for the slave. When the meal is prepared, they do not eat with the slave; only if he [the slave] is well known, will they eat together.[133] [translation and additions in brackets by the author]

This quotation brings out the entanglement of social, religious and commercial factors that arose during the transfer of slaves from one owner (and his family) to another. In the case above, a ritual was performed in order to tie the slave symbolically to his new 'family'. The ceremony arguably represents a 'rite of passage',[134] a symbolic transition from one social status to another, but the sources are silent as to when, where and, above all, to what extent the ritual described above was actually performed. Without further information, however, it is difficult to come to more general conclusions.

When the link to kin and community was severed at the point of enslavement, the person in question was stripped of his or her social value – and indeed died a 'social death',[135] sometimes even a physical one, since he or she was 'heartbroken' as Livingstone phrased it. In one of the most moving passages in his journal, Livingstone described the capture of a group of young men, noting that:

> they had endured the chains until they saw the broad river Lualaba roll between them and their free homes; they then lost heart. Twenty-one were unchained as being now safe; however, all ran away at once, but eight, with many others still in chains, died in three days after the crossing. They ascribed their only pain to the heart, and placed the hand correctly on the spot.... Some slavers expressed surprise to me that they should die, seeing that they had plenty to eat and no work ... it seems really heart-brokenness of which they died.[136]

Yet, such cases were the exception and more often than not the newly enslaved stayed with their new owners for a considerable period of time, in many cases their whole lives. Others were traded several times over long distances until they were given a more permanent residence. In any case, the moment slaves remained in a particular locality, they sought and acquired new social ties, which they hoped would ensure them more security. As will be shown in the next section, the various ways in which these new social ties developed over time determined the life chances of slaves in their new social environment.

Social Life

An unknown number of the newly enslaved were ransomed by their relatives during the first few months after their capture or purchase. The vast majority, however, remained slaves. In the period immediately after their arrival in Unyamwezi, most slaves were said to be regarded as 'strangers' or 'foreigners'. [137]

The generic term for slave in ki-Nyamwezi was *msese* (pl. *basese*), while slave owners were known as *ise bugonzo*. The latter were mostly elderly men who, as head of the household, exercised a large measure of control over the human and material resources of the household, especially labour.[138] During the initial period of ownership, the masters perceived their slaves primarily as a commodity, as a convenient means of storing wealth or as a medium of exchange, since no social ties existed between the two.[139] This was the period when slaves were most eager to escape, so that they were frequently tied up or chained to prevent their flight.[140] The power of the owners over their newly acquired slaves was apparently unlimited, since in Unyamwezi, as elsewhere in East Africa, a slave had 'no creature he can appeal to', as one contemporary observer noted.[141] Yet, over time their relationship changed, not least because the slaves and their owners worked together in the fields, shared the same house and ate from the same bowl.[142] They also wore the same attire and, more often than not, there were no visible marks that distinguished the two groups. To the outside observer, there was usually no discernible difference between the lifestyle of owners and slaves, at least as far as 'ordinary' slave owners were concerned.[143] It is likely, though, that 'insiders' had a much clearer view as to what constituted social difference.

The majority of slaves in Unyamwezi were women.[144] They were believed to be more 'docile' than men. Burton explained that in the southeasterly regions of Unyamwezi, from where huge numbers of slaves were imported, adult men were rarely sold because they were thought to have 'obstinate and untameable characters' since 'many of them would rather die under the stick than level themselves with women by using a hoe'.[145] It was also argued that female slaves were less likely to flee since it was more difficult for them to improve their circumstances by this option.[146] Male adult captives were evidently more likely to attempt to return home than female slaves and were thus often sold 'abroad', to the coast.[147] In this context it should be mentioned that most contemporary accounts agree that female slaves in Unyamwezi were considerably higher priced than male slaves of the same age.[148] Female slaves, it seems, were easier to control and were valued as agricultural labourers, sexual partners and potential mothers whose children belonged to the owner's household. This applied especially to young women of childbearing age, although the sources do not state explicitly that female slaves were generally more expensive because they could be absorbed more expediently than male slaves into kinship groups.[149]

After capture, the transformation of the relationship between owners and slaves proceeded along distinct gender and age lines within the owner's household. Adult male slaves usually lived in their own quarters, especially in households with large numbers of slaves.[150] A few even gained their own homesteads, in particular those who had lived for some time with their owner, had acquired some wealth or had managed to marry a 'free-born' woman. According to a later observer, however, such marriages were not usually allowed.[151] In such cases, the relationship between slave and owner was reduced to acknowledgement of the master's higher social standing, and assistance during harvest time.[152] In a few instances, male slaves in this situation were formally manumitted, albeit rarely, and significantly only in Usoke which was close to the 'coastal' town of Tabora where the influence of coastal 'manners' and practices was particularly strong.[153] Thus, on the whole, it was possible for male slaves to advance considerably in Nyamwezi society, especially when they worked as porters or trade agents for their owners or were employed by chiefs in the administration of the territory under his (in some cases her) control.[154] In this way, some male slaves even managed to accumulate a measure of wealth, including slaves, in their own right.[155]

Yet, the fortunes of these few obscure the fact that a larger proportion of male slaves remained within the ambit of the owners' households. They were treated as distant non-kin in everyday life, especially if their owners had allowed them to marry a female slave. Despite their intimate entanglement with the owners' household, they, and more importantly their children, were regarded as slaves and not as members of the immediate family.[156] They worked primarily on their owners' farms. Male slaves could own property, but as long as they belonged to the owners' household, they themselves were not allowed to buy slaves. After their death, not their own children but their owners inherited their material possessions.[157]

The situation for female slaves was remarkably different. In contrast to male slaves, women frequently became part of their owner's family. They were usually addressed as 'children' or 'relatives', a term which more than likely covered several meanings.[158] The work of female slaves and slave girls was no different from the work performed routinely by other female members of the household, such as working in the fields, grinding corn, cooking, cleaning the house, looking after the children, fetching water and collecting firewood.[159] Younger female slaves are said to have usually worked in the house, whereas older female slaves were more frequently seen toiling on their owners' farms.[160] Some owners formally married their own slaves, and the rise of bridewealth payments for 'free' women in the second half of the nineteenth century probably induced an increasing number of less affluent Wanyamwezi men to do so. However, since no bridewealth was paid for female slaves, their social status within the household was lower than that claimed by 'free' wives.[161] Women did not own slaves, as they were excluded from holding property except for that which they had brought with them into their marriages. Nevertheless, such 'customary' stipulations were occasionally disregarded in practice.[162]

If a Nyamwezi man married a slave woman, he was not required to pay bridewealth to the owner. The children of these marriages belonged to the slave owner's household.[163] If, however, an unmarried female slave had children by her owner, she and her children were 'free' in the sense that 'under normal circumstances' they would not be sold and were thus equal to the other female members of the household.[164] In exceptional circumstances, such women even lived separate lives from their owners.[165] Yet, in periods of famine or in cases of judicial compensation, debt and inheritance settlements, slave wives were still the first in the household who had to face the threat of sale or re-enslavement.[166] As Marcia Wright has argued, 'the kinship idiom cut both ways. It could give comfort to the woman who knew her vulnerability as a slave ... or it could obscure the peril of one who regarded herself as at home.'[167] The grandchildren of female slaves, however, were regarded as free from any obligation arising out of their grandparents' status.[168]

Slave boys faced different perspectives.[169] When they were young, they performed the same kind of work as other boys living in the household, helping in the construction of houses, fetching firewood and working in the fields. Yet, on growing older, a number of them were relieved from agricultural and household work and sent by their owners on trading expeditions as agents or porters. This displayed enormous trust between these slaves and their owners, which is arguably explained by the fact that male slaves who had grown up in the household had no 'relatives' other than their owner's family whom they could turn to in periods of crisis; this necessarily deepened their personal dependence.

Male court slaves played a special role in Wanyamwezi society. They belonged to the chief or had lived for long periods of time in his, sometimes her, settlement. People owned by the chiefs were known as *vanikulu (banyikulu)* in ki-Nyamwezi.[170] They worked as tax collectors, messengers and soldiers (widely referred to as *ruga-ruga*). They usually shared the spoils of their employment and could thus acquire considerable wealth and prestige.[171] The most trusted ones were sometimes even installed as advisers to the chief (in ki-Nyamwezi *mgawe)* or even as sub-chiefs (in ki-Nyamwezi *vanachalo*).[172] Yet, it would be misleading to portray slavery in Unyamwezi as a 'compassionate relationship', as a number of German colonial officials argued.[173] Slaves were despised for their lack of knowledge of local 'customs' and manners of speech, for example.[174] Both female and male slaves were constantly faced with the threat of sale. Owners could use slaves as debt and bridewealth settlements, in commercial exchanges, as well as for compensation purposes.[175] Moreover, owners could punish their slaves. Disobedient slaves, especially those who had attempted to flee, were either severely beaten or put into chains or the slave stick, sometimes for considerable periods of time.[176] In certain circumstances, owners were even allowed to kill their slaves with impunity.[177]

Yet, despite the potential or actual social marginalisation of slaves, there was a precarious balance between the kind of demands owners could impose on slaves and the probability that slaves would seek to escape.[178] The owners' power over their slaves was limited, perhaps more in practice than in 'legal' terms, which were virtually comprehensive. Slaves had little means of internally disputing the 'customary rights' that kinship ideas attributed to the household head. However, if slaves felt they had been treated badly enough by their owners, subjected to physical abuse, for instance, or refused even minimal access to household resources, they resolved to escape or at least attempted to do so.[179] This argument is supported by some tentative evidence regarding the existence of substantial fugitive slave communities in areas adjoining Unyamwezi.[180] The incidence of flight, however, depended not only on the desire of individual slaves to escape their harsh treatment but also to a considerable extent on local circumstances beyond the control of both the slave and their owners. In general, slaves were reluctant to 'free' themselves by flight if they felt that their personal safety was likely to be threatened by their immediate re-enslavement.[181] Running away meant taking great risks,[182] because, from as early as the mid-nineteenth century, Unyamwezi was an area in which 'slaves and muskets were the stranger's sole protection', as Burton put it.[183]

Though there is little evidence on this point, it is likely that there was a divergence in the 'exit options' for male and female slaves. For the latter, running away often meant having to find a new male patron or husband, whereas for the former it was easy to join runaway communities independently or to find employment in Tabora and Ujiji, where traders from Zanzibar and the coast were always looking for soldiers and male porters.[184] In any case, slaves usually only attempted to escape when their security and economic survival were reasonably assured.[185] Thus, for instance, areas with economies deeply involved in translocal commerce provided slaves with an opportunity to offer their services as porters, servants and, in the case of female slaves, temporary wives to passing caravans without the consent of their owners. According to the traveller Reichard, who visited Unyamwezi in the early 1880s, slave owners were usually glad to see such slaves returning from trading journeys and often abstained from punishing them.[186]

Thus it appears from available sources that in Unyamwezi, as in various other parts of East Africa in the latter half of the nineteenth century, servility was primarily understood and expressed in terms of kinship relations (even if these were largely fictive for the great majority of female and male slaves).[187] Kinship facilitated the absorption of large numbers of 'outsiders' into Wanyamwezi society.[188] Though this did not work particularly well for male slaves, who were kept at a distance, female slaves became part of their owner's family, which involved having the same set of rights and obligations as the natal members of that family.[189] The intersection between the position of women and female slaves within households becomes apparent in the sources that describe how slaves and 'free' women responded to particularly 'bad' treatment from the household head.[190] According to these accounts, female slaves and 'free' women could seek the protection of the chief by touching or damaging certain insignia such as the royal drum. Both would instantly become court slaves, the former 'free' women joining the ranks of the chief's slave wives.[191] Only after payment of a heavy fine were such slaves or women returned to the household head. Incidentally, orphaned children also became court slaves.[192]

Moreover, it appears that, according to almost all accounts in Unyamwezi, especially in the more prosperous parts of Unyanyembe,[193] household heads were equally reluctant to sell servile and natal members of the larger family in periods of crisis such as famine. Selling children, whether slaves or 'free', was regarded as shameful and dishonourable.[194] Finally, there is tentative evidence that suggests that women who, according to perceived local standards, had seriously misbehaved were treated as slaves. According to records concerning a meeting to discuss the position of women in Unyamwezi 'customary' law, a participant is quoted to have said in 1930 that 'in former times a woman leaving her husband without just cause was sold into slavery if the dowry could not be returned to her husband by either herself, her father or her relatives'.[195] This again underscores the argument that in Unyamwezi there was no clearly defined social boundary between those who were regarded as family members in the natal sense and slaves who had acquired fictive kinship rights. Kinship, arguably, provided a mode through which people moved in and out of servility.[196] Hence, as far as Unyamwezi in the nineteenth century is concerned, kinship and slavery should be seen as social frontiers that shifted historically according to the particular political and economic circumstances governing everyday life. Importantly, these 'subtle gradations of unfreedom' were grounded in the minute arrangements of residence and work.[197]

In Unyamwezi the majority of slaves, mostly women, lived, ate and worked together with their owners, some of whom became 'proper' wives in the process. Over time, these women thus gained the recognised status of intimate kin group members of their owner's household. The position of male slaves was more ambivalent. The majority of male slaves, especially the older ones, remained in a social limbo, with no opportunity for social mobility. They could neither become kin members of the household nor could they achieve greater personal autonomy, as opportunities to participate in commerce and politics, and thus establish client relationships, were limited.

In Unyamwezi, as elsewhere in East Africa at the time, absorption into kin or community was a contradictory process of 'peaceful' acculturation and assimilation, and of contestation, conflict and violence.[198] Slavery could not have succeeded as a system of social and work relations merely on the basis of violent coercion; it needed a degree of consent from those who were enslaved. That consent was forthcoming partly because slaves were made to believe in the rectitude of their own marginality, for instance through their upbringing, through the imposition of a specific spatial order on their residence, and through restrictions governing social intercourse with their owners.[199] Yet, slavery also depended on allowing slaves the possibility of potentially reducing their social marginality. Social mobility and the permeability of social boundaries, that is, the feasibility of achieving the degree of personal autonomy 'free' born members of society claimed, were thus not the antithesis of slavery or quaint local 'customs'. On the contrary, as slaves could not be freely replaced as a rule without incurring substantial social, political and economic costs, social mobility was arguably the very condition on which slavery rested, given that other means of keeping slaves in their place or preventing them from running away, such as a strong police force, were largely lacking in Unyamwezi, as elsewhere, in the second half of the nineteenth century. The major deterrent to flight was the lack of alternatives. The exit option was arguably only chosen if slaves felt they could escape immediate re-enslavement and somehow solve the problem of economic survival after the event. However, as has been shown above, the material and social opportunities open to female and male slaves differed a great deal, and widened as commercial expansion progressed.[200]

Social Change

Because of the relative paucity of historical sources, the analysis of slavery and nineteenth-century social change in Unyamwezi poses great difficulties for the historian. Some tentative suggestions, nevertheless, seem to be appropriate. As has been argued above, the militarisation of Wanyamwezi society at the political level, subsequent to commercial expansion and the rise of locally resident slave populations, primarily concerned the emergence of powerful warlords, particularly in Unyanyembe. These warlords sustained and enlarged their position at the cost of neighbouring chiefdoms which were raided by armed bands of young men for cattle, ivory and women. At the social level, this development primarily involved the movement of people to stockaded villages and fortified settlements. At the same time, however, agricultural production expanded, not least because of the greatly increased use of slave labour on farms located near these new villages and settlements. As the security situation deteriorated in Unyamwezi in the second half of the nineteenth century, village chiefs and household heads gained unprecedented control over subjects and family members, including slaves and other dependants such as unmarried female relatives, changing the terms but not necessarily the idiom of incorporation into kinship groups.[201] This was also happening in other parts of East Africa at the same time.[202]

As has been pointed out above, the actual living circumstances of slaves and dependants were determined to a considerable degree by their ability to reject the claims of household heads, especially in periods of crisis. Although kinship and patronage relations, according to Willis and Miers, 'continued to provide some weapons of the weak as they sought to improve the terms of their incorporation',[203] the social and material conditions on which sustained incorporation into kinship groups and, thus, effective social mobility rested, apparently declined in the second half of the century, particularly in the 1870s and 1880s.[204] Flight or the movement away from rapacious chiefs, for instance, became a less viable option to better one's life. Moreover, as the number of slaves working on farms and in homesteads increased, household heads, village headmen and chiefs were able to lessen the constraints arising from kinship obligations. Their free dependants became ever less important as a means of sustaining or enlarging their position vis-à-vis their neighbours. Moreover, wealth and prestige were increasingly measured in the number of cattle, women and slaves a chief could command.[205] This development was at its most pronounced in Unyanyembe, the most prosperous but also the most militarised area of Unyamwezi where in the early 1860s chained gangs of slaves were actually seen doing agricultural work in the fields under the supervision of an overseer.[206]

The disparities between the social and economic opportunities for male and female slaves seem to have widened in the course of the second half of the century. Chiefs increasingly recruited slaves and other male dependants into armed bands of young men (*ruga-ruga*) to defend and expand their chiefdoms.[207] In turn, these men were able to extract not only wealth and status from their 'profession', but also the ability to reject demands from chiefs and household heads for labour and obedience. This is probably why European travellers were surprised to see groups of armed young men in the villages and settlements who were apparently doing little else beyond smoking tobacco and hemp and amusing themselves by taunting elderly people, presumably household heads and their dependants.[208] Such 'opportunities' were not available to women, at least not on a comparable scale. Furthermore, in the second half of the century, the status of women, including female slaves who had acquired fictive kinship rights, generally declined, as it did in other parts of East Africa at the time.[209] Women were no longer merely 'exchanged' as wives in marriage agreements between families but increasingly exploited as commercial and political 'properties' in transactions involving local office-holders. As the second half of the century progressed, women and slaves were sold in rapidly increasing numbers to slave traders, exchanged for goodwill from hostile neighbouring chiefs or pawned to local big men, village headmen and chiefs.[210] Thus, while the life chances of 'free'-born women generally deteriorated, some even becoming a 'commodity' in the process, a significant number of male slaves gained the social position of 'free'-born men.

In summary, it appears that the commercial expansion and accompanying rise in the number of slaves resident in Unyamwezi changed the patterns of rights and obligations construed by locally defined sets of kinship relations.[211] This was the result of a process whereby one particular 'cluster of rules' was not simply replaced by another but was rather the outcome of negotiations, disputes and even struggles between those who wished to defend and expand their perceived rights and those who wanted to do away with them. As far as Unyamwezi is concerned, but arguably also in general terms, kinship and patronage relations should thus not be seen merely as a continuum comprising a variety of different social relations. They are also fields of social conflict whose substance and meaning were constantly reworked, particularly when the social, political and economic conditions by which they were shaped underwent significant change.[212]

Thus, nineteenth-century commercial expansion in Unyamwezi brought wealth to the few, but misery to the many, especially to dependants and slaves whose life chances of becoming respected members of kinship groups and patronage networks in the last decades of the nineteenth century notably declined. This process only came to an end with the advent of colonial rule and the emergence of an increasingly wage-based colonial economy.[213]

Notes

1 P. Reichard, 'Die Wanyamwezi', *Deutsche Kolonialzeitung*, 3 (1890), p.277.
2 Bundesarchiv Abteilungen Berlin, Reichskolonialamt (hereafter BAB RkolA), 7382/27, p.88, 'Berichte der einzelnen Verwaltungsstellen in Deutsch-Ostafrika über die Sklaverei', Station Tabora, Berichterstatter: Hauptmann Puder, n.d. [1900].
3 See, for instance, the criticism of Reichard's estimate by F. P. Nolan, 'Christianity in Unyamwezi, 1878–1928', (unpublished Ph.D. thesis, University of Cambridge, 1977), p.143. For a detailed compilation of population figures according to administrative district, see R. Hermann, 'Statistik der farbigen Bevölkerung von Deutsch Afrika, III. Ostafrika', *Koloniale Monatsblätter*, 16, 4 (1914), pp.172–6.These figures seem to suggest that Puder probably underestimated the number of people resident in Tabora district.
4 Other contemporary observers reported similar numbers not just for Tabora district, but also for the neighbouring districts of Ujiji and Mwanza. See *Stenographische Berichte des Reichstages: Anlagen*, p.13. Legislaturperiode, 1. Session 1912/14, Aktenstück Nr. 1395, p.2888 (hereafter *RTA* 1912/14, no. 1395, p.2888) 'Denkschrift über die Hausssklaverei in Deutsch-Ostafrika' by Governor H. Schnee, 20 February 1914. See also BAB RKolA 7382/27, pp.82–4, 'Berichte der einzelnen Verwaltungsstellen in Deutsch-Ostafrika über die Sklaverei', Station Muanza, Berichterstatter: Hauptmann Schlobach, n.d. [1900].
5 For a fuller discussion of these themes see J.-G. Deutsch, *Emancipation without Abolition in German East Africa, c. 1884–1914* (Oxford, 2006).
6 For a brief discussion of the 'insider/outsider' problem, see J. Glassman, 'The bondsman's new clothes. The contradictory consciousness of slave resistance on the Swahili coast', *Journal of African History*, 32 (1991), pp.279, 283f., 289, 298.

7   The phrase 'radical uncertainty' was first used by D. B. Davis in an article in the *New York Review of Books* about the transatlantic slave trade (17 October 1996, p.51). It is cited in M. I. Finley, *Ancient Slavery and Modern Ideology* (Princeton, NJ, 1998), p.13. On the problem of defining 'freedom' in the context of slavery in Africa, see J. Iliffe, *Honour in African History* (Cambridge, 2005), p.120.
8   For a brief introduction to the history of slavery and the slave trade in East Africa in the nineteenth century, see S. Feierman, 'A century of ironies in East Africa (c. 1780–1890)', in P. Curtin, S. Feierman, S. Thompson and J. Vansina (eds), *African History. From Earliest Times to Independence* (London, 1995), pp.352–76. See also J. Iliffe, *A Modern History of Tanganyika* (Cambridge, 1979), pp.40–88.
9   Iliffe, *Modern History*, p.50.
10 J. Glassman, *Feasts and Riot. Revelry, Rebellion, and Popular Consciousness on the Swahili Coast, 1856–1888* (London, 1995), p.36
11 A. D. Roberts, 'Nyamwezi trade', in R. Gray and D. Birmingham (eds), *Pre-Colonial African Trade in Central and Eastern Africa before 1900* (London, 1970), p.49. This and the following paragraphs have greatly profited from R. G. Abrahams, *The Peoples of Greater Unyamwezi, Tanzania. Nyamwezi, Sukuma, Sumbwa, Kimbu, Konongo* (London, 1967); A. D. Roberts, 'The Nyamwezi', in A. D. Roberts (ed.), *Tanzania before 1900* (Nairobi, 1968), pp.117–50; A. M. H. Sheriff, *Slaves, Spices & Ivory in Zanzibar. Integration of an East African Commercial Empire into the World Economy, 1770–1873* (London, 1987), pp.155–200; and S. J. Rockel, '"A nation of porters". The Nyamwezi and the labour market in mid-nineteenth century Tanzania', *Journal of African History*, 41 (2000), pp.173–95. This essay has greatly profited from Stephen Rockel's unpublished Ph.D. thesis, 'Caravan porters of the *Nyika*. Labour, culture, and society in nineteenth-century Tanzania' (University of Toronto, 1997). Apart from the article cited above, some further material can be found in 'Relocating labour. Sources from the nineteenth century', *History in Africa*, 22 (1995), pp.447–54, 'Wage labour and the culture of porterage in nineteenth-century Tanzania. The central caravan route', *Comparative Studies of South Asia, Africa and the Middle East*, 15 (1995), pp.14–24, and 'The roots of a nation. Integration in nineteenth-century Tanzania', *History and African Studies Series*, University of Natal, Pietermaritzburg, 30 September 1998, pp.1–18.
12 Iliffe, *Modern History*, p.80.
13 Nolan, 'Christianity', p.21.
14 For the first contemporary discussion of the problem, see R. F. Burton, *The Lake Regions of Central Africa, a Picture of Exploration* (London, 1860), pp.280–4. He asserts that the term Unyamwezi was already in use in the seventeenth century, probably even in the sixteenth century. For subsequent attempts to define 'Unyamwezi' see Reichard 'Wanyamwezi', pp.228f.; F. Bösch, *Les Banyamwezi. Peuple de l'Afrique Orientale* (Münster, 1930), pp.3–21; W. Blohm, *Die Nyamwezi*, 2 vols (Hamburg, 1931–1933), vol. I, pp.6–10 and RHO Micr Afr 472 R.19/MF 42, Tabora Regional Book, 'Notes on Banyamwezi', 6 May 1932. For the history of the nineteenth-century 'exploration' of Unyamwezi, see Blohm, *Nyamwezi*, vol. I, p.2.
15 Abrahams, *Peoples*, p.24; Nolan, 'Christianity', pp.23f. See also Rockel, 'Nation', p.175.
16 In early colonial times the great majority of the inhabitants of Tabora district were believed to be ki-Nyamwezi speakers, but it should be noted that other language groups lived among them. See RHO Micr Afr 472 R.19/MF 42, Tabora Regional Book, 'Notes on Banyamwezi', 6 May 1932.
17 The first Nyamwezi word list was probably compiled by Bishop Edward Steere. See E. Steere, *Collections for a Handbook of the Nyamwezi Language as Spoken in Unyanyembe* (London, 1871).
18 Burton, *Lake Regions*, p.284. See also Roberts, 'Nyamwezi', p.120.
19 See, for instance J. H. Speke, *Journal of the Discovery of the Source of the Nile* (Edinburgh, 1863).
20 Burton, *Lake Regions*, p.285.
21 For more details on cattle in Unyamwezi, see H. Kjekshus, *Ecology Control and Economic Development in East African History. The Case of Tanganyika 1850–1950* (London, 1996, [first published 1977]), pp.44, 62–4.

22 RHO Micr Afr 472 R.21/MF 46, Kigoma District Book, 'Native Administration: The Wajiji', 13 July 1931. See also J. A. Grant, *A Walk Across Africa, or Domestic Scenes from my Nile Journal* (London, 1864), p.51 and Blohm, *Nyamwezi*, vol. II, p.36 [extract from interview, n.d. (pre-1914)].
23 Pieces of cloth bearing a trademark such as 'Massachusetts Sheeting' were particularly sought after. According to Grant, *Walk Across Africa*, p.87, 'the man who got the stamped portion was thought a considerable swell.' For the local cotton-weaving industry, see Reichard, *Wanyamwezi*, p.276.
24 For a recent summary (and a comprehensive bibliography), see Rockel 'Nation', pp.175–9.
25 For an extensive contemporary description of mid-nineteenth-century commercial practices, see Burton, *Lake Regions*, pp.527–44, especially pp.538–40 (ivory trade). For the later period, see also C. Velten (ed.), *Desturi za Wasuaheli na Khabari za Desturi za Sheri`a za Wasuaheli* (Göttingen, 1903), pp.284–301.
26 Tippu Tip, 'Autobiographie des Arabers Schech Hamed bin Muhammed el Murjebi, genannt Tippu Tip', ed. and tr. by H. Brode, *Mitteilungen des Seminars für orientalische Sprachen* (Berlin, 1902), pp.175–277, (Berlin, 1903), pp.1–55 [for elephant hunting, see p.268]. The same text has also been translated into French by Bontinck. See F. L. Bontinck, *L'autobiographie de Hamed ben Mohammed el-Murjebi, Tippo Tip, ca. 1840–1905* (Brussels, 1974) [with comprehensive notes and an extensive bibliography]. For an English translation Tippu Tip, *Maisha ya Hamed bin Muhammed el Murjebi Yaani Tippu Tip*, ed. and tr. W.H. Whiteley (Nairobi, 1966).
27 J. L. Krapf, *Reisen in Ostafrika ausgeführt in den Jahren 1837 bis 1855*, 2 vols (Kornthal/Stuttgart 1964 [first published 1858]) vol. II, pp.181, 279. See also Roberts, 'Nyamwezi trade', p.50.
28 Sheriff, *Slaves*, pp.78–115.
29 For a contemporary depiction of these porters, see Sheriff, *Slaves*, p.178, plate 27. They are also described in great detail by Burton, *Lake Regions*, pp.153, 169, 186, 237f. See also Krapf, *Reisen*, vol. II, p.182, and V. L. Cameron, *Across Africa*, 2 vols. (London, 1877), vol. I, p.78 and Tippu Tip, 'Autobiographie', p.198.
30 Burton reports that in Unyamwezi caravan leaders or guides were also called *kirangozi* in ki-Swahili. See Burton, *Lake Regions*, p.240.
31 Roberts, 'Nyamwezi trade', p.66. See also Tippu Tip, 'Autobiographie', p.208.
32 Roberts, 'Nyamwezi', p.128. For an extensive discussion on the payment of bridewealth in Unyamwezi, see Bösch, *Banyamwezi*, pp.348–99 and Blohm, *Nyamwezi*, vol. II, pp.90–9. See also RHO Micr Afr 472 R.19/MF 42, Tabora Regional Book, 'Extracts from Nyamwezi Law and Custom by H. Cory', 1952, p.6. According to Blohm (*Nyamwezi*, vol. II, p.90) bridewealth payments consisted of cattle, guns, slaves, cloth and iron hoes; see also M. H. Löbner, 'Fragebogen-Beantwortung für ganz Wanyamwezi durch Missionar M. H. Löbner, stationiert bei Tabora [Usoke, March 1910]', cited in A. Gottberg, *Unyamwesi. Quellensammlung und Geschichte* (Berlin, 1971), p.149f. For the original reports by Löbner, see BAB RKolA 4997/432, 'Beantwortung des Fragebogens über die Rechte der Eingeborenen in den deutschen Kolonien'. In this essay I have used the texts reprinted in Gottberg for reference purposes, since that text is more easily accessible. For the increase in bridewealth following commercial expansion in the hinterland of Mombasa in the nineteenth century, see J. Willis, *Mombasa, the Swahili and the Making of the Mijikenda* (Oxford, 1993), pp.69f.
33 Burton, *Lake Regions*, p.235.
34 Roberts, 'Nyamwezi trade', p.66.
35 P. Reichard, *Deutsch-Ostafrika. Das Land und seine Bewohner, seine politische und wirtschaftliche Entwicklung* (Leipzig, 1892), p.485 and R. Kandt, *Caput Nili. Eine empfindsame Reise zu den Quellen des Nils*, third edn (Berlin, 1914), pp.45, 139f. According to colonial records, in the year 1900/1901 exactly 35,665 adult porters left Tabora for the coast, of whom 2,858 were said to be women. See 'Jahresbericht der Station Tabora 1900/1, Bezirkschef Gansser 20. Juni 1991', cited in H. Dauber (ed.), *"Nicht als Abentheurer bin ich hierhergekommen..." 100 Jahre Entwicklungs-"Hilfe". Tagebücher und Briefe aus Deutsch-Ostafrika 1896–1902* (Frankfurt/Main, 1991), p.255. For female traders and caravan porters in

precolonial Kenya, see C. Presley, *Kikuyu Women, the Mau Mau Rebellion and Social Change in Kenya* (Boulder, CO, 1992), p.20.
36 See Grant, *Walk Across Africa*, p.43 and Reichard, *Deutsch-Ostafrika*, pp.465, 485. See also M. Wright, *Strategies of Slaves and Women. Life-Stories from East/Central Africa* (London, 1993), p.182 and Rockel, 'Roots', p.17.
37 By the mid-nineteenth century, consumption patterns in Unyamwezi began to change. The local cotton cloth industry is a good example of this process. It apparently suffered severely from competition with imports manufactured in India, the US or Europe. People attached special social prestige to the consumption of imported cloth, and as more and more people were able to afford it, local cloth industries declined. See Grant, *Walk Across Africa*, p.87. See also Kjekshus, *Ecology*, pp.105–9.
38 Roberts, 'Nyamwezi trade', p.66.
39 *Ibid.*, p.68.
40 Cameron, *Africa*, vol. II, pp.117f., 168. See also A. D. Roberts, 'Firearms in North-Eastern Zambia before 1900', *Transafrican Journal of History*, 1 (1971), p.9, D. B. Birmingham, *Central Africa to 1870* (London, 1981), pp.131–3 and Wright, *Strategies*, pp.156–60.
41 Sheriff, *Slaves*, p.182. For a different view, see Rockel, 'Nation', p.186.
42 Burton, *Lake Regions*, p.238.
43 *Ibid*, p.46. See also K. Toeppen, 'Handel und Handelsverbindungen in Ostafrika', *Mitteilungen der Geographischen Gesellschaft in Hamburg* (1885–86), p.225.
44 See Burton, *Lake Regions*, pp.538–40, Reichard, *Deutsch-Ostafrika*, pp.435–44.
45 This movement is already noted by Burton who visited Unyamwezi in 1857. See Burton, *Lake Regions*, p.318. See also Grant, *Walk Across Africa*, p.48.
46 When Burton visited Kazeh in 1857, its 'Arab' population probably did not exceed a dozen households. He counted some six *tembe*, although there were others in a village nearby. It is not entirely clear whom Burton regarded as 'Arab'. See Burton, *Lake Regions*, p.228. See also Tippu Tip, 'Autobiographie', p.180. It should also be noted that the population of Kazeh fluctuated heavily during the trading seasons. Thus it is difficult to estimate with any degree of accuracy the size of the Arab population in the interior in the second half of the nineteenth century. The best description of Ujiji in the late 1870s is in E. C. Hore, *Missionary to Tanganyika, 1877–1888*, ed. by J. B. Wolf (London, 1971), pp.66–151. For a description of Tabora in the early 1870s, see D. Livingstone, *The Last Journals of David Livingstone in Central Africa, from 1865 to his Death*, ed. by H. Waller, (London, 1874), p.182 [3 May 1871]. For the early 1880s, see Reichard, *Deutsch-Ostafrika*, pp.344f. For a detailed drawing of a *tembe*, see Cameron, *Africa*, vol. I, p.131.
47 Sheriff, *Slaves*, p.179. See also B. Brown, 'Muslim influence in trade and politics in the Lake Tanganyika region', *International Journal of African Historical Studies*, 4 (1971), pp.617–29.
48 RHO Micr Afr 472 R.20/MF 44, Tabora District Book, 'Notes on an Interview with Jaba bin Zaid by Assistant District Officer N. Burt', 24 May 1927.
49 See Burton, *Lake Regions*, p.227. For a map, see Sheriff, *Slaves*, p.191, Map 5.1: The Hinterland of Zanzibar, c. 1873. For further detail, see C. F. Holmes, 'Zanzibari influence at the southern end of Lake Victoria. The lake route', *International Journal of African Historical Studies*, 4 (1971), pp.477–503.
50 Tippu Tip, 'Autobiographie', pp.183, 201–3. Even after Nyamwezi traders had lost their predominant position in the wholesale trade, independent small-scale trade with the coast continued for some time, although on a reduced scale. It came to an end in the early colonial period when Indian retail traders arrived in Tabora and drove Nyamwezi traders out of the local market. See Blohm, *Nyamwezi*, vol. I, p.171. See also Rockel, 'Nation', pp.186–9. On the role of Indian financiers in the caravan trade, see C. Tominaga, 'Indian immigrants and the East African slave trade', *Seri Ethnological Studies Osaka*, 43 (1996), pp.295–317. For a contemporary report, see J. F. Elton, 'On the coast country of East Africa, south of Zanzibar', *Royal Geographical Society Journal*, 44 (1874), pp.227–52. For the organisation of the Nyamwezi trade in early colonial times, see Graf H. von Schweinitz, *Deutsch-Ostafrika in Krieg und Frieden* (Berlin, 1894), pp.18–20.
51 Cameron, *Africa*, vol. II, pp.20–32. For more details, see Tippu Tip, 'Autobiographie',

pp.248f., 258. See also N. R. Bennett, *Mirambo of Tanzania, 1840?–1884* (New York, 1971); idem, *Arab versus European. Diplomacy and War in Nineteenth-Century East Central Africa* (New York, 1986), pp.112–18, F. Renault, *Tippo-Tip*. *Un Potentat Arabe en Afrique Centrale au XIXème siècle* (Paris, 1987) and I. Hahner-Herzog, *Tippu Tip und der Elfenbeinhandel in Ost- und Zentralafrika im 19. Jahrhundert* (München, 1990).
52 Cameron, *Africa*, vol. I, p.307.
53 Rockel, 'Caravan porters', p.57.
54 Roberts, 'Nyamwezi trade', p.68. See also Velten, *Desturi*, p.225.
55 Glassman, *Feasts and Riots*, p.60.
56 Burton, *Lake Regions*, p.236. For a different view, see Glassman, *Feasts and Riots*, p.64.
57 This figure is, of course, at best a rough estimate, as data that are more precise are not available for this period. For contemporary estimates, see F. Stuhlmann, *Mit Emin Pascha ins Herz von Afrika. Ein Reisebericht* (Berlin, 1894), p.89 and F. Coulbois, *Dix Années au Tanganyka* (Limoges, 1901), p.41. See also O. F. Raum, 'German East Africa – changes in African tribal life under German administration, 1892–1914', in V. Harlow and E. M. Chilver (eds), *History of East Africa*, vol. 2 (Oxford, 1965), p.170 and Sheriff, *Slaves*, p.182.
58 Burton, *Lake Regions*, p.257.
59 Reichard, 'Wanyamwezi', p.241.
60 Burton, *Lake Regions*, p.236.
61 Bennett, *Arab versus European*, p.36.
62 For a detailed description, see Livingstone, *Journals*, pp.124f [18 May 1871]. Livingstone notes that the market was attended by about 3,000 (!) female traders. See also A. C. Unomah and J. B. Webster, 'East Africa. The expansion of commerce', in J. E. Flint (ed.), *Cambridge History of Africa*, vol. 5, (Cambridge, 1976), pp.296f.
63 Abrahams, *Peoples*, p.68; Bösch, *Banyamwezi*, pp.440f; Blohm, *Nyamwezi*, vol. I, p.166.
64 Sheriff, *Slaves*, p.182.
65 According to the missionary Burgess, slavery was already very common in Unyamwezi by the late 1830s. Therefore it cannot be argued that slavery developed in this particular area exclusively in response to the increasing demand for slaves in other parts of the world economy. See 'Letter from Mr. Burgess, dated 11. Sept. 1839', reprinted in Gottberg, *Unyamwezi*, pp.95–7.
66 Roberts, 'Nyamwezi trade', p.59. See also Unomah/Webster, 'East Africa', pp.284–5 and Sheriff, *Slaves*, p.181. In this context it should be noted that slave-holding was an alternative to holding cattle as a means of storing wealth. Rockel notes that in the first half of the nineteenth century cattle were extensively used for that purpose. After the mid-century, slaves seem to have become a more commonly sought alternative. See Rockel, 'Caravan porters', p.110.
67 Reichard, *Deutsch-Ostafrika*, p.468.
68 Nolan, 'Christianity', pp.49, 141f.
69 Burton, *Lake Regions*, p.299.
70 A. J. Swann, *Fighting the Slave Hunters in Central Africa. A Record of Twenty Six Years of Travel and Adventure round the Great Lakes and of the Overthrow of Tip-Pu-Tip, Rumaliza and Other Great Slave-Traders* (London, 1969 [first published 1910]), p.62. See also Nolan, 'Christianity', p.142. In Unyamwezi the title of chief covered a great variety of different office holders. On the difficulties of defining chiefship in Unyamwezi, see the lengthy discussion in RHO Micr Afr 472 R.19/MF 42, Tabora Regional Book, 'Notes on Banyamwezi', 6 May 1932. For a rather different account, see Bösch, *Banyamwezi*, pp.493–504.
71 Roberts, 'Nyamwezi trade', p.59 and Nolan, 'Christianity', p.49.
72 Roberts, 'Nyamwezi trade', p.50.
73 Burton, *Lake Regions*, p.299.
74 *Ibid*, p.301. For the Bunyoro-Buganda-Unyamwezi trade, see also P. L. Jones-Bateman (ed.), *The Autobiography of an African Slave Boy (Martin Furahani)* (London, 1891), p.17. Nyamwezi slave traders are also mentioned in the life story of Chisi-Ndjurisiye-Sichyajunga in Wright, *Strategies*, pp.100f. See also the description of enslavement through capture following a raid by the soldiers of Mirambo in the life story of Anton in H. Krelle, *Anton und seine Anna* (Berlin, 1929), pp.9f.

75 Bösch, *Banyamwezi*, p.442. See also J. Becker, *La Vie en Afrique, ou trois ans dans l'Afrique Centrale*, 2 vols (Paris, 1887), pp.220–2 and Grant, *Walk Across Africa*, p.48. For a similar view, see RHO Micr Afr 472 R.19/MF 42, Tabora District Book, 'Extracts from Nyamwezi law and custom by H. Cory', 1952, p.6.
76 RHO Micr Afr 472 R.19/MF 42, Tabora District Book, 'Extracts', p. 6..
77 Nolan, 'Christianity', p.142.
78 For a description of a slave auction in Tabora in 1874, see Cameron, *Africa*, vol. I, p.144.
79 Burton, *Lake Regions*, pp.182, 212, 214f., 539. For more detail on slavery in Ugogo see A. Hermann, 'Ugogo – Das Land und seine Bewohner', *Mitteilungen aus den deutschen Schutzgebieten*, 5 (1892), pp.191–203 and H. Claus, *Die Wagogo. Ethnographische Skizze eines ostafrikanischen Bantustammes* (Leipzig, 1911), pp.58, 60.
80 Nolan, 'Christianity', p.161. See also H. von Wissmann, 'Araberfrage und Sklavenhandel. Ein Vortrag', *Deutsche Kolonialzeitung*, 1 (1888), p.352. For a similar argument concerning the Shambaa kingdom, see S. Feierman, *The Shambaa Kingdom. A History*, (Madison, WI, 1974), pp.168–84. See also Iliffe, *Modern History*, p.49f.
81 Burton, *Lake Regions*, pp.295, 321, 479. The nineteenth-century arms trade with East Africa has not yet been fully explored; in particular, German archival sources have not been used for this purpose. For an example of German arms export to East Africa in the 1850s, see Burton, *Lake Regions*, p.479.
82 Cameron, *Africa*, vol. I, p.175. See also Reichard, *Deutsch-Ostafrika*, pp.325, 374, 480. For an overview, see R. W. Beachey, 'The arms trade in East Africa in the late nineteenth century', *Journal of African History*, 3 (1962), pp.451–67. In this connection it should be noted that, according to an official estimate, annual imports of firearms in East Africa in the late 1880s amounted to between 80,000 and 100,000 (!) single items, most of which were light guns. For this estimate, see Euan Smith to Salisbury, 28 June 1888, in Great Britain, *Parliamentary Papers. Further Correspondence respecting Germany and Zanzibar*, C. 5603 (London, 1888), p.26, cited in *Traite des esclaves en Afrique. Renseignements et documents recueillis pour la Conférence des Bruxelles, 1840–1890* (Brussels, 1890), p.153. Incidentally, children in Unyamwezi were already playing with toy guns by the 1860s. For this observation, see Grant, *Walk Across Africa*, p.99. For a similar observation by D. Livingstone in 1872, see Roberts, 'Firearms', p.9.
83 *Ibid*, p.71.
84 For the term 'militarization', see Wright, *Strategies*, p.6; Iliffe, *Modern History*, p.50.
85 Löbner, 'Fragebogen', cited in Gottberg, *Unyamwezi*, p.172. According to Löbner, the sub-chiefdoms (in ki-Nyamwezi *gunguli*, pl. *magunguli*) consisted of distinct sets of villages, named *makayas*. The sub-chiefs ruling over the *makayas* were called *vanachalo*.
86 A. Shorter, 'Nyungu ya Mawe and the empire of the Ruga-Ruga', *Journal of African History*, 9 (1968), pp.235–59. See also Tippu Tip, 'Autobiographie', p.210; Grant, *Walk Across Africa*, p.57; Cameron, *Africa*, vol. I, 175; Reichard, 'Wanyamwezi', p.263f. Reichard also noted that the construction of houses had changed. They were bigger and thus easier to defend against slave raiders. For a description of defensive 'housing' in north-eastern Tanzania, see K. Fosbrooke, 'The defensive measures of certain tribes in North-Eastern Tanganyika, Part 2', *Tanganyika Notes and Records* (1954), pp.36, 50–7.
87 Burton, *Lake Regions*, p.176. See also Cameron, *Africa*, vol. I, p.190.
88 Nolan, 'Christianity', p.50. See also Bösch, *Banyamwezi*, p.493.
89 Nolan, 'Christianity', pp.90f.
90 *Ibid*, p.39. For a detailed description of such villages, see Grant, *Walk Across Africa*, p.65; Reichard, *Deutsch-Ostafrika*, pp.168f.
91 Nolan, 'Christianity' 1977, p.51. This is an important point since the mobility of the local population greatly increased in early colonial times.
92 Abrahams, *Peoples*, pp.26, 38f. For further detail on this aspect, see Sheriff, *Slaves*, pp.181, 194 and Unomah, 'Christianity', pp.86–96.
93 Roberts, 'Nyamwezi trade', p.71.
94 Tippu Tip, 'Autobiographie', p.214.
95 A social history of the *ruga-ruga* troops remains to be written. They were not only used by African chiefs and coastal merchants as their main standing fighting force but also by

the German *Schutztruppe*. As unofficial auxiliary troops they did most of the actual fighting in the conquest period, during the Maji Maji War and the First World War. Some material on precolonial *ruga-ruga* troops can be found in Shorter, 'Nyungu', pp.235–59 and M. E. Page, 'The Manyema hordes of Tippu Tip. A case study in social stratification and the slave trade in Eastern Africa', *International Journal of African Historical Studies*, 7 (1974), pp.69–84. For a detailed contemporary description of the *ruga-ruga*, see Capt. E. Storms, 'L'esclavage entre le Tanganyika et la côte est', in *Traite des esclaves*, pp.110–11. In this connection, it is interesting to note that one of the first ki-Nyamwezi grammars, produced in the early 1890s by the Moravian missionary R. Stern, was based on a local dialect called *kirugaruga*.

96 Reichard, *Deutsch-Ostafrika*, p.479. According to Reichard, the most successful chief attracted the most ferocious 'warriors' by this mechanism.
97 Wright, *Strategies*, p.6.
98 Blohm, *Nyamwezi*, vol. II, p.36 [extract from interview, n.d. (pre 1914)], p.37.
99 Another notable Nyamwezi warlord was Chief Fundikira whom Burton met in 1857. See Burton, *Lake Regions*, p.300.
100 For more detail on the fractious relations between Nyamwezi chiefs and Tabora merchants, see Bennett, *Arab State*, p.8.
101 On Mirambo, see Becker, *La Vie*, II, p.174, F. Spellig, 'Die Wanjamwezi. Ein Beitrag zur Völkerkunde Ostafrikas', *Zeitschrift für Ethnologie*, (1927/28), pp.205–9; Bennett, *Mirambo*; and J.-P. Chretien, 'Mirambo. L'unificateur des Banyamwezi (Tanzanie)', in C.-A. Julien et al., *Les Africains*, vol. 6, (Paris, 1977), pp.127–57.
102 Burton, *Lake Regions*, p.284.
103 Sheriff, *Slaves*, p.180.
104 Roberts, 'Nyamwezi', p.134.
105 For an overview by contemporaries, see A. Le Roy, *Mehr Licht in die Zustände des dunklen Weltteils. Die Sklaverei und ihre Bekämpfung* (Münster, 1890); Freiherr von Eberstein, 'Rechtsanschauungen der Eingeborenen von Kilwa', *Mitteilungen von Forschungsreisenden und Gelehrten aus den deutschen Schutzgebieten*, 9 (1896), p.177; and Velten, *Desturi*, pp.305f. For a comparative perspective, see C. Meillassoux, *The Anthropology of Slavery. The Womb of Iron and Gold* (Chicago/London, 1991) [originally published in French as *Anthropologie de l'esclavage. Le ventre de ver et d'argent* (Paris, 1986)], pp.143–56 ; and I. Kopytoff, and S. Miers, 'Introduction. African "slavery" as an institution of marginality', in S. Miers and I. Kopytoff (eds), *Slavery in Africa. Historical and Anthropological Perspectives* (Madison, WI, 1977), pp.12–14.
106 For examples, see Tippu Tip, 'Autobiographie', pp.185, 216, 225, 232, 243.
107 For this argument, see Wright, *Strategies*, p.7. For a detailed description, see the life story of Tatu Mulondyelwa in the same volume. See also the 'trade biographies' of slaves in Captain P.H. Colomb, *Slave Catching in the Indian Ocean. A Record of Naval Experiences* (London, 1873), pp.28f.; Jones-Bateman (M. Furahani), *Autobiography*; Velten, 'Autobiographie', p.306; and Nolan, 'Christianity', p.141. For a different view, see, for instance, Coulbois, *Tanganyika*, pp.99–112, who described nineteenth-century enslavement in East Africa as an Arab 'razzia générale'.
108 Reichard, *Deutsch-Ostafrika*, pp.462f.
109 *Ibid.*
110 For a photograph of a man wearing a slave stick, see Blohm, *Nyamwezi*, vol. I, p.209, photograph no. 16. For a detailed description, see Cameron, *Africa*, vol. I, p.284.
111 See, for instance, Tippu Tip, 'Autobiographie', pp.44, 194 and RHO Micr Afr 472 R.19/MF 42, Tabora Regional Book, 'Extracts from Nyamwezi law and custom by H. Cory', 1952, p.6; see also Livingstone, *Journals*, p.149 (11 August 1871).
112 Blohm, *Nyamwezi*, vol. II, p.36 [extract from interview, n.d. (pre 1914)]; Bösch, *Banyamwezi*, p.442.
113 Blohm, *Nyamwezi*, vol. II, p.63 [extract from interview, n.d. (pre 1914)]. See also H. Waller [1876], in Great Britain, *Parliamentary Papers. Royal Commission on Fugitive Slaves*, C. 1516, (vol. I, p. 35–8), cited in *Traite des esclaves*, p.132. See also Wright, *Strategies*, p.151.
114 Reichard, *Deutsch-Ostafrika*, p.484. See also the description of the journey to the coast by Jones-Bateman (M. Furahani), *Autobiography*, pp.18–20.

115 See, for instance, the highly biased description of the East African slave trade in Evangelischer Afrikaverein, *Das Deutsche Reich und die Sklaverei in Afrika!*, Stenographischer Bericht der am 18 Januar 1895 in der Tonhalle zu Berlin auf Veranlassung des ev. Afrikavereins abgehaltenen Versammlung (Leipzig, 1895); E. Baur and A. Le Roy, *À Travers le Zanguebar. Voyage Dans L'Oudoé, L'Ouzigoua, L'Oukwèré, L'Oukami et L'Ousagara* (Tours, 1886), pp.97–106; and E. Krenzler, 'Sklaverei und Sklavenhandel in Ostafrika', *Jahresberichte des Württembergischen Vereins für Handelsgeographie*, 5–6 (1886–88), pp.71–4.

116 Reichard, *Deutsch-Ostafrika*, p.484. For a similar view, see Burton, *Lake Regions*, pp.318, 326; Livingstone, *Journals*, pp.345 (13 November 1868), 348 (19 November 1868) and 351 (27 November 1868); Cameron, *Africa*, vol. II, p.31; Tippu Tip, 'Autobiographie', p.208; C. Velten, 'Sitten und Gebräuche der Suaheli', *Mitteilungen des Seminars für orientalische Sprachen. Afrikanische Studien*, I (1898), p.7; and Velten, *Desturi*, p.306. See also E. Steudel, 'Die ansteckenden Krankheiten der Karawanen Deutsch-Ostafrikas, ihre Verbreitung unter der übrigen Bevölkerung und ihre Bekämpfung', *Koloniales Jahrbuch 1894* (Berlin, 1895), pp.171–202, RHO Micr Afr 472 R.20/MF 44, Tabora District Book, 'Notes on an Interview with Jaba bin Zaid by Assistant District Officer N. Burt', 24 May 1927; and Nolan, 'Christianity', p.141. For a different description of a slave caravan on the move, see Elton, 'Coast Country', pp.242f.; Toeppen, 'Handel', p.231; S. T. Pruen, 'Slavery in East Africa. Letter from Dr. Pruen, Mpwapwa', *Church Missionary Intelligencer*, 13 (1888), pp.661–5; idem, *The Arab and the African. Experiences in Eastern Equatorial Africa during a Residence of Three Years* (London, 1891), pp.220f; and the life story of Swema as recorded by Pater Horner in 1866 and translated by E. A. Alpers in Alpers, 'The story of Swema. Female vulnerability in nineteenth-century East Africa', in C. C. Robertson and M. A. Klein (eds), *Women and Slavery in Africa* (Madison, WI, 1983), pp.185–219. For an interesting discussion of the highly ambivalent origin of that particular text, see P. V. Kollman, *The Evangelization of Slaves and Catholic Origins in Eastern Africa* (New York, 2005), pp.130f.

117 Iliffe, *Modern History*, p.81.

118 I. Kopytoff, 'The cultural context of African abolition', in S. Miers and R. Roberts (eds), *The End of Slavery in Africa* (Madison, WI, 1988), p.500 has argued that there is no substantive meaning to the term 'free', as slavery as much as kinship is embedded into a 'continuum of dependency'. Arguably, there are different kinds of dependency, for instance, only some forms of kinship in nineteenth-century East Africa allowed a person to become a 'commodity'. Thus, the term 'free' is used here primarily to denote a person's status that precluded his or her outright sale under 'normal' circumstances.

119 The term 'family' is used loosely here in order to denote a kinship group or members of a household. Moreover, the status of freedom in opposition to enslavement is misleading to some degree because it does not do justice to its fragility and ambiguity.

120 Bösch, *Banyamwezi*, p.444; Grant, *Walk Across Africa*, p.48; and A. Seibt, 'Fragebogen-Beantwortung für ganz Unyamwezi durch Missionar A. Seibt, in Urambo stationiert [January 1910]', cited in Gottberg, *Unyamwezi*, p.198. For the original reports by Seibt, see BAB RKolA 4997/467. I have used the texts reprinted in Gottberg for reference purposes since the text is more easily accessible. Further detail can be found in RHO Micr Afr 472 R.20/MF 44, Tabora District Book, 'Records of Meeting Held from the 2nd October to 5th October 1932'.

121 Tippu Tip, 'Autobiographie', pp.2, 251.

122 For examples, see Burton, *Lake Regions*, p.110; Velten, *Desturi* [citing Baraka bin Shomari], p.378; Löbner, 'Fragebogen', cited in Gottberg, *Unyamwezi*, pp.161, 163, 166; and Seibt, 'Fragebogen', cited in Gottberg, *Unyamwezi*, p.193. For a more theoretical discussion of pawnship in Africa, see R. Roberts and S. Miers, 'Introduction', in Miers and Roberts (eds), *The End of Slavery*, pp.46f.; and T. Falola and P. E. Lovejoy, 'Pawnship in historical perspective', in T. Falola and P. E. Lovejoy (eds), *Pawnship in Africa. Debt Bondage in Historical Perspective* (Boulder, CO, 1994), pp.1–26. See also the contributions by F. Morton, 'Pawnship and slavery on the Kenya coast. The Miji Kenda Case', pp.27–42 and J. L. Giblin, 'Pawning, politics and matriliny in Northeastern Tanzania', pp.43–53, *ibid*. Burton notes that people in Unyamwezi were sometimes compelled to sell themselves into slavery because they had run up personal

Slavery & Social Change in Unyamwezi, c. 1860–1900

debts by playing 'bao' (a board game) for too high a stake! See Burton, *Lake Regions*, p.462.
123 See Kirk to Granville, 13 April 1885, in Great Britain, *Parliamentary Papers. Correspondence Relating to Zanzibar*, C. 4776 (London, 1886), p.119, cited in *Traite des esclaves*, pp.116f. For a review of the vast literature on the household as a joint production and consumption unit, see J. L. Guyer, 'Household and Community in African Studies', *African Studies Review*, 24 (1981), pp.87–137.
124 C. S. Smith, *Explorations in the Zanzibar Dominions* (London, 1887), p.103.
125 Bösch, *Banyamwezi*, p.445. For a different perspective on pawning by household heads, see Willis, *Mombasa*, pp.132f. and 'The administration of Bonde 1920-60. A study of the implementation of indirect rule in Tanganyika', *African Affairs*, 92 (1993) pp.66, 58.
126 Blohm, *Nyamwezi*, vol. II, p.38. Arguably, a distinction can be drawn between pawns and slaves depending on the distance between their place of origin and their new residence. However, European sources are frequently unspecific on this point, as differences of this kind were hardly discernible to the outside observer. For more details, see also the illuminating report concerning the practice in the Kilwa hinterland in BAB RKolA 4997: 497, 'Fragebogen über die Rechte der Eingeborenen in den deutschen Kolonien (Wakitu)', Bezirksamt Kilwa, 23 October 1910.
127 Blohm, *Nyamwezi*, vol. II, p.38.
128 For a description of the Ujiji slave market, see *Traite des esclaves*, p.106. See also Burton, *Lake Regions*, p.318.
129 Reichard, *Deutsch-Ostafrika*, p.475.
130 Cameron, *Africa*, vol. I, p.144. For a detailed description of the Zanzibar slave market, see W. C. Devereux, *A Cruise in the 'Gorgon'* (London, 1869), pp.103–5.
131 See, for instance the description of such 'relay' trade in Colomb, *Slave Catching*, pp.28f.; Jones-Bateman (M. Furahani), *Autobiography*; and the life story of Namwaga in Moravian Archives Herrnhut, 'Nachlaß T. Bachmann', vol. III, pp.180f. For comparative material, see also the life stories in Wright, *Strategies*.
132 For a detailed description of commercial transactions of slaves, see Reichard, *Deutsch-Ostafrika*, p.472. See also Grant, *Walk Across Africa*, p.48; and Blohm, *Nyamwezi*, vol. II, p.37 [extract from interview, n.d. (pre 1914)]. For the buying and selling of slaves by caravan porters, see Burton, *Lake Regions*, pp.154f., 454.
133 Blohm, *Nyamwezi*, vol. II, p.37 [extract from interview, n.d. (pre 1914)]. As the text was translated by W. Blohm from ki-Nyamwezi into German and then by the author into English, it is likely that the more subtle meanings of some words have been lost in the process. It is probably worth noting that Blohm does not state in which part of Unyamwezi the person he interviewed had grown up. For a description of the outright sale of a person in the vicinity of Ujiji, see M. Joachim, 'Sizia oder Schicksale einer Negersklavin. Von ihr selbst erzählt', *Afrika-Bote*, 1905/6, pp.109–15.
134 For the term 'rites of passage', see A. Van Gennep, *The Rites of Passage*, transl. by M. B. Vizecom and G. L. Caffee (Chicago, 1960).
135 For the term 'social death', see O. Patterson, *Slavery and Social Death. A Comparative Study* (Cambridge, MA, 1982).
136 Livingstone, *Journals*, p.93 (28 December 1870).
137 Nolan, 'Christianity', p.49. Unfortunately, Nolan does not provide the ki-Nyamwezi words for 'foreigner' or 'stranger', which would have helped to compare their meaning with the appropriate ki-Swahili terms. The ki-Swahili word *mgeni* (pl. *wageni*) [stranger/foreigner] for instance, does not convey a derogative meaning.
138 Bösch, *Banyamwezi*, p.440; and R. G. Abrahams, *The Political Organization of Unyamwezi* (Cambridge, 1967), p.95. See also the short, yet informative article by Spellig, 'Wanyamwezi', pp.212f.
139 Blohm, *Nyamwezi*, vol. I, p.168, vol. II, p.36 [extract from interview, n.d. (pre 1914)].
140 Reichard, *Deutsch-Ostafrika*, p.474. See also Burton, *Lake Regions*, p.383.
141 Pruen, *Arab and African*, p.235.
142 Nolan, 'Christianity', p.49; see also Kopytoff, 'Cultural context', p.490.
143 BAB RKolA 7382/27, p.89, 'Berichte der einzelnen Verwaltungsstellen in Deutsch-Ostafrika über die Sklaverei', Station Tabora, Berichterstatter: Hauptmann Puder, n.d.

[1900]; and Blohm, *Nyamwezi*, vol. II, p.37 [extract from interview, n.d. (pre 1914)], p.38. See also Löbner, 'Fragebogen', cited in Gottberg, *Unyamwezi*, p.142. It is unlikely, however, that chiefs, important headmen or royal courtiers would be seen together with their agricultural slaves.

144 Löbner, 'Fragebogen', cited in Gottberg, *Unyamwezi*, p.12; and Nolan, 'Christianity', p.145. For a comparative perspective, see C. Robertson and M. A. Klein, 'Women's importance in African slave systems', in idem (eds), *Women and Slavery in Africa* (Portsmouth, NH, 1997 [first published Madison, WI, 1983]), pp.3–25.

145 Burton, *Lake Regions*, p.215. This quotation does not allow generalisation, because it is too unspecific about perceived gender roles in agricultural production in other neighbouring regions of Unyamwezi. However, Burton also noted that 'Adults fetch no price, because they are notoriously intractable, and addicted to desertion'. Burton, *Lake Regions*, p.355.

146 See, for instance, Burton, *Lake Regions*, pp.329, 355, 520; and Bösch, *Banyamwezi*, p.441. See also Roberts and Miers, 'Introduction', p.39.

147 Nolan, 'Christianity', p.146.

148 See, for instance, Burton, *Lake Regions*, p.383.

149 For this argument, see Wright, *Strategies*, p.154.

150 Blohm, *Nyamwezi*, vol. I, p.89. See also the report by Hauptmann Puder [1899], cited in Gottberg, *Unyamwezi*, p.237.

151 Nolan, 'Christianity', p.147. See also Abrahams, *Peoples*, p.68.

152 Bösch, *Banyamwezi*, p.445.

153 Blohm, *Nyamwezi*, vol. I, p.3, vol. II, p.36 [extract from interview, n.d. (pre 1914)]. See also Seibt, 'Fragebogen', cited in Gottberg, *Unyamwezi*, p.187. Arguably, from a structuralist perspective, kinship ties and the formal manumission of slaves are mutually exclusive. The former are acquired by birth and descent. These ties can be extended to non-natal kin, for instance to slaves, or reduced, but they cannot be broken except through the act of (re)-enslavement. For a similar argument, see also Kopytoff, 'Cultural context', p.495.

154 Blohm, *Nyamwezi*, vol. II, p.36 [extract from interview, n.d. (pre 1914)], p.64. See also Nolan, 'Christianity', p.49.

155 *Ibid.*, p.146. See also Abrahams, *Political Organization*, p.95.

156 Blohm, *Nyamwezi*, vol. II, p.36 [extract from interview, n.d. (pre 1914); and Abrahams, *Political Organization*, p.95. Yet, see also Bösch, *Banyamwezi*, pp.440f who states that all children of slaves were regarded as 'free'. For a different view, see RHO Micr Afr 472 R.19/MF 42, Tabora District Book, 'Extracts from Nyamwezi law and custom by H. Cory', 1952, p.6. Cory reports that all children of slaves had the same status as 'free' born children.

157 Blohm, *Nyamwezi*, vol. II, p.36 [extract from interview, n.d. (pre 1914).

158 BAB RKolA 7382/27, p.89, 'Berichte der einzelnen Verwaltungsstellen in Deutsch-Ostafrika über die Sklaverei', Station Tabora, Berichterstatter: Hauptmann Puder, n.d. [1900]; and Löbner, 'Fragebogen', cited in Gottberg, *Unyamwezi*, p.152. See also Blohm, *Nyamwezi*, vol. II, p.36 [extract from interview, n.d. (pre 1914)]. It is unfortunate that Blohm does not provide a ki-Nyamwezi translation of these terms, as this would allow a comparison with other authors, such as Bösch. For comparative material, see BAB RKolA 7382/27, pp.82–4, 'Berichte der einzelnen Verwaltungsstellen in Deutsch-Ostafrika über die Sklaverei', Station Muanza, Berichterstatter: Hauptmann Schlobach, n.d. [1900].

159 For a description of female slave work, see the life story of Msatulwa Mwachitete in Wright, *Strategies*, p.65. Whether female slaves actually worked for the 'free' women of the household in daily life rather than for the male household head cannot be decided on the basis of the available sources, but it seems likely, given the gender division of labour. For this argument, see also Robertson and Klein, 'Women's importance'.

160 BAB RKolA 7382/27, p.89, 'Berichte der einzelnen Verwaltungsstellen in Deutsch-Ostafrika über die Sklaverei', Station Tabora, Berichterstatter: Hauptmann Puder, n.d. [1900].

161 For a comparative perspective, see Willis, *Mombasa*, p.70.

162 Löbner, 'Fragebogen', cited in Gottberg, *Unyamwezi*, p.152. On this point, see also B. Ankermann, 'Ostafrika', in E. Schulz-Ewerth and L. Adam, *Das Eingeborenenrecht. Sitten und Gewohnheitsrechte der Eingeborenen der ehemaligen deutschen Schutzgebiete in Afrika und Übersee* (Stuttgart, 1929), pp.212f.
163 Moravian Archives Herrnhut, R 15 M, 'Jahresbericht Urambo 1899'; Löbner, 'Fragebogen', cited in Gottberg, *Unyamwezi*, p.153. See also Nolan, 'Christianity', p.49. For a different view, see RHO Micr Afr 472 R.19/MF 42, Tabora District Book, 'Extracts from Nyamwezi law and custom by H. Cory', 1952, p.6.
164 Bösch, *Banyamwezi*, p.441.
165 Blohm, *Nyamwezi*, vol. II, p.36 [extract from interview, n.d. (pre 1914)].
166 Löbner, 'Fragebogen', cited in Gottberg, *Unyamwezi*, p.154.
167 Wright, *Strategies*, p.43.
168 Bösch, *Banyamwezi*, p.441.
169 Blohm, *Nyamwezi*, vol. II, p.36 [extract from interview, n.d. (pre 1914)].
170 Löbner, 'Fragebogen', cited in Gottberg, *Unyamwezi*, p.152; and Abrahams, *Peoples*, p.58. See also RHO Micr Afr 472 R.20/MF 44, Tabora District Book, 'Tribal Government' [1933].
171 Bösch, *Banyamwezi*, p.442f. See also Reichard, *Deutsch-Ostafrika*, p.479.
172 Blohm, *Nyamwezi*, vol. II, p.36 [extract from interview, n.d. (pre 1914)], p.64. See also Grant, *Walk Across Africa*, p.50; and RHO Micr Afr 472 R.20/MF 44, Tabora District Book, 'Tribal Government' [1933]. See also Wright, *Strategies*, p.36.
173 See, for instance, BAB RKolA 7382/27, p.88, 'Berichte der einzelnen Verwaltungsstellen in Deutsch-Ostafrika über die Sklaverei', Station Tabora, Berichterstatter: Hauptmann Puder, n.d. [1900].
174 Nolan, 'Christianity', p.146.
175 Löbner, 'Fragebogen', cited in Gottberg, *Unyamwezi*, p.153.
176 Blohm, *Nyamwezi*, vol. II, p.124; Grant, *Walk Across Africa*, pp.50, 61, 73.
177 Bösch, *Banyamwezi*, p.440. For a different view, see Löbner, 'Fragebogen' 1910, cited in Gottberg, *Unyamwezi*, p.152.
178 Blohm, *Nyamwezi*, vol. II, p.38 [extract from interview, n.d. (pre 1914)].
179 Idem, vol. II, p.37 [extract from interview, n.d. (pre 1914)]. See also Löbner, 'Fragebogen', cited in Gottberg, *Unyamwezi*, p.152 and Reichard, *Deutsch-Ostafrika*, pp.462f., 466f.
180 Cameron, *Africa*, vol. I, p.184.
181 On the dangers of travelling alone in Unyamwezi, see Grant, *Walk Across Africa*, p.102. See also Tippu Tip, 'Autobiographie', p.277.
182 See the life stories of Grandmother Narwimba and Chisi-Ndjurisiye-Sichyajunga in Wright, *Strategies*, pp.50–2, 83–5.
183 Burton, *Lake Regions*, p.259.
184 For this argument, see Wright, *Strategies*, p.4. See also Robertson and Klein, 'Women's importance', p.18.
185 See, for instance, the life story of Sizia as recorded by Joachim, 'Sizia', pp.109–15.
186 Reichard, *Deutsch-Ostafrika*, p.465.
187 See, for example Kopytoff and Miers, 'Introduction', pp.14–18; and Robertson and Klein, 'Women's importance', pp.2–25. See also J. Willis and S. Miers, 'Becoming a child of the house. Incorporation, authority and resistance in Giryama Society', *Journal of African History*, 38 (1997), pp.480f.
188 For a striking example, see Abrahams, *Political Organization*, p.95f.
189 Pruen, 'Slavery', pp.662f; Pruen, *Arab and African*, p.217. See also Wright, *Strategies*, pp.25f., 169. Whether kinship ideology was consciously used as a means of social control in lieu of coercion is a matter of debate. See, for instance, Meillassoux's reading of Kopytoff and Miers, 'Introduction', pp.3–81 in *Anthropology of Slavery*, pp.12–14.
190 Bösch, *Banyamwezi*, p.445. See also P. Broyon-Mirambo, 'Description of Unyamwezi and the best routes thither from the East Coast', *Proceedings of the Royal Geographical Society*, 22 (1877–8), p.32, cited in Gottberg, *Unyamwezi*, p.118.
191 Löbner, 'Fragebogen', cited in Gottberg, *Unyamwezi*, pp.152, 168. See also Reichard, *Deutsch-Ostafrika*, p.467.

192 Bösch, *Banyamwezi*, p.443.
193 Nolan, 'Christianity', p.147.
194 For this argument see RHO Micr Afr 472 R.19/MF 42, Tabora District Book, 'Extracts from Nyamwezi law and custom by H. Cory', 1952, p.6f.
195 The Nyamwezi elders present at the meeting strongly favoured the re-introduction of this punishment for runaway wives. RHO Micr Afr 472 R.20/MF 44, Tabora District Book, 'Records of Meeting Held from the 12th to 14th October 1930'.
196 Wright, *Strategies*, p.9. For a completely different view on the relationship between kinship and slavery, see C. Meillassoux, 'Female slavery', in Robertson and Klein, *Women and Slavery in Africa*, p.64; and idem, *Anthropology of Slavery*, 14f., 99f. Meillassoux argues that female slaves were exclusively used as agricultural workers. This might be a matter of definition, since he also argued that at the moment that female slaves became part of a kinship group, they ceased to be 'slaves'.
197 Iliffe, *Modern History*, p.43. See also Glassman, *Feasts and Riots*, p.23, following R. I. Pouwels, *Horn and Crescent. Cultural Change and Traditional Islam on the East African Coast, 800–1900* (Cambridge, 1987), p.196, who writes that on the coast 'discursive struggle over [Islamic] ritual constituted a major forum for the contestation of power' between slaves and their owners in the late nineteenth century. However, whether this particular field of conflict was of equal importance to other fields, such as everyday disputes over working and living arrangements, for instance, might be a matter of debate. Moreover, written contemporary documentation is largely silent on this subject and, for this reason, a detailed discussion of the issue has been omitted from this study.
198 For these distinctions, see Willis and Miers, 'Child of the house', pp.480, 485; and Glassman, 'Bondsman', pp.283, 289, 297. See also Kopytoff, 'Cultural context', p.491.
199 For the observation that the upbringing and insecure circumstances of slaves explain their 'apathy', see Pruen, *Arab and African*, pp.237f. On the connection between spatial order, power and ideology, see T. Mitchell, *Colonising Egypt* (Cambridge, 1988), pp.34-62. For an excellent introduction to the literature on power and practice, see A. Lüdtke, 'Einleitung. Herrschaft als soziale Praxis', in A. Lüdtke (ed.), *Herrschaft als soziale Praxis* (Göttingen, 1991), pp.9–63.
200 Wright, *Strategies*, p.2.
201 RHO Micr Afr 472 R.19/MF 42, Tabora Regional Book, 'Extracts from Nyamwezi law and custom by H. Cory', 1952.
202 Willis and Miers, 'Child of the house', pp.481f. On this aspect see also J. M. Lonsdale, 'The conquest state of Kenya, 1895–1905', in B. Berman and J. M. Lonsdale, *Unhappy Valley. Conflict in Kenya & Africa*, vol. 1 (London, 1992), p.21.
203 Willis and Miers, 'Child of the house', pp.481f., 485, 489.
204 On the subversive impact of the expansion of slavery on the ideology and practice of kinship relations in general, see P. Manning, *Slavery and African Life. Occidental, Oriental and African Slave Trades* (Cambridge, 1990), p.119.
205 Blohm, *Nyamwezi*, vol. I, p.168, vol. II, p.35 [extract from interview, n.d. (pre 1914)]. See also, Willis and Miers, 'Child of the house', p.481.
206 Grant, *Walk Across Africa*, p.61.
207 Shorter, 'Nyungu', p.252.
208 See, for instance, Grant, *Walk Across Africa*, p.61.
209 Wright, *Strategies*, p.152. See also Feierman, 'A century of ironies', p.364.
210 Wright, *Strategies*, p.152. See also Willis and Miers, 'Child of the house', p.485.
211 Iliffe, *Modern History*, p.74; Willis and Miers, 'Child of the house', p.481. For a different view, see Meillassoux, *Anthropology of Slavery*, p.327.
212 Similar views on kinship relations have been expressed much more eloquently, for instance, by F. L. Cooper, 'The problem of slavery in African studies', *Journal of African History*, 20 (1979) 1, p. 103; and J. Comaroff, 'Sui Generis. Feminism, kinship theory and "structural" domains', in J. F. Collier and S. J. Yanagisako (eds), *Gender and Kinship. Essays Towards a Unified Analysis* (Stanford, CA, 1987), p. 84.
213 For a fuller account of the end of slavery in central Tanganyika, see Jan-Georg Deutsch, *Emancipation without Abolition in German East Africa, c. 1884–1914* (Oxford, 2006).

Three

Slavery & Forced Labour in the Eastern Congo 1850–1910

DAVID NORTHRUP

Introduction

From the mid-nineteenth century, outside forces transformed the once isolated eastern Congo. Zanzibari traders established a commercial empire there in the 1870s. The new Congo Free State of King Leopold II of Belgium then absorbed the region by legal annexation in 1887, initially making the Zanzibari leader Tippu Tip its governor, before formalising its control through military conquest in 1892–94. In the first third of the twentieth century the territory formed the Congo's populous and productive Province Orientale.

Besides their political and economic impacts, each of these regimes substantially affected labour relations. The Zanzibari rulers markedly increased enslavement for labour purposes. Although the European regimes were pledged to ending slavery, their efforts to command the resources of the region employed forced labour on a large scale.[1] To understand the dynamics of slavery in the eastern Congo one needs to respect the complexity and fluidity of these circumstances and of the perspectives of the participants. As researchers have stressed, slavery in Africa was a range of subordinate institutions, whose particular traits changed with historical conditions.[2] Moreover, the line between free and unfree labour was also shifting in Western minds during the course of the nineteenth and twentieth centuries.[3]

Pre-colonisation

Gender and social status largely defined the division of labour that existed in eastern Congo on the eve of colonisation. The fundamental separation of tasks into men's and women's work was strictly adhered to, at least among free persons. A large share of the ordinary work of farming fell upon women, as did a considerable share of the carrying tasks, from babies to bananas. Crafts, such as the making of cloth, pottery and baskets, also generally came under the heading of women's work. Men hunted, fished, herded cattle, cleared land for farming, smelted and smithed, and went to war.[4]

Social status varied much more than gender roles in the region. The region's isolation, low population densities, and limited economic development inhibited the formation of a slave population in most areas, although degrees of servitude may have existed among some riverain populations such as the Wagenia, a fisherfolk on the upper Congo, and among the Yalusuna agriculturalists west of Kisangani. A Wagenia chief at Nyangwe in 1874, for example, was willing to sell canoes to the explorer V.L. Cameron only in exchange for slaves, although his explanation that slaves were valuable both as capital and labour whereas the cowrie currency would simply lie idle may well reflect already altered circumstances.[5]

The greatest concentration of slaves occurred in the Uele savannahs of the north as a by-product of the Mangbetu, Babwa and Zande conquests in the nineteenth century. Prisoners of war, if not ransomed, became slaves for life. Among the Mangbetu at least, a majority of these slaves were women acquired by commoner lineages to build up their numbers and by royal lineages to produce the food used in royal largesse. Rulers also distributed slave wives as a way of attracting followers, a practice particularly important among the Zande. Slave status was not hereditary and, while the position of slaves was inferior to that of free persons, the growing subordination of free commoners to the royal clans in Zande and Mangbetu states in the late nineteenth century led to a blurring of that distinction. Colonial officials often considered that the claims a Zande or Mangbetu ruler was able to make on the labour of his subjects made them his slaves in effect, if not in law.[6]

More widespread was the purchase or capture of women as wives, although it is not clear how much their status differed from wives acquired from the payment of bridewealth. On his travels through Maniema in the southeastern portion of the region in 1869, David Livingstone found that the only interest in slaves was in females intended as wives; male slaves were considered more troublesome than valuable, being generally criminals, troublemakers, and sorcerers sold by their own people.[7] Likewise, in the Kivu region male prisoners of war were generally either killed or ransomed, whereas females were incorporated as wives.[8] Even allowing for the sparseness of the historical record, examples of economically motivated slavery were rare before the influence of the Afro-Arab intruders.

Zanzibari colonisation

Beginning in the 1860s armed traders and conquerors from the Nile region, Angola, Zanzibar and Europe disturbed eastern Congo's isolation and disrupted or destroyed its social structures. What distinguished these intruders from the earlier Mangbetu and Zande in the northern savannah of the region was their access to the world market. The initial goal for all these intrusions was to obtain the ivory which eastern Congo's elephant population produced and which its human population had long collected. Modern firearms provided the means by which this prize might be obtained at modest cost.

Ivory traders from the upper Nile had reached the Uele valley by 1865. Traders from the Angolan networks also began moving into the south-western frontiers of eastern Congo in the 1860s and 1870s in search of ivory.[9] The penetration of the Zanzibaris appears to have been spurred by a rise in ivory prices in 1856–57 and was facilitated by their possession of firearms. Skirting the formidable kingdoms of Rwanda and Burundi, traders crossed Lake Tanganyika by canoe from Ujiji. The earliest Zanzibari outpost in the eastern Congo was at Uvira on the northwest shore of that lake. From there the traders advanced into Maniema and established a modest outpost on the upper Congo (Lualaba) River at Nyangwe. Trade and alliances with powerful local leaders dominated the early acquisition of ivory, but from 1868 the Zanzibaris had enough men and arms to conquer the small communities of the region and pillage their ivory. As tons of ivory went east to Zanzibar, new Zanzibari adventurers flooded into the region.[10]

The arrival of Tippu Tip in eastern Congo in 1874 began a period of consolidation and further conquests. An experienced trader with family ties to the Omani Arabs, coastal Swahili, and inland Nyamwezi traders, Tippu Tip used his access to Indian capital and arms to establish political and economic dominance of the region. Though warmly welcomed by the Zanzibaris at Nyangwe, he chose to set up his own headquarters to the south at Kasongo, where some of his kinsmen were already located. After repairing relations with local African communities, whose mistreatment had led them to boycott trade, Tippu Tip was able to acquire an immense quantity of ivory, which he took back to Zanzibar in 1881. Upon his return to eastern Congo at the head of a large and well-armed caravan, Tippu Tip set about expanding and consolidating his dominion. He moved his headquarters to Kisangani, at the bend in the river, from where he dispatched twenty caravans into neighbouring districts in search of ivory and alliances.[11]

Those who were slow to cooperate felt the power of his arms. Conquests led to a great increase in captives, who were incorporated into Zanzibari armies, caravans and settlements. Detached from their roots and cultural restraints, the new slaves were often guilty of the most brutal rapine and pillage of the countryside. Young men were turned into servants and soldiers. In 1876 Tippu Tip had about fifty youths whom he was training 'as gun-bearers, house servants, scouts, cooks, carpenters, house-builders, blacksmiths, and leaders of trading parties'.[12]

Though forced to meet the labour demands of the growing trade, captives might also experience rapid assimilation, which had been possible for some of the slaves the Zanzibaris had brought with them. For example, Tippu Tip's slave Ngongo Lutete became governor at Kasongo after his master moved on to Kisangani. Indeed, the Zanzibaris appear to have had a preference for free porters, who were less inclined to flee. Most of the captives who survived the caravan journeys to Ujiji or Unyanyembe, Cameron asserted in 1874, then hired themselves out as 'free porters'. Of course, once they were across Lake Tanganyika the impressed porters would have had little hope of returning home alone, so their willingness to sign on with a new caravan may have owed as much to their needing a means of livelihood as to their liking the work. In any case, European explorers noted, slave porters, though bound to slave forks, were not otherwise cruelly treated.[13] In 1885 Tippu told a State agent that it was a number of years since captives had last been captured in order to carry ivory to and from Kisangani . Instead, what he termed 'domestic slaves' conveyed the ivory from Kisangani south to Nyangwe, from where other porters took it as far as Ujiji, and so on to the coast, each team of porters returning to its home base.[14] By that time free Maniema porters were also relatively common, with those Tippu Tip supplied to Stanley in 1887 deserting when they were abused.[15]

A similar mixture of impressment and assimilation marked the use of slaves in the major Zanzibari settlements in eastern Congo. On the settlements' plantations slaves were worked hard, fed little and tended to die within a year.[16] However, the women who were incorporated by the hundreds into the Zanzibari leaders' harems might expect a less harsh existence.[17]

Free State Colonisation

European explorers, Christian missionaries and agents of King Leopold's Congo Free State followed in the wake of the Zanzibaris. On the basis of Henry Morton Stanley's descent of the Congo in 1876 and his subsequent travels on behalf of the International Congo Association, the Berlin Conference accorded Leopold sovereignty over the Congo basin in 1885, although the Free State had only a feeble presence in the eastern Congo for another decade.

The Free State forces broke Zanzibari resistance by 1894, but took over much of the personnel and policies that the Zanzibaris had created in the eastern Congo. While explicitly condemning slavery, the Free State continued the forced labour practices of the Zanzibari for reasons that are not hard to find. First, the understaffed and underfunded Free State was ill equipped to undertake any substantial reforms in the vast area that it now claimed. Second, viewed from the most generous perspective, its administrators were charged with fundamentally contradictory policies of reform and profit. Less generously, one could argue that the Free State was more sincere in its pursuit of profit than of reform. Finally, Free State leaders were ill prepared philosophically and economically to create a viable alternative to compulsion as a mechanism for labour mobilisation. Put another way, they lacked a vision of free labour that was a viable alternative to slavery.[18]

The descent of the Free State into disgrace is well known.[19] The revelations that shocked even other imperialists came initially from reports of the British consuls in the Free State, of which Roger Casement's was the most explosive, from foreign missionaries, and from E.D. Morel's Congo Reform Association. The Free State's fate was sealed when the international commission of inquiry that Leopold himself appointed in 1905 returned a report whose mild tone made the abuses it confirmed even more devastating. In 1908 Belgium was forced to assume direct responsibility for the colony.

Details of the labour situation in the eastern Congo are less well known than those to the west. Casement never reached the eastern Congo and the international commissioners only touched its western edge. A review of the situation on the ground makes it easier to understand the complex socio-economic issues beneath the moral outrage. In particular, it exposes the wide gap between the Free State's stated mission and its actual performance. From the beginning the Free State had described its mission as ending slavery, extending liberal Western values and uplifting African lives. According to Secretary of State Baron Edmond van Eetvelde in 1897, the Free State's labour policies were intended to 'regenerate the native', and introduce him or her to the equitable remuneration that came from commercial cultivation and the collection of wild rubber and other forest products. Should the civilising lure of the market prove insufficient, however, Africans would be driven to work by requisitions of goods and services for which the Secretary of State promised remuneration.[20] In practice, the Free State's first resort was to compulsion. In their pursuit of profit its agents used methods that approached the Zanzibaris' in brutality and surpassed them in scope and duration. With remarkable candour Governor General Théophile Wahis described the regime in the eastern Congo about 1893 as 'in short just about what had been created by the Arabs. The division of territory is what they had established. The personnel, who occupy the regions here and there, are those whom they sent there.'[21] He might have added that the Free State's labour recruitment policies resembled those of the Zanzibaris, except that slavery was no longer officially recognised.

A cornerstone of the Free State's early recruitment of labour was the redemption of slaves. The Free State encouraged its officers to meet their labour needs by redeeming former Zanzibari captives and taking new captives. Over the course of several years at Stanley Falls, one early agent bought and freed some 2,000 Zanzibari slaves. Meanwhile, the Free State's military campaigns against the rebellious Zanzibaris and their African allies were producing large numbers of new captives, who were pressed into state service. In the three years of the campaigns more than

5,000 captives arrived at the military camp at Lusambo in Kasai, which served the eastern Congo – so many that some had to be parcelled out among local chiefs or given to individual soldiers. In 1894–5 the commander of Tanganyika district hanged a number of slave traders and diverted the hundreds of slaves 'freed' from their caravans into service in the Force Publique or the production of food for government outposts. Youths too young to go directly into military service were given to Catholic missions or trained for future military service.[22]

Those 'recruited' into the Force Publique served as sentries and auxiliaries in the villages beyond Free State outposts. Untrained, ill-supervised, loyal to neither the African villagers nor the Free State, these individuals often abused their power, much as their counterparts under the Zanzibaris had done. So long as the quotas in rubber, ivory, and other goods were met, European officials largely ignored the excesses. In 1905, the head of the Province Orientale lauded the services such auxiliaries had provided in the early years of the Free State, while assuring investigators that they were no longer used.[23]

Liberated Africans and other forced recruits served many other functions. The plantations the Zanzibari had established along the Lualaba from Stanleyville (as Kisangani had been renamed) to Kasongo continued to provide the rice and citrus on which the Europeans depended. A former Free State employee, the American E.J. Glave, described the Free State's labour policies along the river in 1894–5. Glave generally accepted the need for harsh measures, 'to beat the natives into submission', and to habituate them to steady work for the State. But, he found, payment for labour was as lacking as it had been during Zanzibari rule:

> The State conducts its pacification of the country after the fashion of the Arabs, so the natives are not gainers at all. The Arabs in the employ of the state are compelled to bring in ivory and rubber, and are permitted to employ any measures considered necessary to obtain this result. They employ the same means as in the days gone by, when Tippu Tib was one of the masters of the situation. They raid villages, take slaves, and give them back for ivory. The state has not suppressed slavery, but established a monopoly by driving out the Arabs and Wangwana competitors.[24]

The relationship between the African chiefs and the Free State also resembled the relationship the chiefs had had with the Zanzibaris. To supply the labourers and military recruits demanded by the State, the chiefs drew upon their domestic slaves, former slaves and other defenceless persons among their subjects just as they had done for the Zanzibaris.[25] In 1905 the chief of one such village of unfree labourers had complained to the international commission that a Catholic missionary was telling his men that they were legally entitled to leave him, either to sign labour contracts with the State or to return to their homes. The chief went on to explain that he had been given these men by one Lieutenant Lothaire at the end of the 'Arab' wars in 1894, and that the chief still needed them and their descendants to work his coffee and rice plantations and to provide the porters requisitioned by the State.[26]

Along the trail eastward from Stanleyville settlements of *arabisés* (Islamicised Africans) provided porters and provisions to the European officials much as they had to their former Zanzibari masters. A British vice-consul reported as follows:

> In some instances these porters are literally slaves, and are considered so both by their masters and themselves. They formerly belonged to Bangwana [waungwana] raiders. When the slaves were emancipated they were supposed to leave their masters, though hardly any did so, and they immediately returned. The State then made the masters 'Chiefs' and when porters are wanted these Chiefs are called upon to supply them. They naturally send these former slaves, who cannot refuse to go.[27]

In 1909 former Zanzibari dependants still furnished rice and porterage along the eastern part of the main road from Stanleyville to Lake Albert.[28]

Despite Leopold's systematic destruction of the Free State's archives on the eve of the Belgian takeover, evidence suggests that the Free State's imposition of heavy labour demands on the general population near government posts and along porterage routes was widespread. In the Lado enclave, a part of the Anglo-Egyptian Sudan administered by the Congo, British observers found a situation of 'tyrannical compulsion' very similar to that Glave described along the Lualaba.[29] Although the demands and methods appear to have been much more moderate in the densely populated territories between Lakes Kivu and Tanganyika, the Free State's agents there were under special instructions to avoid any actions that might disturb the local people and thus jeopardise their claim to an area also claimed by Germany.[30]

Some African societies and chiefs were able to use the Free State's presence, as they had the Zanzibaris', to enhance their positions. In the territory of Isangi just west of Kisangani, for example, the Yalusuna, already slave-holders before their conquest by the whites, subjected some additional villages in order to meet their rubber quotas without doing the collection themselves. Eventually, their slaves sought colonial protection from these excesses. Mangbetu rulers in Uele also used their enhanced coercive powers in the early colonial period to exact more work and goods from their own subjects for themselves as well as for the state, and to assert their authority over neighbouring peoples, such as the Mamvu. Increasingly it seemed to their subjects, as well as to outside observers, that the distance between subject and ruler resembled closely that between slave and master.[31]

An indirect way to measure the magnitude of the work obligations on Africans is from the records of the state's exactions in ivory and rubber. Official records indicate that exports of ivory from the Free State's own territories averaged 233 metric tons a year in 1893–7, 244 tons in 1898–

1902, and 189 tons in 1903–7. About 40 per cent of the total came from the eastern Congo, initially from accumulated stocks of 'dead' ivory and then from the hunting of live elephants.[32]

The porterage of ivory, as well as of requisitioned food and building materials, was widespread and burdensome in the 1890s. There was also a growing head and canoe porterage on the routes that brought supplies to the Lualaba from the Nile and from Lake Tanganyika. As with other kinds of exactions, force was regularly employed in securing this labour. Along the Uele east of Bima, for example, two armed attacks were employed in 1891 to convince the Bakango to furnish canoemen for the state.[33] In 1896–7 small villages of Kibali were raided for porters, who were led off tied together, leaving behind 'a good number' of killed and wounded.[34] An indication of volume is the estimate that the transport service westward from Rejaf on the Nile moved 4,000 two-man loads in six months in 1899 'without too much resort to arms'.[35]

As ivory supplies dwindled, the state imposed far greater labour prestations in the form of compulsory wild rubber collection. The eastern Congo exported between 1,350,000 and 1,800,000 kilos of rubber a year between 1901 and 1907, as the region's share of the Free State's rubber exports rose from 22 to 38 per cent.[36] To meet their assigned quotas administrators had to press more and more African villages into service. The disagreeable nature of the collecting and the time and work necessary to meet the ever rising quotas made the rubber tax the most generally hated aspect of Free State rule and provoked a number of rebellions. The first major revolt against excessive rubber quotas in the region, in Aruwimi in 1895, was punished by the imposition of fines in rubber on top of the rubber quotas.[37] That district also saw new turmoil in 1903.[38] Other revolts in western Uele were put down by the military, which enforced rubber collection. Uere-Bili zone, for example, had produced 2,800 kilos of rubber in December 1903, but a year later monthly returns jumped to 6,200 kilos after a military occupation of Likafi and Zia territories, and averaged 8,600 kilos a month during the spring of 1905.[39]

Revolts such as these stirred critics in Belgium and raised a storm of protest in Britain. In response, the Free State undertook the first major reform of its labour tax. By a decree of 18 November 1903 prestations were limited to a maximum of forty hours a month per adult male. However, district administrators were told that their contributions to the Treasury 'must not be less than those of the previous year'; on the contrary, an increase must be aimed at.[40]

Not surprisingly, the international commission's report, published in November 1905, did not consider the reform law of November 1903 to have produced significant improvements. The emphasis on sustaining and increasing production led to exactions in goods that almost everywhere exceeded the forty-hour limit. The commissioners found that demands for food and building materials and labour corvées for maintaining roads and telegraph routes were frequent, widespread and very much disliked by

Africans, especially those close enough to government outposts to be called upon constantly or at short notice.[41]

During the years of its administration, the Free State forced Africans to produce for the international economy, yet it did little to create a free market in labour or goods. In place of slavery and tribute, it relied on a system of forced labour and forced requisitioning of goods. The negative effects of these prestations on labour recruitment were felt in three main areas: (i) the depression of real earnings because labour was often paid in arbitrary assortments of overvalued goods, (ii) the depression of wage rates generally, but especially for government employees, and (iii) shortages (especially of food) resulting from disincentives to the operation of local markets because of these low wages.

The payment of wages in kind, instead of in currency, was bound up with the state's dominance of the economy generally. Since the state almost monopolised exports, employment and imports, it made sense (at least to the bookkeepers) not to introduce a money economy. Payment in kind reinforced the state's control of the economy by depriving Africans of any loose change they might be tempted to spend on the baubles of itinerant peddlers. Despite its simplicity the system did not work smoothly. At one government station in Upper Ituri zone, for example, 60 per cent of the goods stored for labour payments in January 1906 consisted of beads of no value or interest to the local inhabitants. Later that year a state inspector reported that porters and canoemen at another station went unpaid because there had been no goods in stock for seven months. Five years later at a third station there was 'continuous lack of goods'.[42] Even where there was an abundance and variety of goods, the individual worker, as a practical matter, had no hope of exercising the free choice of goods he was promised by law. As a British vice-consul noted: 'It is impossible for a busy chef de poste to escort from 50 to 100 natives around the store, and they have to take what he gives them.'[43] Finally, the values assigned to the goods were often artificially high, in practice making the already low wage rates even lower.[44]

The new Belgian Congo promised to alter this system, though real change was slow to come. Just as the Free State had long followed Zanzibari practices, this new administration also inherited attitudes and patterns of behaviour from the Free State. One of the main legacies was the tendency to ignore the problems caused by a lack of incentive and freedom in the labour system and to blame the Africans instead for the failings of the system. Throughout this period, when called upon to justify the extension of this quasi-feudal economy that preferred direct obligations in labour and goods to a money economy, colonial authorities had a ready answer. Africans must be brought out of their native indolence and taught the value of work.

How long the process of education need last was a difficult question; some would still be talking publicly in those same terms in the 1950s! Coercion and restriction of economic choice clearly suited purposes that went far beyond this civilising mission and that were far less idealistic. Thus reform came slowly and reluctantly, more in response to external political pressures than to the dynamics of the internal process of 'education' under way in the colony. Indeed, pressures from below for moving on to the next stage seemed to trouble administrators, not please them. For example, in March 1909 an official circular explained to puzzled local administrators how they were to deal with Africans who wanted to produce more rubber than their tax quotas. The vice-governor general informed officials that the government was in favour of voluntary labour 'in principle' but his description of the free market was identical to tax collection: voluntary labour should be paid at the same low rate as remuneration for the rubber tax and chiefs should likewise receive the standard indemnity of 5 per cent of the value. Why this peculiar model of a 'free market' economy? The vice-governor's explanation showed he esteemed cheap labour over free labour: 'Thus, in rewarding voluntary labour at a rate above that of the tax, we would risk *artificially* raising the local salary rate and giving an *unjustified* increment to the products of native industry.'[45] The British vice-consul was of the opposite opinion. He declared 'Give the native the opportunity of freely earning money and he will be only too glad to get quit of his obligation to the State by the payment of two francs per month.'[46]

Conclusion

The history of slavery in the eastern Congo between 1850 and 1910 is full of blurred boundaries and ambiguity. In precolonial societies slave wives and free wives shared many disabilities. Ordinary subjects of powerful rulers often found it hard to differentiate their subjection from slavery. The Zanzibari conquest produced large numbers of captives who, if not redeemed, became a servile labour force. Of these new slaves some were soon dead from disease, combat wounds or overwork. Others earned their freedom by surviving a term as porters, while a third group remained in bondage to the Zanzibari and chiefly allies.

The Congo Free State emancipated some male slaves but generally assigned them to a lifetime of service to the state. The Free State also created new forced-labour systems that Africans and outside observers found it hard to distinguish from slavery. Under the Free State and Belgian rule neither slave wives nor male slaves who remained under the control of African masters experienced much change in status.[47]

Like the colonial administrators, modern historians might arbitrarily designate one part of this complex spectrum of servitude as 'slavery' and insist the rest were 'free' people, but the resulting definitional clarity would serve to obscure the larger historical dynamic. Even the more thoughtful colonial officials suspected that the line between their forced recruitment and the Zanzibaris' slave raids was arbitrary and self-serving.[48]

Slavery & Forced Labour in the Eastern Congo 1850–1910

Recognising the ambiguities inherent in African and colonial institutions of subordination and in modern notions of freedom enhances understanding of the historical processes at work in the eastern Congo as it passed through multiple regimes, all intent on profiting from its human, animal and mineral resources.

Notes

1. This history is recounted more fully in David Northrup, *Beyond the Bend in the River: African Labour in Eastern Zaire, 1865–1940* (Athens, OH, 1988); David Northrup, 'The ending of slavery in the eastern Belgian Congo', pp.462–82 in Suzanne Miers and Richard Roberts (eds), *The End of Slavery in Africa* (Madison, WI, 1988); and P. Ceulemans, *La question arabe et le Congo (1883–1892)* (Brussels, 1959).
2. Igor Kopytoff and Suzanne Miers, 'Introduction. African "Slavery" as an institution of marginality', in Suzanne Miers and Igor Kopytoff (eds) *Slavery in Africa: Historical and Anthropological Perspectives* (Madison, WI, 1977), pp.3–14; Claire C. Robertson and Martin Klein, 'Women's importance in African slave systems', in Claire C. Robertson and Martin Klein (eds), *Women and Slavery in Africa* (Madison, WI, 1983), pp.3–17; Paul E. Lovejoy, *Transformations in Slavery: A History of Slavery in Africa* 2nd edn (Cambridge, 2000), pp.1–15, 283–7.
3. Robert J. Steinfeld, *The Invention of Free Labour: The Employment Relation in English and American Law and Culture* (Chapel Hill, NC, 1991); Tom Brass and Marcel van der Linden (eds), *Free and Unfree Labour: The Debate Continues* (Bern, 1997); Stanley L. Engerman (ed.), *Terms of Labour: Slavery, Serfdom, and Free Labour* (Stanford, CA, 1999); and David Eltis (ed.), *Coerced and Free Labour: Global Perspectives* (Stanford, CA, 2002).
4. Northrup, *Beyond the Bend*, pp.16–19. An early study of the Lega is Charles Delhaise, *Les Warega (Congo Belge)* (Brussels, 1909), pp.41, 63.
5. Verney Lovett Cameron, *Across Africa*, new edn (London, 1885), p.290. Cameron makes clear that most Wagenia had no interest in owning slaves, a point that is also stressed by Sidney Langford Hinde, *The Fall of the Congo Arabs* (London, 1897), p.157.
6. G. De Bauw, 'La zone Uere-Bomu', *Belgique Coloniale*, 17 February 1901, pp.73–4; C. R. Lagae, *Les Azande ou Niam-Niam. L'organisation zande. Croyances religieuses et magiques. Coutumes familiales* (Brussels, 1926) pp.46–53; D. T. Lloyd, 'Precolonial economic history of the Avongara Azande c. 1750–1916' (unpublished PhD dissertation, University of California, Los Angeles), pp.254–74; Curtis A. Keim, 'Women in slavery among the Mangbetu c. 1800–1910', in Robertson and Klein, *Women and Slavery*, pp.144–59.
7. David Livingstone, *The Last Journals of David Livingstone, in Central Africa from Eighteen Hundred and Sixty-five to his Death*, ed. Horace Waller (New York, 1875), pp.305, 310.
8. Birhakaheka Njiga, 'La principauté de Nyangezi: essai d'histoire socio-économique (1850–1960)', mémoire de licence en histoire, Institut Supérieur Pédegogique, Bukavu (hereafter ISP), 1978, 1, pp.142–3; Assan Kabemba, 'Les rapports entre Arabes et Manyema dans l'histoire du XIXe siècle', *Cahiers du CERUKI*, séries C2 (Sciences Humaines), No. 1 (1979), p.45; Cyr. Van Overbergh, Preface to Delhaise, *Warega*, pp.xiv–xv.
9. Curtis Keim, 'Long distance trade and the Mangbetu', *Journal of African History*, 24 (1983), pp.1–22; Livingstone, *Last Journals*, pp.428, 431; Cameron, *Across Africa*, pp.319–28; Tippu Tip, *Maisha ya Hamed bin Muhammed el Murjebi yaani Tippu Tip*, supplement to East African Swahili Committee Journals, 28.2 (1958) and 29.1 (1959) [also Nairobi, East African Literature Bureau, 1966], p.111.
10. Livingstone, *Last Journals*, pp.292–396; Henry M. Stanley, *In Darkest Africa, or the Quest,*

Rescue, and Retreat of Emin, Governor of Equatoria (London, 1890), Vol. 2, pp.84–7; Kabemba, 'Rapports entre Arabes et Manyema', pp.31–46.

11 Tippu, *Maisha*, pp.99–107.

12 Musée Royal d'Afrique Centrale, Section Historique (hereafter MRAC), R.G. 1078, L. N. Chaltin, Notes redigées sur la question arabe, carnet 1, p.20; Belgium, Ministère des Affaires Etrangères, Archives Africaines, Brussels (hereafter AA), D(387)4, Dhanis to Fivé, 1893?; cf. Senga Ongala, 'Les arabisés Kusu et la création et l'évolution du poste de Walikale (1901–1954)', Travail de fin d'études, ISP, Bukavu, 1978, pp.32–34; Henry M. Stanley, *Through the Dark Continent* (London, 1878), 2, pp.129–30.

13 Cameron, *Across Africa*, pp.256, 305; Norman R. Bennett (ed.), *Stanley's Despatches to the New York Herald, 1871–1872, 1874–1877*, (Boston, MA, 1970), Nyangwe, 28 October 1876, pp.324–5.

14 Camille Coquilhat, *Sur le Haut-Congo* (Paris, 1888), pp.415–16.

15 Tippu Tip to Mahomed Masood and Seif bin Ahmed, Stanleyville, no date. Translation in Great Britain, Public Record Office, Foreign Office, FO 84/1975 No. 8, received 21 December 1888.

16 AA, BMC(46)11, Isidore Tobback, Journal, p.18; Chaltin, Notes, pp.20, 34; Le Clement de St.-Marcq, *Mouvement Géographique*, 25 May 1890, p.42; Senga, 'Les arabisés Kusu', p.34; Hinde, *Fall of Congo Arabs*, pp.183–5.

17 Cameron, *Across Africa*, p.285; Richard Stanley and Alan Neame (eds), *The Exploration Diaries of H. M. Stanley* (London, 1961), 7 November 1876; Stanley, *Through the Dark Continent*, 2, pp.117–20, 30; Coquilhat, *Haut-Congo*, p.427.

18 Northrup, *Beyond the Bend*, pp.29–33.

19 The most recent of a large number of works is Adam Hochschild, *King Leopold's Ghost: A Story of Greed, Terror, and Heroism in Colonial Africa* (Boston, MA, 1998).

20 Van Eetvelde, 'Rapport au roi', 25 January 1897, *Bulletin Officiel de l'Etat Indépendent du Congo* (1897), pp.47–9.

21 In Ceulemans, *Question arabe*, pp.53–4.

22 *Ibid.*, pp.225, 233–34; Tobback, Journal, p.20; AA, AE(200)4, Capitain Descamps to GG, Mtoa, 12 December 1894 and 8 February 1895. For the missions see David Northrup, 'A Church in search of a State: Catholic Missions in Zaïre, 1879–1930', *Journal of Church and State*, 30 (1988), pp.313–19.

23 AA, AE(350)528, No. 330, 21 January 1905; the commissioner had given the order, but compliance was not universal: in 1906 an agent named Moro in Upper Ituri was still stationing armed African sentinels in isolated posts, as a result of which orders were given not to renew his contract. AA, IRCB(722)73/II, 29 September 1906.

24 'Cruelty in the Congo Free State. Concluding extract from the journals of the late E. J. Glave', *Century* 54 (September 1897), pp.705–6.

25 See the remarks of the Rev. A. De Clercq, former Provincial of the Scheut missionaries in the Congo Free State, and Captain R. Dubreucq, a Free State administrator, Conseil Colonial, *Compte Rendu Analytique* 1908/9, pp.165–7. Their indications of the importance of slaves in providing a labour force apply specifically to the Kasai and Equator provinces, but suggest the practice was more general. For the Aruwimi district of the eastern Congo see Mitchell to Nightingale, Stanleyville, 27 November 1907, Great Britain, *Parliamentary Papers*, Africa (No. 1), No. 29, p.59.

26 AA, AE(349–350)528, Commission d'Enquête, dispositions, No. 346.

27 Mitchell to Nightingale, Bafwesendi, 18 September 1907, Great Britain, *Parliamentary Papers*, Africa, No. 1(1908), No. 23, p.48.

28 FO403/417 in No. 35, Gerald Campbell, 'Report on a tour of the Province Orientale, Aruwimi, and Equator Districts', p.60.

29 'Report by Dr. Milne on the administrative methods of the Congo Free State in the Upper Nile Valley', 1899; FO 403/304 in No. 97, pp.202–3. Reginald Wingate, 'Note on the present Administration in the Lado Enclave', Khartoum, 23 November 1904, FO 403/364, p.25.

30 Zaire, Archives de la Sous Région du Kivu, Uvira: Rapports de reconnaissance, Luvungi, 1904–9, *passim*; Emile J. Vandewoude (ed.), *Documents relatifs à l'ancien district du*

Kivu (Léopoldville, Section Documentation, Bureau Archives, 1959), No. 1 Instructions concernant territoires litigieux, 1900; Instructions, 1902, No. 48 Rapports mensuels sur la situation générale, Uvira, 1903–5.

31 AA, D(385), Rapport d'enquête, chefferie de Yamfira, territoire d'Isangi, district d'Aruwimi, no date.
32 *Bulletin Officiel de l'Etat Indépendent du Congo* 1894, p.50; 1895, p.10; 1896, p.44; 1897, p.116; 1898, p.60; 1899, p.80; 1900, p.45; 1901, p.113; 1902, p.64; 1903, p.71; 1904, p.65; 1905, p.25; 1906, p.83; 1907, p.432; 1908, p.139.
33 Lieutenant Gustin, 'Vers le Nil', *Mouvement Géographique* (1898), col. 229; cf. G. De Bauw, 'La Zone Uere-Bomu', *Belgique Coloniale*, 17 February 1901, p.74.
34 H. Bodart, 'Journal Personnel', pp.27–8; AA, D(382)9/1.
35 Chaltin, Journal, 7 October 1899.
36 Northrup, *Beyond the Bend*, p.58, Table 3.2.
37 Glave, 'Journal [19/20 February 1895]', 54:706; Chaltin, Journal, 10 September 1895.
38 *Tribune Congolaise*, 27 August 1903.
39 AA, IRCB(772)73: Extracts from monthly reports of Uere-Bili.
40 Costermans à MM les Commissaires de district et Chefs de zone, Boma, 29 February 1904, No. 1283/g, enclosed testimony of H.A. Delhaye, 20 October 1904, Commission d'Enquete, procès verbal No. 15, AA, AE(349)528.
41 Janssens, 'Rapport d'enquête', pp.169, 184–5.
42 AA, IRCB(722)73/II, Rapport par M. Lund d'un inspection, 2 May 1906 and Rapport d'Inspection, Poste de Rungu, Zone de Bomokandi, April 1906; MRAC 50.30.1, Rapport sur l'inspection du Poste de Zobia, transports, 10 February 1911.
43 FO403/410 in No. 43, Gerald Campbell, 'Report on a Tour in the Aruwimi and Haut Ituri, Districts of the Congo State', p.67. MRAC 50.30.517, records from the Buta station, Rubi zone, in October and November 1911 show workers received standardised bundles of Americani cloth, belts, spools of thread, needles, pieces of *coteline*, glasses and indigo cloth.
44 FO403/425, in No. 16 Jack Armstrong, 'Report on the Condition of the Natives of Uele District', 30 September 1910, pp.22–23.
45 MRAC 50.30.66, Vice-governor general, circular No. 2074, Boma, 17 March 1909; emphasis added.
46 Michell to Nightingale, 23 March 1907, Great Britain, *Parliamentary Papers*, Africa No. 1 (1908) in No. 2.
47 E. De Jonghe, *Les formes d'asservissement dans les sociétés indigènes du Congo belge* (Brussels, 1949); Keim, 'Women in slavery', pp. 154–7.
48 See Northrup, 'The ending of slavery in the eastern Belgian Congo', in S. Miers and R. Roberts (eds), *The End of Slavery in Africa* (Madison, WI, 1988).

Four

Legacies of Slavery in North West Uganda
The story of the 'One-Elevens'

MARK LEOPOLD*

Introduction

Following the seizure of power in Uganda by General Idi Amin Dada, on 25 January 1971, the country plunged into a decade of chaos. As Amin's rule went on, it rested increasingly on the support of a small group of people known in Uganda as 'Nubians' or 'Nubi', to which Amin himself was considered to belong. There is now a certain amount of historical literature on the Nubi,[1] who were believed to be the descendants of former slave-soldiers from Southern Sudan. These slave-soldiers had come into what is now Uganda in the late 1880s under the command of a German-born officer known as Emin Pasha, General Gordon's Governor in Equatoria Province of Sudan at the time of the Mahdi's Islamic uprising. It was these soldiers, taken on in 1891 by Frederick Lugard of the Imperial British East Africa Company, who formed the core of the forces used to carve out, not just Uganda, but much of Britain's East African Empire.[2]

In this essay I examine the changing meanings of 'Nubi' identity, from its roots in the Sudanese slave-soldier system to the present day, through a focus on the role of the Nubi in the area of Uganda to which Emin took his troops, known in the colonial era (and still widely referred to in Uganda today) as West Nile district,[3] where I carried out archival and ethnographic research between 1995 and 1998. West Nile is the area north of Lake Albert, to the west of the Nile River as it flows northwards to Sudan. Today this is the north-west corner of Uganda, by the borders with Congo-Zaire and Sudan. In the early twentieth century this area changed imperial hands three times; part of King Leopold's Congo territories until his death in 1909, it reverted to Sudanese authority (then under the Anglo-Egyptian Condominium) before being exchanged with the Uganda Protectorate for a parcel of territory to the east (occupied by the Bari people).[4]

During the Amin era, Ugandans referred to his Nubian supporters as the 'One-Elevens', because many of them had three vertical lines scarred on their cheeks. These scarifications were said, probably correctly, to have originated as marks made by nineteenth-century Sudanese slave-soldiers to identify their captives. At various times, and for different reasons, the 'One-Eleven' markings had been adopted by members of local West Nile 'tribes', such as the Lugbara, the Madi and the Kakwa, for whom over the course of the twentieth century 'Nubi' identity provided an elective, strategic, potential alternative 'ethnicity' to their original ones. Indeed, in many ways, as Omar Kokole suggests,[5] it may be better to see the Nubi as a 'club', rather than as an ethnic group. Membership of the club was based on professing the Muslim faith, and on speaking (not necessarily as mother tongue) a language known as 'KiNubi', a form of southern Sudanese Trade Arabic.

In West Nile, Nubian officers were used as district and county 'Chiefs' to impose British administration and taxation, and came to dominate long-distance trading and much of urban life. The three facial marks of the Nubians, and their lifestyles as traders and soldiers, were increasingly adopted by Lugbara and other local people, becoming, from a fairly early stage in the British administration, a sign of relatively high social status.[6] The district was maintained as a 'closed area' from which outsiders were excluded and cash crops were discouraged, and it became a labour reserve, supplying unskilled labour for the sugar and other plantations in the south of the country. The West Nilers were regarded elsewhere in Uganda as strong, primitive and potentially violent people,[7] and the military role of the Nubi was partially transferred to them, as they became disproportionately involved in the colonial army and other coercive institutions, such as the police and prison services. This was the background from which Idi Amin sprang.

The striking image of the both inscribed and embodied 'One-Eleven' facial markings and their evolving meanings crystallises the complex legacies of slavery in North West Uganda. The story of the Nubi raises many issues about the relationship between slavery and other forms of unfree labour (such as military conscription and forced labour), and about the continuities between precolonial, colonial and postcolonial social forces and formations in the region. In this chapter I explore these issues, from the 1860s to the present day, through an examination of the role of the Nubi in the former West Nile district of Uganda.

The Sudanese Slaving Heritage

Sudanese slaving traditions, as they evolved and adapted to different historical conditions over the centuries, exhibit some unique features in relation to other forms of slavery in the Great Lakes region. Chief among these is the military focus, which adapted to successive state systems and established ways of life and social identities that persisted long after the end of formal slavery. The very name 'Sudan', and indeed the term 'Nubian' (and their cognates, 'Nubi', 'Nuba', 'Nubia', 'Sudi'), although they have meant different peoples and places at different times, nevertheless all derive from terms which connote, basically, both 'Slave', and 'Black'.[8]

The independent Sudanese kingdoms of Darfur, Sennar and Tegali had been based on military slavery since long before the Turko-Egyptian invasion of the Sudan in 1820, while the Egyptian army itself had for centuries had a central core of Black slave troops.[9] From service under the Egyptians, these Sudanese slave-soldiers went on to fight for a succession of different states and independent armed bands. As Douglas H. Johnson summarises their history:

> During a period of about a century, these Sudanese soldiers were sent to many parts of the world. They fought in Greece on the side of the Ottoman Sultan, and in Syria against him: some were lent to Napoleon III as part of Maximilian's army in Mexico: some were sold to the Germans in 1888 to put down the Bushiri rising in Tanganyika: some manned Egyptian garrisons in Somalia, Uganda and Ethiopia. Independent slave armies raised by Sudanese merchants and often incorporating slave soldiers from the Egyptian army, carved out their own empires, the most famous being that of Rabih ibn Fadlallah in what is now Chad, defeated by the French in 1900. Slave soldiers deserted to the Mahdi in the Sudan, or fought stubbornly on the side of Egypt. Sometimes the same soldiers did both....
>
> It was an indigenous institution which was taken over and used by a series of imperial powers (Egypt, Britain and Germany, to name but three). In using it, they changed it, but they also adapted themselves to it.[10]

Military slavery was an important aspect of Sudanese slave systems, but it was not, of course, the only one. There had always been an export trade to the Middle East and elsewhere, and after 1850 slavery in southern Sudan (and later northern Uganda) received a massive boost from the ivory trade based in Khartoum. Slavery and ivory went together, since the raiders (many of whom had been slave-soldiers) could ransom captives for ivory, use them to carry the tusks and other supplies, sell them on as slaves once they reached Khartoum, or indeed recruit them to their ranks (or marry them). Although the trade is usually associated with Muslim Arabs, many Europeans were also involved, among them the first to explore the areas north of Lake Albert, and to discover the upper Congo and the Uele rivers.[11]

Much of the literature treats the trade in terms of a bipartite exchange system of people and tusks (with a remarkably consistent exchange rate of one young slave, male or female, per tusk).[12] In fact, however, there was a third factor in the equation, which had its own consequences; this was guns and ammunition, which could be bartered for either of the other two, and were indeed necessary for the acquisition of both. As Dr Stuhlmann, an official of German East Africa, put it in 1895, in a deposition in the case of the British ivory trader, Charles Stokes, who had been executed by Belgian forces in the Congo for selling arms to a slave:

> The most experienced African travellers consider that it is impossible to separate the trade in ivory from the trade in arms; when an ivory trader starts on an expedition, he must take with him trade arms (and also arms for his defence) a fact which induced the Powers which signed the Brussels Act to make the trade in muzzle-loaders, &c, free.[13]

Given the role of guns in the tripartite exchange relationship, the ivory regime is perhaps best seen as another mutation of the military slavery system, in which arms, whether (as in the Turko-Egyptian army) owned by the state or by the individual soldier, also played a central role. The possession of guns allowed slave-soldiers to transfer their loyalties elsewhere if necessary, either to another state, or to service in one of the armed commercial companies of slavers based in armed camps known as *zara'ib*. Arms also made possible the system of 'living off the land' (i.e. whatever could be extracted from local populations and wildlife), rather than paid service. This, in turn, together with the role of slave-soldiers themselves in capturing and enslaving others (often young women and children), led to the characteristic social structure of these 'armies', which consisted of a relatively small number of armed men accompanied by a much larger number of slaves, porters, wives, children, semi-retired ex-soldiers, and others. All these factors, as I shall show, persisted as legacies long after slavery itself disappeared. Through many mutations, the descendants of the Sudanese slave-soldiers remained simultaneously 'Soldiers, Traders and Slaves',[14] though from time to time one or other of these factors became pre-eminent or faded away.

Two other important and contrasting factors must be mentioned in summarising Sudanese slaving traditions; one is the Islamic element, the other the issue of ethnicity. Soghayroun points out that the Sudanese slavers in Equatoria were mostly followers of the *Maliki* school of Islamic jurisprudence. He suggests that this code (in comparison, for example, with that of the Zanzibari slave traders) is relatively paternalistic in its attitude to the slave-master relationship, and gives (male) slaves some of the same rights as a freeman; for example, slaves could own property, claim their freedom if treated cruelly, act as *Imam*, and even have some rights in arranging their own marriages.[15] If the religious factor allowed a degree of dignity in slave status, however, the ethnic factor limited this. The slave might be a fellow Muslim (indeed, Soghayroun suggests that conversion was one of the slavers' motivations),[16] but he was also a Black African, not an Arab. The Sudanese slaving system fed on a long-standing racial theory, that of 'martial races', biologically and culturally suited for warfare.[17] The persistence of this racialised image of the slave-soldiers is well captured by Idi Amin's British former commanding officer in the King's African Rifles, Iain Grahame, reminiscing about a particularly exhausting route march in the 1950s:

As we finally passed the finishing post, Idi Amin was marching beside me at the head of the column, head held high and still singing ... for all he was worth. Across one shoulder were two bren guns and over the other was a crippled askari. It reminded me of a translation of another KAR marching song:

> It's the Sudi, my boy, it's the Sudi
> With his grim-set, ugly face:
> But he looks like a man and he fights like a man
> For he comes of a fighting race.[18]

Sudanese Slavery in Southern Equatoria

The arrival of the slavers, probably some time after 1850, was (as far as anyone knows) the first encounter the people of what was to become West Nile district, then seen as the southern tip of Sudan's Equatoria Province, had with outsiders who possessed radically different technologies (especially guns) and came from a very different kind of society. The West Nilers were members of small-scale, decentralised societies of the kind social anthropologists used to call 'acephalous segmentary lineage systems'. Although John Middleton, the anthropologist of the largest West Nile group, the Lugbara, claimed that they were little affected by slavery, Lugbara speakers from the north of the district have distinct oral historical traditions of slavery (Middleton's main fieldwork site was further south). Samson Ayub Geria from Maracha County was, at the time of my fieldwork, Principal of a Teacher Training College in Arua town (the capital of West Nile District). In 1973, he produced an undergraduate dissertation for the History Department of Makerere University, based on extensive oral research in his home county, which is worth quoting at length, for its viewpoint from the position of the enslaved population, rather than the more frequently seen perspective of the slave society.[19]

Geria identifies two groups of slavers, the first (known locally as *Tukuria* or *Kuturia*) in his informants' grandparents' generation (c1841–68), the second (the *Wolo-Wolo* or *Jahadia*) later on:

> The activities of both the Tukuria and Wolo-Wolo, according to the Northwestern Lugbara, were identical. Both groups came principally for slaves and cattle. Each group brought with it black attendants, who were most probably Nubians and Bari.
> The Arabs usually made surprise attacks on villages, usually at daybreak. They would first shoot their guns in the air to frighten the villagers, who would panic and run off into hiding, leaving behind their cattle and children. The Arabs would kill all the children of tender age but would take away the older children as slaves. They would capture all able-bodied men who were not able to run away in good time or were discovered in their hiding places. They killed all senile people. They drove away all the abandoned cattle, and either ate or took away a lot of the abandoned food

and foodstuffs. Lastly, they set houses and granaries on fire, leaving the place completely desolate.

The captured slaves were tied together by their necks and were taken into the Sudan. To help them identify their run-away slaves, the Arabs marked their captures' cheeks by making three deep vertical cuts on each cheek. The slaves walked the whole distance to the Sudan and were forced to carry heavy loads including ivory. However, children were allowed to ride cattle as they were too young to walk such a long distance. Any slave who became too weak to continue the journey was either left in the wilderness to die a slow death or was shot down.

The main slave route passed through the following stations: Rubu, Gbegbe, Bangule, Pilima (now in Zaire), Yei, Juba and Khartoum. However, some of the slaves stopped at Yei which was the main slave-market for the southern regions of the Sudan. On reaching the markets and Yei and Khartoum, the slaves were sold as domestic slaves.[20]

Geria's informants also spoke of local resistance to the slavers:

The Northwestern Lugbara elders say that many people picked up courage to fight back against the Arabs with just bows and arrows, or managed to escape safely because as they put it, 'when the gunner was busy loading and pounding his gun, in the meantime one got ample time to run away.' Furthermore, these guns could be put out of action by rain, thus rendering their users defenceless. Lastly, what commonly encouraged the Northwestern Lugbara to resist the Arabs was when the latter ran out of ammunition. In such a case many Arabs would be killed and the killers managed to rescue their relatives and any cattle the Arabs might have captured. It is said that the guns which the local people took away from the dead and run-away Arabs were used in various non-military ways. They were dismantled and their wooden parts were used as hoe handles or walking sticks, and their metal parts would be smelted and forged into bracelets and earrings.[21]

Sir Samuel Baker also wrote of resistance to slavery among the Lugbara's neighbours, the Madi, citing 'the destruction of a station belonging to Abou Saood in the Madi country. This Zareeba had been under the command of a vakeel named Jusef, who had exasperated the natives by continual acts of treachery and slave hunting. They had accordingly combined to attack the station at night, and had set fire to the straw huts, by shooting red-hot arrows into the inflammable thatched roofs.'[22] In December 1877, the German/Russian adventurer, Wilhelm Junker, accompanied the slaver Ahmed Atrush, on a raid into 'Lubari [ie Lugbara] Land'.[23] He describes a raid from the viewpoint of the slave camp itself:

As soon as it [the Eid feast on 15–18 December] was over the raids were continued. At cockcrow the camp was all alive and the men told off for the ghazweh set out. The many voices in the early concert bore witness to a large community of fowls. There could not have been less than a thousand of these stolen birds; Atrush alone had eighty, and all the officers and Nubian soldiers had their poultry yard.

To the losses of the natives in oxen, goats, and sheep, to the wasting of their fields, and destruction of their huts, was added the theft of women and children. In the hunt for slaves neither age nor sex is spared. Whatever fell into the hands of the robbers was driven to the camp, and of course the men were able to get away more easily than the women and children. The Makarakas were not above taking even the old women from their homes, so long as they were capable of working in the fields, but those who were disabled or too weak were set at liberty again.[24]

Emin Pasha and the Ethnogenesis of the Ugandan Nubi

The eradication of these slaving gangs, which were raiding throughout the southern part of what was then Sudan's Equatoria Province, was the task given to the Province's new Governor, Emin Pasha (a friend of Junker's) in 1878. A German doctor, christened Eduard Schnitzer, he had converted to Islam and adopted the Turkish form ('Emin') of the fairly common Arabic name (usually transliterated 'Amin') signifying 'Faithful'. His main interests were in natural history, and he continued to collect specimens throughout his adventures.[25]

In the early 1880s, an Islamic revolt against Egyptian rule in Sudan, led by Mohammed Ahmed, known as the Mahdi, swept across Sudan. Slave-soldiers fought on both sides. Emin and his troops (many of whom were former slave-soldiers)[26] were forced south, towards the southern tip of Equatoria, to the area later known as West Nile, with garrisons in the ports of Dufile on the Nile and Wadelai by Lake Albert. By 1885, Emin and his men were surrounded by hostile African forces – Mahdists to the north and the Bunyoro kingdom to the south. For four more years, they lived 'off the land', until the Welsh-American adventurer Henry Morton Stanley, sponsored by a variety of imperial interests, arrived from the west coast of Africa with the 'Emin Pasha Relief Expedition', and took him off to the east coast,[27] leaving behind most of his soldiers under two rival commanders, Selim Bey and Fademulla (or Fadl el Maula) Bey.[28] According to Kokole,[29] the former was a member of the 'Makaraka' [Azande?] tribe, the latter a Lugbara. In 1998, I was proudly shown by an ageing Nubian man in Arua an illustration of Selim in his Egyptian uniform.

Two years after Emin's departure with Stanley, in August 1891, Frederick Lugard, in charge of a force of the Imperial British East Africa Company (IBEAC) arrived at Selim's base (Fadl el Maula having rebelled and gone off with a number of the troops) in search of the men he considered to be 'the best material for soldiery in Africa'.[30] Lugard described Selim as 'an enormous Sudanese, stout, and of a giant's stature ... [H]e struck me ... as a man of very considerable character.'[31] After some persuasion, Selim agreed to join Lugard's troops, pending the approval of the Egyptian ruler, the Khedive. By this time, Selim had some 600 armed men, each of whom (in keeping with the traditions of the slave armies) had 'an average of eleven unarmed followers. These followers consisted of (1) women (wives, concubines, and female slaves), children and men slaves; (2) the similar establishments of those who had died or been killed in the Sudan; and (3) the Lendu [locally recruited slaves and "servants"].'[32] By this stage, they also included several second-generation 'Nubians'. As O.W. Furley put it:

> Lugard was unable to offer the Sudanese any establishment in the service of the Company and could only offer them regular pay at such time as the Company and the Khedive might agree, and Lugard was fully aware that such agreement might take a year to materialise. Lugard's idea was that the troops and their followers should meanwhile live off the land... The troops had had no pay for ten years, living on plunder meanwhile, while the newer recruits had never been under proper military control. In some companies, self-promotions had been prolific, and majors, captains, sergeants and corporals abounded, to the confusion of a handful of luckless privates. This was the task facing Lugard then; he... had to lead a whole community into fresh territory and settle them there, knowing full well that their habit was to plunder and loot wherever they went.[33]

While most of Selim's men went off with Lugard, Fadl el Maula and his force remained by the Nile alternately allying themselves with, and fighting, the Mahdists. According to Collins, around 800 of Fadl el Maula's people went south to join up with Selim's forces in 1891, and when the Belgian Congolese officer Captain Van Kerkhoven arrived in the area in 1892, only some 500 men were left in the area that was to become West Nile. It is in this place that the focus of the present study lies, so I will not discuss the involvement of the Sudanese troops in the 'Uganda Mutiny' of 1897, nor their wider role in the creation of the various colonial states of East and North-east Africa and their establishment of settlements around the region (in Uganda, notably in Bombo, Hoima and Entebbe), all of which are topics that have been covered extensively elsewhere.[34] In Arua town, this wider history is reflected in the names of the various suburbs associated largely with the Muslim population, names such as Kenya Village and Tanganyika Village, which speak of the British military service record of their Nubian inhabitants. It was also reflected in many of the conversations and interviews I had with their descendants in the late 1990s.[35] As Soghayroun emphasises, the Sudanese in this period acted as Muslim missionaries in the area, where many settled permanently, in some cases after retiring from British military service.[36] They also brought their *lingua franca*, KiNubi. In 1899, a British officer remarked on the high number of 'natives' who spoke a 'low-class Arabic', while a Christian missionary source noted that 'As a general rule the tribes living in the vicinity of the Nile north of Wadelai know a fair amount of Arabic.'[37]

While the British were busy with their Nubian allies to the east and south, the area north of Lake Albert and west of the Nile was occupied after 1892 by troops of King Leopold's Congo Free State. Now referred to as the 'Lado Enclave', it changed hands several times in the course of the scramble for Africa, reverting to the (then Anglo-Egyptian) Sudan in 1910 on Leopold's death, and finally ceding its southern part (the future West Nile) to the Uganda Protectorate in 1914. Leopold's rule was harsh but intermittent and faded away after the Anglo-Congolese Agreement of 1906, which ended any realistic prospect of continued Belgian control.[38] The area became prey to European commercial ivory hunters, as the last place in Africa where they could evade all game laws and take as much ivory as they could get hold of.[39] The local population was once more terrorised by the demand for ivory and its corollaries of forced labour, looting and an influx of guns. The historian of British imperial hunting, John MacKenzie, describes the Lado Enclave in this period as being the scene of 'the swansong of the professional European ivory hunter'.[40] The Sudanese period was brief and there was little attempt to administer the district, despite the efforts of the former hunter, C.H. Stigand, Governor of Mongalla Province, who, in a posthumously published book, described 'the Lugware [i.e. Lugbara] country' as:

> [I]n a state of utter disorganisation, practically every village was hostile to its neighbours, whilst it had been the practice of the better armed and more organised tribes on the north and east to make continual raids on them, seizing women and children, stock, and all moveable property.
>
> On the coming of the Sudan Government these raids ceased and the Lugware began to recover from the continual persecution to which they had been subject, but they had fallen into such a lawless state that every man's hand appeared to be turned against his neighbour....
>
> The country ... still remained in a disintegrated state.... Such a state of affairs makes it impossible to institute an effective administration.... The Lugware have been credited with such an evil and truculent disposition.... Their bad reputation has been chiefly fabricated for them by the neighbouring tribes, who have made profit out of their helplessness and capital out of the supposed necessity of inflicting on them incessant punishment.[41]

The Nubi in West Nile, 1914–61

This, then, was the situation faced by the new British District Commissioner of West Nile District, A.E. Weatherhead, whose arrival coincided with the outbreak of the First World War. This meant that it was not until after 1917 that he could begin to try to collect taxes, a process which met with some opposition. For Weatherhead, the solution was obvious. Wherever such resistance occurred, he removed the local 'chiefs' (who had mostly been appointed by the Belgian and Sudanese administration) and replaced them with Nubians loyal to the British. In

1920, he placed the Lugbara as a whole under the rule of a Nubian 'Agent', a post that was not abolished until the late 1920s.[42]

An exemplary Nubi career was that of Fademulla Murjan of Aringa County, born some time around 1886. His father, Murusalli Jalbudelli, a Bari speaker, had been one of Emin Pasha's troops who had settled in Aringa, while his mother was a Lugbara woman. The young Fademulla and two of his older sisters were captured by slave soldiers and taken to Yei, where the girls were sold off as wives to other Nubians (they eventually settled in Nairobi and Bombo). The boy remained with the soldiers, who in 1891 joined up with Lugard's newly formed Uganda Rifles. As the boy grew bigger, he enlisted as a bugler and took part, at the age of about 13, in the battle of 1899 in which Kabaleega of Bunyoro was captured. He went on to fight in Somalia for the 4th Battalion of the King's African Rifles, before returning to Aringa in 1915, shortly after Weatherhead's arrival. In 1916, the latter appointed him Wakil (sub-county Chief) of Rumogi, then in 1927 he became Sultan (County Chief) of Logiri and in 1947 Sultan of Aringa, before retiring in 1951.[43]

The complex relationship between the military slavery heritage and the new demands of the colonial state, is illustrated in an account given by Doka Ali Kujo, a retired District Education Officer, who carried out oral research in Aringa County for his (unpublished) history of Islam in Uganda, written in the 1990s. He tells the story of the coming of Islam to Aringa:

> During the captivity period, two sons of Aringa happened to be captured by the same Jaddyas, who took them to Dufele, which was their bigger barracks of Egyptian-Sudan government in the present Moyo district. Those were Akutre Anyule and Azabo Uruta. They were captured while looking after Urute's cattle at Aliape village in Aringa county. Aringa by then was not yet a county as such, but the name of Aringa of course had already existed in the district before. The boys' funeral rites were ceremonially performed and the people of Aliap gradually forgot about the two boys. As the people at home believed that the boys were taken and killed, it did not happen, as they thought. Akutre and Azabo were still alive and they joined the Sudanese army to serve under Egyptian in various places in Uganda. Here in West Nile, they were at Wadilai, later they moved to Mahagi and Kavillis [all Emin Pasha's forts] . These two places are on the Western side of Lake Albert.
>
> Akutre and Azabo became Muslims and they were moved to Kampala by Captain Lugard with the permission of Egyptian leader Ismail Khedive. Akutre then was given a new name of Islam, he was called Fadimula Ali, while Azabo was called Bilali. After having retired the service of the British Uganda Rifles, Fadimula Ali made an attempt to come to Adjumani, hunting game. He happened to meet Nuwa of Goa clan and talked with him about the people in Aringa and he (Fadimula Ali) promised to come back soon. Fadimula Ali when he returned from Buganda to Aringa he was already a married man. He came in 1912 and settled at Bujo.

In Doka's account, Fadimula met some British officers who were surveying the district prior to its incorporation into the Uganda Protectorate and, due to his knowledge of KiSwahili, was able to act as translator for them:

> Fadimula was a very significant figure to look at when he met with those whites, the whites straight away had interest in him as being someone knowledgeable and civilised. Fadimula then received a nickname with whom he was popularly called in Aringa. He was called Aduu.... Aduu was in time to come home to have the chance of becoming one of the County Chiefs of West Nile District.... The county Administrations started with the demarcation of counties. Aringa became one of the counties of West Nile and Fadimula Ali Aduu then took the chance of a chiefship of Aringa. It was after when he became a county chief, the idea of Islam came to his mind in 1916... As County Chiefs had their Central Lukiko [council] meetings in Arua, Fadimula Aduu used to come for the meetings and he would come with his food stuffs, enough to take him for one or two weeks before he returned to Aringa. Since he did not eat dead animals, or else an animal slaughtered by a non-Muslim, he was doing all this slaughtering himself. He one day felt he needed some youngmen to assist him in slaughtering animals. But these youngmen must first of all be circumcised so as to become Muslims. One evening at his home, he called the youngmen by name Pale and Ariga. He told them that he (Aduu) would like to Islamise them so they could slaughter the animals for him... So the first batch, who were circumcised at Kulacara were as follows:- Abdala Pale, Musa Kuri, Muhamadu Ariga, Daudi Waiga, Abdula Tula, Abdu Afua and Yusufy Gbagbe...After having heard that Fadimula Ali was appointed a county chief of Aringa, the Nubis with whom they had lived together followed him immediately and settled first in Aringa before they moved to Arua town. As the new Muslims were Islamising in great numbers, the Nubians found it fit for them to stay with their Muslim brothers and sisters. They started marrying Aringa girls and they went on teaching Islam to new Muslim converts.[44]

The Nubi, then, became closely associated with British rule. The earlier interchanges between local people and the Sudanese ensured that, from the start, the role became one that could be adopted by Muslim West Nilers, and it clearly conferred many advantages. In 1925, R.E McConnell, a military doctor who had been in West Nile with Weatherhead in 1918[45] and was stationed in Madi country on the east bank of the Nile as early as 1911,[46] published in the *Journal of the Royal Anthropological Institute of Great Britain and Ireland* an article entitled 'Notes on the Lugwari tribe of Central Africa', in which he noted that 'The Nubi (Mohammedan) distinctive marks of three linear marks on each cheek are also now frequently appearing. These were originally the marks distinguishing the slaves of the invading Nubi troops and are now inseparably connected with being Mohammedanised, and convey some social distinction.'[47] He also remarked of the Lugbara that 'In the King's African Rifles, during the war, they furnished some excellent soldiers. The officers have told me they despaired of them at the beginning, but that when their minds did at last awake to the meaning of their instructions they were among the best of the native soldiers.'[48]

Increasingly, the military way of life of the Nubians became available to West Nilers as one of the few ways, along with migrant manual labour on the plantations of southern Uganda, in which they could earn money and thus pay their taxes. In a sense, over the colonial period the West Nile district as a whole became to some extent 'Nubified', and West Nilers became prominent, not only in the army *per se*, but in the other coercive trades of the state, as police officers, security guards, prison warders, and so on. This became apparent in several of my interviews with elderly men in the late 1990s. One man, for example, told me about working in the Kabaka of Buganda's prison in Mengo in the 1950s and 1960s. West Nilers, he told me, were hired for this work because 'They were frightened of us, the Bantus, so they used us also to frighten their prisoners.'[49]

The relationship between the British and the Nubi was not, however, an unproblematic one. Hansen outlines how, at the Protectorate level, concern rose over the growing numbers of Nubi ex-soldiers, especially in Buganda. They were seen as an immigrant group, which had rendered great services to the government, but which nevertheless represented a potential threat to order. The Nubians were first, after 1923, confined to special areas; to district capitals or to Bombo, north of Kampala, the largest Nubi settlement in the country. Long discussions took place over how they were to be defined, and the initial restrictions applied only to ex-soldiers and their immediate dependants.[50] At the local level, in West Nile, this meant the exile of much of the Aringa Nubi leadership to Arua town (founded by Weatherhead on a site suggested by Stigand). The Nubi chiefs in place throughout the district were replaced from the mid-1920s with Lugbara, Madi, Alur or Kakwa notables. In Aringa, however, enough converts had been made to ensure the continuity of Islam among the leadership of, and throughout, the county.[51]

The concentration of Nubians throughout the major towns of the Protectorate speeded up a process that had begun much earlier: the use of their national and regional networks to develop trading opportunities. They became traders as much as, or more than, soldiers. Hansen quotes the Provincial Commissioner, Eastern Province in 1933, '"The Nubi community as a whole have long since forfeited any right to special consideration", by now, the majority were petty traders or "mere Drones" of no real use to the community.'[52] Schemes to deal with them, however, continually foundered on the problems of defining the Nubians as a group. The administration had to concede that the term could not solely be defined with reference to military service, and that a process which Hansen terms 'Nubianization' had taken place. The definition therefore included not only forces of Emin Pasha, their dependants and descendants, but also 'individuals who, through association with the Nubi community over many years (by adopting Islam and assuming Nubian dress and face markings) "have lost all connection with the tribes from which they originally sprang".[53] The real situation was considerably more complex and dynamic than such a definition could encompass, however, and undoubtedly many people were Nubi when trading in town (or serving in the forces), and Lugbara or Kakwa when they returned to the villages of West Nile.

Increasingly, the Nubis did indeed turn to trade rather than military careers. When the anthropologist John Middleton arrived in Arua town in 1949 he found that:

> The town consists largely of Nubis who are said to be the descendants of Emin Pasha's Sudanese troops... Today, however, there are very few pure-blooded Arab or Sudanese Nubis in Arua, most of them being Lugbara, Kakwa or members of other tribes who have become Muslims and married into Nubi families. They control the hide and skin trade, and deal in other goods in which the profits are too small for larger traders. In addition they control the illicit gin trade in Arua, perhaps the most profitable trade in the district.[54]

The Nubi's links with the military did not, however, disappear, and nor did their propensity to recruit from the people of north-west Uganda, while continuing to reproduce themselves as a group. As the anthropologist of the Alur, Aidan Southall, summarised their role, in an article on the historical roots of Amin's coup:

> The core tradition of the Ugandan army is a Nubi tradition. Any members of those ethnic groups from which the Nubi originally derive... are in the most fundamental sense Nubi as soon as they join the army, especially if they are – or become – Muslim as well ... Nubi culture is as hard to define as Swahili, to which it has several similarities. It is essentially urban and Muslim, tied to the army and to other kinds of service, such as railway station officials, institutional guards, and night watchmen, with shopkeeping and small-time real estate business as adjuncts for those who do not serve or have retired. Although they are cut off from their Sudanese origins, the northwest Uganda peoples, such as the Kakwa, Lugbara and Madi, are not only a direct extension of that culture area, but are also present in the Congo and neighbouring parts of Zaire.[55]

West Nile in the Postcolony, 1962–2000: Idi Amin and the Ethnosuicide of the Nubi

When Uganda attained independence in 1962 there were, famously, only two Ugandan Commissioned Officers in the army, one of whom was Idi Amin. His origins are a matter of speculation; many Ugandans and others claim that he was born outside the country, but there is no evidence of this. His mother was a Lugbara, possibly with Nubi links, his father a Kakwa (from the far north-west of West Nile district, around Koboko). As

Legacies of Slavery in North West Uganda

an upwardly mobile young Muslim West Niler, it was natural for him to join the army and take up the Nubi identity available to him.

I do not intend in this essay to summarise the well-known history of post-Independence Uganda,[56] nor the massive amount of literature on Amin.[57] Elsewhere I have discussed the popular image of Amin, in the West and in Uganda, and its connection with a persisting association of the whole West Nile region with violence and marginality, an association which may be traced back to the period of the slavers' first incursions in the area, and indeed perhaps earlier to the first European fantasies of what lay in the 'Heart of Darkness' that Central Africa was believed to be, long before white people actually went there.[58] Here I want to focus on the Nubi association with Amin's regime and its consequences for the people of West Nile.

Much of both the popular and the academic literature on Amin portrays him and his regime as quintessentially Nubian phenomena.[59] Perhaps the most interesting debate on the character of his rule was the contemporaneous one between Aidan Southall and Ali Mazrui, both based at Makerere University at the beginning of the Amin period, both relocated to Chicago by the end of it. Broadly speaking, Mazrui celebrated Amin, at least at first, as a powerful, masculine African leader, an heir to the Zulu king, Shaka, while Southall deprecated such views.[60] They agreed, however, on the fundamental nature of the regime. Halfway through the Amin period, in 1975, Southall wrote 'Central to my interpretation is the fact that General Amin is a Nubi, and that the history of the Nubi is important for the understanding of contemporary events. The present regime is more and more predominantly a Nubi regime, and its core strength is a Nubi strength.'[61]

Mazrui thinks Southall exaggerates, pointing out that at no time, before or after Independence, were the Nubi a numerical majority in the Ugandan army, but he agrees that:

> the Nubi presence in the Ugandan army is not a sudden alien intrusion but is solidly part of the history of that army from the beginning, and is inextricably linked to the pattern of ethnic affiliations between the West Nile district of Uganda and the adjoining areas of Sudan and Zaire. The Nubi factor in the domestic balance of power in Uganda simply reaffirms once again that the boundaries drawn up by the colonial powers were arbitrary.[62]

As Amin's rule progressed, his power base in the army was progressively reduced to a core group of Nubi (and southern Sudanese) soldiers. Even the other West Nile groups in the army, the non-Muslim Madi, Alur, Lugbara and Kakwa, became successively persecuted. The one-time markings of the Nubi slaves, the three vertical lines scored on each cheek, became a symbol of loyalty to the President, H.E. Field Marshall al Hajji Idi Amin Dada, CBE (Conqueror of the British Empire), etc., etc. Those who wore them were known among the Baganda as the

'One-Elevens'.[63] As the regime began to crumble, even Amin's English henchman, 'Major' Bob Astles, demonstrated his dedication by inscribing the 'One-Elevens' into his face. Illustrating its article by a photograph of Astles showing the marks on his cheek, the African magazine *Drum* commented that 'Such scars are gaining popularity in Uganda and reports have reached *Drum* that people from other tribes have also gone in for this practice and are also learning the Nubian language in order to survive.'[64]

By this time, the very nature of the army had changed. A military career once again became one which involved the opportunity to live 'off the land' (or off the backs of the civilian population), a process which intensified after Amin's notorious expulsion of Uganda's Asian population. If the Nubians had specialised, in parts of Uganda at any rate, in petty trade and small businesses, then the Asians had dominated large- and medium-scale trade and business since the beginning of the colonial era. Their businesses were distributed among Amin's supporters, especially the Nubi troops, and the military life once again gave way to the advantages of trade (especially smuggling and other illegal trades, known in Uganda as *Magendo*).[65] One professional soldier at the time, a Christian West Niler, explained the results to me (with some disgust in his voice) in an interview in 1997.

> I was in the army, but personally I knew by 1977-78 there was no army. The situation we were in really showed militarily... Because at that time, all soldiers were now acquiring big shops, otherwise they had factories. In every town they were just celebrating. The military life, that way of life got lost completely. They were living extravaganza lifestyles, and civil ones, not military at all.[66]

Small wonder, then, that so little opposition was offered when the Tanzanian Army invaded Uganda in 1979. Amin's troops were quickly driven back to, then through, the West Nile, into southern Sudan. Shortly afterwards, the majority of the West Nilers, persecuted by forces from elsewhere in Uganda who took over from the Tanzanians as an occupying force in the district, joined the remnants of the Uganda National Army over the borders into exile in southern Sudan and north-east Zaire. They were joined by West Nilers living elsewhere in the country. Odoga ori Amaza, a Madi medical student at Makerere at the time, found that '[N]o sooner was Amin overthrown than everybody from West Nile became not only Amin's agents, but even a foreigner. We were variously labelled Sudanese, Nubians or Anyanya. People from West Nile, the Kakwa, Lugbara and Madi, in particular, found themselves being singled out as those responsible for Amin's misdeeds.'[67]

The experience of the West Nilers as refugees and their repatriation to the district after 1985 are, perhaps surprisingly, well-researched topics.[68] In exile and later, a key issue became the need to distance themselves from the Amin regime, a particularly important matter for the Kakwa and the Nubians. Virmani describes the latter as being 'especially bitter' about being collectively associated, regardless of their individual affiliations and actions, with the former regime. Many believed that this led to their being neglected by the UN aid agencies after 1979.[69] Among their southern Sudanese hosts, 'the Aringa clan of the Lugbara were praised as excellent petty traders, while the Nubians (a group that included many Kakwa, Lugbara and Madi) were known as entrepreneurs who could see business opportunities "around the corner".'[70] Harrell-Bond reports the Nubis' resistance to agricultural settlement programmes. By 1982, their settlement, known as Tore, had become 'notorious for its ability to subvert food aid ... Relief food was being supplied for a population of over 2,000, while the actual numbers were certainly less than half. With the surplus, some of the settlers were reconstructing their lives around their normal occupation of petty trade and hawking.'[71]

The victory of Yoweri Museveni's National Resistance Army/Movement in 1986 was broadly welcomed, both by West Nilers who had returned to the district and most of those still in Sudan. However, while the vast majority of the West Nilers then returned, a handful of Amin's lieutenants remained in exile with their followers. One of these was Juma Oris, a Nubi of Madi origin who had been one of Amin's cabinet ministers and had close connections with the Sudanese intelligence services.[72] I have discussed elsewhere the consequences of his creation, under Sudanese sponsorship, of a rebel group called the West Nile Bank Front, which raided across the border from Sudan in the mid-1990s, together with a splinter group named the Uganda National Rescue Front Part II.[73] These groups reinstated a pattern familiar from the nineteenth century; attacking West Nile from the north, abducting children, driving away livestock and burning homesteads, until their defeat in 1997. Like their nineteenth-century predecessors, and like their better-known rivals to the east, the Holy Spirit Movement/Lord's Resistance Army, they recruited in part by abducting young boys and training them to kill. Unlike the HSM/LRA, which developed a syncretic religious faith deeply embedded in Acholi traditions,[74] the WNBF and UNRF II were based solidly in the Nubian Muslim traditions of the slave-soldiers. On one occasion, I spoke to a British aid worker who had briefly been captured by a group of WNBF rebels. They told her they were fighting for what they called 'The Lado Republic', a term that meant nothing to her, but something to me.

For the vast majority of West Nile Muslims, however, the Nubi heritage was not, after their return, something to recreate or celebrate. During my fieldwork between 1995 and 1998, only a few older men still showed the 'One-Eleven' scars, and few people called themselves Nubi or Nubian. Since the period of exile, the favoured self-designations have become 'Muslim Madi', 'Muslim Kakwa', 'Muslim Lugbara', etc. Even more common than the latter, 'Aringa' is no longer just the name of a county, but has become an ethno-religious designation meaning 'Muslim Lugbara' and covering much the same people as would in the past have called themselves 'Nubis'. An even stronger sign of the vanishing salience of the term 'Nubian', and the Nubis' re-absorption into the indigenous groups from which most of them came, occurred after I had returned to the UK from fieldwork. I learned from two different sources that in 1999 the Lugbara elders recognised a new clan, created for and by Lugbara-speaking former Nubis and their offspring, a sign of their re-admission to the 'tribal' fold as 'Lugbara Muslims'. The end of the Nubians, as a West Nile group at any rate,[75] seems to be in sight. In retrospect, perhaps, the Amin era, the point at which they appeared as actors on the national scene for the first time since the Uganda Mutiny, may have been an act of ethno-suicide for the imagined descendants of the slave-soldiers.

Conclusion: Legacies of Slavery

In this chapter, I have examined continuities and changes in the Nubi tradition, in terms both of historical events and of how Nubi identity was imagined (by group members themselves and by others) at different times. The metaphor of the 'One-Eleven' markings serves to illustrate a general point about Nubi identity, whether we consider the latter as an ethnicity or a 'Muslim club'. At first sight, the scarification seems like an empty, floating signifier, connoting at different times 'slave', 'colonial soldier', 'trader/smuggler', 'Amin supporter' or whatever meaning the pressure of events might call forth, the only constant being the Islamic faith and a form of Arabic speech. However, a closer look shows that there are tight limits to the range of possible meanings, rooted in the Sudanese slaving traditions of the nineteenth century and in the wider context of these traditions, the relationship between expanding states and the stateless societies on their peripheries.[76] Against this background emerged the various elements of the Nubi tradition: the simultaneous roles of soldier, trader and slave; the tripartite exchange of ivory, slaves and guns; the incorporative social and family structures of the *Zara'ib* armed camps; the pillaging skills involved in 'living off the land'. The salience of these different elements varied over time, but only around a central coherence, creating a tradition that can truly be called a legacy.

Notes

*   This chapter first appeared in modified form in *Africa* 76, 2 (2006), pp.180–99. It is reproduced here with the kind permission of the editorial board and Edinburgh University Press. The research on which this essay is based was funded by the UK Economic and Social Research Council (Research Studentship Award R00429534198), and by the Ioma Evans-Pritchard Junior Research Fellowship at St Anne's College, University of Oxford. My use of 'legacy' in the title reflects my debt to Douglas H. Johnson's 'The structure of a legacy: military slavery in Northeast Africa', *Ethnohistory*

36, 1 (Winter 1989), pp.72–88 and, by the same author, 'Sudanese military slavery from the eighteenth to the twentieth century', in L. Archer (ed.) *Slavery and Other Forms of Unfree Labour* (London and New York, 1988); and 'Recruitment and entrapment in private slave armies: the structure of the Zariba in the Southern Sudan', *Slavery and Abolition* 13, 1 (April 1992), pp.162–3.

1   See I. Soghayroun, *The Sudanese Muslim Factor in Uganda* (Khartoum, 1981); H.B. Hansen, 'Pre-colonial immigrants and colonial servants. The Nubians in Uganda Revisited', *African Affairs* 90 (1991), pp.559–80; O.H. Kokole 'Idi Amin, "the Nubi" and Islam in Ugandan Politics, 1970–1979', in H.B. Hansen and M. Twaddle (eds), *Religion and Politics in East Africa* (London, 1995); and M. Leopold, *Inside West Nile: Violence, History and Representation on an African Frontier* (Oxford, 2005). Earlier work is referenced below.

2   F.D. Lugard, *The Rise of Our East African Empire: Early Efforts in Nyasaland and Uganda* (Edinburgh and London, 1893), Vol.2. See also H. Moyse-Bartlett, *The King's African Rifles: a Study in the Military History of East and Central Africa, 1890–1945* (Aldershot, 1956).

3   West Nile District is now three separate Ugandan Districts: Arua, Moyo and Nebbi.

4   This latter exchange was, of course, *de facto* within the British empire even if there were *de jure* differences between a Condominium and a Protectorate. However, on the ground there were significant differences between the two administrations.

5   Kokole, 'Idi Amin', p.48.

6   See R.E.McConnell, 'Notes on the Lugwari Tribe of Central Africa', *Journal of the Royal Anthropological Institute of Great Britain and Ireland*, 55 (July to December 1925), pp.439–67.

7   I have discussed the image of the West Nilers in Uganda as a whole in M.Leopold, '"The War in the North": Ethnicity in Ugandan press explanations of conflict 1996–97', in T. Allen and J. Seaton (eds), *The Media of Conflict; War Reporting and Representations of Ethnic Violence* (London and New York, 1999).

8   See Johnson, 'Sudanese military slavery', p.151; P.M. Holt and M.W. Daly, *A History of the Sudan*, Fifth edn (London, 2000), p.17; H. Erlich and I. Gershoni, *The Nile: Histories, Cultures, Myths* (New York and London, 2000), p.177.

9   J.J. Ewald, *Soldiers, Traders and Slaves, State Formation and Economic Transformation in the Greater Nile Valley, 1700–1885* (Madison, WI, and London, 1990); R.S. O'Fahey 'Slavery and the slave trade in Dar Fur', *Journal of African History* 14, 1 (1973), pp.29–43. Holt and Daly, *A History*, p.17; Johnson, 'Structure of a legacy', p.73.

10 Johnson, 'Sudanese military slavery'; see also G. Prunier, 'Military slavery in the Sudan during the Turkiyya', *Slavery and Abolition*, 13, 1 (April 1992), p.132; Ahmad Alawad Sikainga, 'Military slavery and the emergence of a Southern Sudanese diaspora in the Northern Sudan, 1884–1954', in J. Spaulding and S. Beswick (eds), *White Nile, Black Blood; War, Leadership and Ethnicity from Kampala to Khartoum* (Asmara, Eritrea, and Lawrenceville, NJ, 2000).

11 R.W. Beachey, 'The East African ivory trade in the nineteenth century', *Journal of African History* 8, 2 (1967), pp.269–90. See also Holt and Daly, *A History*, pp.61–3.

12 See e.g. Sir S.W. Baker, *Ismailia: a Narrative of the Expedition to Central Africa for the Suppression of the Slave Trade Organized by Ismail, Khedive of Egypt* (London and New York, 1895), p.320; E.D. Moore, *Ivory, Scourge of Africa* (New York and London, 1931), Introduction; Beachey, 'East African Ivory trade', p.282; cf. H.J. Fisher, *Slavery in the History of Muslim East Africa* (London, 2001), p.109.

13 'Inclosure 3 in No.308, Memorandum by Dr Stuhlmann', United Kingdom Public Record Office (UKPRO), FO403/218, p.250.

14 Cf. the title of J.J. Ewald, *Soldiers, Traders and Slaves: State Formation and Economic Transformation in the Greater Nile Valley, 1700–1885* (see note 9). This focuses on the pre-colonial Taqali (or Tegali) state in the Nuba Hills region of Sudan.

15 Soghayroun, *Muslim Factor*, p.6 fn.22, citing J.S. Trimingham, *Islam in East Africa* (Oxford, 1959), p.134.

16 Soghayroun, *Muslim Factor*, p.6.

17 See Johnson, 'Sudanese military slavery'.

18 I. Grahame, *Amin and Uganda; a Personal Memoir* (London, 1980), p.39.

19 This point is made, in a different context, in W. James, 'Perceptions from an African

slaving frontier', in L. Archer (ed.), *Slavery and Other Forms of Unfree Labour* (London and New York, 1988), p.131.
20 S.A. Geria, 'A traditional history of the Northwestern Lugbara of Uganda' (unpublished BA dissertation, Department of History, Makerere University, Kampala, 1973), pp.80–81. (A copy of this is in the library of the Makerere Institute for Social Research (MISR)).
21 *Ibid.*, p.81.
22 Baker, *Ismailia*, p.268.
23 W. Junker, *Travels in Africa during the Years 1875–1878*, Trans. A.H. Keane, 3 vols, (London, 1890), p.466.
24 *Ibid.*, pp.467–8.
25 A reliable if now outdated bibliography of the extensive literature on Emin Pasha is D.H. Simpson (ed.), 'A bibliography of Emin Pasha', *Uganda Journal* 24, 2 (1960), pp.138–65. Some more recent works are listed below (the bibliography in I.A. Smith, *The Emin Pasha Relief Expedition* (Oxford, 1972) is particularly helpful).
26 Stigand divides Emin's forces into three groups '(i) Kutiria, who were Dongolan irregulars recruited from the disbanded Nubian forces of the old ivory and slave raiders. These were armed with percussion guns, (ii) Dragomans, local natives armed like the Kutiria ... (iii) Jehadia, or Egyptian regulars, armed with Remingtons. Of these there were comparatively few.' Major C.H. Stigand, *Equatoria, the Lado Enclave* (London/Bombay/Sydney, 1923), p.171. According to Stanley's assistant, Jephson, Emin's soldiers were 'for the most part men belonging to the Dinka, Madi, Boru, Shefalu, Maru Maru, Bongo, Makraka, Mongbutee or Moru tribes' (quoted in Soghayroun, *Muslim Factor*, p.29). As Soghayroun points out, these were closely related to the Southern Equatorian tribes from which many of their 'followers' came. Emin himself wrote of 'the greater part of our soldiers, coming as they do, from our own districts (Makaraka, Dinka, etc.) and having never seen Egypt' (letter to Schweinfurth, 3 March 1886, quoted in Smith, *Emin Pasha*, p.30).
27 On the Relief Expedition, see e.g., Smith, *Emin Pasha*; F. McLynn, *Stanley, Sorcerer's Apprentice* (London, 1991).
28 'Bey', like 'Pasha', is a Turko-Egyptian military rank. On Selim Bey and Fadl el Maula Bey, see R.O. Collins, *The Southern Sudan 1883–1898; a Struggle for Control* (New Haven, CT and London, 1962), pp.70–71, 80–117; Soghayroun, *Muslim Factor*, pp.27–29; O.W. Furley, 'The Sudanese troops in Uganda', *African Affairs* 58, 233 (1959), pp.311–13.
29 Kokole, 'Idi Amin', p.49.
30 Lugard, *Rise*, vol.2, p.134; Moyse-Bartlett, *Rifles*, p.50.
31 Lugard, *Rise*, vol.2, p.209.
32 *Ibid.*, p.217. On the Lendu see also p.205, fn.1.
33 Furley, 'Sudanese troops', pp.311–28, (quote from pp.315–16).
34 Collins, *Struggle for Control*; Furley, 'Sudanese troops'; Moyse-Bartlett, *Rifles*; Soghayroun, *Muslim Factor*.
35 E.g. written statement of Mr K.G., Arua, 27 January 1997 (manuscript in my possession).
36 Soghayroun, *Muslim Factor*, p.13.
37 Both cited in *ibid.*, p.163.
38 R.O. Collins, 'Anglo-Congolese negotiations, 1900–1906', *Zaire* 12, 6 (1958), pp.479–512.
39 R.O. Collins, 'Ivory poaching in the Lado Enclave', *Uganda Journal* 24, 2 (1960), pp.217–28.
40 J.M. MacKenzie, *The Empire of Nature; Hunting, Conservation and British Imperialism* (Manchester, 1988), p.164.
41 Stigand, *Equatoria*, pp.78–9.
42 J.F.M. Middleton, 'Some effects of colonial rule among the Lugbara', in V. Turner (ed.), *Colonialism in Africa, 1870–1960* (Cambridge, 1971).
43 His story is told in E.C. Lanning, 'Sultan Fademulla Murjan of Aringa', *Uganda Journal*, 18, 2 (1954), pp.178–80. There were other Fademulla Murjans, including one who

became overall Agent.
44 Doka Ali Kujo, 'The Coming of Islam in Uganda 1830–1843' [sic] n.d. (photocopied typescript in my possession), pp.6–8.
45 See A.E. Weatherhead, Diaries, Rhodes House Library, Oxford, mss.Afr.s.1638. Entry for 21 August 1918 and subsequent entries.
46 See Provincial Commissioner Northern Province to Chief Secretary, 7 October 1911, Uganda National Archives, Entebbe, Secretariat Minute Papers 1910–1929, 2nd Series, A46/165/item 59.
47 McConnell, 'Lugwari', p.447
48 Ibid., p.433.
49 Interview, B.D., Arua town, 16 March 1997. See my 'The roots of violence and the reconstruction of society in North Western Uganda' (unpublished D.Phil thesis, University of Oxford, 2001).
50 Hansen, 'Pre-colonial immigrants', pp.567–8.
51 Doka, 'Islam', pp.8–9. See also J. Middleton, *The Lugbara of Uganda*, second edn (Fort Worth, TX and London, 1992), p.5.
52 Hansen, 'Pre-colonial immigrants', p.569.
53 Ibid., pp.569–70.
54 John Middleton, 'Trade and markets among the Lugbara of Uganda', in P. Bohannon and G. Dalton (eds), *Markets in Africa* (Chicago, 1962), p. 571.
55 A. Southall, 'General Amin and the coup: great man or historical inevitability?', *Journal of Modern African Studies*, 13, 1 (1975), p.89.
56 On which see especially the collections edited by H.B. Hansen and M. Twaddle: *Uganda Now* (London, 1988); *Changing Uganda* (London, 1991); *From Chaos to Order: the Politics of Constitution-making in Uganda* (London, 1995); *Developing Uganda* (Oxford, 1998).
57 M. Jamison, *Amin and Uganda: an Annotated bibliography* (Westport, CT and London, 1992), p.xiii, citing 406 'scholarly, research level works [on Amin and the period of his rule in Uganda] in English and housed in libraries in North America'.
58 Leopold, 'Roots of violence'.
59 See especially the works by Southall and Mazrui listed below, and also Hansen, 'Pre-colonial immigrants'; Johnson, 'Sudanese military slavery'; D. Pain, 'The Nubians, their perceived stratification system and its relation to the Asian issue', in M. Twaddle (ed.), *Expulsion of a Minority* (London, 1975); J.A. Rowe, 'Islam under Idi Amin: a case of *déjà vu*?', in Hansen and Twaddle, *Uganda Now*; P. Woodward, 'Uganda and Southern Sudan', in Hansen and Twaddle, *Uganda Now*.
60 The debate is in A.A. Mazrui, 'The resurrection of the warrior tradition in African political culture', *Journal of Modern African Studies* 13, 1 (1975), pp.67–84; Southall, 'General Amin and the coup'; A.A. Mazrui, 'Religious strangers in Uganda: from Emin Pasha to Amin Dada', *African Affairs* 76, 302 (1977), pp.21–38; the contributions by both Southall and Mazrui (and others) to A.A. Mazrui (ed.), *The Warrior Tradition in Modern Africa* (Leiden, 1977); and A. Southall, 'Social disorganisation in Uganda before, during and after Amin', *Journal of Modern African Studies* 18, 4 (1980), pp.627–36.
61 Southall, 'General Amin and the coup', p.85.
62 Mazrui, 'Religious strangers', p.23.
63 See, e.g., H. Kyemba (a former Cabinet Minister under Amin) *A State of Blood: the Inside Story of Idi Amin* (London, 1977), p.111.
64 *Drum*, January 1979, reprinted in A. Seftel (ed.), *Uganda: The Rise and Fall of Idi Amin* (Lanseria, South Africa, 1994), p.213.
65 On *magendo* see (in addition to previously cited sources) especially, R.H. Green, *Magendo in the political economy of Uganda: pathology, parallel system or dominant sub-mode of production* (IDS Discussion Paper, Institute of Development Studies, University of Sussex, 1981); G. Prunier, 'Le magendo', *Politique Africaine* 9 (1983), pp.53–62. On the informal economy in West Nile at a later date, see K. Meagher, 'The hidden economy: informal and parallel trade in northwestern Uganda', *Review of African Political Economy* 47 (1990), pp.64–83; also M. Leopold, 'Roots of violence', Appendix.
66 Interview, O.N., Arua town, 6 February 1997.

67 O.O. Amaza, *Museveni's Long March from Guerilla to Statesman* (Kampala, 1998), p.xiv.
68 See, e.g., B.E. Harrell-Bond, *Imposing Aid* (Oxford, 1986); J. Crisp, 'Ugandan refugees in Sudan and Zaire: the problem of repatriation', *African Affairs* 85 (1986), pp.163–80; T. Allen, 'A flight from refuge, the return of refugees from Southern Sudan to Northwest Uganda in the late 1980s', in T. Allen (ed.), *In Search of Cool Ground: War, Flight and Homecoming in Northeast Africa* (London, 1996); A.M. Virmani, 'The resettlement of Ugandan refugees in Southern Sudan, 1919–86' (unpublished PhD dissertation (Field of Political Science), Northwestern University, Evanston, IL, 1996).
69 Virmani, 'Resettlement', pp.229, 251.
70 *Ibid.*, pp.313–14.
71 Harrell-Bond, *Imposing Aid*, p.35. Most of the Nubi refugees were, however, self-settled among the local population rather than in assisted settlements, a process facilitated by the close relationship between KiNubi and the southern Sudanese *lingua franca* known as 'Juba Arabic' (*Ibid.*, p.34).
72 Harrell-Bond, *Imposing Aid*, pp.38, 141; *Africa Confidential*, 2 November 1983.
73 Leopold, 'Roots of violence'; Leopold, 'Ethnicity'; M. Leopold, '"Trying to hold things together": international NGOs caught up in an emergency in north western Uganda', in O. Barrow and M. Jennings (eds), *The Charitable Impulse: NGOs and Development in East and North East Africa* (Oxford, 2001).
74 See, e.g., H. Behrend, *Alice Lakwena and the Holy Spirits: War in Northern Uganda 1986–87* (Oxford, 1999).
75 The Nubians in Bombo, and elsewhere in East Africa, may well be a different matter.
76 Cf. James, 'Perceptions'.

Five

Human Booty in Buganda
Some observations on the seizure of people in war, c.1700–1890

RICHARD REID

Introduction: Prisoners-of-War or Slaves Forever More?

Slavery and warfare were indelibly intertwined in the nineteenth-century Ganda kingdom (see Map 3), part of the process by which Buganda sought to impose itself on the surrounding region, effect commercial control over its neighbours' economies, achieve external security as well as internal cohesion, and develop its own peculiar form of 'national identity'. Slavery as an institution was fundamental to the effective functioning of the internal political and economic systems; slaves also became, after the 1850s, Buganda's primary commercial export. Slaves themselves were, at least in part, a product of the cycle of expansionism which had been operative since the seventeenth century. War was the vital instrument in the acquisition of slaves for both the internal and the external market. It should be observed, however, that the Ganda rarely waged war for the sole purpose of acquiring slaves: their military policy, indeed their entire military ethos, was much more complex than this. War was a method of achieving political and economic dominance, and of controlling and maximising use of regional resources. But more than this, warfare underpinned Ganda identity. Many of the signs and symbols of Ganda national identity were to be found in the kingdom's highly sophisticated military culture, which glorified the bearing of arms and emphasised the Ganda people's superiority over their neighbours, which in turn justified the fact that the bulk of the slaves in Ganda possession were drawn from those same neighbours. The violence of the Ganda state, therefore, was both explicit – in its celebration of the achievements of war – and implicit – in the integral belief in the right of the Ganda to dominate and enslave surrounding peoples.

Extensive slave-ownership in Buganda undoubtedly developed in parallel with the kingdom's expansion during the seventeenth and

145

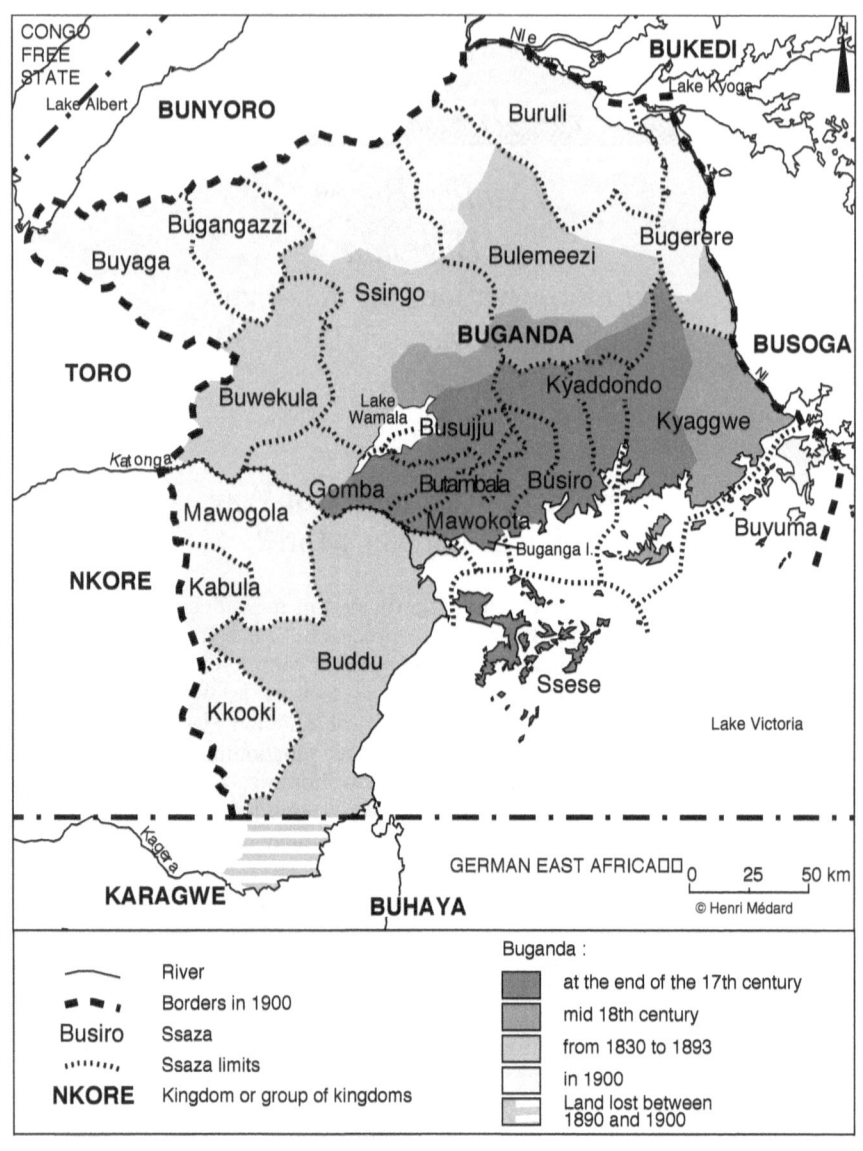

Map 3 Buganda's expansion (c.1640–1900)

eighteenth centuries to the point of regional dominance. It may reasonably be supposed that during the same period the complexities of the slave system also developed, including the emergence of slave hierarchies and divisions of labour within the broad institution of slavery itself. It is not a straightforward matter to define who or what constituted a 'slave' in the nineteenth-century kingdom. As a term it can reasonably be used to cover everyone from the humble *bazaana* – domestic female slaves – to certain *bagalagala*, the young and mostly male pages serving at the centres of political power who belonged within the system of what we might term 'privileged indentureship'. Distinctions also existed between the *abanyage*, those who were captured in war, and the *abagule*, those who were purchased. Some slaves had greater privileges and opportunities than others. Yet at the most generalised level in terms of the structure of Ganda society, we can say that the cardinal right of the *bakopi*, or free peasantry, was freedom of movement: they were able to enter and leave the patronage of a chief at will, and to transfer their skills and labour according to their own needs and wishes. Slaves could not do this. In some situations they were accorded certain 'physical' rights, but in general they had little influence over their personal circumstances or geographical location.

It is clear that slaves in all spheres were critical to Ganda social and economic life. They served as the personal and political attendants to powerful chiefs, sometimes being groomed for future political status themselves; they performed agricultural labour for wealthier peasants, and probably, although there is comparatively little direct evidence for this, also worked in some of the more skilled industries such as iron-working. They were also, it seems, extensively used in war, a theme to which we shall return below. A number of contemporary accounts of conflict suggest that slaves formed a significant part of the Ganda army's auxiliary forces. This would seem to be an indication of the degree to which slaves were integrated into Ganda society.

The seizure of people in war – either as a primary objective or as a by-product of wider conflict – was of critical importance to Buganda, as to other African states in the eighteenth and nineteenth centuries, on a number of levels. People thus captured had an eminently practical, economic function, in that they were either absorbed into the domestic economy or exported;[1] but the seizure of people was also a critical means by which the Ganda asserted themselves on the battlefield, and in so doing articulated a continually developing sense of ethnic or even 'national' superiority and imposed a particular identity across the region. It is a commonplace that so-called 'predatory' states such as Buganda regularly captured people in war, and that these people were thereafter, if they were not already, 'slaves'; and indeed that such 'predation' (for the activity has frequently been deemed unworthy of the term 'warfare') was carried out with the very purpose of capturing people. This is simply what such states *did*. In fact, both the practice of seizing human booty, and the prosecution of warfare itself, were rather more complex than this textbook view might suggest. To examine the relationship between slaves and warfare in Africa in general, and for our purposes here Buganda in particular, goes in many ways to the very heart of both the nature of the institution or practice of slavery and the nature of warfare in African states and societies. Who were the people captured in war, and exactly what purpose did they serve? Can they all be described as 'slaves', or might some more accurately be described as 'prisoners-of-war'? Was there anything to distinguish slaves captured in war and those acquired through more peaceful, i.e. commercial, channels? In the region of the Great Lakes in the nineteenth century, we often do not have the evidence to answer all these questions satisfactorily or definitively, even for the relatively well-documented state of Buganda. But it is nonetheless important to pose them, if only to compel us to think more critically about the relationship between slavery and warfare.

Turney-High made what was in many ways the classic statement of the late nineteenth- and early twentieth-century Western perception of so-called 'primitive war' when he suggested that '[m]ilitary slaving as an economic enterprise also belongs on levels above the lowest primitivity. It is certainly more productive to enslave a war captive than to kill him or to eat him.'[2] (This may be so, although it would surely depend on the circumstances surrounding capture, as well as on the war captive him- or herself.) Taking an 'example' from West Africa, Turney-High opined that 'what the Dahomeans called wars were no more than large-scale slaving enterprises'.[3] One of the problems confronting the historian of African warfare is that the relevant contemporary sources were usually of the same opinion. Certainly, in most studies of African warfare, there is an at least implicit assumption that there was in fact no such thing as a 'prisoner-of-war', at least as most people understand the concept today, and that the vast majority of generically termed 'war captives' were indeed to be considered as 'slaves'; and furthermore, that such war captives indeed constituted the sole or primary aim of the conflict in the first place. Comparisons from other parts of the continent where similar research has been undertaken are instructive, however. Among the Yoruba of the nineteenth century, Robert Smith and J.F. Ade Ajayi observed how it 'has been assumed, and still seems probable, that captives from the wars provided the bulk of the slaves exported via the markets of Dahomey and the Lagos lagoon'. Significantly for our purposes, they cautioned against the 'further assumption' that conflicts among the Yoruba were themselves prompted by the external demand for slaves, an assumption which 'overlooks the important political and economic issues of the wars'. At any rate, Smith and Ajayi felt able to assert that 'not all captives were enslaved. Some were imprisoned ... The least fortunate were put to death ... The most fortunate were redeemed [against payment] or even released freely.'[4] Elsewhere the authors noted the 'exchange of notable prisoners',[5] but the implication here is that – as in eighteenth- and nineteenth-century Ethiopia, for example – what we might understand as a 'PoW' was very often a figure of some importance, perhaps a military commander or a political personage unfortunate enough to be seized in the course of an attack. In a separate, and seminal, work, Smith modified his earlier argument somewhat in a wider West African context: '[c]aptives were always regarded in West Africa as part of the booty of war ... [M]any – almost certainly, from the seventeenth century onwards, most – captives were retained or sold as slaves.' He now largely rejected the notion that the 'prisoner-of-war' was in any way common, and offered a rather novel explanation for this: 'it must be remembered that enslavement represented a considerable mitigation of the harshness of war, for slavery of any kind was preferable to violent and often hideous death and also probably preferable to imprisonment – which was an alternative rarely offered to any but the most important captives.'[6] This assertion – that enslavement was a 'mitigation' – seems to be open to serious question, but the idea is certainly an interesting one.

In the context of precolonial Buganda, there is little evidence for the existence of 'prisoners-of-war'; so the aim of this essay is to examine the links between slavery and warfare in Buganda in the eighteenth and nineteenth centuries, the period which saw the kingdom at its height in terms of territorial expansion and military might. Our overarching questions must therefore be: to what extent, and why, was slavery apparently the usual consequence of war captivity? And what were the conventions and circumstances governing the fate of war captives? In other words, is 'slave' an appropriate term to apply to the myriad of groups and individuals encompassed within the generic circumstance of 'war captivity'? Clearly, in terms of military activity, an important influence in this context was the nature of the military action being undertaken: the distinction would be made, where possible, between single battles which were fought within defined combat zones and which were limited in range and scope, and actions which formed part of larger campaigns involving territorial expansion and the incorporation of conquered peoples. Unfortunately, however, precise evidence for these conditions at any given time is frequently lacking; and thus we are reduced to the precolonial historian's familiar tools of intelligent guesswork and speculation.

Understanding the African Context

The treatment of the 'enemy populace' in the context of the aims and nature of conflict in the region under study is worth considering for a moment, relative to how we might understand similar themes in 'Western' warfare. We are working on the basic assumption that those taken in war were, with a few exceptions, rarely returned to their home societies and communities under recognised conventions at the conclusion (or at least suspension) of hostilities. To begin with, although it may seem a little gratuitous, we need to remind ourselves that the notion of a 'prisoner-of-war' is, in its modern definition at least, a uniquely Western concept. In its broadest sense, a prisoner-of-war must be understood as a status related to the following: to the bi- or multilaterally-accepted duration of a conflict, presumed to be a finite period of time, or at least of the stages of a prolonged conflict; to the recognition of 'combatant', whether professional or semi-professional, as a status enjoying certain universally recognised rights and protection; and to the idea that war was a special set of circumstances requiring a distinct legal framework (although one sharing certain universal principles with its 'peacetime' counterpart) which would serve to mitigate the harsher aspects of human combat, the brutalities inherent in war. At this point we might note again Smith's argument that 'enslavement' represented just such a mitigation, although Smith himself demurs on the issue of whether or not this was a deliberate mechanism. While African warfare was indisputably governed by customs and conventions, rules and regulations,[7] the notion of a captured person being a 'prisoner-of-war' seems rarely to have been among them. It is, again, a Western concept, and a relatively modern one at that, developing through the eighteenth and nineteenth centuries and coming to be enshrined in a series of international conventions, the violation of which is today regarded, in principle, as a heinous crime (although this is scarcely regarded as sufficient reason not to violate them). In other words, even to attempt to discuss the notion of 'prisoner-of-war' is a non-starter in the African context; it is the unique product of the peculiar circumstances of Western industrial and nationalist warfare over the past two centuries and holds no relevance for the African experience.

In understanding the African context, moreover, the omnipresent issue of demography is extremely pertinent, particularly when it is recognised that issues of population in Africa were on one level really about resources and raw materials. In an under-populated continent — and in this we must also include the comparatively densely populated region of Buganda and its immediate neighbours — in which combat over resources and people was in truth a matter of life and death for the communities and states involved, and in which the maximisation of labour, fertility and production was critical (as well as being an objective of war policy in itself), prisoners-of-war were not merely an expensive luxury: they were, in socio-economic terms, illogical. Why bother to maintain a prisoner-of-war class when within a distinct social and cultural framework they can be 'enslaved', stripped of key rights and freedoms, incorporated (to various degrees and in various ways) into the 'host society', and their labour and skills utilised? Why bother, indeed, when this is accepted and conventional practice on both sides? In the African context, slave incorporation is wholly rational and logical; and the retention and eventual exchange or ransom of key 'prisoners' only takes place when some decided political, social or economic advantage thus accrues.

We need also to consider the conventions governing war, and here, for the sake of convenience and an attempt at brevity, some generalisation is required. In the region under study, conventions governing both war and diplomacy again clearly existed, and in this sense war did indeed, as in Europe, come to be perceived as a special set of circumstances requiring a distinct set of rules and regulations. But we might suggest that among a number of African societies war was not regarded as 'special' enough to warrant such regulations as governed the treatment of human beings, especially considering that the capture and exploitation of people was a natural feature of combat. It might be the case that war and combat were more 'natural' extensions of the politico-social entity – the state, the kingdom, the community – in parts of Africa, that they were less 'special' or 'unusual' than they had come to be perceived in Europe, and that therefore there was less effort made to protect those involved from the brutality of war. In Europe, for example, there had been a process of separating and distinguishing war from the 'normal' functioning of society; in large parts of Africa, including the region under study, this may not have been the case. In relation to the rules of war, of course, there is the critical question of who was actually captured in combat: specifically, was a distinction made between combatant and non-combatant? If not, beyond the practical implication that an active combatant was perhaps more likely to be put to death, then there were no obvious conventions governing *who* or *what* constituted a 'war captive': the status, like the term, was generic and all-encompassing. But into this discussion, to which we shall return below, we must introduce such factors as gender, one of the most obvious sources of differentiation among those captured in the process of conflict.

Finally in this context, and closely linked to the last point, we have the issue of the actual *aims* of warfare. If Buganda is to be understood as an 'expansionist' state, then we must consider its expansionism on several levels: territorial, in other words spatial, through the physical extension of boundaries; political, i.e. the enlargement of the structures and institutions of the state; economic, meaning the physical seizure of, or at least establishment of what I have elsewhere termed 'informal control' over,[8] the means or sources of agricultural and industrial production and trade; and of course human, connected to each of the above, namely, the incorporation and utilisation of people for a range of purposes and in a variety of ways, not least – as noted at the beginning of the essay – in terms of their material contribution to the state, and in terms of the extension of the ideology and identity associated with the Ganda state. Those captured in war, in different ways, were a critical part of this expansionism. The assumption that Buganda was a society, like several others in the region, which was based on slavery is at best somewhat misleading and at worst dangerously incorrect. A number of scholars, Michael Twaddle among them,[9] have certainly been correct to point towards the great importance of slavery in Ganda society, and to emphasise the complex nature of slavery itself. Again, I have also attempted this elsewhere.[10] I would argue, however, that slavery was only one means by which the Ganda state in a broader sense utilised its human and material resources in the pursuit of external security and internal cohesion.

Slavery and War in Buganda

The links between slavery and war were fundamental to the functioning of the Ganda state – and this is commonly accepted through the use of the slaves-guns/cloth model in much of the literature – but they were rather more complex than perhaps is generally realised. The seizure of our generically termed 'war captives' was regarded as a basic component of military practice in Buganda and throughout the wider lacustrine region. Yet war captives faced a number of possible fates, and it is necessary to consider these in relation to the types of people captured and the status in which they were thus held. It is important to observe at this juncture that, although Buganda acquired slaves through other channels, most importantly through trade,[11] during the period under examination, we are concerned here solely with warfare and war policy. While it is clear that Ganda war policy was usually influenced by wider strategic objectives, war captives were either a by-product of conflict, or themselves represented a key objective of conflict. It is therefore important to identify whether any distinction was made between those captured in these ways; to examine differentiation between combatant and non-combatant; and, to some degree linked to the second point, to identify distinctions made in terms of gender.

Four distinct fates are envisaged for all war captives during the period under study, fates which were clearly affected by internal or domestic needs as well as external pressures, and which also provide some clues, at least intuitively, to the status of those captured. The first scenario, and one to which we have already alluded as relatively rare, involved the return of captives to their place of capture or homeland following a period of detention, which may or may not have involved a particular activity, such as forced labour or other services. They may have been either sold back – or ransomed – or returned gratis. This scenario permits the identification of such captives as 'prisoners-of-war', probably if not exclusively male, while military and political considerations – notably related to the rank of the prisoner – can be assumed to have factored in this situation. The second scenario, again probably relatively unusual, involved captives being executed or 'sacrificed' following capture, influenced by political, military or what we can broadly call 'cultural' factors. Human sacrifice did occur in Buganda, and despite contemporary European accounts which surmised that innocent freemen were dragged randomly from highways for this purpose,[12] it seems likely that the practice invariably involved slaves. Students of slavery in other African societies have shown that slaves used for human sacrifice were usually fresh captives held in limbo by the state.[13]

Thirdly, and much more commonly, there is the domestic market scenario, involving varying degrees of incorporation into society in a range of capacities. Such captives can, in the broadest possible sense, be categorised as 'slaves', both male and female, although the gender balance is highly debatable and virtually impossible to ascertain, while in any case it probably varied over time. Status would vary widely, from relatively low – for example, individual captives working on peasant homesteads, serving rank-and-file soldiers who return to their plantations following conflict – to relatively high, notably those captives in the service of chiefs or the *kabaka* [king] himself with what we might describe as 'privileged portfolios'. Influencing factors in this scenario would include the level of skills and expertise of the captives in particular fields; sexual possibilities (mostly but not, it would seem, exclusively female); perhaps military rank at the time of capture; and personal and 'favoured' qualities more generally. The open and competitive nature of Ganda society is also clearly significant in this context. And, finally, we have the option of export out of Buganda. This could have taken place in the context of a local or regional slave trade, but in the second half of the nineteenth century it is much more likely that this scenario involved the long-distance slave trade and that it was powerfully influenced by emerging commercial circumstances, the result of internal responses to external demand and the commercial opportunities thus offered. It is furthermore critical to assess the influence of these changing commercial circumstances on Ganda war policy more widely.

The relationship between warfare and slavery can therefore be regarded as a complex one. Slaves were, at least in part, the product of warfare, a core component in the cycle of expansionism which had been taking place since the seventeenth century, and thus war became a vital instrument in the acquisition of slaves for both the internal and the external market. Yet, as mentioned earlier, the Ganda appear to have rarely waged war for the *sole purpose* of acquiring slaves: their military policy, indeed their entire military ethos, was much more complex than this. War was primarily a means to achieving political and economic dominance. The 'violence' of the Ganda state was both explicit – in its celebration of the achievements of war, and of the act of war itself – and implicit, in the integral belief in the right of the Ganda to dominate and, indeed, enslave surrounding peoples. Nonetheless, this second assertion must be understood in light of the fact that Buganda was simultaneously a markedly open and competitive society which welcomed – indeed to a very real degree depended upon – expertise and new skills from the very societies over which the kingdom claimed hegemony and superior status. Therefore, in many ways the practice of war captivity and the institution of slavery moulded the apparent paradox into a more coherent and logical whole. Slaves were accumulated in war for export; but there were also 'internal' factors which had a powerful influence on how the Ganda regarded those captured in war, and doubtless indeed *how* they captured slaves in war: ethnicity (which might be regarded as a kind of precolonial nationalism); the requirements of foreign policy, in the best Clausewitzian tradition; and domestic economic and indeed political requirements, including the need to maintain the political establishment and to supply slaves for internal consumption and the development of a broad base of economic resources (and both of these involved the control of people). The words used by Ganda to distinguish between slaves purchased in commercial transactions, *abagule*, and those captured in war, *abanyage*, do not hint at the specific functions or roles played by such slaves; they seem simply to represent semantic differentiation. But the fact that there are indeed different terms which refer to slaves' origins might seem to suggest that the two categories were regarded differently in Ganda society and performed different functions or occupied different statuses. It is, of course, impossible to assess with any precision the extent of slave ownership in the nineteenth-century kingdom. While a poor stratum of free society may have been excluded from the slave ownership system, it is possible to suggest that a significant proportion of wealthier peasants and non-chiefs owned at least one or two serviles,[14] and that this came about in large part through participation in military campaigns.

Most slaves in nineteenth-century Buganda, though by no means all, were either foreign or of foreign descent.[15] By this time, there had come into existence a substantial slave population which was descended from war captives. This group of slaves, who were born in Buganda to foreign, captive parents, adds to our understanding of Buganda's reputation for absorbing (and even exalting) foreigners in the precolonial past. There would have been a clear distinction made between such slaves and those of more recent import who were still living on the edges of Ganda society and culture and whose alienness was as yet undiluted.[16] Yet the enduring nature of slave status in Buganda, the fact that it could be inherited at least through one generation, demonstrates the power of identity of origin in Ganda society. There was clearly, therefore, an ethnic dimension to Ganda slavery; it is not difficult to find evidence of a sense of ethnic superiority, or perhaps seniority, among the Ganda. Much of their military ethos was founded upon such a sense – and they were by no means unique in this – and important spheres of their material culture somewhat mendaciously preserved notions of the innate supremacy of Ganda civilisation. It is impossible to say with certainty which came first, i.e. whether this sense of supremacy formed a core component of Ganda identity prior to the systematic enslavement of foreigners, or whether such haughtiness was actually prompted and fuelled by increasing military success. But they certainly grew in tandem. The term *mudokolo*, for example, an insulting and generic reference to anyone from the north, is revealing, while one Ganda chronicler states that 'it was the custom of the Baganda to despise other tribes, and any person of any of the other tribes they called him Munyoro'.[17] Ganda attitudes might appear at first glance to be somewhat contradictory, when we contrast the willingness to absorb outsiders and foreign skills with this sense of 'tribal' superiority. Again, however, on

Human Booty in Buganda

another level – that of slavery and war captivity – it is clear that these attitudes were in fact perfectly complementary.

Notably, slaves were also, it seems, extensively used in war, a fact which takes on a particular relevance considering that they were mostly foreign in origin and might therefore have found themselves fighting on the Ganda side against their own home societies. A number of contemporary accounts of conflict suggest that many slaves served in the Ganda army's auxiliary forces, as carriers of weapons and supplies or personal attendants to chiefs. It is unclear how far back this practice can be traced, but by the second half of the nineteenth century large numbers of slaves appear to have been thus utilised: Stanley, undoubtedly exaggerating, mentions 50,000 slaves accompanying the Ganda army in the field against Buvuma in 1875.[18] Roscoe mentioned 'servants' accompanying chiefs to war, and Mackay described chiefs and their slaves when observing an army being organised.[19] The use of slaves in this way is germane to the more general question of their effective integration into Ganda society. It is difficult to imagine, for example, that the Ganda would have risked attacking Bunyoro with recently enslaved Banyoro forming a major part of their military force. It seems likely that only the most loyal of slaves accompanied their masters on such expeditions: in other words, those who were descendants of war captives or who had been captured in childhood, and whose loyalty to their adopted culture transcended all others. Presumably the opportunities for personal advancement presented by war played a vital role in persuading slaves that they too had a 'stake' in the success of the Ganda state. Their former identities perhaps became subsumed within that of Buganda in a manner akin to the absorption of conquered peoples by the Zulu, for example.[20]

Again, the fact that most slaves in Buganda were foreign in origin – Nyoro and Soga, mostly, although also sometimes from societies to the west of Buganda – tended to underpin the Ganda sense of ethnic superiority. At the same time, however, foreign skills and influence were welcomed in the development of certain key industries, notably iron-working: blacksmiths from Bunyoro, and from the former Nyoro province of Buddu especially, were brought to the capital to work, and while some of these may have been, in the first instance, war captives, their skills were highly prized and must have brought them relatively high status. It seems safe to assume that it was precisely because they had such expertise that they were targeted as war captives. As in iron-working, so it was with regard to the history of pottery in Buganda: Nyoro influence, again, was brought to bear on the industry in the kingdom from at least the late eighteenth or early nineteenth centuries, apparently following the arrival at the capital of a Nyoro slave who made a profound impression on *Kabaka* Kamanya.[21] There is also evidence that the Ganda may have imported herding skills from neighbouring societies, and, like those who worked in iron and clay, these would probably in the main have been captured in war, targeted precisely because they possessed skills which the kingdom needed.[22]

War captivity leading to slavery, therefore, can be seen as the means by which Buganda's apparent paradox was resolved: in other words, through the institution of slavery, their sense of ethnic superiority and professed chauvinism[23] was underpinned and indeed empowered – i.e., it was self-perpetuating – while many of the skills which the Ganda themselves lacked were thus acquired. As Buganda expanded, it therefore built upon its existing resource base and pool of skills by bringing in foreigners. Again, a great many of these were brought in by force, such as the Nyoro potter who may have been set free as a reward for his skills and service but who equally may have been retained as a slave with privileged status,[24] something which a number of slaves in Buganda seem to have enjoyed. They were not 'prisoners of war', in our understanding of that term; but they were a particular kind of war captive, enslaved through military means to serve a particular function in Ganda society based on their skills and region of origin.

In the second half of the nineteenth century heightened demand for slaves from export-oriented foreign traders in Buganda brought unprecedented pressure to bear on the domestic servile system. This clearly weakened the internal slave system which had served the kingdom so well for so long, and there is evidence of an anxiety – in the capital, at least – that too many slaves who would normally have been retained for domestic use were being sold abroad.[25] It seems that increasing numbers of actual Ganda slaves – rarely exported before – were being sold. We have observed that slaves had always been a significant by-product of war; warfare was the 'natural' means by which the Ganda slave population, both male and female, was sustained, and it is clear that this remained the case as late as the beginning of the 1890s. In the second half of the nineteenth century, however, slaves for export were also being drawn from this broad band: this meant that either more Ganda had to be enslaved to sustain the indigenous slave population, or that more foreign captives had to be brought in specifically for export. What actually happened appears to have been a combination of these developments, but the second was unquestionably the more important and dramatic. Now, there is little evidence that the Ganda actually fought more wars, or carried out more external slave-raiding expeditions, during this period, to meet demand. Wars continued to be fought, for a variety of strategic and political reasons, as they had before the external demand for slaves. Instead the gathering of foreign captives during military expeditions must have become more widespread and more systematic than had been the case before the 1850s.[26]

The ability to own and indeed sell slaves had long meant social and economic power in Buganda, and had served to reinforce critical ideas about domination, particularly, although not exclusively, along lines of gender and ethnicity. The injection of long-distance commercial impulses served to strengthen these ideas, and made the selling of slaves even more lucrative. But while slavery had been, for most of the kingdom's history, a source of social, political and economic strength, the long-distance trade in slaves in the decades prior to colonial rule was actually a source of weakness. Buganda's reliance on the slave trade, brief but intense, was inimical to the kingdom's long-term economic development; at the same time, the exaltation of the firearm, the most valued commodity received in exchange for slaves, led to enervating political factionalism and the blunting of the army's effectiveness on the battlefield. Guns were not used to any great effect in war before the 1880s, and in any case they were often unreliable;[27] yet at the same time gun-wielding, politically ambitious young men – products of intrigue at the royal court rather than military experience – were taking the place of more expert spearmen as the army's strike force.[28] 'War captives' had long made an important contribution to Ganda society and economy, in the knowledge and expertise they brought to particular fields and activities, the manner in which they swelled the ranks of the army as loyal retainers, and, for female slaves at least, the enormous contribution they made in terms of the kingdom's reproductive capacity. All of these indicate the importance of slave accumulation. The large-scale export of such people in the 1870s and 1880s must only have served to undermine the kingdom's internal strength, while in any case, of course, the slave trade itself was doomed.

Finally in this context, the element of gender is clearly critical in helping explain how war captivity led to slavery, although it is impossible to quantify in terms of a precise male-female ratio through time. It seems significant that, while references to male war captives appear consistently throughout Buganda's history, women and children figure so prominently in the contemporary sources for late nineteenth-century slavery. We have alluded already to the significance of the sexual dimension to war captivity. It appears that during the eighteenth and nineteenth centuries, the number of women attached to the royal enclosure, for example, increased dramatically, at least according to indigenous sources.[29] It seems safe to assume that a significant proportion of these women were seized violently in war. The missionary Gorju suggested that it was in the middle of the eighteenth century that chiefs began to take foreign female slaves who had been seized in war as concubines,[30] and this is certainly plausible, coinciding as it does with the era of Buganda's greatest military success. Certainly, by the 1870s and 1880s, women formed a significant part of captives brought into the capital following military campaigns, indeed it seems that at times they formed the bulk of such batches. I would suggest that, although women had always been captured – largely, before c.1850, for domestic consumption – the late nineteenth century saw a marked increase in the number of female captives, largely because of the expansion of the long-distance slave trade. Women formed the bulk of the fresh captives described in the capital in 1879 and 1880,[31] while the price of women was increasing from the late 1870s onward, owing to the increased preference for them among coastal traders.[32] Pastoralist Hima women, notably, were commonly sold to the coastal merchants, and were regarded as being exceptionally beautiful.[33] While many of these would have been seized within Buganda itself — and such 'internal' raids were particularly common during the reign of Mwanga in the 1880s — there can be little doubt that equally a sizeable proportion would have come from Bunyoro or the societies to the west.

Concluding Remarks

It is clear, then, that slaves were not usually the primary objective of Ganda warfare, and therefore for most of the kingdom's history before the middle of the nineteenth century the export trade did not significantly influence the provenance, nature or indeed the frequency of Ganda war-making. However, slaves were an important by-product of conflict, and the gathering of captives — for a range of functions and purposes — was an intrinsic component of the practice of warfare. Domestic demand for such captives was considerable, and the 'act' of war-making needed to take full account of this internal dimension. It is worth noting that the domestic dimension was crucial in determining the fate of war captives, and indeed the latter cannot be understood without placing them in the context of Ganda domestic exigencies and cultural requirements: only by doing so can we understand how such captives were 'slaves' rather than 'prisoners-of-war'. Moreover, there was huge differentiation among captives taken in war, in terms of social status and 'profession', and this is directly linked to the nature of Ganda society itself, which was simultaneously inclusive — characterised by a desire to incorporate those with new and vital skills — and exclusive, driven by and organised around a sense of 'ethnic superiority', with a number of neighbouring peoples regarded collectively as inferior to the Ganda themselves.

At the same time, the practice of war captivity can be seen as the most effective, although by no means the only, means of reinforcing the twin pillars of the centralised Ganda state in the nineteenth century, namely, the maintenance of the ideology of ethnic — or perhaps proto-national — supremacy and regional hegemony, and the absorption of skills and expertise which the Ganda lacked or needed to build upon. Thus conflict abroad brought together foreign and domestic policy strategies, and the violent capture of people is perhaps the clearest demonstration of the ways in which war was, for Buganda, viviparous, a dynamic, living thing, through which the kingdom grew both internally and externally.

Notes

1   Elsewhere, I have more fully examined the practice of slavery itself: see my *Political Power in Pre-Colonial Buganda: Economy, Society and Warfare in the Nineteenth Century* (Oxford, 2002).

Human Booty in Buganda

2   H.H.Turney-High, *Primitive War* (New York, 1949), p.178.
3   *Ibid.*, p.180.
4   R.S. Smith and J.F. Ade Ajayi, *Yoruba Warfare in the Nineteenth Century* (Ibadan and Cambridge, 1971) pp.51–2.
5   *Ibid.*, p.121.
6   R.S. Smith, *Warfare and Diplomacy in Precolonial West Africa* (London, 1989), pp.36–7.
7   Even nineteenth-century observers who would repeatedly emphasise the curious amalgam of savagery and pointlessness of African warfare would nonetheless usually also point to the 'ritual' nature of combat, attended by a range of 'taboos': see for example J. Roscoe, *The Baganda: an Account of their Native Customs and Beliefs* (London, 1911).
8   See, for example, my 'The Ganda on Lake Victoria: a nineteenth-century East African imperialism', *Journal of African History*, 39, 3 (1998).
9   See, for example, M. Twaddle, 'The ending of slavery in Buganda', in R. Roberts and S. Miers (eds), *The End of Slavery in Africa* (Madison, WI, 1988); and 'Slaves and peasants in Buganda', in L.J. Archer (ed.), *Slavery and Other Forms of Unfree Labour* (London, 1988).
10 Reid, *Political Power*, chapter 6.
11 Grant, for example, described a thriving regional slave trade: J.A. Grant, *A Walk Across Africa* (Edinburgh and London, 1864), p.117. This commerce functioned at the highest level, with Mutesa receiving slaves from Kabarega in return for cloth, copper, brass and glass beads: G.Schweinfurth et al. (eds), *Emin Pasha in Central Africa* (London, 1888) p.115.
12 See G. Casati, *Ten Years in Equatoria* (London and New York, 1891) II, p.51; A.M. Mackay (ed. by his sister), *A.M. Mackay: Pioneer Missionary to Uganda* (London, 1890), p.197.
13 S. Miers and I. Kopytoff (eds), *Slavery in Africa* (Madison, WI, 1977), pp.129, 316; R.C.C. Law, 'Human sacrifice in pre-colonial West Africa', *African Affairs*, 84 (1985), pp.53–87.
14 Grant was told that the average Muganda owned a hundred slaves: while clearly a gross exaggeration, it conveys some idea others had of the extensive nature of Ganda slave ownership: Grant, *A Walk*, p.55
15 Roscoe, *The Baganda*, pp.14–15.
16 See, for example, White Fathers: C13/5 Livinhac to Lavigerie, 24 September 1879; and again Roscoe, *The Baganda*, pp.14–15. Both sources refer to slaves achieving favoured status the longer they spent with the same household, though timescales are not mentioned. Speke told the story of Uledi, the slave of a coastal merchant, who eventually inherited his late master's property and achieved a position of some political importance: J. Speke, *Journal of the Discovery of the Source of the Nile* (London, 1863), p.276.
17 B.M. Zimbe [tr. F. Kamoga], *Buganda ne Kabaka* (MS, c.1939), p.53.
18 R. Stanley and A. Neame (eds), *The Exploration Diaries of H.M. Stanley* (New York, 1961), p.99.
19 Roscoe, *The Baganda*, p.350; Mackay, *Pioneer Missionary*, p.111.
20 J.Guy, *The Destruction of the Zulu Kingdom* (Pietermaritzburg, 1994), p.xviii; J.D.Omer-Cooper, *History of Southern Africa* (London, 1987), p.57.
21 A. Kagwa [ed. M.M. Edel, tr. E.B. Kalibala], *Customs of the Baganda* (New York, 1934), p.159. There are other examples of foreigners being 'brought to the capital' to work, for example the iron-workers from Buddu and Bunyoro in the eighteenth century, although in these cases it is not explicit that the craftsmen were war captives: *ibid.*, p.160.
22 Reid, *Political Power*, pp.162–3.
23 In this, it should be noted, Buganda was not unique in the region: the Nyoro also had a keen sense of their own importance in interlacustrine history.
24 Kagwa, *Customs*, p.159. Moreover, a young *mugalagala* enjoyed rather more privileged servitude than a mere *muddu*, being in the service of the *kabaka* or senior chiefs: Zimbe, *Buganda*, pp.96–7; White Fathers: Rubaga Diary 1/13 November 1879; CMS CA6/025/21 Wilson to Wright, 31 May 1878.
25 R.W. Felkin, 'Notes on the Waganda tribe of Central Africa', *Proceedings of the Royal*

159

Society of Edinburgh, 13 (1885–86) pp.746, 753–4; C.T. Wilson and R.W. Felkin, *Uganda and the Egyptian Soudan* (London, 1882) I, p.190. A missionary noted in 1879 that slaves had become a scarce commodity: White Fathers: C13/5 Livinhac to Lavigerie, 24 September 1879. Slave-stealing and kidnapping increased – White Fathers: Rubaga Diary 2/12 August 1881 – and in this same period Mackay estimated that some 2,000 slaves per year were being exported from Buganda: Mackay, *Pioneer Missionary*, p.435.

26   For example, Speke, *Journal*, p.361. Missionary accounts from 1879 and 1880 describe in gruesome detail the arrival of batches of fresh war captives from Busoga: CMS CA6/019/13 Pearson to Wright, 29 September 1879; CMS G3 A6/0 1881/22 Pearson to Mackay, 29 July 1880.

27   For example, CMS CA6/025/8 Wilson to Wright, 6 July 1877; White Fathers: Rubaga Diary 3/23 February 1886.

28   J.R.L. Macdonald, *Soldiering and Surveying in British East Africa* (London, 1897), pp.142–3; see also R.J. Reid, 'War and militarism in pre-colonial Buganda', *Azania*, 34 (1999) pp.53–4; M. Twaddle, 'The emergence of politico-religious groupings in late nineteenth-century Buganda', *Journal of African History*, 29, 1 (1988).

29   See, for example, Kagwa, *Customs*.

30   J. Gorju, *Entre le Victoria, l'Albert et l'Edouard* (Rennes, 1920), p.123.

31   CMS CA6/019/13 Pearson to Wright, 29 September 1879; CMS G3 A6/0 1881/22 Pearson to Mackay, 29 July 1880.

32   Schweinfurth et al., *Emin Pasha*, p.117; Felkin, 'Notes on the Waganda tribe', pp.753–4.

33   C. Peters [tr. H.W. Dulcken], *New Light on Dark Africa* (London, 1891), p.402; W. Junker [tr. A.H. Keane], *Travels in Africa during the Years 1882–1886* (London, 1892), p.550.

Six

Stolen People & Autonomous Chiefs in Nineteenth-Century Buganda
The social consequences of non-free followers

HOLLY HANSON

Introduction

A new form of chiefship, the *ekitongole*, emerged in the Buganda kingdom in the eighteenth century. An *ekitongole* (pl. *ebitongole*) was a collection of people under a chief organised to do a particular work on a particular piece of land. While older chiefships bore the name of their territory or a name which asserted an ancient service of the chief to the monarch, the names of *ebitongole* announced their purpose. The *Ekikinakulya*, for example, was created and named 'for the purpose of things to eat', and *Ekibukula Mabira*, 'for the purpose of opening up of the forests', was created to supply hunters who were needed to drive away elephants and buffaloes that were attacking people. *Kabakas* (kings) created the first *ebitongole*, but chiefs who grew wealthy through trade created their own *ebitongole* in the late nineteenth century.

The implications of the emergence of a new form of chiefship tied particularly to production raise fascinating issues which have not yet been fully explored by historians of Buganda. This essay argues that *ebitongole* chiefship became a mechanism for organising the labour of war captives, and that this incorporation of war captives in *ebitongole* profoundly destabilised the Buganda kingdom.

This interpretation challenges well-accepted habits of thought about Buganda. It suggests an alternative to the idea that *ebitongole* chiefships were part of a consolidation of royal power, the making of a 'modernising bureaucracy', in which royal power replaced clan authority.[1] Although historians M.S.M. Kiwanuka, John Rowe and Michael Twaddle[2] have all noted that this concept oversimplifies the relationship of kings, clans and chiefs, the idea of the modernising Baganda continues to appear in scholarly works – most recently as 'defensive modernisers' in Philip Curtin's study of imperialism.[3] The increasing power of kings to allocate land in chiefships does not tell the whole story of *ebitongole*, however. This emerging institution can also be understood as an attempt to institutionalise enslavement which contributed to increasing social violence and the collapse of patterns of reciprocal obligation that had previously drawn the polity together. The underlying premise of my argument is that the masses of captive people brought into Buganda during its wars of expansion represented a significant challenge to the polity; they caused a crisis in the ordering of the kingdom, and led to a drastic decline in the status of ordinary Baganda, especially women.

While the meagre written sources on war captives (slaves) in Buganda support this interpretation, it rests primarily on an analysis of the social logic of the Buganda kingdom based on an examination of exchanges of land and labour from the origins of the kingdom to the early colonial period.[4] Using evidence of tribute and gift obligations that emerged some time after 1700, explanations for kings' gifts of land to followers in the late nineteenth century, records of conflicts over remuneration for work and chiefs' efforts to meet colonial demands for labour between 1900 and 1920, that larger work argues that people built the Ganda polity by wielding gifts of land and labour that created relationships of reciprocal obligation. The patterns of exchange that characterised *ebitongole*, evident in the histories of particular *ebitongole* told before the 1924 Commission of Inquiry into Butaka Land, represent a sharp break from earlier patterns.

Ebitongole chiefship emerged in Buganda as part of the effort to respond to the instability caused by the massive influx of captives as a result of the post-1700 wars of expansion. Unlike mid-nineteenth-century captives, who were enslaved in order to be sold, the large numbers of captives brought into Buganda in the late eighteenth century were settled on particular areas of land as non-free followers of the king or particular chiefs. The presence of thousands of non-free people in Buganda undermined the social contract of the kingdom in three ways. First, it diminished the bargaining power of followers in relation to their chiefs. Second, it lessened chiefs' leverage over the king, because kings made themselves independent of labour provided by chiefs by creating entire political units made up largely of non-free people. Finally, because chiefs themselves subsequently began to create their own land units settled by non-free people, the king began to lose control of the centre of the kingdom.

The Social Logic of a Coalescing Polity

The social contract challenged by *ebitongole* originated in the conjunction of the ecological conditions of the region north of Lake Victoria and enduring interlacustrine Bantu understandings of rulership. In the consistently fertile land that became Buganda, where permanent cultivation of bananas replaced a mixed agricultural system about a thousand years ago, people gradually knitted together a kingdom out of smaller polities, probably before the seventeenth century.⁵ Because land was abundant but some land was better for cultivation than other land, the essential dynamic of power in Buganda was that chiefs needed followers and followers could leave their chiefs.⁶ This led to political heterarchy: people held power over others in many different ways in the distant Ganda past – as leaders of clan branches, leaders of cults, and leaders of followings without clan or cult origins. All these different kinds of leaders competed for followers. Leaders had to be constantly alert to the possibility that their followers might desert them if other leaders in the same neighbourhood treated their people better.

Incessant competition among chiefs for followers characterised Ganda politics. This is evident in the dense, overlapping webs of patterns of tribute and allegiance in the oldest parts of the kingdom.⁷ Chiefs did not necessarily have authority over the people who lived on the land they controlled. As the kingdom developed, the critical axis of conflict in Buganda had been between chiefs for followers, and chiefs had often succeeded in winning other chiefs' followers from underneath them. Effective chiefs had to be skilled in resolving disputes in ways that seemed just to all parties; they had to be able to obtain and redistribute goods in ways that satisfied both their superiors and their followers; and they had to develop working relationships with other chiefs so that their followers would not be encouraged to leave them.

Several sets of sources suggest that the structures of the Ganda kingdom developed as chiefs who had autonomous authority created relationships of obligation with a ruler whose primary asset was prestige. These sources include chiefly titles, rituals that bound kings to clans, and recorded oral histories which defined Buganda's chiefly hierarchy as a set of relationships that commemorated the king's recognition of services performed for him.⁸ For example, the king's debt of obligation to the Elephant clan was re-enacted early in the reign of a new monarch through a ritual in which the chief royal herdsman, a titled position in the Elephant clan, brought cows into the king's enclosure, and made the king play on a flute that Kimera (Buganda's third *kabaka* [king] in Apolo Kaggwa's dynastic tradition)⁹ had played on and herd the cows for a short time. Members of the Reedbuck clan, who hunted elephants and gave the king tribute in ivory, brought a new king an elephant tusk, which he had to jump over, in order to increase the size of elephant herds.¹⁰ Although dynastic tradition states that the *kabaka* gave out land and authority over people, and in popular memory 'the great Chiefs together with the Bataka [clan heads, s. *Mutaka*] started as the kabaka's servants', a careful reading of tradition and ritual suggests that the kingdom coalesced when chiefs brought their land and people into a relationship of reciprocal obligation with the king.¹¹

Ethnographic observations from the late nineteenth and early twentieth century, as well as stories from dynastic tradition, suggest that chiefs conducted their battles over the prestige that would secure their followers in the court of the *kabaka*. Decisions that went in favour of one chief or clan at one time might be decided in favour of the other party at a later date, when the relative strength of the two parties – the love the *kabaka* felt for them – had shifted.[12] C.W. Hattersley, an early missionary, described the work of repairing a royal building before 1908: 'When the squad of men belonging to a given chief had finished their part of the work they seized a reed and came before their chief, and before the Katikiro [prime minister], to announce the completion of their portion, and danced up and down chanting peculiar refrains and behaving generally like madmen.'[13] This 'madness' conveyed the importance and satisfaction inherent in being men of the chief and of the king, and it also made a claim for the favouring of the presenting chief in relation to all other chiefs.

The ability to withhold allegiance was therefore critical to the social logic of Buganda. Followers could choose to leave their chiefs, and individual chiefs or coalitions of chiefs could, and did, withhold their support from the king. Passive opposition to a king could be extremely effective: the chiefs who met in the gathering place in the centre of the kingdom had the power to offer or withhold tribute and labour, and to choose the peers with whom they would align.[14]

The Challenge of Expansion

The seventeenth-century wars of expansion brought territory and captives into Buganda, and both acquisitions upset the order of the kingdom. The Ganda hierarchy of important chiefs almost doubled in size through the incorporation of the territories of Butambala, Gomba, Kyaggwe, Bulemezi and Buddu over the course of 100 years of wars. This territorial expansion enabled kings to assume a kind of power that had previously belonged to chiefs, that of creating dependants through the allocation of land. In the late seventeenth century, kings began to allocate regions as chiefships in the same way that chiefs allocated gardens for cultivation to followers. This represented a new role for kings, who had distributed prestige, but not land, in earlier generations. Apolo Kaggwa described kings' allocation of land in chiefships as an intentional circumvention of the power of other wielders of authority (at the same time rationalising his own assertion of power over others as a result of the 1900 Uganda Agreement's creation of private property in land (*mailo*)):

> King Mawanda found the whole of the land in the hands of the Bataka. He cut off a bit of land (uncultivated) from a butaka [landholding owned by a clan] and made it *butongole*.... The king wanted to get reports from his own men from various parts of the country so he put them in to a corner of the butaka and told the mutaka you needn't worry to come to see me and report, my man will do it, this was the beginning of the *basaza*, just as now the Government are giving milos.[15]

The perception of Buganda as a 'modernising bureaucracy' derives from the kings' increasing power over both land and the people on the land, and certainly royal power expanded in Buganda whenever kings created chiefships.

The new *ebitongole* chiefships created new kinds of conflict. As more chiefships were created, the share of the kingdom's power wielded by the chiefs of older provinces was somewhat diminished.[16] Yet the *ebitongole* did not recreate power in Buganda as something held by kings and 'king's men', whose only loyalty was to the king who appointed them. In the first place, the older regions still had the greatest prestige and thus a significant voice in decision-making at court. The chief of Kyaddondo, for example, 'was often surpassed by others in wealth, because he could not raise as much in taxes,' but he remained one of the highest-ranking chiefs because his county was one of the oldest in Buganda.[17] Furthermore, while newly appointed chiefs in recently conquered areas might be favourites of the *kabaka*, they still had to win the allegiance of the people who lived there through a long, slow process of creating relationships. Cohen estimates that constructing authority took forty years in Busoga.[18] Kaggwa's explanation may accurately point to the desire kings had to increase their autonomy, but it fails to describe the actual consequences of their actions.

The dynastic tradition records that at the same time that they created new chiefships kings made innovations in ritual in order to connect people more firmly to the centre of the kingdom and to clarify patterns of prestige. One example was the creation of the ritually powerful royal drum, *Kaulugumo*, which *Kabaka* Mutebi had made immediately after his failed attempt to dismiss the hereditary chiefs Mugema and Kaggo.[19] Another was the office of *Kibaale*, a chief whose responsibility was to 'try' a *kabaka* and determine whether he had acted wrongly, which *Kabaka* Mutebi created for members of the Oribi Antelope clan after he had removed the Oribi Antelope clan head from the position of *Mukwenda*, chief of Ssingo county.[20] This constitutional check on the power of *kabakas*, which might have been a form of compensation to the Oribi Antelope clan, or might have been a way of forcing the *kabaka* to admit that he had been wrong to take the Mukwendaship away from them, endured for the next century.

An explicit connection between political disorder and the creation of new ritual is made in the dynastic tradition regarding the installation of *Kabaka* Juuko. 'Diviners prophesied that there would be a rebellion' and told Juuko to create order in the *lukiiko* with a new ritual for seating the chiefs. A child of the *Mugema* (the prime minister to all deceased *kabaka*s and 'father' of the living *kabaka*) was to whip the chiefs who acted in a disorderly way, using a whip made of the sinews of a person sacrificed during the *kabaka*'s installation. According to Kaggwa, 'This position was very much respected, and parliament became much more dignified by the exercise of this power in preserving order.'[21] The need for a new method of keeping discipline, and the fact that this task was given to the son of the chief and clan elder with the greatest autonomy from a *kabaka*, suggests that chiefs had ceased to be able to determine their relative importance.

The disorder in the *lukiiko* was a result of the incorporation of chiefs of newly conquered territories into the gathering of chiefs before the king.

The incorporation of non-free people destabilised the kingdom even more profoundly. Records of royal wives and concubines provide insight into the number of non-free people coming into the kingdom. Kimbugwe, who ruled in the late sixteenth century, had seven women who were not named wives, i.e. who were probably captives. Kateregga, the next king, began the wars of expansion and had 300 such women. For the next hundred years or so, each king had between 100 and 700 women attached to the palace who did not have the status of named wives.[22] At the end of the eighteenth century, the numbers of non-free women in Buganda rose dramatically: Semakokiro had 8,500 non-free women, and his successor Kamanya had over 10,000. Stolen women were distributed to the principal chiefs of the kingdom, chiefs who had led expeditions, and men who had participated in them; female war captives enabled ordinary Baganda to begin to practise polygamy.[23] Ganda women and the free followers of chiefs suffered a drastic reduction in their status as a result of the importation of these massive numbers of non-free people, as the following section explains.

Ebitongole as Collections of Captive People

Captive people brought into the kingdom as a result of wars of expansion allowed both the king and other powerful men to create units of productive labour unhooked from networks of reciprocal obligation. At the height of the dynastic conflict associated with Buganda's territorial expansion, *Kabaka* Mawanda created a new kind of chiefship, *ebitongole*. Direct and indirect evidence suggests that *ebitongole* organised the labour of captive people. In contrast to the old pattern of chiefships which were named after important people or significant interactions in the past, sometimes having the purpose of commemorating a relationship or event, *ebitongole* chiefships were usually named for what they were supposed to accomplish, and they carried the implication of directing resources towards a particular productive activity. *Kabaka* Namugala, who probably ruled in the mid-eighteenth century, established the *ebitongole Ekigalagala* (for the purpose of spreading out) and *Kitamanyang'amba* (for the purpose of knowing what is said). A generation later, *Kabaka* Kamanya established the chiefship *Ekikinakulya* (for the purpose of things to eat).[24] The consolidation of military conquests was the purpose of some of the original *ebitongole* chiefships, which explains why they have been erroneously considered a form of military chiefship.[25] Settling an area in order to incorporate new territory into Buganda was one purpose towards which the *kabaka* directed productive resources, but there were many others. An *ekitongole* in Buganga was called *Ekibukula Mabira* (for the purpose of opening up of the forests) because a local clan elder had asked the *kabaka* for hunters to drive away elephants and buffaloes that were attacking people. The *ekitongole* consisted

Stolen People & Autonomous Chiefs in Buganda

of the uninhabited land that was supplied to the incoming hunters in order to meet their food needs.[26] Other *ebitongole* created in the same area were *Kikwekwesi*, whose purpose was to provide supplies for the head of all the *kabaka*'s servants, and *Kisomose*, the place where the makers of the *kabaka*'s drums and boards for the *mweso* game lived, grew their food, and carried out their work.[27]

The establishment of *Ebitongole* required an extremely large number of people to do work that was dangerous and that no-one would choose to do voluntarily. *Ebitongole* were created on land without people, and opening up new land in this region required immense amounts of labour. Mikairi Kidza's statement to the Butaka Land Commission of 1924 on the origin of the *Ekitongole* 'Ekirwanyamuli' at Golo in Buganga emphasised that *ebitongole* began with unoccupied land: 'The Chief Omulwanyamuli passed through Buganga with the Kabaka and he coveted the place as a good place for fishing and he applied to the Kabaka to give him a place there for this purpose, which the Kabaka did; but he did not turn out any Mutaka from his butaka land but only opened up new and uncultivated land.'[28] This point was also expressed by another prominent Muganda, Shem Spire Mukasa, in 1927. Mukasa asked Kaggwa why he had given himself lands complete with tenants in the post-1900 *mailo* allocation, when 'it was the custom of the country to create new estates by opening up new lands?'[29] According to the historian M.S.M. Kiwanuka, the *kabaka* created special *ebitongole* to open up resource-poor or unhealthy areas, such as the *mbwa* fly region of Kyagwe, and 'people would be obliged to go and settle there'.[30] That large numbers of non-free people were coming into Buganda at the same time that these new chiefships requiring large amounts of labour came into being, suggests that *ebitongole* were created to organise the labour of captives.

In the nineteenth century some chiefs clearly directed the work of the *ebitongole* they controlled towards profit, increasingly for themselves as well as for their king. The historian Michael Twaddle has demonstrated how the great hunter, soldier and chief, Kakungulu, acquired wealth for his own private purposes as well as for the *kabaka* through his *ekitongole*, *Ekirumba njovu*, (for the purpose of hunting elephants).[31] The leading chief of the late nineteenth and early twentieth centuries, Stanislaus Mugwanya, created his own *ekitongole*, as he remembered in 1924: 'Do you know that during the reign of *Kabaka* Mwanga a man named Vivi took part of this estate at Katende, and his headquarters was Chief Muwanda's old headquarters; and that I also took part of it and appointed my own Kitongole called Kirima Ntungo ('Sim sim [sesame] cultivators') at this place?'[32] Mugwanya may have been exporting sesame seeds to Bunyoro or producing them for the caravan trade; other people in East Africa began to organise slaves to produce food for the caravan trade at this time. The focused purpose of *ebitongole* – to cultivate sesame seeds, to obtain food at a fishing site, to hunt elephants – suggests specialised, organised labour, controlled more thoroughly than the free followers of chiefs.[33]

There is also some direct evidence that *ebitongole* consisted of non-free people. We know that the *Ekisalosalo*, one of the military regiment *ebitongole*, was formed 'for a body of pages captured in war'.[34] Similarly *Kabaka* Ssuna assigned an *ekitongole* for captured Nyoro potters.[35] In the late nineteenth century the *Mukwenda*, chief of Ssingo county, created an *ekitongole* named Ekirumba, in memory of Ddumba, Ssingo's previous county chief. The title of the head of this new *ekitongole* was *Mulumba*, and the first holder of this post was an enslaved Musoga man who had been captured in his childhood.[36] Apolo Kaggwa described free people joining *ebitongole* in search of security and wealth, but that happened later in the nineteenth century, after increasing enslavement for sale had changed *ebitongole* in ways that are described below.[37]

Ebitongole chiefships and stolen women undermined the practices of gift exchange and service which had previously connected the nodes of power in the Buganda polity. Eventually, the unobligated, non-free labour turned the logic of prestige in the capital upside-down. Kings who used non-free *ebitongole* to accomplish their goals did not need to ensure that the ancient, high-status chiefs of the kingdom would continue to supply tribute labour. At the same time, chiefs who controlled their own *ebitongole* became less reliant on the 'love' of the king. For example, a late nineteenth-century missionary observed that the king was intensely jealous and angry about the 'handsome houses and neat fences' in the capital which chiefs built using their *ebitongole*.[38]

These new avenues to prestige undermined the king's task of maintaining balance among chiefs through distribution, and led to escalating social violence inside Buganda. Chiefs were no longer competing amongst themselves for prestige, but instead began to join together in coalitions to place their preferred candidate on the throne. Thirteen *kabaka*s held power inside of five generations between around 1670 and 1812,[39] as princes and their factions fought each other for control of the spoils of expansion. Dynastic traditions provide mundane explanations for many of these regicides, but the fact that the habit of regicide began at the same time as expansion and incorporation of war captives suggests that coalitions of chiefs were trying to put 'their' prince on the throne in order to benefit most fully from the flow of captives. The security of chiefs (many of whom were also clan leaders) in office also became much more tenuous, as kings tried to reward their allies and punish those who aligned themselves against them. The perception that clans lost power and kings gained it during Buganda's expansion ignores the very short lifespan of kings of these generations. Kings may have been taking away many lineage privileges but lineages were killing many kings.

Since non-free people diminished the value of free followers to their chiefs, *ebitongole* and stolen women profoundly undermined the status of ordinary people in Buganda. Chiefs who had slave wives and slave workers had less need to prove by their behaviour that they were more generous and just than neighbouring chiefs in order to retain followers. The problem posed for free followers is evident in the increasing coercion of dependants which appears to have accompanied the expansion. The dynastic history regarding this period recorded a higher level of violence against followers than had occurred earlier and it is important to note that the dynastic history condemned that violence. [40] A gap opened up between the social power of followers asserted by Ganda proverbs, stories, and expressed views regarding social relations, and the character of those social relationships described by nineteenth-century visitors and participants.[41] Either Ganda people wrongly believed their society to allow women to choose their husbands and people to choose their chiefs, or the influx of non-free people with the expansion wars seriously disrupted practices of reciprocal obligation which people considered to be ordinary and unremarkable.

Kabaka Semakokiro, who ruled at the end of the eighteenth century, attempted to solve the problem of unending conflict among rivals for the throne by killing all the princes except for a few, who were instead imprisoned as insurance against the *kabaka* dying heirless. The historian Michael Wright was told by a clan elder, Kalikuzinga, that this solution had been considered so abominable that the priest of the god Mukasa had insisted on making the suggestion to the king with no one listening.[42] This drastic action not only ended competition for the throne, but also, by removing potential foci of opposition, eliminated some of the constraints on *kabakas*' actions. Nineteenth-century visitors to Buganda observed a kind of daily coercive violence which suggests a social order falling apart. Chiefs and the king mutilated their followers as a form of punishment for seemingly trivial offences. Followers' capacity to leave chiefs who did not treat them well had clearly eroded.[43] Killing people who attended the *kabaka*'s court appeared to be an almost casual occurrence. The foreigners who observed this assumed that Buganda had always been this way, but the Ganda chroniclers who wrote about it remembered the violence as something that became much worse during their lifetimes. Kaggwa wrote: 'On the whole this killing reached terrible excesses. Sometimes the king put to death his own children, brothers, and sisters. Sometimes it was the other way round, several of the children conspiring together to kill their father. The chiefs killed their servants for next to nothing. The death penalty became so ordinary that it often put the chiefs in a dilemma.'[44] The large-scale incorporation of non-free people set up a spiral of competition that led to this apparently unstoppable social violence.

The capacity of chiefs to exert pressure on the *kabaka* had been diminished by *ebitongole* created by the *kabaka*. On the other hand, *ebitongole* created by the chiefs undermined their need to please him. Meanwhile, free people had less bargaining power with chiefs who had masses of captive followers. All these factors contributed to escalating violence, even before people began to be sold for cloth in the second half of the nineteenth century.

Ebitongole in the Era of Firearms and the Slave Trade

In the deteriorating social conditions of the reign of *Kabaka* Mwanga (1886–97), the nature of *ebitongole* changed. Mwanga began to raid his own people to sell them into the slave trade, and those in the kingdom who had the means began to do the same thing. Extraction of wealth through violence became the primary activity of *ebitongole*; young men who controlled guns, rather than older leaders who controlled people and land, began to form them. Mwanga took large areas of land from county chiefs between 1886 and 1888 in order to create four new *ebitongole*, which he placed under the control of young men who already had armed followings. These were the *Ekitongole Ekiwuliriza* (the chiefship of listening carefully); the *Ekitongole Ekigwanika* (the chiefship of wealth); the *Ekitongole Ekijasi* (the chiefship of guns); and the *Ekitongole Ekiyinda* (the chiefship of menacing noise).[45] According to Southwold, these *ebitongole* represented Mwanga's attempt to remove power from the established chiefs and give it to young chiefs whom he could control more easily.[46] In fact, Mwanga was not in control of these chiefs, he was merely naming as chiefs the new men who already held power as autonomous controllers of people and guns, and thus attempting to assert authority over them.[47] That free people joined these new *ebitongole*, which had the character of private armies, does not negate the possibility that *ebitongole* had originally begun as organisations of primarily non-free people.

Conclusion

In Buganda, as in so many other African societies, enslavement led to profound transformation of the social order. Structures built on visible assertions of reciprocal obligation became less effective. The status of some followers – especially women – never recovered. The capacity of chiefs to make their voice heard became much more chaotic and arbitrary when the focus of chiefly competition switched from the prestige which attracted free followers to the power that controlled the distribution of non-free followers.

Buganda's wars of expansion, the incorporation of stolen people, and the creation of *ebitongole* did contribute to an increase of the *kabaka's* power and a diminution in the bargaining capacity of chiefs. The means through which this happened, however, was not the development of forms of efficient bureaucracy. Rather, Buganda's eighteenth- and nineteenth-century experiment with efficiency involved the concentrated labour of non-free people directed towards a particular purpose, and that specialisation had destabilising consequences for the Ganda polity. How the productive capacities of *ebitongole* might compare with many other innovations in labour organisation people made in the same period is a topic which historians have not yet considered.

Notes

1. Martin Southwold, *Bureaucracy and Chiefship in Buganda: The Development of Appointive Office in the History of Buganda*. East African Studies No. 14 (Kampala, n.d.).
2. M.S.M. Semakula Kiwanuka, *A History of Buganda from the Foundation of the Kingdom to 1900* (New York, 1972), pp.120–1; John Rowe, 'Revolution in Buganda 1856–1900' (unpublished PhD dissertation, University of Wisconsin, Madison, 1966), pp.25–6. Michael Twaddle observes that the one time when a distinction among *bakungu*, *batongole*, and *bataka* might make sense was in the 1880s when *kabakas* attempted to regain control of the polity by creating many new *ebitongole* chiefships. 'Muslim revolution in Buganda', *African Affairs*, 71 (1972), p.58.
3. Philip D. Curtin, *The World and the West, The European Challenge and the Overseas Response in the Age of Empire* (Cambridge, 2000), pp.116–27.
4. Holly Hanson, *Landed Obligation: The Practice of Power in Buganda* (Portsmouth, N.H., 2003).
5. Christopher Wrigley, *Kingship and State in Buganda* (Cambridge, 1996) suggests how this might have happened, and David Schoenbrun's works document the social and political resources of the early residents of the interlacustrine area. David Lee Schoenbrun, *A Green Place, A Good Place: A Social History of the Great Lakes Region, Earliest Times to the 15th Century*, (Portsmouth, NH, 1997); idem, *The Historical Reconstruction of Great Lakes Bantu Cultural Vocabulary: Etymologies and Distributions* (Köln, 1997).
6. Christopher C. Wrigley, *Crops and Wealth in Uganda: A Short Agrarian History* (Kampala, 1959), pp.2–3; J.M. Fortt and D.A. Hougham, 'Environment, population and economic history', in Audrey I. Richards, Ford Sturrock, and Jean M. Fortt (eds) *Subsistence to Commercial Farming in Present-Day Buganda* (Cambridge, 1973), p.18; J.M. Fortt, 'The distribution of the immigrant and Ganda population within Buganda', in Audrey I. Richards (ed.), *Economic Development and Tribal Change* (Cambridge, 1954), pp.83–84.
7. John Roscoe, *The Baganda: An Account of Their Native Customs and Beliefs* (1911, Reprint, New York, 1966), p.241; Martin Southwold, 'Leadership, authority, and the village community', in Lloyd Fallers (ed.), *The King's Men* (New York, 1964), p.214; Richard Waller, 'The traditional economy of Buganda' (Master of Arts Essay, University of London, School of Oriental and African Studies, 1971); Michael Wright observed that 'low tension' characterised Ganda political interactions, differences were not pursued to the point at which conflict would become necessary, *Buganda in the Heroic Age* (Nairobi, 1971), p.51. This perception stands in contrast to that of Lloyd Fallers that the lack of clearly delineated functions of each of the multiple office holders would have increased the power of the *kabaka*, 'Despotism, status culture and social mobility in an African kingdom', *Comparative Studies in Society and History*, 2 (1959), pp.4–32.
8. Kiwanuka, *History of Buganda*, pp.112–13; Julien Gorju, *Entre le Victoria, l'Albert et l'Edouard* (Rennes, 1920), p.136.
9. Apolo Kaggwa, *The Kings of Buganda*, M.S.M. Kiwanuka, trans. and ed. (Nairobi, 1971), p.195.
10. Roscoe, *The Baganda*, pp.147, 168.
11. Bataka Land Commission, Entebbe Secretariat Archives of the Uganda Protectorate, Secretariat Minute Paper, No. 6902, Danieri Serugabi, p.540 (hereafter 'Commission' followed by the name of the witness).
12. John Roscoe and Apolo Kaggwa, 'Enquiry into native land tenure in the Uganda

Protectorate', 1906, Rhodes House, Bodleian Library, Oxford, Shelfmark MS Africa s 17, pp.27, 70. This is one of the themes of the testimony of clan elders before the Bataka Land Commission in 1924; see for example the testimony of Daudi Basudde, Commission, p.352.

13 C.W. Hattersley, *The Baganda at Home* (London, 1968 [first published 1908]), p.20.

14 The story of the rise and fall of the servant Kiyanzi, which carried on for several generations, is an example of this. Kaggwa, *Kings*, pp.146–9.

15 It is useful to consider that the kings-over-clans perception of it gained currency in the context of twentieth-century politics. Apolo Kaggwa provided this explanation while he was being questioned about his actions in allocating land five years earlier. Half a century later, as the British Protectorate of Uganda gave way to a British-styled independent Uganda, Martin Southwold wrote about Ganda chiefship as a modernising bureaucracy. Roscoe and Kaggwa, 'Enquiry', p.4; Southwold, *Bureaucracy and Chiefship*, pp.9, 13.

16 Kiwanuka, *History of Buganda*, pp.115, 117.

17 Apolo Kaggwa, *Empisa za Baganda* (1907, partially translated by Ernest B. Kalibala under the title *The Customs of the Baganda*, May Mandelbaum, ed.) Columbia University Contributions to Anthopology, no. 22. (New York, 1934), p.162; Fallers, 'Social stratification in traditional Buganda', in Fallers, *King's Men*, p.96.

18 David William Cohen, *Womunafu's Bunafu: A Study of Authority in a Nineteenth-Century African Community* (Princeton, NJ, 1977), p.159.

19 Kaggwa, *Customs*, p.28; Kaggwa, *Kings*, p.144.

20 Roscoe and Kaggwa, 'Enquiry into native land tenure', testimony of Zachariah Kisingiri, p.10.

21 Kaggwa, *Customs*, p.78.

22 Nakanyike B. Musisi, 'Women, "elite polygyny", and Buganda state formation', *Signs*, 16, 4 (1991), pp.757–86.

23 Kaggwa, *Customs*, p.68; Gorju, *Entre le Victoria*, p.120.

24 'Bataka Land Commission', letter of Lukiko, p.563. 'Kabaka Namugala created two chieftainships called Ekigalagala and Kitamanyang'amba....Kabaka Kamanya created the chieftainship called Kinakulya...Kabaka Suna II created many new chieftainships such as Ekirumbya, Kisuna, Kitutumuzi, Kikebezi, Kintwa and many others...'

25 Kiwanuka makes this point, *History of Buganda*, p.120.

26 Commission, Mikairi Kidza and Stanislaus Mugwanya, pp.400–1. 'Q. Do you know the Kabaka's Kitongole called Ekibikula which was on Buganga? A. I know it. When the elephants and buffaloes attacked us in Buganga at that time our father Lusekera applied to the Kabaka for some hunters to drive away these elephants and buffaloes, and on their arrival in Buganga they were given this Kitongole called 'Ekibukula Mabira' (which means 'opening up of the forests').'

27 *Ibid.*, p.401. 'Q. Do you know the Kitongole called Kikwekwesi which was the head of all the Kabaka's servants? A. This Mutongole was merely allowed a temporary shelter at this place together with some others whom I have already mentioned. Q. Do you know Kimbugwe's man called Kisomose, the maker of drums and 'mweso' boards who lives at Buganga? A. I do not know him, and he never turned us out of our butaka land at Buganga.'

28 Commission, Mikairi Kidza, p.401.

29 Commission, Shem Spire Mukasa, questioning Kaggwa, p.522.

30 Kiwanuka, *History of Buganda*, p.119. Mbwa flies are vectors of several serious diseases.

31 Michael Twaddle, *Kakungulu and the Creation of Uganda 1868–1928* (Athens, OH, 1993), p.20.

32 Commission, Stanislaus Mugwanya, p.395.

33 Commission, Mikairi Kidza, p.401; Stanislaus Mugwanya, p.305.

34 M. Wright, *Buganda and the Heroic Age* (Nairobi, 1971), p.26.

35 Commission, Yosiya Sensalire, p.472. 'Q. Do you know that Kabaka Suna gave this estate Sanda to the Banyoro potters? A. I know that the potters occupied one part of it; but afterwards the Kabaka removed them from this estate and collected them together

and gave them the estate called Nakigala to settle there.'
36 Rev. J.F. Faupel, *African Holocaust: the Story of the Uganda Martyrs* (London, 1962), pp.29–30.
37 Apolo Kaggwa, *Basekabaka be Buganda* (typescript of English translation by Simon Musoke, Africana Collection, Makerere University Library), pp.340–1.
38 Robert Pickering Ashe, *Chronicles of Uganda* (New York, 1895), pp.27, 94–5; Bartolomayo Musoke, *Buganda ne Kabaka* (Mengo, 1939: typescript translation, 'Buganda and the King', Cambridge University Library), p.82.
39 Henri Médard, 'Croissance et crises de la royauté du Buganda au XIXe siècle' (unpublished PhD dissertation, University of Paris I, 2001), p.29.
40 Kaggwa, *Basekabaka be Buganda*, pp.71/126.
41 One of Mutesa's first foreign visitors commented on this gap. C. Chaillé Long, *Central Africa* (London, 1876), pp.129, 131.
42 Wright, *Heroic Age*, p.2.
43 Cosmas Gitta, 'International human rights: an imperial imposition? A case study of Buganda, 1856–1955' (unpublished PhD dissertation, Columbia University, 1998), p.123; Alexander M. Mackay, *A. M. Mackay: Pioneer Missionary of the Church Missionary Society in Uganda* (London, 1890), p.199.
44 Kaggwa, *Customs*, p.84.
45 Kiwanuka, *History of Buganda*, pp.198–9; Kaggwa, *Basekabaka*, pp.99/143.
46 Southwold, *Bureaucracy and Chiefship*, pp.15–17.
47 Kiwanuka, *History of Buganda*, p.199. According to Twaddle, the purpose of these new *ebitongole* chieftaincies was to guard Mwanga, but the information available about them suggested the *ebitongole* acted in their own interest. *Kakungulu*, p.59.

Seven

Women's Experiences of Enslavement & Slavery in Late Nineteenth- & Early Twentieth-Century Uganda

MICHAEL W. TUCK

Introduction

The subject of slavery remains one of the key issues in African studies and, as the Introduction to this book makes clear, the subject of slavery and slave trading in East Africa has been relatively understudied. I would go even further to contend that the aspect of slavery about which we have the least detailed information is the lives of people in slavery. One problem has been a lack of sources. Recently I uncovered some material which, when added to known sources, will help to shed light on women's enslavement and their lives as slaves in Uganda, especially in the kingdom of Buganda. This chapter focuses on women because of their importance to the institution of slavery within Africa, and to societies in Uganda.

Since the strength of this essay is the sources, some explanation of them is required. The major sources used are descriptions of the lives of fifty-five women who were slaves or held servile status in Uganda in the latter part of the nineteenth century. The women, or the men to whom they were connected, were preparing for Catholic baptism and the accounts are attempts by the Catholic missionaries to sort out their marriage histories. These accounts, known as 'Marriage Cases', were recorded by priests from the Saint Joseph's Foreign Missionary Society, known more colloquially as the Mill Hill Mission.[1] While the individual accounts are not as long or detailed as some well-known sources from East Africa,[2] the main value here is the number of examples. Most sources on slavery in Buganda consist of statements about categories of slaves and generalisations about what slave status was like. These records give us the best view we have of women's actual lives in slavery, and allow us to make general statements on a firmer foundation. Going beyond that, having fifty-five accounts means that we can see patterns in women's experiences that individual accounts cannot offer. Another point that makes these sources valuable is that they come from areas not only outside the capital, but even outside the centre of Buganda. Most of the sources we have hitherto had on slavery in Buganda recorded the observations of people in the capital, and consequently tell us little about how life may have differed in more remote areas.

Unfortunately, although the information in the accounts seems to be accurate, it was not recorded verbatim from the women or men. The priests wrote the accounts in the third person which robs them of the potential power and immediacy that first person accounts would likely have had. Therefore, although we have the data, we do not hear the women's voices directly. Another major caveat about the sources is that they only describe the lives of women kept within the region, and not of those who were exported. However, as I shall show below, their lives do demonstrate some of the mechanisms of slave transfer, and the implicit attitudes regarding women slaves. In addition, following Paul Lovejoy, I argue that the evidence shows that the impact of the long-distance slave trade caused a transformation in slavery within Uganda, which in turn affected practices of servitude and economic exchange, and ultimately the status of women within Ganda society in particular.[3]

Definitions of Slavery

Before looking at the lives of women, it is first necessary to note how scholars have defined slavery in Buganda. They agree that Ganda society was hierarchical and that servility and patron/client relationships governed many social interactions. Slaves were at the bottom of the hierarchy, but there are different views on the fundamental characteristic of slavery. Twaddle emphasised slaves' alien status and lack of kin connections.[4] Reid saw the right of freedom of movement as the characteristic which distinguished *Bakopi* (peasants) from slaves, while identifying most slaves as either foreigners or of foreign origin.[5] Both recognised a variety of occupations and statuses of slaves, and the importance of routes of enslavement to future treatment. Twaddle quotes Mulira at length on categories of slaves, and it is worth repeating here:

> Peasants were rewarded for valour in battle by the present of slaves by the lord or chief for whom they had fought. They could be given slaves by relatives who had been promoted to the rank of chiefs, and they could inherit slaves from their fathers. There were the *abanyage* (those pillaged or stolen in war) as well as the *abagule* (those bought). All these came under the category of *abenvumu* or true slaves, that is to say people not free in any sense. In a superior position were the young Ganda given by their maternal uncles into slavery [or pawnship], usually in lieu of debts... Besides such slaves both chiefs and king were served by sons of well to do men who wanted to please them and attract favour for themselves or their children. These were the *abasige* and formed a big addition to a noble household.... All these different classes of dependents in a household were classed as

abaddu (male servants) or *abazana* (female servants) whether they were slave or free-born.[6]

In addition, Twaddle described slaves' occupations, from labourers and porters to administrative slaves.[7] Twaddle and Reid agree that women constituted the majority of slaves in Buganda, and that they were mainly held in domestic servitude as cultivators, wives and concubines.

Mulira's description (in addition to other sources) points out some of the basic arguments that scholars before now have made about slavery in Buganda. The historiography emphasises that there was a hierarchy among slaves, and that how persons became enslaved was important, and had a significant impact on their subsequent lives. These distinctions were apparent to Baganda, and people could be categorised based on their path to bondage. Each category had terms to describe it, which were well-known. People's roles or occupations in slavery varied, and also affected their social position. Finally, there was a gendered dimension to slavery, with some of the higher status positions, such as those in administration, nearly always being limited to men.

Becoming a Slave

Based on the discussions of slavery sketched out above, it is important to consider how women ended up in slavery. What becomes apparent is that the strict categorisation offered by Mulira does not match with women's real experiences as revealed in the missionary records. Table 7.1 shows a breakdown of how the fifty-five women originally became slaves, although, of course, individuals also may have been sold, exchanged, or kidnapped after becoming slaves.[8]

Table 7.1 How women became slaves

Method	No.	%
Kidnapping/stolen	20	36.4
Sale or exchange	18	32.7
Gifts	8	14.5
Inheritance	2	3.6
Debt/bondage/pawn	1	1.8
Not recorded	6	10.9

The first point that is apparent is the large percentage of women who were kidnapped or stolen, which sets Uganda apart from other areas studied. Scholars argue that most enslavements occurred as a result of different types of violence. In descending order of importance such violence involved warfare conducted for political purposes, state-directed slave raids, and kidnapping or raiding by individuals without state support.[9] Although the women who related their stories (and the priests recording them) did not always specify, evidence suggests that most of the kidnapping was done by individuals conducting raids without the oversight of the *Kabaka* or his court. The most important piece of evidence is that, among the women kidnapped into slavery, only five detail the type of distribution indicative of Ganda formal warfare or state-directed raids, where captives were taken to the *Kabaka*'s enclosure and then given to followers, or distributed by senior chiefs.[10] All of the other women, and the men who were often the informants, described women being kidnapped directly from their families. This should not be too surprising, given the context of the wars and the civil unrest of the later nineteenth century, as will be discussed below. I argue that the large percentage of women who were kidnapped by individuals, rather than as part of formal war parties, indicates the lawlessness of the border areas, and the freedom of operation that chiefs and other individuals enjoyed in these areas. Such kidnapping also implicitly supports Reid's assertion that the central Ganda state in this era was in decline. One would have expected a strong *Kabaka* to control raids from the capital so that he could direct the warfare as well as disburse the booty to followers. This evidence underscores Twaddle's depiction of late nineteenth-century Buganda as experiencing a 'spiral of violence' to feed the domestic and export trades in slaves, although, as Reid points out, that violence was not necessarily state warfare.[11]

While the Mill Hill marriage cases come mainly from Buganda and therefore are most likely to contain the accounts of women enslaved elsewhere and brought to Buganda, they also contain evidence of women who were enslaved or held elsewhere in the region. Twelve of the records mention the location where the woman was kidnapped. Of these twelve women, seven were kidnapped in Busoga, most then being taken to Buganda. One Ganda woman had been exported to Busoga, while another was taken from one area of Buganda to another. Two of the women were Banyoro, one being held in Buganda, the other in Buvuma. The final case was captured in Buvuma and brought to Buganda. These cases give us some indication of how widespread the phenomenon of slave raiding was, primarily in the border areas.

It is also important to note when most of the women were enslaved. Dates were always given as approximates, usually in the terms the women themselves gave, such as in 'the beginning of Mwanga's [1884–97] reign'. Even without exact dates their testimony does help us establish a time period during which many kidnappings occurred. Those which gave some idea of dates were clustered in two groups: the largest group corresponded to the reign of King Mwanga, especially the early years of 1884–86. The second group referred to the 'Mahometan war', or Karema's reign, which would be c. 1888–90. A few scattered references were made to dates even further in the past, from c.1870 to c.1880. This information supports the general assumptions in the literature that the unrest of the religious wars was a fruitful time for enslavements, and that Buganda's raids on its neighbours under Mwanga and his predecessors were also a source of slaves. To emphasise that enslavements by kidnapping did not end under the British protectorate, the most recent case to cite a date occurred in about 1895. It is also relevant that these dates correspond to the major years of the export trade out of Buganda, where these women kept in the country may well have been replacements for women exported. Reid says that Buganda was exporting 1,000–2,000 slaves per year from the early 1880s, but that the export had pretty much come to an end by about 1890.[12] But beyond simply confirming general accounts in the literature, the dates and routes to enslavement lend important insights into political and social conditions in late nineteenth-century Buganda, such as the status and roles of women, the range and extent of patriarchal authority, and the intersection of slavery with patron-client relationships.

Sale or exchange, the second most common route to enslavement, indicates women who were sold for money or goods, or who were traded for other women. In both cases the important point is how, due to the exchange of females in the region, women had come to be commodities and virtually interchangeable.

Table 7.2 Prices of women/girls sold into slavery

Name (Case number)	Age at sale	Date of sale	Price
Mwanika (14)	about 9 years old	c. 1895	1 gun
Mwamirembe (15)	about 9 years old	c. 1895	9000 shells
Tulinomubezi (28)	very young	c. 1888	1 cow
Tibwantusa (46)	young girl	c. 1885	5 or 7 cows

Whereas these people were sold in an internal or domestic slave system, purchases made with cowrie shells, a gun or other imported goods do indicate the influence of the external long-distance trade system in the region. The importation of shells and firearms, and their adoption as currencies of a sort, shows the interconnectedness of the internal and external markets for slaves. It also seems likely that if Buganda was exporting about 2,000 slaves a year during the later nineteenth century, this would have increased prices internally as well. These prices mostly correspond well with Henri Médard's compilation of slave prices,[13] keeping in mind the caveats of differences in exchange rates of imported goods and domestic livestock, as pointed out by Reid.[14]

The only glaring difference is in the price for Tibwantusa from Kome Island. Rather than see this as possibly in error, I think it represents an important corrective to the data collected from around the capital or other major trading centres. In that case it is not surprising that a remote area like the Kome Islands, with presumably greater transportation costs and lower supply, would have unusually high prices.[15] Similarly, in the 1860s it seems that prices for slaves in northern Singo were about twice what they were in the Ganda capital.[16] In addition, it is significant that none of the women who were sold mentioned any type of slave market. While that level of detail could simply be missing from the data, all indications are that the sales were privately conducted between two individuals. This corresponds to Roscoe's statement that 'slaves were not often taken into the market-place for sale, but were sold by private arrangement'.[17] Such evidence provides a correction to the impression given in Twaddle's work from his discussion of the slave market operating at Gublas in Busoga.[18] While slave markets did undoubtedly exist, the evidence indicates that they were not a major factor in internal slave transfers, but perhaps operated for the export trade.

Women also found themselves in bondage as a result of being given by one man to another. Six of the eight women were given away as gifts to service a network of patronage, being shunted up or down the political ladder, either from a follower to a chief, or from a chief to a follower. In three of the cases women were given away by their relatives, either their father or their brother. Whereas the giving of women did not necessarily entail slave status, in the majority of these cases the women clearly were given without their consent, and the normal bridal dowry which would have signified a free and legitimate marriage was not paid. The evidence supports the conclusion that these were previously free women being given into bondage, a conclusion which holds for the women who were inherited into slavery, as well as the woman who was given away to satisfy a debt. In trying to explain why a father would give away his daughter, we can turn to Lovejoy's observation that '[t]here were also cases of men pawning or selling free children and other relatives, even when slaves were available, but this was done to protect personal wealth at the expense of the lineage.'[19] Thus, we may well be seeing a situation of the triumph of individual drive over the needs of the lineage, again something which could well be a partial result of the impact of long-distance trade. In the meantime, these examples of women being used as gifts to superiors or subordinates demonstrates how the slave and patron-client systems overlapped in an important way. Rather than seeing slavery supplant clientship, we see examples of the transfer of women into bondage to support the patron-client relationship. We shall discuss a similar feature of the social system below, where women were being given away or transferred after being enslaved.

Women's Lives in Bondage

We need to look at what the sources tell us about women's actual lives in slavery and servitude, and how that compares with descriptions of normative behaviour and treatment from the secondary literature. The literature often discusses women's experiences in terms of categories: as wives, concubines, labourers and so on. I instead looked for patterns in the women's experiences, whether there were commonalities such as slave women being mainly in larger households or smaller ones, or whether they were more likely to be a man's first or later partner, or anything that could be termed a normal or average experience for a woman in bondage in Buganda. I could find almost none. This in itself tells us something: that the phenomenon of enslaved women was so widespread, among all status levels and in all social niches, that concepts of categories do not accurately reflect historical experience. Almost the only commonality was women's domination or control by men, but even that was not a given, since there is evidence of women's resistance, and also a few cases of women owning women.

But just as problematic as definitions of slavery were definitions of wife and marriage, and the distinctions between wives and slaves. All the women in my data set performed almost the same tasks in a household, primarily cultivation, cooking and child-rearing. The differences came in their rights and how they could express them, and in the control men had over these women. The nature of the marriage, or in general the relationship between the slave and the owner or master, largely determined the rights the woman had, and the restrictions placed on her. There was a continuum of marriage relationships among the Baganda which ranged from a marriage where the woman had full social rights and few restrictions to a marriage in which the woman was virtually a slave. The different marriage relationships were predicated on how the woman came into the relationship, the social relationship between her family and her husband's family, and how the marriage was consecrated or acknowledged.[20] In fact, although the missionary priests refer to domestic slaves or servants as 'cooking women', in Ganda culture wives literally were cooking women. One of a woman's primary duties was cooking for her husband. In Luganda, as in other Bantu languages, the word used for a woman to be married to a man was the passive form of the verb meaning 'to cook'.[21]

Thus, the terminology describing women's slave status is not necessarily explanatory. Neither, it turns out, is the term 'slave wife' which is used in the literature, and which we must discuss. There is an assertion in the literature that women could be kidnapped to become wives, a status that was presumably distinct from that experienced by domestic slaves. For example, Twaddle explains that, although the Protestant Ganda leaders signed a pledge in 1893 not to take more slaves, they only meant chattel slaves, and not slave wives for distribution among subordinates.[22] Other secondary literature suggests that women taken to be 'slave wives' were not a single, homogeneous group, arguing that it was possible to distinguish both between slave and regular wives, and between women who were enslaved to become wives and those enslaved for other purposes.[23] However, the idea that women were ever enslaved to be made wives is not supported by the evidence. First, there is little evidence of a pattern of experience that corresponds to the image of a slave wife who was kidnapped and then retained by her capturers' chief, or given to a follower who had to keep her. In fact, women who were kidnapped presumably with the intention that they would become wives in practice were often sold on or given away (see below), and their experience in this regard was no different from that of women who were enslaved by other means. Second, no matter what one's definition of a slave wife might be, very few of the women seem to have been treated as wives.

Almost none of the women were considered to be full wives, who had gone through the rituals of gift exchange between two families. In fact, in an example of the maxim of 'the exception that proves the rule', according to the records only three or four of the women did have their relationships with their masters regularised by performance of marriage rituals, in one case almost two decades after being kidnapped.[24] However, these reports of regularised marriage came solely from the men, and may have been an attempt to legitimise their relationships to the priests. The story that sounds the most plausible came from a man named Nkakata who told how he was given Yanyiriza, when he and she were both about fifteen years old. She was given to him by *Kabaka* Mutesa [1856–84], after which Nkakata 'took a goat to her people at Jinja, Busoga. He also gave them a *lubugo* [barkcloth] and a parcel of salt.'[25] Since at the time the story was recorded he was trying to get rid of her, and thus had all the motive in the world to deny any formal relationship, the fact that he reported a gift given to her parents rings true. It also corresponds precisely to Roscoe's explanation of a man's duties after being given a woman by the *Kabaka* or a chief.[26] However, it is necessary to point out that in other cases where women were given by chiefs or royals the men did not bother to pursue this action. We can therefore conclude that these exceptions are just that, and only point up the lack of formalised marriages of any type among the rest of the women and men in the accounts.

If women were not primarily wives for the men and mothers for their children, it becomes apparent that most were domestic servants and helpers. In the words of one of the accounts: 'Alirwa is a woman of Batume but was not married to him – her work is to kulima [cultivate] and to cook Balume's food.'[27] There was an accepted status of women in Buganda who cooked food and cultivated for men, but who were not their wives. Similarly, women were given or lent to visitors, including merchants and missionaries, to help with cultivation, cooking and other domestic service. While there may have been sexual aspects to some of those relationships, there is little evidence that it was a common feature. As pointed out below, such relationships seem rarely to have resulted in children, and the women's primary duty was domestic service, so they should not really be defined as concubines. Even the Mill Hill priests who recorded the slave accounts had their own 'cooking women', and there is certainly no evidence that there were sexual relationships in those cases.[28]

Names can also shed light on the tasks women were expected to perform. Two of the slave women were named *Tulinomubezi*, which translates as 'we have a helper'.[29] Both of these women were acquired as children, and while they may have been so named by their parents, it seems more likely, especially given their childhood entrée to bondage, that they were re-named by their masters. This tells us something about how they were viewed within the households in which they lived. And whereas the literature on women in Africa emphasises women's dual contributions to production and reproduction, what is apparent in Buganda is that all women were valued for their domestic service, which could be considered production but which was rarely production for a market. The most important task was cultivation and preparation of *matoke*, the steamed plantain dish which was the *sine qua non* of Ganda-ness. Women could find themselves serving individual men or larger households of chiefs or prominent individuals who needed women to produce food for followers and guests.[30] On occasion, women were in bondage to other women, in one case it seems as a slave to a slave, but their duties were the same, and the evidence shows that female owners were no different from male owners in their control or transfer of slave women.[31]

It is not surprising that men would not seek to make slave women full wives, since that would reduce their control over them. Women had very little they could do to change the situation. Some scholars of slavery suggest that having children with a master would improve a woman's status, but there is no evidence of that for Buganda. There is a record of only eight of the fifty-five women having living children with the men who controlled them at the time their cases were considered. While not all records are complete, the priests would have considered this significant information, and would have enquired about it. A few of the other women had had children, but these did not survive. Of the eight, only one had what might be called a stable marriage, where both partners wanted to stay together. In all other cases either they were already estranged, the woman was seeking to leave, or the men had driven the women away. In most of the eight cases the women went back to their families in spite of having to leave the children behind with their fathers' kin group. Slave women who were not full wives could be disposed of at any point, especially when they got older and were unable to work as much or were past child-bearing. Unlike free wives, slave women driven back to their families did not get the bridewealth returned, since none was normally paid. In fact, if they married another man he would probably have had to pay the bridewealth to the woman's master or former master. Men could also keep any children from the relationship without any interference from in-laws, and simply send the women away, or if possible sell them. Younger women could still be given to followers and junior lineage members. In this time of civil unrest and economic shifts, the men who controlled slave or dependent women wanted maximum flexibility in deciding whether to keep, distribute or sell them.

Evidence supporting the assertion that men wanted flexibility in distributing women can be found in the fact that, even after their initial enslavement, women were often exchanged or transferred, sometimes through many hands. Twenty of the women belonged to two or more people as slaves. Women changed owners in many ways: they were sold, pawned, inherited, given away, kidnapped, or recaptured after running away. One example was Tatenda, who was given away as a child by her father to pay off a debt, which initiated a sequence of exchange in which she passed into the possession of three different men by the time she turned eleven. The further exchange of women also underscores how women were increasingly treated as commodities. That was certainly true of Tatenda, who as a pawn should have stayed with the person or lineage to whom the debt was owed, and not been further transferred. Other cases also showed how women were treated as interchangeable objects. Perhaps one of the most extreme, but also very instructive, examples was the case of Marta Alibanlide.

> Marta ... says she was stolen when a child by Bagya, who sold her to Kimpeme, who in his turn sold her to or rather gave her in exchange to Nasaza who had lent Kimpime a woman whom he sold in Bunyoro. Nasaza sold her again to Musagala Kibuwuka for another woman who had rebelled. Now Kibuwuka agrees he got her from Musagala in change [sic] but Musagala is his brother and had got her from Senkezi who robbed her in Busoga.

In most cases the continued exchange of women also had the effect of making their eventual return home very difficult. This was especially true of those enslaved as young girls. This may have been one reason for the frequent movement of women away from the area in which they were enslaved, something which was a common technique in West Africa for establishing control over an enslaved individual. The further they were from home the less likely they would be to try to escape, and the more likely that they would obey their master because they had few alternatives. Four of the women whose data I have, though, did know where their families were, or their families had news of them.[32]

The continual exchange of women also points out their importance in Buganda beyond their contributions to the domestic sphere. Reading the accounts it is clear that men did not willingly live without women; even males as young as sixteen were lent or given women to serve them. These exchanges became the underpinnings of a network of reciprocal arrangements that occurred between social, political and lineal juniors and seniors. Ultimately women were the social glue that bound men to one another in patron-client relationships, and also which bound families, clans and lineages to one another. The case of Yanyiriza, cited above, was probably a classic example of the gift of a woman by a *Kabaka* to one of his followers.[33] The gift of a woman from a superior carried with it presumed loyalty in exchange. A slave woman, Kangao, was given by a chief to a man called Sekibobo, but she was taken back by the chief because Sekibobo 'refused to become a man of his'.[34] In fact, one could go further and argue that chiefs were under some obligation to provide women for their followers. In two instances chiefs gave women to their followers, and when those women died the chiefs supplied other women to replace them.[35] Exchange also worked in the other direction, such as with Alimonya, who was given by her father to a chief because 'he was a man of that chief'.[36] Although one could argue that a transfer from a subordinate to a superior was more in the nature of an apprenticeship for the child involved, for girls it more likely shifted them into a situation where they were domestic help and future wives for the head of the household, but without the bridal dowry and protection of being full wives.

One conclusion that we can draw from the frequent transfer of women is that slavery in this period meant instability for women: enslaved women were often traded, sold or re-sold, and clearly could not count on maintaining ties with any one individual or group. Since the societies of this area determined citizenship by social ties, whether to family or clan, this essentially meant that slaves were without kin and therefore without membership in the society. Nor could enslaved women count on assimilation to ameliorate their condition. In fact, it is hard to find evidence of assimilation, either attempts at it by slave owners or desire for it by slaves. Again, the cases of the small number of women who had children with their masters indicate that this was not a route to integrating into the new homestead or society. The only evidence that looks like masters attempting to assimilate slave women is the fact that a number of women were renamed by their new owners, usually it seems to correspond to more common names in the areas where they now lived, such as Nalugonda, a Musoga woman, whose name was changed to Alirwa after she was taken to Buganda.[37] However, renaming was probably less an attempt to allow the women to fit in than it was a means of breaking their connections with their points of origin and past lives. In fact, we see the opposite of assimilation, which was the inheritance of slave status from one generation to another.[38]

It is worth noting that, in spite of the overall restrictions women may have faced, a number of them displayed a great deal of courage and strength in resisting. One woman, Cecilia, ran away twice and refused to go back.[39] A woman who was enslaved in Bunyoro took advantage of the chaos after Kabaleega's [1871–99] deposition to flee, and an unnamed woman at Nazigo in northern Buganda also ran away twice from her 'husband'.[40] In these types of cases we need to consider what we mean by resistance. Since we can recover something of the women's actions but not necessarily their thoughts, it is hard to come to conclusions about their consciousness. Given the context of widespread acceptance of slavery in the region, it seems likely that what the women were resisting was not slavery *per se*, but the particular circumstances or conditions in which they found themselves. One example was Mujemula who specifically told the priest that she fled a man that she did not like. However, she did not achieve freedom, being kidnapped by other men while on the run.[41] Thus, when fleeing slavery women often only ended up in another situation of bondage, unless they could get back to their families. Perhaps the ease with which women were transferred from one man to another also made it easier for women who fled a man to find another situation. Although, as argued above, most women would have found it difficult to return to their families, they were quite successful in finding better situations. When Cecilia fled her master she did not know where to run, and headed back to a previous master. Even this type of resistance is an important correction to the reports of contemporary European observers who described women slaves as largely passive, and resigned to their fate.[42] We do not have many examples of day-to-day types of resistance in the marriage cases, but perhaps the best evidence is the number of cases themselves. The large number of women who sought to become Christians, and use that as a route out of bondage and dependent relationships, is a testament to their intelligent response to circumstances as they used the availability of the priests to win their freedom.[43]

Discussion and Conclusions

Quoting Macdonald from 1897 that 'a woman was an article of barter', Reid reviews the evidence and concludes that '[t]he commonness of a trade in female slaves is thus suggested'.[44] I would argue that this chapter conclusively demonstrates such a trade, and the wide extent of slavery of women within Buganda, to a degree not before known. All of the evidence, including that in this essay, shows that there were profound transformations in slavery in the nineteenth century. The categories of slaves and definitions given by Mulira appear to have broken down under the increasing slave raiding of the late nineteenth century. There has been little consideration given before now to how the meanings of these terms may have changed over time; thus, we have previously been presented with a static picture of what the Baganda thought about slaves, and how they categorised them. By moving beyond terms and categories, this chapter has shown that for women of the region the late nineteenth century was a time of widespread vulnerability and dependence.

Lovejoy's synthesis examined the transformations that occurred in domestic slavery and slave trading as a result of the impact of the external trade in slaves across Africa. Whereas he argues that much of that transformation was in the use of slaves for production, for Eastern Africa he concluded that 'In contrast to the West African coast, the domestic economy [in Eastern Africa] did not experience the kind of transformation to "legitimate" trade that could result in the exploitation of slaves in a productive capacity. Consequently, slavery in many parts of the interior reinforced a social order based on dependency but not on the exploitation of slaves to produce commodities.'[45] That was true for Buganda, but I would add that the increased exploitation of slaves not only reinforced the social order, it also changed it. It had a deleterious effect on the status of women, and it underpinned the power of senior individuals at the expense of the lineage or social group. Senior men were able to use gifts or loans of slave women to extend their patronage. As a result, power in Ganda society also came to be more masculinised, with even senior women operating in the same fashion. This was one cause of the decline in women's power in the late nineteenth and early twentieth centuries.

Going further, we also see the transformation in the status of women in society, the legacy of which affected women certainly throughout the first half of the twentieth century. In Buganda it was clear that the expansion of and transformation in slavery came about in co-ordination with the clientship system already in place, and not as a result of external demand for products. This may be because of Buganda's distance from the coast, and the unprofitability of producing goods for export in the nineteenth century. It may also be that in the turmoil of the later nineteenth century individuals in Buganda, primarily senior men, decided to increase their social standing if not their wealth *per se* by concentrating on the control of dependants, including slaves and others, through the use of slaves. This would translate into wealth via production for export in the twentieth century when many of the senior men of Buganda would be able to use their control of labour, along with their access to newly instituted freehold land tenure, to produce cotton for export. I would argue that we need to look for the roots of the patron-client and labour systems of the early twentieth century in the slave systems of the late nineteenth century.[46]

Notes

1 The records of these cases can be found in Mill Hill Mission archives in two locations. Forty-three cases were found in Jinja, Uganda, in three separate files among the Mill Hill papers kept in a small archive at the Bishop's office. The files were labeled: 'History I, 1894–1899'; 'M/15/3, Marriage Cases 1896-1901'; 'M/15/3, Marriage Cases 1902/1903'. The other twelve cases were described in books one through four of the Nsambya Diaries, kept at the main archives of the Mill Hill mission at their headquarters in north London. They were catalogued as 'UGA-Box 5-File a'. Subsequent references in this chapter to specific women or cases will cite the appropriate source for that information, along with the woman's name when known. Although an argument can be made for changing or suppressing the women's names, I think that using them reveals more accurately their historical experience, and makes it easier to see them as real people, and not just as cases.

2 Perhaps the best accounts can be found in Marcia Wright, 'Women in peril: A commentary on the life stories of captives in nineteenth-century East-Central Africa', *African Social Research*, 20 (Dec. 1975), pp.800–19; Edward A. Alpers, 'The story of Swema: female vulnerability in nineteenth-century East Africa,' in Claire C. Robertson and Martin A. Klein (eds), *Women and Slavery in Africa* (Portsmouth, NH, 1997), pp.185–219.

3 Paul E. Lovejoy, *Transformations in Slavery: A History of Slavery in Africa*. 2nd edn (New York, 2000), *passim*.

4 Michael Twaddle, 'The ending of slavery in Buganda,' in Suzanne Miers and Richard Roberts (eds), *The End of Slavery in Africa* (Madison, WI, 1988), p.121.

5 Richard Reid, *Political Power in Pre-Colonial Buganda* (Oxford, 2002), pp.113–14.

Women's Experiences of Enslavement & Slavery in Uganda

6   A.I. Richards, *Economic Development and Tribal Change* (Cambridge, 1954), pp.170-1, quoted in Twaddle, 'Ending of slavery,' p.123.
7   Twaddle, 'Ending of slavery,' p.122.
8   In some cases it is not clear if the woman was already a slave before being sold or given to her current owner; in those cases the first known type of transaction is used.
9   Lovejoy, *Transformations in Slavery*, pp.3–4; Patrick Manning, *Slavery and African Life: Occidental, Oriental, and African Slave Trades* (Cambridge, 1990), pp.88–9.
10 Mujemula, 16 November 1901, and Yanyiriza, 6 February 1900, in file 'M/15/3, Marriage Cases 1896-1901'; Alibadzewa, 31 May 1901, Nsambya Diary, Book 1, 24 May 1901- 30 June 1901; Tulibantu, Nsambya Diary, Book 3, 9 August 1901-12 Sept. 1901; Nalugonda or Alirwa, Nsambya Diary, Book 4, 13 September 1901-10 October 1901. Royal distribution of slaves is described in Reid, *Political Power*, p.116.
11 Twaddle, 'Ending of slavery', pp.119, 122; Reid, *Political Power*, p.162.
12 *Ibid.*, pp.160–4.
13 Henri Médard, 'Croissance et crises de la royauté du Buganda au XIXe siècle' (unpublished PhD dissertation, Université Paris I Pantheon Sorbonne, U.F.R. d'Histoire, 2001), pp.781–5.
14 Reid, *Political Power*, p.163.
15 The sources do not detail the place of origin of the other women mentioned in this table. Since they typically did comment if the woman was from far away it seems likely that they were from eastern Buganda or Busoga.
16 J.A. Grant, *A Walk Across Africa* (Edinburgh & London, 1864), p.258, as cited in Reid, *Political Power*, p.162.
17 John Roscoe, *The Baganda: an Account of their Native Customs and Beliefs*, 2nd edn (London, 1965), p.456.
18 Twaddle, 'Ending of slavery,' p.132.
19 Lovejoy, *Transformations in Slavery*, p.248.
20 For marriage in precolonial Buganda see Lucy Mair, *Native Marriage in Uganda* (London, 1940); and Roscoe, *The Baganda*, pp.82–97.
21 R.P. Ashe, *Two Kings of Uganda* (London, 1889), p.303.
22 Twaddle, 'Ending of slavery,' pp.133–4.
23 Reid, *Political Power*, p.126, quoting Roscoe, *The Baganda*, pp.14–15.
24 Tulinomubezi, 12 January 1902, 'File M/15/3, Marriage Cases 1902/1903'; also Yanyiriza, 'M/15/3, Marriage Cases 1896-1901', and Tulibantu, Nsambya Diary, Book 3, 9 August 1901– Sept. 12, 1901, and maybe an unnamed woman, Book 2, Nsambya Diary, Book 2, 1 July 1901–5 August 1901.
25 Yanyiriza, 'M/15/3, Marriage Cases 1896–1901'.
26 Roscoe, *The Baganda*, pp.92–3.
27 Nalugonda or Alirwa, Book 4, Nsambya Diary, Book 4, 13 September 1901-10 October 1901.
28 Note from Nagalama post, 21 January 1898; File 'History I, 1894–1899', Mill Hill Papers at Bishop's office, Jinja.
29 Tulinomubezi, 9 April 1901, 'M/15/3, Marriage Cases 1896–1901', and Tulinomubezi, 12 January 1902, 'File M/15/3, Marriage Cases 1902/1903'. Thanks to Mikael Karlström for discussing translations with me.
30 Note from Nagalama post, 21 January 1898; File 'History I, 1894–1899', Mill Hill Papers at Bishop's office, Jinja; see also Roscoe, *The Baganda*, p.95.
31 Kabedja had an unnamed slave woman, 21 January 1898; 'History I, 1894–1899'; other slave-holders seemed to be elite women.
32 Includes an unnamed woman, 2 March 1898, 'M/15/3, Marriage Cases 1896–1901'; Tulinomubezi, 12 January 1902, 'M/15/3, Marriage Cases 1902/1903'; Anna, 5 July 1901, Book 2, Nsambya Diary, July 1, 1901–August 5, 1901; Nalugonda or Alirwa, Book 4, Nsambya Diary, 13 September 1901-10 October 1901. Wright also mentions this phenomenon, 'Women in peril', p.814.
33 Yanyiriza, 'M/15/3, Marriage Cases 1896–1901'.
34 Kangao, 16 October 1901, 'M/15/3, Marriage Cases 1896–1901'.

35 Nabula, 11 December 1901, 'M/15/3, Marriage Cases 1896–1901'; and Cecilia, 23 June 1901, 'M/15/3, Marriage Cases 1896–1901'.
36 Alimonya, undated, 1901, 'M/15/3, Marriage Cases 1896–1901'.
37 Nalugonda or Alirwa, Book 4, Nsambya Diary, Book 4, 13 September 1901–10 October 1901. Wright talks about renaming, but draws different conclusions; 'Women in peril', p.812.
38 Tusaba–omu [sic], October 1901, 'M/15/3, Marriage Cases 1896–1901' and Taliba, 2 July 1901, Book 2, Nsambya Diary, 1 July 1901–5 August 1901; inheritance of slave status is mentioned by Twaddle, 'Ending of slavery', p.121; and Reid, *Political Power*, pp.125–6.
39 Cecilia, 23 June 1901, 'M/15/3, Marriage Cases 1896–1901'.
40 Zwafrumambi [sic], 21 January 1898, 'History I, 1894–1899'; and unnamed woman, 13 June 1902, 'M/15/3, Marriage Cases 1902/1903'.
41 Mujemula, 16 November 1901, 'M/15/3, Marriage Cases 1896–1901'.
42 Reid, *Political Power*, p.127.
43 Women's efforts at emancipation will be the subject of another article based on these same sources.
44 Reid, *Political Power*, p.162, quoting J.R. Macdonald, *Soldiering and Surveying in British East Africa* (London, 1897), p.143.
45 Lovejoy, *Transformations in Slavery*, p.246.
46 Sunseri does an excellent job of this for Tanganyika, albeit for a system more dominated by European planters; see Thaddeus Sunseri, *Vilimani: Labor Migration and Rural Change in Early Colonial Tanzania* (Portsmouth, NH, 2002).

Eight

Slavery & Other Forms of Social Oppression in Ankole 1890–1940

EDWARD I. STEINHART*

Introduction

Among all the kingdoms and societies of East Africa, itself an under-researched region, the claim can reasonably be made that the least studied and worst understood servile institutions were those of the precolonial kingdom of Nkore and its western neighbours that would be merged into the colonial district and Kingdom of Ankole (see Map 4).[1] The reasons for this obscurity and an attempt to make a belated assessment of slavery and other forms of servitude in Ankole are the subject of this chapter.

Searching for Slaves

In 1940, Kalvero Oberg, a Brazilian anthropologist, published what would become a classic study of the political system of Ankole. Lying at the western edge of the kingdoms area of the Great Lakes region, Ankole, like its southern neighbours, Rwanda and Burundi, was described in terms of the sharp divisions of class or caste. The gulf that separated Bahima pastoral rulers from their so-called Bairu agricultural countrymen would come to dominate the politics and literature of colonial Ankole down to the present. The result for the study of slavery and other forms of dependent labour in Ankole, as Oberg succinctly put it, was that 'Very little could be learned about slavery in Ankole.'[2] This chapter proposes to examine why so little has been learned about slavery in Ankole, despite the growth of interest in that institution in Africa and globally in the second half of the twentieth century.[3] In doing so, we may come to learn more about slavery *per se*, about other forms of unpaid and dependent labour, and perhaps even about the nature of the complex, class-based and conflict-ridden society that was the Ankole kingdom from the late nineteenth century until its end in 1966.

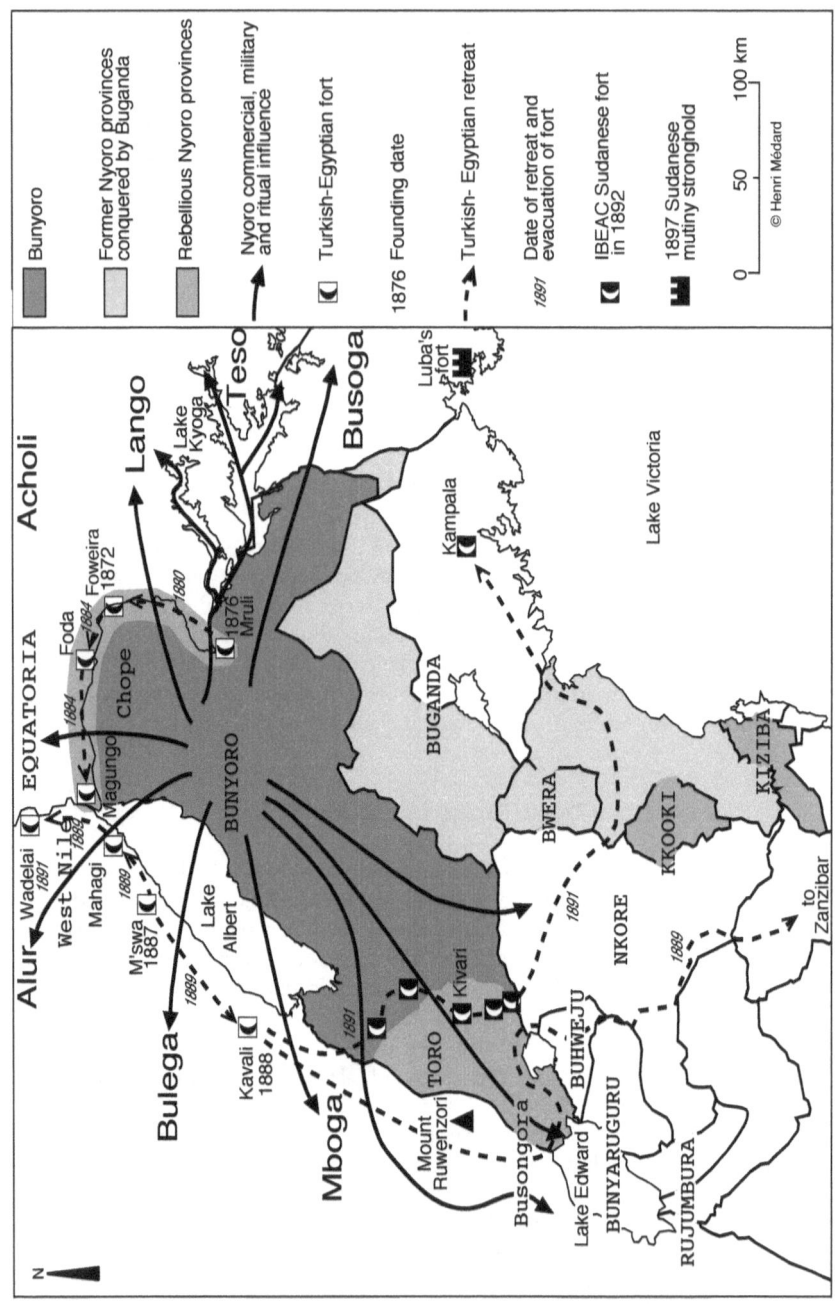

Map 4 Bunyoro, Nkore and the Sudanese (1870–1900)

Why, then, is the history of slavery in the Ankole kingdom and district so obscure? I will offer three explanations for the difficulties faced by Oberg in the 1930s and by other researchers ever since. The first has to do with the mis-description of the so-called Bairu as 'serfs' and sometimes as 'slaves' in the earliest literature which also portrayed the Bahima as if they were the only free citizens or subjects of the Nkore kingdom.[4] In these ethnographic works, Bahima informants predominated and the result was a description of the Banyankole majority as dependent labourers, living among and at the sufferance of their pastoral masters. Indeed, the question of 'Bahima-Bairu relations' has plagued the study of Ankole politics and society from the very beginning of European observation to today.[5] With the focus firmly on the Bairu as an underclass of servile labourers, little if any attention was given to true slavery where it existed, or other forms of 'social oppression' found between rich and poor, exploiters and exploited, within 'traditional' and colonial Ankole.[6]

Secondly, slavery and the slave trade had made a very small impact on both the pastoral and agricultural societies of the Nkore kingdom and its western neighbours by the end of the nineteenth century. While slavery had emerged as an important social and political institution in neighbouring Buganda and the coastal slave trade had made significant inroads into the eastern and southern lacustrine areas,[7] neither indigenous slave institutions nor the effects of external trade in slaves appear to have cut very deeply into the fabric of precolonial Ankole. Thus, the kingdom's historians, both vernacular and Western-trained, have largely ignored servile institutions in favour of the political history of the monarchies or the problem of Bahima-Bairu relations.[8] This appears to be even more the case among the observers of Ankole's colonial history and institutions. Slavery in Ankole has flown beneath the radar of modern social science.[9]

Finally, we might have expected the early missionaries and colonial administrators to have conducted an extensive search of Ankole society to locate and uproot those servile institutions that qualified as slavery, given the place of both anti-slavery and anti-slave trade ideology in the initial motives for exploration, conquest and the establishment of missions and *bomas* (local colonial headquarters). If so, we would be severely disappointed. The early missionaries left a remarkable gap in their accounts, both published and private, of the status of servile labourers. Some even prided themselves on their ability to command the labour of domestic servants drawn from the Bairu underclass and enabling them to live in the manner of their social superiors among the English aristocracy at home.[10] Similarly, the overriding concerns of the early administrators were not with the suppression of the slave trade, but rather with the flow of arms and ammunition into the country and the interdiction of Arab trading caravans illegally exporting ivory, a key source of colonial revenue. And when disputes arose between the wealthy and powerful and their servile labour force, who had 'become little more than slaves ready to work for the chiefs when ordered', the reaction of seasoned administrators like George Wilson was to side with the elite in insisting on deference from the workers, noting that 'the peasantry require discipline in even greater degree'.[11] The result of this imperial attitude favouring deference to authority and subordination of the servile to 'duly constituted authority' militated against any serious consideration of the status and condition of slaves and other dependent workers at least down to the era of the Great Depression and the beginnings of colonial reform.

Definitions and Attributions

It would be customary at this point to introduce a working definition of slavery for the purposes of the exposition that follows. However, rather than reiterate what has been said in the Introduction and various other contributions to this volume, I propose to offer instead a brief discussion of four key attributes of slavery as found in the area that became Ankole district and as it was understood by my respondents.[12] The first and most obvious is that slavery (*ubuhuuku* and *okuzaana*) and several other forms of dependent labour (*okushumba* in the precolonial period, and *akashanju* and *oruharo* in the colonial period) found in Ankole were considered to be unpaid labour. Thus, even when it was clear that food, clothing and shelter were being offered to the labourer and his dependants, if any, my informants, with only one exception, insisted that offering milk to drink was not in fact compensation for work. It was in the minds of the givers rather a form of charity offered to the destitute, who were, in turn, offering to work for the bare necessities. Neither the employer nor the employee appeared to have considered this as the payment of wages.[13]

Second, my respondents uniformly believed that coercion was a central element in the conditions of enslavement and the maintenance of slavery. In most cases, the coercion was physical or legal-political in nature. In one case, that of the status of *okushumba*, the coercion was social and economic. As we shall see, the *abashumba* were thought of as voluntary workers, usually employed by wealthy herdsmen and chiefs. This has led me to consider them as analogous to the 'indentured servants' of colonial North America in the seventeenth and eighteenth centuries and therefore as another form of social oppression.

The question of the commoditisation or marketability of Ankole slaves, and hence their status as chattel, raises several difficult questions. Unlike neighbouring Buganda, which had become monetised and had a degree of market orientation by the late nineteenth century,[14] Ankole's pastoral-dominated society remained largely outside the reach of markets and the money economy that had been penetrating the lakes region from the eighteenth century. Nonetheless, the widely held idea that the head of the household (*mukamawe*) had the power to command not only the labour but also the persons of the slaves, to give them as gifts, to use them to repay debts, to transfer them permanently to the ownership of another would appear to me to constitute these Ankole slaves as chattel.

Finally, my respondents emphasised the ideas of alienation and degradation that Orlando Patterson has explored in great depth in his seminal work, *Slavery and Social Death*. For Patterson the key to understanding the nature of slavery is the idea of what he calls 'natal alienation' and the lack of honour suffered by the slave.[15] In the case of Ankole, the central manifestation of these constituent elements of slavery was the sense of humiliation and degradation experienced by the slaves that continues to embitter the social relations and political struggles of contemporary Nyankole society. Let us now turn to the various forms of servile labour, first in precolonial Nkore and its environs and then in the colonially created 'Kingdom of Ankole'.

Servants, Slaves and Handmaidens

Abashumba: The term that was most commonly mentioned when I asked my respondents to tell me about slaves was *abashumba*.[16] This is somewhat ironic in that it is the one category of unpaid labourer that fails to meet the other three attributes of slave status (coercion, commoditisation and degradation).

Abashumba were and are destitute peasants or, more usually, herdsmen, who voluntarily seek employment herding the cows of rich cattle owners. From the perspective of the owners of large herds, there was need for men to do the arduous and 'dirty' work of tending to the cattle and the kraal. The daily tasks of watering and grazing the cattle, of sweeping the enclosure and removing cow dung were those most frequently assigned to *abashumba*. Various domestic tasks such as churning milk into ghee (clarified butter), collecting grass for mats and so on would be assigned to *abashumbakazi* (female servants).[17] It would appear, however, that Hima households required far more male than female labour, because of the arduous nature of herding and grazing cattle.

The work of the slaves was not only arduous, but often unpleasant, and therefore shunned by those with the freedom, wealth and power to do so. Again from the cattle owners' point of view, the employment of *abashumba* was looked upon as an act of charity.[18] Destitute herdsmen and peasants would come in search of something to drink, i.e. milk, the basic form of sustenance among the Bahima cattle keepers. And the owner would allow them to look after cattle, thus maintaining the herdsmen's status as Bahima. Moreover, they got clothing and shelter within the cattle owner's homestead. However, these bare necessities were not offered as payment, but simply as an act of common decency towards a fellow cattle keeper. In the end or after a period of service, the owner might also offer the gift of a cow, and, in exceptional cases, several cows to allow the *omushumba* herdsman who had been faithful and disciplined to rebuild his own herd.

This was always described as a gift, given freely, and not as compensation for labour.[19]

From the perspective of the *abashumba* themselves only dire necessity would send one in search of the unrewarding work of tending another's cattle. The loss of one's own herd through disease, theft or drought was a common cause of this form of indenture. For young men especially, the inability of their families to provide them with cows for the required bridewealth might lead them to seek work as herdsmen, in the hope of earning the gift of cows or of being able to purloin some of the owner's cattle. Indeed, according to retired Bishop Yoramu Bamunoba:[20]

> I have not known of a person who got gifts and became rich. But I have known some *abashumba* who became rich by secretly stealing animals of their masters. One of the things you should know if you were *bashumba*, there were two classes of *bashumba*. There were *bashumba* who were poor cattle keepers, who by accident their fathers have died and he came to support himself. And then he would move to another person's [place], and then this particular person would probably be given gifts. A person of the Bahima class would be given gifts out of sympathy and finding to the connections [sic] ... these people sometimes they have got his distant uncle or distant friends and the *bashumba* there but then they would have sympathy for doing the work for the master. That is [one of] the better class than this one, who came from the Bairu, who has no connections. [One] who had no connections would not be treated with gifts. Just work and work and if he were clever enough he might steal one or two cows..., whereas the other one would get gifts one by one and eventually form up his own herd.

Attracted by the prospect of 'gifts' of cattle or the possibility of acquiring cattle by theft, the *abashumba*, of both the Bahima and the Bairu groups, were clearly willing entrants into the relationship. They appear also to have been able to end the relationship at their discretion. Their freedom to move, to change masters, to return home or to strike out on their own clearly distinguishes them from slaves, as well as from true indentured labourers. But this freedom of choice may have been socially illusory as it was most often the cattle owner who would terminate the relationship in one of two ways. He might send away an unsatisfactory worker, one lacking in deference, energy or discipline. Or he might, after some years of faithful service, send away a *mushumba* with enough cows to be independent even if he did not want to go. As Dixon Kamukama put it:

> To me as long as the pastoralists had need for them they would have them [stay] and in most cases, to the contrary of what you found out, ...it used to be the pastoralist's place, after you have worked for him for so many years, at one point or another he will say you have worked for him, you have had your own children, and the family is now getting into the other family. And now he says: 'And now I think it is time for you to be on your own.' He says you take maybe ten or so head of cattle and be on your own.

You find that maybe it is his children who remain working for the other persons. At times it 'okushumba' was not negative. At times ... someone would gain out of it. "I am omushumba today, tomorrow I may not be omushumba."

Many respondents asserted that the *abashumba* were treated as members of the cattle owner's family. It is simple to dismiss these statements as paternalistic apologetics. But perhaps we should ask what precisely was the family life of *abashumba* like. Were their marriages honoured? What was the status of the children of *abashumba*? Was the position or status of unpaid worker and servant passed on to their children? As many *abashumba* came for employment when they were single and in search of bridewealth, it is clear that the patron/owner had a great deal of influence in determining the servant's ability to marry. The patron would often specify the time and assist in finding a suitable wife for his *omushumba* from among the young women of the poorer families of the community. Nevertheless, Bahima sexual mores were such that any women within the household, other than one's own mother, were accessible to all the male members of the family, including *abashumba*. There is no reason to believe that this would not have been true of the wives and nubile daughters of the patron.[21]

What, then, was the status of the children of *abashumba* living in close contact with the patron's family? Once again, it was frequently asserted that they were treated as members of the family, growing up as the playmates and putative brothers and sisters of the *mukamawe*'s own children. This would be equally true of the children of other servile women *(abazaana)* who bore children for the family of the owner. To all outward appearances, the children of female servants, whether of *abashumbakazi* or *abazaana*, would be raised as the biological children of the owner of the house. During the colonial era, the children of *abashumba* would frequently be sent to school by their patron as well as provided with bridewealth.[22]

The status of *okushumba*, then, was neither permanent in one generation nor heritable in the next. No caste of *abashumba* existed in precolonial Nkore, neither was the class of impoverished 'indentured' workers composed exclusively of cattle-less Bahima herdsmen nor destitute and family-less Bairu agriculturalists. During the colonial era, the term would increasingly be seen as one of abuse and be replaced by the more neutral term *abakosi* or (wage) worker. The position of *abashumba* has largely disappeared from Ankole life, except within the remotest regions of the predominantly pastoral county of Nyabushozi.

Omuhuuku: The term *omuhuuku* has similarly disappeared from usage in the Runyankole language, as has the status to which it referred. It is this term that comes closest to fulfilling the meaning of slave and exhibiting all four of the key attributes we are applying. To begin with, the labour of *abahuuku*, who were always men, was unpaid. In this regard they did not differ from *abashumba*. However, there is no doubt that the labour of *abahuuku* was coerced labour. In most instances, in precolonial Nkore, the *abahuuku* began as war captives (*abakwatwa*).[23] Only one of my respondents flatly denied that *abahuuku* were captured, believing that they were only sold or pawned into servitude.[24] The idea that *abahuuku* were also bought and sold is generally agreed, with the special circumstance of the sale or transfer of delinquent young men from their families to the families of the wealthy also being noted.[25] Another way in which *abahuuku* might be transferred was by gift. This derives from an especially monarchist version of the nature of *ubuhuuku* (slavery). It argues that all *abahuuku* were the property of the *Mugabe* (king), and that he could and did give them as gifts to whomsoever he pleased for services rendered, particularly in warfare, or just to show his pleasure and power.[26]

It was also firmly established that, after capture or purchase, *abahuuku* were forced to work. They would be forced to do the most demeaning of jobs and could refuse nothing. No excuses were accepted for not working, such as illness. None of my respondents mentioned the use of corporal punishment, but in that, as in the nature of the agricultural, pastoral and domestic tasks that they were forced to perform, there was little to distinguish them from *abashumba* or even socially inferior members of the patron's family.[27]

One important distinction in the treatment and status of *abahuuku* was the fact that they could be and generally were 'branded' by the excision of all or part of one or both ears. Initially this was done to prevent them from escaping and mixing unnoticed among free Banyankore, who were no different in appearance or language from the slaves from neighbouring areas. But it is also clear that 'cutting the ear' was a form of humiliation and an expression of the absolute power of the owner over the person of the *omuhuuku*.[28] Another task required of *abahuuku* was the dehumanising obligation to attend his master during sexual intercourse and assist him by 'holding the thigh' of his sexual partner, often enough a female slave (*omuzaana*).[29] Unpaid and coerced labour, purchase and sale and alienation and humiliation were all evident in the status and roles of the *abahuuku*.

Abazaana: The female counterparts of the *abahuuku* were referred to as *abazaana*. *Abazaana* were both far more numerous and far more important to the economic and social life of the Bahima household than were the *abahuuku*. There were three ways in which *abazaana* might be acquired by wealthy Bahima (and some wealthy Banyankole) households: (i) by capture in war; (ii) by purchase; (iii) by debt bondage of the destitute.[30] These women were drawn from the agricultural class and their work was principally the domestic work of cleaning, cooking, gathering wood and water, etc., which they would share with the women of the family and with *abashumbakazi*, if they were present.

The work and burdens of the *abazaana* were those dictated by sex and gender. As a result of the gendered roles of women in Nkore society, their subordination to the men of the household was guaranteed. As slaves or 'handmaidens', they also came under the authority of the free women of the household and especially the wives of the householder. But most significant, as a result of the sexual mores of the Bahima family, they became sexually available to all the adult men of the homestead. This double exploitation of female slaves will come as no surprise to students of slavery elsewhere. But the difference that Nkore sexual custom made was significant. According to Hope and Merabu Kivengere:[31]

> they would be like workers in the house, but as soon as [they] had children [the children would] belong to the man. Not only that, as soon as a woman starts having children then the head of the household would build a house for her. Before she was a child ... Because in those days each wife would have a house and then there was a main house. So the *omuzaana* would live in the main house but as soon as she produced a child then she would also get her own house. So then she would become a wife in her own right.

Therefore, the status of *abazaana* was not usually life-long. *Abazaana* were typically young women and girls and older childless women. Once they began to bear children for their owner, they would make the transition to being a wife. Needless to say, in terms of the sexual and labour burdens that they bore, that transition was not very marked.

As with the children of *abashumba* born within the household of the patron, the children of *abazaana* were the responsibility of the owner and would be raised as his children, 'the children of the house', alongside the children of his wives and daughters-in-law. It is very revealing that unmarried *abazaana* who gave birth within their patron's household were not punished. This stands in marked contrast to the treatment of unwed daughters of a Muhima patron who became pregnant. Informants, on being asked about such situations, reported that 'This could never happen, because the penalties for out-of-wedlock pregnancy were so severe', describing the imposition of a penalty of death on the pregnant woman and her foetus, specifically at the hands of her closest brother. No one contested the idea that historically pre-marital pregnancy among free women was punishable by death, although there was disagreement on two elements of unwanted pregnancies. First, the question of whether abortions might be induced to prevent the draconian solution of the killing of the woman and foetus was debated by a gathering of male Bairu respondents. After asserting that abortions did not occur, they relented when confronted with the idea that the patron's wives might help their daughters escape punishment by keeping the pregnancy secret from him and providing the abortifacient drug derived from the *omuhoko* tree (*Diospyros abyssinica*). The women, they admitted, could be the only ones to know of this.[32]

The second issue was whether the killing of pregnant, unmarried Bahima women was done out of shame and the loss of family honour or out of the purely economic consideration of the loss of value in bridewealth that would be suffered by the family and specifically by the 'favourite' brother, who would now lose a large proportion of his sister's bridewealth cattle that he would have used to obtain his own bride. The preponderance of evidence was that family honour was very much at the root of the harsh treatment of unwed prospective mothers in both Bairu and Bahima cultures.[33]

This diversion into the questions raised by pre-marital pregnancy in precolonial Ankole societies serves to underscore the idea that only the 'legitimate daughters' of the family were capable of dishonouring the household through their sexual misconduct. The *abazaana* were seen to be without honour and therefore incapable of bringing shame on the father and head of the household or its other male members. I believe the condition of being 'without honour' is a key indicator of the slave status of the *abazaana*. Similarly, *abahuuku* were also dishonoured because, as captives or kinless individuals, they had lost the inherent capacity of free family members to possess honour.

In conclusion, the status of slaves as distinct from other forms of dependent labour in precolonial society was far more a matter of the alienation of honour rather than the alienation of labour. Servants and slaves, domestic workers and women of the family differed little in the work that they did or their subordinate position in the social hierarchy. What separated the slaves from the free was fundamentally their lack of honour, resulting in the continual humiliation of slaves, and their physical, sexual and emotional abuse by the wealthy and well-born, especially the Bahima aristocrats who were the politically and socially dominant elite of the pastoral society of Ankole. In colonial times, this pattern of alienation, dishonour and abuse would extend to two new categories of coerced labour, as we shall see below. More important, however, would be the development of a culture of humiliation, dishonour and abuse by the Bahima elite over the so-called Bairu 'servants' within the new colonial kingdom of Ankole.

Slave Trading and Raiding

Before we turn to the colonial era and its impact on slavery, we must examine the watershed decade of the 1890s and specifically the impact that the external slave trade had on Ankole and its slave institutions. It should be borne in mind that the decade beginning in 1891 was one of dislocation and seemingly endless crises. Environmental and health crises caused by rinderpest and smallpox were contributing factors to the political crisis that preceded the death of Ntare V in 1895 and the interregnum crisis that followed it.[34] In this context, the relatively late arrival of coastal Arab-Swahili merchants in the western Uganda region had a limited impact. This is in sharp contrast with the experience of Buganda in the second half of the nineteenth century.[35] There the arrival of Arab-Swahili merchants seems to have had a profound impact on both the cultural and economic life of the Baganda. The presence of large numbers of enslaved workers, especially women, at both the Ganda royal court and the chiefly establishments around the country, created a regular pool of servile labour that could be sold in exchange for the goods offered by the coastal traders. In contrast, Ankole had neither the pool of labour nor the demand for imports of arms, cloth or cowries noted for Buganda. This is both a function of the smaller scale of the Nkore and other pastoral kingdoms in the west and the narrower distribution of wealth within them. It is perhaps significant that sale to foreign merchants was typically conceived of as a punishment for anti-social behaviour among *abahuuku* and *abazaana* rather than being motivated by a desire for profit.[36] With fewer households holding fewer slaves, the Ankole pastoral region became a corridor through which coastal caravans passed *en route* to Buganda and Bunyoro where slave markets had become established earlier in the nineteenth century.

The limited commercial impact of Arab-Swahili trade on Ankole slavery was matched by the marginal effect that both the slave trade and slave raiding had in the region. The principal object of the east coast merchants who came to Nkore and its neighbourhood appears to have been to procure ivory rather than slaves, the demand for which could be more readily satisfied elsewhere. In exchange for ivory, coastal merchants offered guns and powder, cowrie shells and cloth. But these goods had a very shallow penetration within Ankole societies, affecting only the wealthiest of chiefly and pastoral households. In the western margins of Ankole, two groups of coastal merchants, known locally as *Basumbwa* and *Barunganwa*, engaged largely in peaceful trade in obtaining slaves as well as ivory.[37] Another group, deriving from the Manyema slavers of the Lake Tanganyika region and called *Bavuntu*, carried out plundering and terrorist raids against the people of that region.

In addition, Khartoumer slavers never reached the Ankole kingdoms area, stopped by the power and hostility of the Bunyoro kingdom to the north. In any case, the Khartoum slave trade was based far more on slave raiding than on mercantile activities. In all, the trade in slaves and slave raiding seem to have made little impression on the Nkore state and its neighbours, their *abahuuku* and *abazaana* slaves or on the historical memories of that era.

To the extent that Ankole societies were affected by the violence associated with the acquisition of slaves, they should be regarded as both victims and perpetrators of the raiding economy. As victims, Nkore and its western neighbours seem to have suffered from increasing *Bavuntu* and Baganda slaving expeditions during the last three decades of the nineteenth century. But these raids seem to have been aimed primarily at Bunyaruguru, a largely agricultural area northwest of Nkore near the Kazinga channel.[38] Curiously, the most important raids against Ankole's pastoral kingdoms continued to be the cattle raiding expeditions carried out by Banyoro from the north and Banyarwanda from the south. While men encountered in these raids were usually killed, women might be taken by the raiders as *abazaana*. This, however, was tangential to the main purposes of the raids as well as inconsequential for the processes of enslavement in the region.[40]

Nkore and its fellow pastoral kingdoms did also become raiders for slaves during this chaotic period at the end of the nineteenth century. Several prominent Banyankole political families claim descent from captives brought back in precolonial times to the Nkore kingdom from Bunyaruguru and Busongora to the northwest. Bahima women and girls were particularly prized as captives for their beauty and reputations for sensuality, but they were seldom enslaved. If they came from elite families, class would trump their status as *abakwatwa* and they would be taken in marriage by their captors or passed on to suitable marriage partners among the Bahima elite of the region and sometimes beyond. Many lowborn women from both the Bahima and the Bairu appear to have been captured and retained by the Bahima elite.[40] But within Nkore itself, raiding for slaves was by and large the by-product of other kinds of expeditions aimed at procuring cattle or political advantage vis-à-vis other pastoral kingdoms. Nonetheless, the growing violence and commercialism of the period do seem to have increased the vulnerability and insecurity of slaves held in the region. The only kingdom in the area which seems to have responded with major structural reforms to the new opportunities and dangers of the late nineteenth century was Rujumbura. Rujumbura's king, Makobore, organised a force, armed with firearms and commanded by an able officer named Muranda, for the purpose of both defending the kingdom from raids and instituting raids of its own. It was chiefly due to the power of this military force that Makobore was able to escape the clutches of the expanding Ankole kingdom during the transition to colonial rule and maintain Rujumbura's independence from Ankole, if not from their British overlords.[41]

Colonialism and Slavery

The connection between nineteenth-century anti-slavery ideology and the exploration and colonisation of Africa is a commonplace. Uganda was no exception, and opposition to the slave trade was prominent among the justifications for the sending of both missionaries and administrators to Buganda and its environs in the last half of that century.[42] Even the most egotistical and eccentric of Uganda's early European explorers, men like Henry Morton Stanley and Emin Pasha, found in the anti-slavery impulse a useful ally.[43] It is therefore all the more surprising, then, that men like Frederick Lugard and Bishop Alfred Tucker seem to have ignored that impulse when it conflicted with other objectives. Lugard's backtracking on domestic slavery and even his loss of interest in the suppression of slave raiding have been well established.[44] Tucker's indifference to the burning issue of enslavement is made apparent by his only passing references to it in his memoir, *Eighteen Years in Uganda and East Africa*. Even these brief references to slaves indicate that a slave boy was still part of the bishop's entourage as he passed through Ankole in c.1910, and that his interest in emancipation seemed little more than sentimental.[45] It must be said in Tucker's defence and that of the Anglican missionaries in general that the purchase of slaves and the creation of freed slave communities as part of the strategy of evangelisation had been seriously debated. The presence of slaves at mission stations and as part of the mission personnel in Uganda may derive from this strategy.

The problem with the emancipation of slaves was compounded by two imperatives of colonial rule. The first was the need to entrench alliances of collaboration with the occupying power by bolstering chiefs who had been appointed or recognised by the colonial state. In Ankole this involved reinforcing the authority of the Bahima pastoral elites over the subordinate peasantry, the Bairu, and extending the central control of Nkore's Bahinda ruling dynasty and its leading collaborating chief, Nuwa Mbaguta, over the congeries of other pastoral kingdoms and chieftaincies in the region.[46] Secondly, the colonial state required the recruitment of labour for the development of the strategic and economic infrastructure of the regime, principally, road building and maintenance, and the construction and upkeep of government buildings and the headquarters of the hierarchy of colonial chiefs, who would be responsible for the collection of taxes. In the absence of a sufficient supply of money, especially in commercially undeveloped areas of the new Uganda protectorate like Ankole, this meant the use of unpaid labour. During the course of the first forty years of colonial rule in Ankole, two systems of forced labour would be instituted: *akashanju* and *oruharo*. Neither would meet our criteria for being called slavery. However, in the minds of those affected by them, coerced, unpaid and abusive labour regimes of the colonial period were tantamount to slavery, and might, as Michael Twaddle (borrowing from Hugh Tinker) has suggested for Buganda, constitute 'a new system of slavery'.[47]

Akashanju: The roots of this practice of coercing labour for government projects and public works appear to lie in the recruiting practices of the Baganda chiefs who enjoyed significant early influence in Ankole, especially over the *Nganzi* (prime minister or favourite), Mbaguta. A number of my informants were at pains to point out that the term itself was identical to and derived from the Luganda term, *kasanvu*. They agreed that it derived from the term for '7000', indicating the large (or indeterminate?) number of people making up these new labour gangs.[48] Men and boys from about the age of 16 were dispatched by their local village (*miruka*) chiefs to sub-county (*gombolola*) and county headquarters and to the royal palace and government headquarters at what is today Mbarara, in order to be assigned various tasks of hard, manual labour. Work on the chiefs' enclosures seems to have been a continuation of precolonial systems of political tribute. What was new was the demand from colonial officers for work on roads and in head porterage.[49]

Before *akashanju* was introduced in the first decade of the twentieth century, a less formal system of recruitment called *akarezi* seems to have existed. But it was under the *akashanju* regime of large-scale recruitment that the abuse of the workers led them to consider that they were being treated 'as slaves'.[50] It was not simply the absence of pay that was resented, but the heavy demands for hard labour, which often resulted in death and which deprived those at home of the labour and protection of able-bodied men for extended periods of time. Unlike the later instituted system of *ruharo*, *akashanju* had no fixed term of employment, workers being recruited for the duration of the project. This surely contributed to the system's reputation as a kind of slavery.

But it was the physical and personal abuses suffered while performing *akashanju* tasks that are at the heart of the institution's slavery-like image. Men would not willingly work without compensation and so had to be physically coerced into the *akashanju* labour gangs.[51] Moreover, once recruited they could be made to do any work that the chiefs or officials required of them. The system was frequently abused by forcing *abashanju* to do work for the personal benefit of the chiefs. *Nganzi* Mbaguta was particularly known to have abused the system in having a two-storey house built for himself using forced labour, just as he might earlier have used slaves for such tasks.[52] The reputation for the personal abuse of workers by the Bahima chiefs as well as for the regimen of hard, menial labour caused many young men to flee from Ankole district, especially to Buganda, to avoid recruitment as *akashanju* 'slaves' and instead seek paid employment.

The First World War and the recruitment of Banyankole for military service as porters and menial labourers seemed to have brought *akashanju* to an end. Its demise may also have been hastened by the increasing availability of cash in the economy and the decreasing need for head porterage and road construction workers as a basic network of rudimentary roads and motorised transport was completed. Road maintenance, though, would remain a major source of demand for unpaid labour for many years under the postwar system called *ruharo*.

Ruharo: After the war, a more closely administered system of labour recruitment was instituted. According to one informant, it was begun in Kigezi district to the west of Ankole as early as 1914. This, however, may have been confused with the system of wartime recruitment (*ekinkumu?*) that preceded *ruharo*.[53] Basically, *ruharo* was a non-commutable system of *corvée* labour for public projects instituted in lieu of payment of taxes in cash. It frequently involved heavy labour on road gangs and in the construction of public buildings and chiefly headquarters. In fact, the area of Kamukuzi, where the *Mugabe* of Ankole's royal enclosure and palace stood, is still called Ruharo to this day. *Ruharo* labour also involved working under the direct supervision of chiefs on private projects, as the line between the chief's personal and political authority remained at best indistinct.[54]

A fixed period of thirty days labour *per annum* was administered under the direction of the District Inspector of Revenue. As one respondent put it, *ruharo* 'was a way of levying tax. One would be taken to work at the gomborora for a month or working on a road and after a month you will be given a ticket for the tax of that year.'[55] In fact, at the end of thirty working days (as distinct from a calendar month), the local administration clerk would enter the taxpayer's name in a register and issue him with a receipt to cover his taxes for the year. At this point, he would be allowed to go home. 'After another month, the clerk sends the names to the D.I.R. with the tickets.'[56]

In as much as only adult males were subject to direct taxation, women were as excluded from this system of 'slavery' as they had been from *akashanju*. However, young boys often found themselves recruited, especially in the early days. This was because, firstly, it was possible for individuals to buy a substitute to do the debasing and difficult month's labour for them. In as much as elders were likely to have the means to avoid such work, it was often juniors who were under age and not themselves subject to tax who would provide the labour.[57]

Secondly, as *ruharo* was introduced well before the issuance of birth certificates became common, proof of age was a rough estimate. According to Festo Karwemera, '[Ruharo] applied to those of tax paying age. This was confirmed by counting your teeth and if they found you had 16 teeth on each jaw then you are fit to pay tax. Because birth certificates came in 1927 and paying taxes started in 1915, so without a birth certificate they would count one's teeth.'[58] Mr Karwemera also explained that the punishment for refusing to perform *ruharo* was a term of imprisonment. So *ruharo* was both unpaid and coerced. It was also humiliating. The counting of teeth to determine age is indicative of the treatment of Banyankole workers like cattle or horses, i.e., as chattel. Their close supervision by the sub-county and county chiefs was also calculated to be humiliating. These chieftaincies were filled almost exclusively by Bahima pastoralists, because the colonial authorities believed they had exercised a monopoly of chiefly power in the precolonial Nkore kingdom. And although both Bahima and Banyankole (so-called Bairu) were subject to *ruharo*, the wealthier cattlemen tended to be able to gain exemptions or to avoid the more onerous tasks as a result of ethnic privilege. This meant that the burdens of the *ruharo* system of forced labour fell heavily on the underclass of poor farmers and were perceived by them to be evidence of Bahima oppression of the Bairu as a class. Among these burdens were the constant exposure to attitudes of superiority and verbal and physical abuse by the Bahima administrators who referred to the workers as servile Bairu, no better than slaves.[59]

Ruharo would be brought to an end by the outbreak of the Second World War. In some cases, however, *ruharo* administrators were reassigned work within the system of recruitment and transportation of forced labour for the war effort after 1939.[60] In any event, the growth of the money economy and especially the growth of mission education worked in tandem to bring colonial forced labour to an end in the period after 1939.[61]

Conclusion and Discussion

A variety of servile institutions existed in precolonial Nkore and its neighbouring pastoral kingdoms. They ranged from the relative freedom of the institution of *okushumba*, which, although unpaid and involving menial and sometimes degrading labour, was considered to be voluntary and not physically coerced, to the statuses of *abahuuku* and *abazaana*, that contained all the constitutive elements of chattel slavery that we have delineated: *abahuuku* and *abazaana* were unpaid, coerced, saleable and 'without honour'. In addition, they were frequently procured by capture in raiding and warfare and deprived of home, kin and the right to control their own lives and deaths, that is to say, they suffered natal alienation, in Orlando Patterson's words. The distinction between the *abashumba* servants and the *abahuuku* and *abazaana* slaves was not, however, just in the degree of un-freedom they suffered.

The *abashumba* were drawn principally, but not exclusively, from among the Bahima pastoral group, albeit from those at the lowest end of the social and economic scale among cattle herders. In contrast, the *abahuuku* and *abazaana* appear to have been drawn virtually entirely from the poorer classes within Banyankole or so-called Bairu society. Is it for this reason that the latter were more systematically abused, humiliated and dishonoured? Or is it perhaps because, from the Bahima elite's perspective, so many slaves were Banyankole peasants by birth and culture that all Banyankole came to be spoken of as 'slaves' or Bairu? Of course, it need not be one or the other. But whatever the explanation, the result was that the stigma of slavery and the status of agriculturalist came to be conflated in the early literature, and the Bahima came to be seen in Western ethnography as the only 'people' of Ankole.[62] These terms and the practices of oppression of both servile and independent agriculturalists would persist well into the twentieth century.

The impact of both Swahili/Arab and European contact seems to have increased the social distance that servility had already accentuated. Although the slave trading and raiding exploits of the coastal traders had been a secondary interest to their commercial activities (at least in comparison with the impact on Buganda), what influence they had appears to have increased the jeopardy felt by slaves, who might now be even further alienated from their natal roots. Moreover, the attitudes of deference to authority and sense of hierarchy exhibited by the early colonial missionaries and administrators appear also to have contributed to the persistence of Bahima attitudes of superiority and Bairu subordination. To this the colonial authorities added new forms of unpaid and coercive labour in the guise of public works and labour taxes that fell heavily on the Bairu. Their sense of exclusion from the benefits of their own labour and their despised status in society would rankle through the decades.

It seems from the expressions of disdain by Bahima and resentment by Bairu in the testimonies of my respondents that the problems of natal alienation and dishonour that were the constitutive elements of slavery in Ankole as elsewhere present a curious conundrum. The fact that slaves were drawn exclusively from the Bairu ethnic communities and served almost exclusively the Bahima aristocracy reinforced the notion that the Banyankole agriculturalists were essentially a servile class. They too were considered by the Bahima to be outsiders, alienated by their birth, and not just their poverty and occupations, from the Bahima owners of cattle, wealth and slaves. The question we set out to answer at the beginning of this essay regarding the obscurity of the question of slavery in Ankole has been answered by the conflation of slave status with the subordinate status imposed on all agriculturalists by the system of pastoral privilege that permeated (and bedevilled) western lacustrine and, in particular, Ankole society.

The second objective we set for this essay was to investigate the actual workings of slavery in Ankole society. The heart of the system of slavery I have argued can be found in the process of natal alienation experienced by Bairu who through capture, purchase or other means became slaves, *abahuuku* or *abazaana*. Traces of this process of alienation can be seen in the bifurcated clan system, which distinguished between Bairu and Bahima branches of the same totemic clans. This placed the Bairu branches in a subordinate position throughout the pastoral domains and subjected the members of the inferior 'Bairu' sub-clans to the possibility of alienation by purchase or forfeiture.[63] Furthermore, evidence is accumulating in support of the idea of a gradual differentiation of the two groups and the slow emergence of pastoral dominance in Ankole. At the heart of this process lay a system of clientage (and I would add the practices of servile labour) through which the Bairu group became alienated, kinless strangers among the Bahima, who in turn came to see themselves and be taken by outsiders as the sole citizens of Nkore and the only full members of Ankole society.[64] As a result, Bairu came to be deprived of the right to seek blood vengeance that was granted to Bahima; various rituals of kinship, such as newly installed kings spitting in the mouths of representatives of a debased Bairu clan, served to emphasise the humiliation of the Bairu as a whole and their collective lack of honour.[65] By equating Banyankole farmers with the status of slaves and by heaping abuse on them as social inferiors and cultural strangers, without kin and without honour, they would become, like Orlando Patterson's slaves, victims of a 'social death'.[66] Rather than a benign institution for acculturating strangers and providing for the gradual adoption of aliens into society, slavery in Ankole contributed to the perpetuation of a system of inequality and oppression, underscoring the divisive and politically charged problem of 'Bairu-Bahima relations' that continues to vex Ankole society and Uganda politics down to the present.

Notes

* My thanks to Texas Tech University for a Faculty Development Leave and the assistance of Makerere University's Department of History and the Department of Women's and Gender Studies, which enabled me to conduct oral history research in Uganda from September to November 2003. Apologies go to Walter Rodney for the appropriation of his phraseology in my title.

1 I shall use the term Nkore to refer to the precolonial kingdom and the term Ankole to refer to both the colonial-era district and kingdom of Ankole and the precolonial region that was subsequently incorporated into this district. That region included Buhweju, Bunyaruguru, Igara, Kajara, Rwampara, and Shema, located to the west of Nkore, which in 2005 comprised the Bushenyi and Ntungamo districts of the contemporary Republic of Uganda.

2 K. Oberg, 'The kingdom of Ankole in Uganda', in M. Fortes and E. E. Evans-Pritchard (eds), *African Political Systems* (London, 1940).

3 The growth of interest in African slavery developed later than the pioneering work on North America, such as Kenneth Stampp, *The Peculiar Institution* (New York, 1956); Stanley Elkins, *Slavery, A Problem in American Institutional Life* (Chicago, 1965); and Eugene Genovese, *Roll, Jordan, Roll* (New York, 1974). The works by S. Miers and I. Kopytoff (eds), *Slavery in Africa* (Madison, WI, 1977) and F. Cooper, *Plantation Slavery on the East Coast of Africa* (New Haven, CT, 1977) on African slave institutions are directly influenced and inspired by this literature, as is that by Paul Lovejoy, *Transformations of Slavery*, 2nd edn (New York, 2000). Works with a broader philosophical perspective that have influenced my thinking on slavery are David Brion Davis's *The Problem of Slavery in Western Culture* (Ithaca, NY, 1966), Robin Blackburn's recent overview, *The Making of New World Slavery* (London, 1997) and especially Orlando Patterson's *Slavery and Social Death* (Cambridge, MA, 1982).

4 J. Roscoe, *The Banyankole* (London, 1911) and his *Twenty Five Years in Uganda* (Cambridge, 1923), p.209. Also, J.F. Cunningham, *Uganda and its Peoples* (New York, 1969 [1905]), pp.3–24 and J. Meldon, 'Notes on the Bahima of Ankole', *Journal of the Africa Society*, 6 (1907), pp.136–53 and 234–49.

5 According to H.M. Stanley, writing in 1889, 'The agricultural class consists of slaves – at least such is the term by which they are designated.' J. Scott Keltie (ed.), *The Story of Emin's Rescue as told in Stanley's Letters* (New York, 1969 [1890]). Cf. Harry Johnston, *The Uganda Protectorate* (London, 1902) and M. Doornbos, *The Ankole Kingship Controversy: Regalia Galore Revisited* (Kampala, 2001), pp.11–24.

6 On the role of the *bakopi* as a subordinate class in blurring the significance of slavery in precolonial Buganda, see M. Twaddle, 'Slaves and peasants in Buganda', in L.J. Archer (ed.), *Slavery and Other Forms of Unfree Labour* (London, 1988), p.121.

7 M. Twaddle, 'The ending of slavery in Buganda', in S. Miers and R. Roberts (eds), *The End of Slavery in Africa* (Madison, WI, 1988), pp.121–4. Cf. R. Reid, *Political Power in Pre-Colonial Buganda* (Oxford, 2002), pp.113–32 and 160–71 and his chapter in this volume.

8 A. Katate and L. Kamugunguru, *Abagabe b'Ankole* (Kampala, 1955); S. Karugire, *A History of the Kingdom of Nkore* (Oxford, 1971) and his 'Relations between Bairu and Bahima in nineteenth-century Nkore', *Tarikh*, 3, 2 (1970), pp.22–33.

9 E.g. M. Doornbos, *The Ankole Kingship Controversy* (Kampala, 2001); J. Muvumba, 'The politics of stratification and transformation in the kingdom of Ankole, Uganda' (unpublished PhD thesis, Department of Government, Harvard University, 1982).

10 Cf. Roscoe, *The Banyankole*; Rev. H. Clayton, 'Extracts of Letters from Ankole' and Hilda Clayton, 'Letters', Microfilms at Makerere University Library, Kampala. My thanks to Rev. Canon Alex Kagume of Mukono Christian University for this observation drawn from the letters of Rev. and Mrs. Clayton, the pioneer missionary couple in Ankole. Personal communication, 18 September 2003 at Mukono.

Slavery & Other Forms of Oppression in Ankole

11 Quoted in E. Steinhart, *Conflict and Collaboration* (Princeton, NJ, 1977), pp.243–4.
12 Oral interviews were conducted in Ankole and Kampala in 2003 among recognised historical authorities, local social and political leaders and older men and women to elicit popular memories of the various categories of unfree labour. In addition, several Ankole-born professional historians and churchmen were also interviewed for their expert knowledge. A complete list of respondents and transcripts of interviews are available from the author.
13 Slavery in Ankole (SLA) interviews 4, A. Mulumba; 5, P. Gabavungo; 6, Y. Bamunoba; 8, J. Kahigiriza; 10, J. Kaishogorize; and 15, Banyankole Cultural Foundation.
14 See Reid, *Political Power*, chapter 8.
15 Patterson, *Social Death*, pp.1–14 on 'natal alienation' and the dishonouring of the enslaved. According to Patterson (p.7) 'what is critical in the slave's forced alienation, [is] the loss of ties of birth in both ascending and descending generations ... a loss of native status, of deracination. It was this alienation of the slave from all formal, legally enforceable ties of "blood", and any attachment to groups or localities other than those chosen for him [sic] by the master, that gave the relationship of slavery its peculiar value.'
16 Background interview 1, Mr. Dixon Kamukama, History Department, Makerere University offered the best overall description of *okushumba*.
17 SLA interview 1, Hope and Merabu Kivengere.
18 See SLA interviews 5, P Gabavungo; 8, James Kahigiriza; and 14, Kezakia Kaitiritimba for examples of this elite point of view.
19 SLA interview 7, Bishop Amos Betungura.
20 SLA interview 6, Bishop Yoramu Bamunoba.
21 Background interview 1, Kamukama. On Bahima sexual mores, see Background interview 2, Alex Bangirana; Christopher Muhoozi, 'Migration and socio economic change in Uganda' (unpublished M.A. thesis, History Department, Makerere University). Muhoozi also points out that only very wealthy cattle keepers with large herds could afford to employ *abashumba*, referring to them as 'rich men' (pp.27–8). I am translating the term *mukamawe* as either owner or patron in referring to such 'rich men', the heads of large pastoral households.
22 SLA interviews 1, Kivengere; 3, Kesi Nyakimwe; 4, Ananias Mulumba; 11, Rev. Lazaro Njunwoha; and 13, Faith Beyaka. Background interviews 1, Kamukama and 2, Bangirana also discuss the status of *abashumba* children.
23 SLA interview 1, Kivengere; 4, Mulumba; 6, Bamunoba; 10, John Kaishogorize; 11, Njunwoha; 14, Kaitiritimba.
24 SLA interview 8, Kahigiriza.
25 SLA interviews 4, Mulumba; 6, Bamunoba; and 8, Kahigiriza.
26 SLA interviews 5, Gabavungo; and 14, Kaitiritimba.
27 SLA interviews 11, Njunwoha; and 15, Banyankole Cultural Foundation. Cf. Background interview 1, Kamukama.
28 SLA interviews 9, H. Mutashwera; 10, Kaishogorize; 11, Njunwoha; 12, F. Karwemera; and 14, Kaitiritimba. Lazaro Njunwoha also provided the names of several people that he has known who were so branded. Mr. Festo Karwemera (SLA 12) provided a number of Runyankole-Rukiga proverbs bearing on the humiliation and abuse of *abazaana*, including their mutilation.
29 SLA interview 17, Eva Rutafa.
30 For methods of enslavement of *abazaana*, see SLA 1, Kivengere on capture and purchase; 6, Bamunoba on poverty and debt bondage. Banyankole is the term used today in preference to Bairu by those who do not identify as Bahima but as citizens of the old Ankole district of the Uganda protectorate.
31 SLA 1, Kivengere. Cf. Background interview 2, Bangirana.
32 SLA 15, Banyankole Cultural Foundation. Cf. SLA 1, Kivengere; and A.B. Katende, Ann Birnie and Bo Tengnas (eds), *Useful Trees and Shrubs of Uganda* (Nairobi, 1995), pp.232 and illustration 233, on the use of *omuhoko*, although no mention is made of its abortifacient capacity.

33 SLA 15, Banyankole Cultural Foundation on 'Bairu' practice; SLA 1, Kivengere on the Bahima. Contrast Background interview 2, Bangirana.
34 Steinhart, *Conflict*, pp.133–48; Karugire, *History*, pp.207–50.
35 For the following section, see Twaddle, 'Ending of slavery', pp.119–24; and Reid, *Political Power*, pp.160–71.
36 SLA interview 6, Bamunoba.
37 E. Kamuhangire, 'The pre-colonial history of south western Uganda' (unpublished Ph.D. thesis, Makerere University, Kampala, 1996), pp.420–9 and 433–6; cf. R. Beachey, 'The East African ivory trade in the nineteenth century', *Journal of African History*, 8, 2 (1967), pp.269–90; and SLA interviews 1, Kivengere; 4, Mulumba; and 6, Bamunoba.
38 Kamuhangire, 'Pre-colonial history', pp.432–4; and SLA interviews 4, Mulumba; and 6, Bamunoba.
39 SLA interview 6, Bamunoba.
40 SLA interviews 6, Bamunoba; 14, Kaitiritimba; and 3, Nyakimwe.
41 SLA interview, 1 Kivengere. Cf. Kamuhangire, 'Pre-colonial history', pp.427–8. Hope and Merabu Kivengere are respectively the granddaughter and daughter of Muranda.
42 R. Oliver, *The Missionary Factor in East Africa*. 2nd edn (London, 1965); R. Robinson and J. Gallagher, *Africa and the Victorians* (New York, 1961).
43 E.g., H.M. Stanley, *In Darkest Africa*, II (New York, 1890), pp.368–71 for Stanley's views on Christian work in Buganda while in Ankole. Also, Iain R. Smith, *The Emin Pasha Relief Expedition, 1886–1890* (Oxford, 1972), pp.34–5, 45–7 on Emin Pasha's anti-slavery connections.
44 M. Twaddle, 'Slaves and peasants', pp.124–5 and his 'Ending of slavery', pp.127–8. Also, M. Perham, *Lugard: The Years of Adventure, 1858–1898* (Hamden, CT, 1968), pp.191–2.
45 A.R. Tucker, *Eighteen Years in Uganda and East Africa* (Westport, CT, 1970 [1911]), pp.278–81. On the question of slaves and freed slaves, see Oliver, *The Missionary Factor*, pp.16–19, 26, 53–6.
46 Steinhart, *Conflict*, pp.191–209.
47 Twaddle, 'Ending of slavery', pp.138, 135–6, and 142–4.
48 SLA interviews 12, Karwemera; 10, Kaishogorize; 11, Njunwoha; and 6, Bamunoba. See also C. Taylor, *A Simplified Runyankore-Rikiga-English Dictionary* (Kampala, 1998), p.39.
49 SLA interview 10, Kaishogorize mentions having to carry white men in litters as well as road constuction. Cf. SLA interviews 11, Njunwoha and 12, Karwemera on road construction.
50 SLA interview 10, Kaishogorize not only makes the analogy with slavery, he also names various individuals known to him who worked as *abashanju* and were his sources of information.
51 *Ibid.*
52 SLA interviews 6, Bamunoba; and 11, Njunwoha.
53 SLA interviews 12, Karwemera; and 14, Kaitiritimba.
54 SLA interviews 13, Beyaka; and 15, Banyankole Cultural Foundation.
55 SLA interview 12, Karwemera.
56 Interview 14, Kaitiritimba, who administered the *ruharo* system as a clerk for five years starting in 1933.
57 SLA interview 11, Njunwoha offers his own experience at age 15 or 16 of substituting for a sick uncle for which the uncle paid him a goat.
58 SLA interview 12, Karwemera.
59 SLA interviews 15, Banyankole Cultural Foundation; and 3, Nyakimwe.
60 SLA interview 14, Kaitiritimba.
61 SLA interview 6, Bamunoba.
62 See above notes 4 and 5.
63 T.M. Mushanga, 'The clan system among the Banyankole', *Uganda Journal*, 34 (1970), pp.29–34.
64 E. Steinhart, 'The kingdoms of the March', in J.B. Webster (ed.), *Chronology, Migration and Drought in Interlacustrine Africa* (Halifax, 1979); and more recently, J. Willis, 'Kinyoni

and Kateizi, the contested origins of pastoral dominance in southwestern Uganda', in J.-P. Chrétien and J.-L. Triaud (eds), *Histoire d'Afrique, les enjeux de mémoire* (Paris, 1999), pp.119–36; and P. Robertshaw, 'The ancient earthworks of western Uganda: capital sites of a Cwezi Empire?', *Uganda Journal*, 48 (2002), pp.17–32.

65 T.M. Mushanga, 'The end of racial inequality in Ankole' (unpublished ms. in the possession of the author, 1994). My thanks to Ambassador Dr Mushanga for the many helpful conversations and the suggestions he made and for his hospitality during the course of this research.

66 See his *Social Death*, Introduction.

Nine

The Slave Trade in Burundi & Rwanda at the Beginning of German Colonisation 1890–1906

JEAN-PIERRE CHRÉTIEN

Introduction

It is difficult to speak about European penetration in Eastern Africa at the end of the nineteenth century without taking account of the question of the slave trade practised between the Indian Ocean coast and the interior of the continent. It was in the name of an anti-slavery crusade that missionaries, Protestants as well as Catholics, decided to involve themselves in this field, in particular the 'White Fathers' of Monsignor Lavigerie.[1] And it was in the name of the fight against the Zanzibari slave trade that the German Reich intervened directly and militarily to support its citizens who initiated colonial enterprises in the 1880s. The campaigns of King Leopold II, as sovereign of the Congo Free State, against the 'Arabs' in the 1890s could also be mentioned. But at the same time, from the period of the first 'explorations' (1850s–1870s), it would have been impossible to travel into the Great Lakes region without the technical support of the Indian, Arab or Swahili caravan organisers of Bagamoyo or other coastal harbours. Yet these financiers, these traders, these caravan foremen were also the entrepreneurs of the slave trade. This contradictory situation continued under German colonisation. It was particularly clear in the case of Burundi and Rwanda which were located in a double border zone, the border negotiated over a fifteen-year period between Germany and the Congo Free State and also the border of the sphere of action of the slavers whose favourite hunting ground from the 1860s was located on the western sides of Lakes Tanganyika and Kivu (see Map 5). Let us go back to the terms of this contradiction.

COLONISATION, ANTI-SLAVERY AND CATHOLIC MISSIONS

The German project in East Africa, initiated in 1885 by Carl Peters' men, was put in danger in 1889 by the so-called Bushiri general rebellion on the Swahili coast. A co-ordinated British and German action was carried out

The Slave Trade in Burundi & Rwanda, 1890–1906

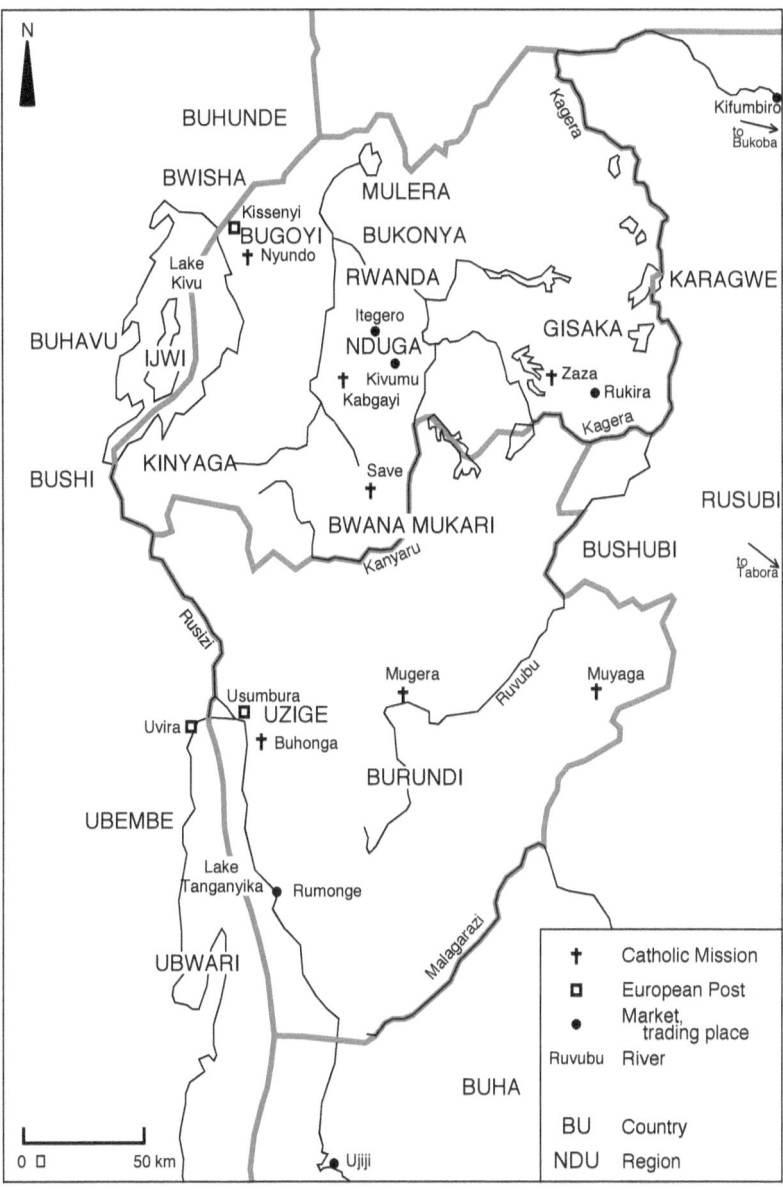

Map 5 Missions and trading places in Burundi and Rwanda (c.1895–1905)

in the name of the fight against slavery, with a blockade of the coast being established to control gun running in particular. This intervention was blessed in Europe by Mgr Lavigerie. The Brussels anti-slavery conference of 1890, inspired to a great extent by him, provided a timely justification for these military deployments and also taxation infringing the rules of free trade concerning the Congo Basin since the Berlin Treaty of 1885. Initially informal, German colonisation became official in 1890 with the creation of a new department at the Ministry for Foreign Affairs (the *Kolonialabteilung*) and the territorial and administrative organisation of the 'protected territory' (*Schutzgebiet*) of *Deutschostafrika* whose governor resided in Dar es Salaam.[2]

The coast was taken under German control, with the sultanate of Zanzibar being restrained to its island territories and soon falling under British protection. The advance into the interior took place gradually, as borders were repeatedly redrawn on paper between 1885 and 1890, always with the pretence of humanitarian action. For example, in 1892 Oscar Baumann (the first European to travel extensively in Burundi) led expeditions aiming to launch steamboats on Lakes Victoria and Tanganyika, which were funded by an 'anti-slavery lottery' supported by members of the Rhine Valley aristocracy and middle class. Berlin also gave its support, without any qualms, to the White Fathers who had settled in the 1870s in Unyamwezi (Tabora) and on the shores of Lakes Tanganyika and Victoria. The White Fathers preferred the Germans to the British, whom they considered henchmen of the Protestant faith, and to the Congo Free State which was, according to them, infiltrated by the Freemasons. In 1895, they reorganised their Vicariates Apostolic according to the new borders established by the German administration. Unyanyembe was headquartered at Ushirombo close to Tabora while South-Nyanza's headquarters was at Kashozi, or Marienberg, near Bukoba. Burundi was included in the first, Rwanda in the second. An intimate link between colonisation and anti-slavery therefore seems obvious.

THE FIGHT TO CONTROL THE 'SECOND SHORE' OF EAST AFRICA: THE TANGANYIKA-KIVU AXIS AGAINST LEOPOLD'S CONGO

Up until 1910, the German administration was troubled by a debate over its western borders due to the contradiction between the theoretical frontier defined in 1885 on sketch maps and the reality of the field (especially concerning the position of Lake Kivu which did not appear on the maps drawn at the end of the 1870s by Henry Morton Stanley, the journalist-explorer). Between 1894 and 1897, after the domination of the Arab chief Rumaliza over the shores of Lake Tanganyika was ended,[3] the first Congolese (Uvira) and German (Ujiji, Usumbura) posts were established there. Later others were founded to the north along the Rusizi valley and on the shores of Lake Kivu. The theoretical border defined in August 1885 in the wake of the Berlin Conference in reality cut across the mountains of Rwanda and Burundi. Yet the Germans insisted that the frontier should follow the natural hydrographic axis, which also had the advantage of globally respecting the western borders of the Rwanda and Burundi kingdoms.

In this German-Belgian[4] confrontation, Leopold's case was that the need to contain Arab slave dealers required a secure border situated to the east of both lakes, whereas the German argument by contrast emphasised freedom of trade along this second shore of the colony and therefore barely hidden support for the Muslim commercial networks from Ujiji to other Swahili centres on Lake Tanganyika. On one side the control of ivory in the Congo basin was at stake, on the other it was the continuation of the draining of this ivory towards the East African coast, as well as Germany's dependence on the technical support provided by Swahili speakers (Islamised Africans called Wangwana and a few Arabs) in establishing their control over the shores of Lake Tanganyika.

Controversy between Hirth and German Government

The South Nyanza Vicar Apostolic, Monsignor Jean-Joseph Hirth, an Alsatian, had fled from the Protestants in Buganda in 1892, after the last 'religious war' and the triumph of the Anglo-Protestant party in that country. He began to implant his mission in Rwanda at the beginning of the twentieth century. The first station was opened by him at Save, in the south of the country, in 1900; then followed Zaza in the east (1900) and Nyundo to the northwest (1901). For the sake of comparison, let us note that Burundi was included in the Unyanyembe vicariate under the responsibility of Mgr François Gerboin. After initial failures between 1879 and 1884 on the shores of Lake Tanganyika because, according to the White Fathers, of Muslim opposition, new stations were founded in the interior of the country between 1898 and 1899 (Muyaga in the east, Mugera in the centre), and then in Buhonga in 1902, near Usumbura, the headquarters of the German military district.

So the missionaries were present in the interior of both countries, whereas, before 1907 and 1912 respectively,[5] the German military were mainly posted on the western periphery of Rwanda and Burundi facing Congo, from Usumbura to Kissenyi (north of Lake Kivu). The whole area was administered from Ujiji from 1896 until 1901, when the district of Usumbura (including Rwanda and Burundi) was created. Usumbura was in turn divided in 1906 into two 'residencies', which neighboured the Residency of Bukoba located to the east.

A DENUNCIATION BY MGR HIRTH (JUNE–OCTOBER 1901)[6]

On 25 June 1901, Cardinal Ledochowski, prefect of Propaganda Fide, met the Prussian ambassador to the Pope, the Marquis Wolfgang von Rotenhau, to whom he gave a letter presenting information provided by

Mgr Hirth. The Vicar Apostolic, following a visit to the country of the 'Mountains of the Moon', in other words after his journey through Rwanda and the establishment of Save, had written an alarming report to the Congregation of Propaganda concerning the 'sad state' of the people of this country 'shortly after coming into contact with Europeans'. According to the missionaries present in the centre of the country, Rwanda was being devastated by the slave trade, the total number of victims reaching 20,000-25,000 per year, with 'the Europeans' support'.[7] In fact these slaves were typically resold four or five times on their journey east and took two to three years to reach the coast. Two-thirds of them would die on the way. As Mgr Hirth concluded, the Germans were allowing this under the cover of 'domestic slavery' (*Haussklaverei*), aiding in this way Islam's corrupting influence. The cardinal, in the name of Propaganda, requested that 'the tribes of Rwanda be spared from these cruel raids against humans, to which they were exposed through the intermediary of Muslims favoured by the Europeans' and that, to attain this objective, the peaceful activities of the missions should be favoured. During the summer of 1901 Canon Hespers, within the *Kolonialrat*, also made known his concerns about this matter. An official inquiry was promised.

The Catholic Church clearly used all its networks to put pressure on the government in Berlin. Mgr Hirth himself wrote directly on 30 July to Governor von Götzen (a letter that reached him only on 3 October), to inform him about his several months' stay in Rwanda and to alert the person who 'opened this country to civilisation' (referring to the von Götzen exploration of 1894) about the 'depopulation' that threatened it in such a senseless manner, since 90 per cent of the slaves died on the way to the coast. Meanwhile, a Dutch missionary active in Burundi (where he founded the missions of Muyaga and Mugera), Johannes-Michael van der Burgt, made use of his stay in Europe (devoted to the editing of his French–Kirundi dictionary) to write on 13 September to Captain Heinrich Bethe, former chief of Usumbura military station, who was also in Germany at that time. He quoted Hirth on the depopulation of Rwanda and Gisaka during 1900, due to the slave trade towards Unyamwezi (in caravans of five to thirty slaves). Van der Burgt called on Bethe, whose friendship he had earned, to ensure that new posts were established in Karagwe, Gisaka and Rusubi in order to better monitor both the 'Wasui' intermediaries in the slave trade and the 'Wasumbwa' markets.[8] This early twentieth-century lobbying was an attempt to exert influence, through German Catholic circles, on the balance of power in Berlin.

THE REACTIONS OF THE DEUTSCHOSTAFRIKA ADMINISTRATION[9]

As early as 13 October, Governor von Götzen, without hiding his scepticism, wrote to Hirth, asking him for a precise report. More officially, on 15 October 1901, the governor's adviser on educational and missionary affairs, Henicke, wrote to Mgr Hirth making the following points: in light

The Slave Trade in Burundi & Rwanda, 1890–1906

of the report from the Holy See on the depopulation of Rwanda, the governor would seek some clarification from the German local authorities on this issue of the slave trade; the administration was being accused of complicity, since the missionary correspondence referred to 'European support'; he would be sorry to see friendly relationships compromised, but according to his experience in Rwanda he did not believe that trade of such an extent existed, and in any case military resources were limited and caution was necessary in dealing with populations which might prove dangerous; finally, the recent creation of the new district of Usumbura would, he concluded, help to strengthen German influence and work more efficiently against slavery.

The enquiry which resulted leaves us today with a very detailed file on the problem of the slave trade in the Great Lakes region during the early twentieth century. The responses written between December 1901 and March 1902 by the men in charge of the districts of the interior were of two types, either offended or nuanced and more questioning.

Offended reactions
• Tabora, 31 January 1902: Captain von Beringe presented a collective report representing the opinions of all local Europeans. He stated that if 20,000 slaves had been exported each year, this would surely have been noticed in the main Arab market of the region. In 1901, 84 slaves were emancipated, of whom only seven were from Rwanda, Ussuwi (Rusubi) or Karagwe. Only four sentences had been imposed in cases relating to the slave trade. The head of the district therefore protested against Hirth's allegations and above all against the theory of a worsening of the situation in Rwanda since European contact. He concluded that this was a libel against the German stations.

• Usumbura, 29 January 1902: Captain Werner von Grawert wrote of missionary rumours. He had never witnessed a trade of more than 20,000 slaves a year! But he was aware that in certain regions parents did sell their children. If such a trade existed, then perhaps it was sourced in the Congo because in the German border sector such an occurrence was impossible. The Catholic Church was obviously using all its networks to pressure Berlin. He concluded by suggesting that Doctor Richard Kandt who had been visiting the Lake Kivu region for several years be consulted. In an appendix, Von Grawert provided a list of slaves emancipated at the station of Usumbura and sent to the Mugera mission. It consisted of children aged four to twelve years old (see Table 9.1).

Over three years only one nine-year–old girl from Rwanda was to be found among a total of 29 individuals. This officer returned to the issue in a letter dated 24 February 1902. There was no slave trade generally speaking in Rwanda, and nothing confirmed Mgr Hirth's allegations. He had never met a slave caravan. Hirth's defamations called for a legal response, in his opinion, and he would be prepared to lodge a complaint.

• Kissenyi, 10 February 1902: Captain Herrmann, head of the

Table 9.1 Emancipated slaves at Usumbura, 1899–1901

Year	1899	1900	1901
Boys	4	1	1
Girls	9	10	4
Babembe	8	1	0
Bavira	2	5	2
Bashi/Banyabungo	2	5	0
Barega	1	0	0
Banyarwanda	0	0	1
'Upper-Congo'	0	0	2

boundary commission, explained that the missionaries believed African gossip. During the last ten years, he wrote, he had observed them exploiting this line to sensitise European public opinion. When they made a mistake no refutation followed; nobody ever believed the authorities and the anti-slavery opinion was based on fantasies. Public opinion was mobilised to pay for a steamer on Lake Victoria to hunt slavers' sailboats which transported, it was said, tens of thousands of slaves. But it turned out that no *dhow* (sailboat) could be found on the lake and that there had been no more than six in previous years. Nevertheless, the Prince of Wied had rallied to this crusade (it was the 'anti-slavery lottery' that had financed Oscar Baumann). Instead of these public campaigns, concluded Herrmann, they should deliver precise facts to the stations! This story of 25,000 slaves in Rwanda was false!

Nuanced reactions
• Bukoba, 31 December 1901: Captain Richter reported that a slave trade was no longer coming from the north (Uganda), but admitted that slave trading from Gisaka remained important (this sentence was underlined in red in Dar es Salaam).
• Mwanza, 21 January 1902: the local official observed that slaves were still coming from Rwanda but in declining numbers. In the time of Captain Herrmann, he went on, the trade was one of entire caravans, whereas today Swahili and Arabs bought groups of between three and five young people, at the price of 6 *doti* of cloth for a boy and more for a girl. The comments were disillusioned: Rwanda was far away and the cattle dealers could indulge in abuses if they so desired.
• On 12 February 1902, in response to Herrmann's request, Richard Kandt (explorer of the shores of Lake Kivu since 1898 and future Resident of Rwanda) made the following comments. A true slave trade from the whole of Rwanda did not exist except in time of famine, when people sold their close relations. For example, in Gisaka, he said, people were sold

during the last famine to 'Wasumbwa and Wasui' traders: that was why Hirth had met a caravan of nine women. Most of the victims would be women already enslaved and sold in emergencies. In fact, he added, slaves were imported into Rwanda from Ubembe (20 per cent) and Uyungu (80 per cent), that is to say from the Congo. The Babembe were brought through South Kivu and the Rusizi valley. There had also been people from 'the place of Gwesche and Kabare', that is to say from Bunyabungu (or Bushi), but that had stopped with the establishment of a Belgian post there. Those from Uyungu arrived through Bugoyi or via Ijwi, because of famines in that Congolese region. Kandt offered an estimate of the volume of the trade: at most 3,000 people were imported per year and 500 exported. He commented, if we cannot help the victims of food shortage then we should not interfere! The figure of 25,000, he concluded, 'carries the seal of falsity', these were rumours caused by missionaries' belief of Africans' small talk and also by the profit they gained from it. He gave the example of a list of French donors to a 'slave redemption' fund which had been published in a bulletin, with each contributor giving one hundred francs when a slave cost at most five francs, which therefore meant a gain of ninety-five francs each time! Missionary letters were for the edification of pious souls!

• Then the new head of Bukoba station wrote to the Governor on 17 March 1902: he had gone to visit the seat of the Apostolic Vicariat at Marienberg, to discuss the allegations raised by Mgr Hirth. He learned that the accusation against Europeans of complicity in the slave trade carried on by Arabs or Swahili concerned the *Safarischeine* delivered by the stations located on the coast and on the caravan routes. This 'travel certificate' allowed people, under the cover of trading in goods, to go from Tabora to Rwanda and to carry out a traffic in human beings. The station of Bukoba had rarely issued such *Safarischeine*, he added, because traders from there were not very numerous and were very well known. The two areas which were incriminated, Karagwe and 'Ussuwi' (Rusubi, that is to say, the region of Biharamulo) and also the Arab hideout at Kifumbiro, the ford across the Kagera river, were, as much as possible, under German control, he claimed, and the rare cases of slave trading had been severely dealt with. Mgr Hirth, he concluded, admitted that the trade could not be exterminated, nor could everywhere be watched over these vast expanses of territory. As for caravans going from Tabora to Rwanda via Ussuwi or Karagwe, these seldom went through Bukoba. Tours, patrols and influence over the 'sultans' (local kings) enabled the administration to avoid anything worse. During his next tour in 'Ussuwi', Von Stuemer promised to take care of this issue and to free slaves originating from Gisaka if he found a great number of them.

Having received this correspondence, on 24 June 1902 the governor sent a circular letter to the heads of the coastal districts of Bagamoyo, Pangani, Saadani and Dar-es-Salaam and asked them for a report on the question within three months.

The responses were as follows:
- Bagamoyo, 16 October 1902: caravan permits issued by that district for a destination further than Tabora or Mwanza, essentially to Bukoba, were very rare. Porters were changed over when caravans reached these two stations, and only 'Wanyamwezi' and 'Wasukuma' served as porters between Tabora and Mwanza and the coast. Therefore traders who might have come from Rwanda with cattle and ivory were very rare in Bagamoyo.
- Saadani, 4 November 1902: the answer was the same, this district only saw incoming caravans of 'Wanyamwezi' cattle traders, who did not operate in the western frontier region and who had no slaves with them. More control should be exerted over the region concerned.
- Pangani, 20 February 1903: large slave caravans had ceased to exist a long time before. Slaves were brought in small numbers and were subject to intensive control, but none had come from Rwanda or neighbouring countries.
- Dar-es-Salaam, 8 May 1903: the head of the district answered the governor in a contradictory manner. Hirth's suggestion that Europeans might have collaborated in the enslaving of people was, he said, concerning the coastal stations, insanity! Caravan certificates were not delivered to people suspected or already convicted of slave trading. Unchecked transfers of property in the form of slaves existed, especially if the slave was described as having always been a slave (in the absence of written records), with the latter probably having been intimidated by his master. In this district, about one hundred slaves originating from the regions of Lake Tanganyika could be found, but they were far from all having been reduced into slavery irregularly. The interior station should be asked to deliver certificates when transfers of property occurred, to make it possible for their legality to be verified. The governor's office added in pencil the note *geheim* ('secret')!

It can be seen that, even though the German administration as a whole was annoyed by the apocalyptic description (thousands of people deported, depopulation, and so on) from the Apostolic Vicariate of South Nyanza, the enquiry revealed that there was no smoke without fire.

THE SEARCH FOR A COMPROMISE

In reality this polemic about the slave trade was associated with other issues. The German military administration (in particular in Usumbura and Bukoba) was unhappy with the White Fathers' interventions in a range of political affairs. Examples included the decision to found a mission at Nyundo to the northwest of Rwanda, right in the middle of a region that was 'contested' by the Congolese and the British, without having asked the authorities' opinion; the adjudication of legal cases; the aggressive attitude towards chiefs; violent incidents provoked by Baganda 'askari–catechists';[10] the activism of missionaries animated by a crusading zeal like the Fathers Brard (at Save) and Barthélémy (at Nyundo);

disagreements with the German decision to support existing local authorities, especially in Rwanda with King Musinga, contacted by Captain Ramsay as early as 1897, and his chiefs. Mgr Hirth could not hide his hostility towards these chiefs who represented the 'Tutsi or Hima' race, responsible in his opinion for a feudal order contrary to the principles of freedom and property. The government also regretted the insufficient number of Germans in the ranks of the White Fathers. Letters were exchanged on these themes in parallel with the debate about slavery.

However, in April–June 1902, there occurred a polite exchange of letters between Hirth and von Götzen, each seeking reconciliation in the well understood joint interests of the European presence in the region. Three letters put an end to the crisis.[11] They revealed the persistence of the other causes of dissension between the mission and the administration, and also the fact that the administration was compelled, at least on the surface, to show some concern about the slavery issue even if it considered that Hirth was exaggerating its extent, and that he had had to water down his complaints.

• Mgr Hirth wrote to the governor on 4 October 1902. The trade, he noted, had diminished in 1902 thanks to the Usumbura station's support for the opening of the missions in Rwanda and to the ordinance concerning *Haussklaverei* dated 29 November 1901. In a year there had been a decline of 80 per cent in the traffic. He recognised that the depopulation of Rwanda had started as early as 1895–6, when Rwanda's reputation for impenetrability had come to an end. But he upheld his estimate that 20–25,000 slaves had been sold in 1901, as a result of the expansion of the trade in the immediately preceding years. In 1899, the missionaries of 'Ussui', he said, had observed the traffic at the ford of the Kagera: 400 to 500 slaves per month (without counting the stowaways). Hirth himself, between 20 and 22 October 1901, encountered on his journey (55km) six caravans with a total of 67 women or children; in January 1900, travelling up the Rusizi valley, 20 boys or girls were offered to his porters at one camp, while the border was uncontrolled.

Hirth explained that the rise of the slave trade in Rwanda would have been a consequence of the closing down of the markets in Uganda and southern Tanganyika between 1890 and 1895; that the tolerance of 'domestic slavery' favoured Islam; and that the trade depended on European complicity, with 'travel letters' being issued to petty traders, who were in reality slave dealers who went to buy slaves in Rwanda for four or five ells of cotton. Swahili, agents of Arab or Indian firms, entered Rwanda looking for ivory, so that it, and neighbouring kingdoms, were infiltrated by Islam. Karagwe over the past forty years was an example of a country ruined by the Arabs. And he evoked his experience of 28 years under the threat of Islam in Uganda: one must, he insisted, prevent the youth from falling under the influence of Islam, which was hostile to 'progress and European influence'. This debate would continue relentlessly between Catholic missions and the German colonists up to 1914.[12]

Hirth's other point on Rwanda was that the chiefs were won over to this new trade because they were greedy for cloth, and so started selling women and children first from Congo, then from 'submitted tribes' within their own country, who were regarded as 'an inferior class of men' and were treated as slaves. Force ruled over the entire Great Lakes region. To eliminate slavery and make 'civilisation and, with her, liberty' advance in these kingdoms, slavery as well as the subjugation of the lower classes must be eliminated and schools must be multiplied! Hirth's analysis confused two separate problems, the slave trade and the social organisation of Rwanda, forgetting that this powerful kingdom was spared the worst form of slave trade that unleashed itself in the east of the future Congo, where societies were less strongly organised.

• The governor sent a circular letter on 10 December 1902 to all districts.[13] It consisted of five points:

– There was 'no doubt' that in Rwanda and neighbouring countries, in sectors far away from military posts, 'the slave trade is still practised' 'and that in particular there are still traders coming from the coast to buy slaves'. 'In one case in Tabora, the station has managed to confound the culprits of this professional slave trade'; the main culprit had been sentenced to the chain gang for life, the sentence being confirmed by the governor.

– Since the traders were very likely to try to bypass the stations to reach the coast, this could be avoided if, during their tours, officials gave priority to reminding the 'sultans' of their district of the existence of the decree of 19 August 1896 that made provision to reward denunciations of infractions and for a discreet surveillance of the suspected regions.

– To fight the slave trade more efficiently, the governor specified that, in the worst cases, the sanction could extend to the death penalty.

– Furthermore, he reminded his administration of the contents of the circular of 17 December 1895 concerning the rigorous control of caravans going to the coast, when issuing permits. In particular, women and children accompanying the caravans would have to be watched.

– Finally, in order to enforce the 29 November 1901 ordinance on domestic slavery (continuing the ordinance of 29 September 1901 on the administrative emancipation of slaves), with particular regard to redeeming slaves if they desired to be freed,[14] he reminded officials that they were required to allow the transfer of *Herrenrecht* (the property rights of the master) only over people who were resident in their own district. So if a slave had come from another district, in particular from the interior, then the authorisation had to be refused. In such cases the rights of the master had to be ascertained and if they were not absolutely clear, then a freedom letter had to be delivered at once, independent of any court action. Slaves had to be interrogated about their situation without their owners being present.

All this, concluded the circular letter, had to be officially announced during a public *shauri* and the population had to be invited to cooperate.

This circular has all the appearance of a cover-up, combining a conciliatory tone, self-justification, verbal agitation and references to existing texts. Governor von Götzen also planned a report on the slave trade in Rwanda for the Ministry. This report was sent to the *Kolonialabteilung* on 8 June 1903 and then made public. Its content was rather cursory. He was sure, he wrote, that in previous years there had been a quite important trade in slaves in Rwanda and in the neighbouring countries and doubtless it continued clandestinely. But Mgr Hirth's claims were exaggerated; they were the fruit of a superficial understanding and a desire to develop propaganda for missionary action in Rwanda, and the bishop had now retreated from his previous assertions. Von Götzen ended by stating that the traffic was in decline and that the application of the ordinance of 29 November 1891 by German stations was serious. All this would appease Hirth, concluded von Götzen, adding that he had asked the station in Bukoba to favour the schools of the missions!

The polemic thus settled down into bargaining between the missions and the administration, without leading to a more in-depth inquiry into the reality of the slave trade in Rwanda.

The Realities of the Slave Trade and Slavery at the Local Level (Rwanda and Burundi)

Documentary sources and recent works enable us to underline the differences between Rwanda and Burundi, according to their respective political and social contexts.

1) IN RWANDA

In the overview of Rwandese society presented by Jan Czekanowski, the Polish anthropologist, after he passed through the country in 1907, slavery was mentioned, but as a marginal institution concerning mostly women and children and arising from famine.[15]

> There are also slaves in Ruanda. But the institution of slavery does not play any role here, though the number of slaves must be really large in Bugoyi[16] and among the Batutsi of Nduga. Here slaves, as far as I know, are mostly women, 'baja'. During the quite frequent periods of famine, they were sold as little girls by their parents in exchange for food. On the social situation of boys sold against foodstuff, I did not manage to obtain anything precise. It seems to me that while growing up they integrate themselves into the mass of clients (*bagaragu*).
>
> Any country periodically hit by famine, like Ufumbiro,[17] for example, supplies slaves who, once they are in a foreign country, are no longer protected by their kin and remain in a situation of inferiority, at the mercy of their masters' protection.... However, the situation of slaves cannot be globally described as bad. Nowhere have I heard about bad treatment.

For a more precise vision of the situation, analysed from the interior, we shall rely on Eugénie Mujawimana's remarkable BA thesis supervised in the early 1980s at the University of Rwanda by Roger Heremans, which dealt precisely with this question.[18] It provides precious evidence on six aspects of the situation at the end of nineteenth century.

The existence of this trade

Firstly, it is possible to find traces of it in the specialised vocabulary of *kinyarwanda*. *Gutunda*, peddler, and *iguriro* or *igerero*, market (literally, in particular in Kinyaga and in Gisaka, the place were one exchanges or the place where one measures), do not apply specifically to 'slave markets'. The latter are found more under the meaning of 'commercial centre', *akagali*, designating houses grouped into a hamlet, an unusual situation in a country of dispersed settlement. Adornments (pearls, metal bracelets, cloth) and slaves were exchanged there. The action of approaching prospective clients was known as *kuregura*. Even more precise terms applied to the slave trade: there existed the verb *kuhanjura* (to negotiate for slaves), in particular in the north, with its derived term *abahanjuzi* (slave traders). Among the *abaja*, slaves, were distinguished war captives (*b'umuheto*, 'from the bow') and those secured by trade (*b'abagurano*, 'from exchange'). *Abahalira* designated young people who had become slaves.

Mujawimana also collected oral testimonies. Among others, that of Nyirangirente who was sold by her paternal uncle, as a young porter, to a trader from Mulera in exchange for seven goats. This trader sold her on to a third person in replacement for a cow that should have been given back in the context of a pastoral contract of the loan of a milch cow. This occurred towards 1905. In the end this young woman married the son of the master, and entered without a dowry into his family.[19]

This type of story complements archival sources, in particular those of the White Fathers. While emancipating slaves in, for example, Mwanza, at the mission in Katoke and in Ushirombo, some slaves coming from Gisaka in Eastern Rwanda were found; this region was divided at the time into three provinces (Migongo, Mirenge and Gihunya) from where they were brought by Basubi or Basumbwa traders.[20]

Favourable factors

Arab-Swahili trade was present in the neighbouring kingdoms, to the east in Rusubi (the 'Buswi' of the Europeans at the time) as well as to the west on Lake Tanganyika and in the Rusizi valley up to Lake Kivu (in particular in Rumaliza's time, during the years 1884–94). This trade favoured the development of networks of small local slave traders.[21]

In Rwanda the attitude of the royal powers themselves added to this tendency. The *mwami* Rwabugiri resided as early as 1856 in Gisaka, a former kingdom annexed by his predecessor Rwogera that became a centre for trade to the east where, at the end of the 1880s, a royal monopoly of ivory exportation was instituted. This trade was carried on with Bazinza peddlers,[22] in exchange for cloth and guns, mediated by chiefs placed by the king in Gisaka. These chiefs were the first slave dealers. The only foreign traders allowed in to trade were black (Bazinza, Basubi, Bahaya, Basumbwa); Arabs did not arrive before the German period. The west of Rwanda was not visited by foreign traders: the atmosphere there was too bellicose. The interests of King Rwabugiri (who died in 1895) and the region's chiefs in this traffic were clear: through it they could acquire cotton cloth, rare ornaments, firearms and other goods that added to their capacity for prestige, exchange or pressure, and so allowed them to acquire larger cattle herds, the most sought-after means of affirmation of power in this country.

At the opposite end of the social structure, another factor played a crucial role in the nineteenth century, the multiplication of calamities and famines.[23] These were recorded in 1892, 1895–6, 1897–8 (due to locust attack), 1898–1901 and 1902–4 due to drought, and then because of excessive rain in 1905–6 and 1907–8. The period from 1908 to 1916 was one of respite. The fostering of children, a normal response to such situations, could easily develop into a slave trade. Local domestic slavery already existed, with young girls being acquired by the wealthy, having been captured during raids, especially during Rwabugiri's wars against his western neighbours. The end of those wars after 1896 led to a growth of trade exchange as a means of procuring slaves (we have already noted the case of Nyiragirente).

The main centres

'Slave markets' did not exist in the strictest sense, but instead there were places managed by traders for the gathering of captives. For example, at Kivumu, in Nduga (in the centre of the country, a region important because of the royal courts established there), local traders had enclosures where they kept slaves to be bartered. They had proceeded in the same way to sell elephant tusks coming from the northwest to Bahaya traders. The slave traffic was induced by demand from Gisaka traders, themselves connected with the Zinza network at the end of the nineteenth century. This specific activity, which took place in a fairly discreet way, hidden behind high fences, was encouraged economically by the proximity of a real market at Itegero, where in particular bows and arrows made by local craftsmen could be found but also food, hoes, tobacco and so on. The White Fathers discovered the site of 'this slave market' on their way to found Kabgayi mission in 1905–6. Father Lecoindre wrote in April 1905: 'I was taken to the exact place where formerly the public slave market was held.'

Eugénie Mujawimana also quotes the testimony of Samson Rwanamiza:

> There was no slave market at Kivumu, not even a market for other products. The only market around was that of Itegero. However, the great

slave traders, including Mulinzi, lived in Kivumu. They bought slaves and sold them in their homes, inside their enclosures, inside their huts even. Every person that managed to kidnap or buy someone went to sell him at Kivumu at those traders' homes when they were not able to bring him to Gisaka.

Another typical example is that of Rukira in Gisaka. The chief of Gihunya (where Rukira is located) was awarded control of the trade with the east around 1887 by the king: some of the king's great traders (*abasasakirago b'uwmami*, 'those who spread the palaver mat for the king') and elephant hunters (*abayovu*), generally Batwa, therefore came to Rukira. Over time traders gradually emancipated themselves from this royal monopoly, keeping to themselves a growing share of the cloth acquired through this traffic. Rukira had previously been frequented by foreign traders coming from the east and also by suppliers coming from the interior. Evidence concerning slaves being held or kept for traders by the local authorities was still being recorded in 1906. But there was no 'market' in this region.

Other centres can be mentioned: Rwanza in Bwanamukali, Byahi in Bugoyi, and Mubuga in Bukonya.

Routes and caravans

Two types of trade routes can be distinguished. Peripheral exchanges, concerning western border regions, were orientated towards Bushi, Buhavu, Buhunde, Bwisha, Gishali (that is to say, regions situated to the west of Lake Kivu) and to a lesser extent towards Burundi. Apart from these there were internal networks which flowed towards exportation to the east, as we have seen. People coming from the north (Mulera, Bugoyi) were sold at sites such as Kivumu or Rukira, in particular during periods of famine. For example in July 1906 the diary of Rwaza notes:[24]

> Pushed by famine, many take into the neighbouring countries their wives, their children, and they sell them for food or cattle. To conduct this trade, the wretched creatures hide themselves because they know that the bulk of the population will not approve of them. It's at night mostly that those bands pass by.

Or again in April of the same year:

> Ku Mbuga [at Mbuga] the great trade is carried out; from there trade goods are sent to Kivumu, then to Kisaka and Ujinja [Buzinza]. Crafty people take the opportunity presented by the famine, take the poor devils in, feed them, and as soon as they have recovered go to sell them in Bukonya.

This 'trade' therefore also used violence, deceit and raids. For example, towards Buhanga (close to Ruhengeri), a place renowned for its ceramics, women buying pots were kidnapped by the bands of a certain Ruvugiro (from the Abalihira clan). At Rukira persons kidnapped from Gisaka itself were sold.

The Slave Trade in Burundi & Rwanda, 1890–1906

Caravans were collective and grouped together several traders with large numbers of porters often led by the sons of the traders. The ferry men and the authorities received tolls. Slaves were relatively well treated with the object of maintaining the trade qualities of the 'commodity', except if they tried to escape.

The actors of the slave trade: professional merchants

Some of these merchants of Gisaka or Kivumu were well known. At Kivumu, according to the diary of Kabgayi in May 1906, nine main traders could be found, including a chief from Bukonya, the remaining eight being Bahutu.[25] Eugénie Mujawimana identified fifteen merchants using her oral sources, of whom Mulinzi and Mushakamba, two brothers, of the Hutu lineage of the Basindi clan, were especially significant. Mulinzi, born around 1870, was the son of an arrow featherer of Kivumu; he himself was a crafts and goats peddler. He practised his trade using contacts established with Swahili traders after 1887. He ended his days in Gisaka. Testimonies exist about his enclosure, which contained many cattle, full granaries, and stocks of cloth and slaves, where he received Bazinza and Basumbwa. Like a chief, he had several wives who wore copper bracelets and necklaces of white and red beads. In the same way this BA thesis provides a list for Rukira, detailing the traders who went to the east and knew Swahili. Other small caravan leaders were allied to the former.

Among this workforce of the slave trade, foreign itinerant traders coming from Rusubi or Buhaya and also some Basumbwa, close to the Banyamwezi, should not be forgotten. Certain local notables also acted as traders, as did, for example, some chiefs and sub-chiefs in Gisaka (such as Muliro, a prince from Gisaka who was the nephew of the last independent king of this country, Kimenyi Getura, and was therefore a fallen aristocrat). Elsewhere political leaders did not trade directly, but were in league with traders who provided them with goods to cover their taxes.

Volume estimates

From 1895 to 1918, in Kivumu, counting about four slaves per trader twice a month for thirteen traders, one arrives at about 1,200 slaves per year, in other words more than 20,000 during the twenty years of this traffic. But at Rukira, at the site of exportation, the estimate would be double or triple this sum; that is, at least 3,000 per year. These numbers are far from Mgr Hirth's estimates, but the flow was not negligible.

2) IN BURUNDI

It was mostly on the shores of Lake Tanganyika in the 1890s that the slave trade can be observed. As early as 1879–81 in Rumonge, in the south of the country, the White Fathers rented or 'redeemed' slaves from the Arabs and the Swahili or from Babwari intermediates (coming from the west bank of the lake), mostly children sold by their families. The travellers of the 1890s described great markets with several thousands of people on the northern shores of the lake, but they mentioned the slave trade only rarely.

During the years 1880–90 Burundi's shoreline served as an entrepot for the slave traffic coming from Congo. For example, to the north of the lake, in Uzige, the Austrian traveller Oscar Baumann witnessed, in September 1892, a slave encampment controlled by followers of Rumaliza, opposite the settlement opened by the latter at Rubenga, on the other shore, close to Uvira:[26]

> The Arab post, composed of several negroes' huts, was full of slaves, mostly women and children, of whom only a few were chained whereas the others went to and fro freely.... A recent arrival, coming from Ruwenga, consisted only of miserable, skinny, wasted shadows.... Most of them were people from Ubwari, Uvira, Ubembe regions repeatedly devastated by the people of Rumaliza....

Salumu, chief of the trading post in Ujiji, after Rumaliza's departure (1894), continued with sailboats making stopovers in different places along the lake's shores. But cotton cloth was rare in Burundi at that time in contrast with Rwanda (Captain Ramsay noticed this in 1897 during his expedition across both countries).[27] Therefore 'external' trade was more limited. However Oscar Baumann,[28] as well as sources used in Jan-Georg Deutsch's chapter, mentions the presence of Barundi slaves in Unyamwezi and Zanzibar but no slaves from Rwanda. It cannot be excluded that Barundi and Banyarwanda, speaking almost the same language, have been in some cases confused or mixed together. Observers in Burundi at the time did notice some cases of a slave trade.

Von Trotha,[29] who crossed Burundi from east to west in 1896, considered that there was neither slavery nor slave trade in the interior of the country. However, he noted that at 'Munkasa' (present-day Bujumbura) market, a 'woman was bought for ten strings of red beads'. And Father Van der Burgt noted in his *Dictionary* that (in 1897–8) there were a few discreet slave dealers in Uzige (in the region of Usumbura), some Bangwana (Islamised people from Unyamwezi or from the Congo basin), Basumbwa, Bavira (from the country of Uvira), or Bayangayanga (peddlers from the south of Burundi specialised, in particular, in the salt and iron trade[30]), and he added that a boy was worth two to four *fundo* or strings of beads, whereas a girl was worth twice as much (a *fundo* was worth 0.30F at the time).

In 1897 a Belgian report about an Arab from Tabora, who had an agent in Buha and who traded as far as Bushi and Rwanda, noted that he was also implicated in slave dealing in Burundi.[31] The same year Captain Ramsay, who had just founded the military post of Usumbura, exposed a traffic in children from Bunyabungo (Bushi), carried out by Congolese traders towards German territory and he warned the Uzige chiefs about this.[32] In spite of this evidence, the Congo state authorities denounced the complicity of 'Wakanya' (Mibakanyi),[33] the local chief. The White Fathers also present in 1897 in Usumbura revealed frequent cases[34] of this border region trade: on 16 May the chief Kiyogoma sold four little girls to the Arabs; on 27 May six slave girls were at the home of *bayangayanga* peddlers of Rumonge; on 1 June a German soldier went after a Muvira trader who was operating on the Burundi shore of the lake; on 24 July a mother complained that one of her kin had sold her son. On 30 November a man from the mission went to Uvira to redeem seventeen children (of whom twelve were girls); on 3 December a Muslim trader of Ganda origin settled nearby (a certain Muhambazi) took away a little girl of 'extraordinary beauty'. The traveller Richard Kandt also noted in 1898 that the chief Kinyoni (on the plain of Rusizi) sold slaves to the Arabs and also mentioned the role of Muhambazi.[35] Early in 1899, the mission diary of Mugera[36] reported a Sumbwa trader who had bought several captives coming from Uvira in Bulamata (to the south of the Ruzizi plain), at chief Mikoni's, and who wanted to transport them towards the east, across Burundi. Following an attack carried out by a chief from the east of the country, these slaves had escaped and some had taken refuge at the mission. It appeared that this trader was the father-in-law of one of the Christians of Mugera! These events reveal a marginal slave trade concerning particular people abducted away in Congo, and mostly organised by foreigners. In his 1916 synthesis, the geographer Hans Mayer echoed the writing of Father van der Burgt (and the controversy we have dwelt on earlier in this essay). He wrote[37]:

> There existed a very active slave trade from Burundi directed outside the country, under the influence of Arabs and of Swahili coastal people, and through Wavira, Bassuwi, Wasumbwa and Wanyamwezi intermediaries living on the western and eastern borders of the country. The Barundi sold as slaves not only their compatriots taken prisoner during internal wars, in particular women and small girls, but also orphans put on sale by their kin or even children sold by their own parents. The transaction was paid in salt, beads and iron hoes; high prices were paid for pretty Tutsi girls who ended up in the harems of Arabs or rich black Swahili or well to do Wanyamwezi.

But he claimed straight away: 'As in Ruanda, there is no, or no more, slavery in Burundi.' He added that it would not have been necessary, since according to him the mass of Bahutu were the 'servants of the batussi lords'. We find here the outline used also by Mgr Hirth at the end of his controversy with the German administration. But this would be another debate.

However, the collective memory in Burundi focuses mostly on Rumaliza's slavers in the mid-1880s. He had in fact led several raids on the shores of Lake Tanganyika, and even, in 1886, an attack towards the interior of the country where warriors of Mwezi Gisabo victoriously opposed him. *Umuja* in Kirundi designates mostly women's domestic work, in particular at the courts of powerful people. It is a depreciative term. But the verb *kuhanjura*, known in Rwanda, as we have seen, and also in Buha (*kuhanzura*), is not used in Burundi. We have found only one occurrence during our field investigations, at Burambi, on the shore of Lake Tanganyika, therefore still in this very peripheral context.

The logic of the passage towards servitude also calls for some attention in Burundi's case. It raises the question of defining the 'slave trade'. It appeared mostly in relation to famines:[38] in such situations people ate what they could gather from the wild, or went searching for food far away, or they could rent out the strength of their arms. In such situations, in Rumonge, for example, on the lake, children were 'sold': a witness whom we interviewed spoke of five children being exchanged for a single root of cassava![39] To bring children to be sold is referred to as *gushora* or *gushorera*,[40] which usually refers to bringing cattle to the drinking place or to the market. Sales could be transacted with a richer person locally: the exchange took the form of a kind of rewarded adoption, or reduced or deferred bridewealth. In the local imagination, the young women given out by their families were compared to heifers. But in this case the matrimonial logic was replaced by a commercial one. For boys the stake was that of labour as a domestic worker (*mushumba*).[41] Paul Bwandondeye, in the region of Ruyigi,[42] in the east of the country, transmitted to us a saying of those days: 'to give one's daughter in exchange for a banana root'. It is very clear that the placement of children or the giving away of a child during difficult periods could be expected in the context of reciprocity or protection networks. It was not a reduction into slavery for the family. However, this gift, in some regions, could turn into a definite departure and a true appropriation by a foreign dealer.

The cases of Rwanda and Burundi help us to analyse a particular situation, that of regions spared for a long time from the slave trade and practising other types of relations of dependence rather than slavery. In these cases the process of the introduction of the slave trade is worthy of attention, in terms of its context, its actors, its victims. The great question is to identify the existence of weaknesses in a society, of fragile and marginalised elements, and of the factors that could lead to the acceptance of the swing towards a radical exploitation, towards total uprooting and subjugation with no escape.

Notes

1   See F. Renault, *Lavigerie, l'esclavage africain et l'Europe* (Paris, 1971).
2   Cf. F.-F. Müller, *Deutschland, Zanzibar, Ostafrika. Geschichte einer Deutschen Kolonialeroberung, 1884–1890* (Berlin, 1959).
3   J. Marissal, 'Mohammed bin Khalfan', in C.A. Julien (ed.), *Les Africains*, Vol. 11 (Paris, 1978), pp.49–71.

4 Or more precisely, German-Leopoldian up to 1908.
5 Dates of the creation of the headquarters of the Residences at Kigali and Gitega.
6 This file is to be found in the German archives of Dar-es-Salaam, Tanzania National Archives (TNA), G 9/18.
7 Passage underlined in red in the letter from the *Kolonialabteilung* received by the governor at Dar-es-Salaam, 27 August.
8 The governor was informed of this demand by Bethe the following November. The Basubi and the Basumbwa controlled the commercial roads between Rwanda and the south of Lake Victoria.
9 TNA, G 9/18 and G 9/19.
10 See I. Linden, *Christianisme et pouvoirs au Rwanda (1900-1990)* (Paris, 1999).
11 TNA, G 9/19.
12 In the 1910s Father van der Burgt accused Muslims of being responsible for a demographic decline in East Africa because of their role in the diffusion of venereal diseases.
13 Prepared by his adviser Franz Stuhlmann, who was knowledgeable about the Great Lakes region.
14 It should be noted that 'domestic slavery' was still not abolished in 1914.
15 J. Czekanowski, *Forschungen im Nil-Kongo-Zwischengebiet, vol. I, Ethnographie Zwischenseengebiet Mpororo-Ruanda* (Leipzig, 1917), pp. 262–3.
16 To the northwest of the country, close to the present border with Congo, whereas Nduga is the central region, that of the royal capitals.
17 Bufumbira, in the southwest of present-day Uganda, was controlled at the end of the nineteenth century by the Rwandese monarchy.
18 E. Mujawimana, 'Le Commerce des esclaves au Rwanda' (Université Nationale du Rwanda, Mémoire Multigraphié, Ruhengeri, 1983) (this unpublished work has sometimes been used by unscrupulous authors without being properly referenced).
19 The equivalence between women and cattle also operated in a number of inter-lineage relationships.
20 Mujawimana, 'Commerce'.
21 On trade and 'markets' in Rwanda at the end of the nineteenth century see B. Lugan, 'Les réseaux commerciaux au Rwanda dans le dernier quart du XIXe siècle', *Études d'Histoire Africaine*, 9–10 (1977–8), pp.183–212.
22 It should be noted that the Basubi (the people of Rusubi, not to be confused with Bashubi, who neighboured Burundi) share the same Zinza culture and descent from a kingdom born from the break-up of an ancient Great Buzinza (see J.-P. Chrétien, *L'Afrique des Grands Lacs* (Paris, 2000), p.130).
23 See R. Botte, 'Ruanda and Burundi, 1889–1930: chronology of a slow assassination', *International Journal of African Historical Studies*, 18, 1 (1985), pp.53–91 and 18, 2 (1985), pp.289–314.
24 References to the diaries come from E. Mujawimana's B.A. thesis.
25 This enables us to better evaluate Mgr Hirth's suggestions linking the Tutsi with a reduction into slavery.
26 O. Baumann, *Durch Massailand zur Nilquelle* (Berlin, 1894), pp.94–5.
27 H. Ramsay, 'Uha, Urundi, Ruanda', *Mitteilungen aus den Deutschen Schutzgebieten*, 3 (1897), pp.177–82. See also J.-M. van der Burgt, *Dictionnaire français-kirundi* (Bois-le Duc, 1903), p.212.
28 O. Baumann, *Der Sansibar-Archipel* (Leipzig, 1897), p.21.
29 L. Von Trotha, *Meine Bereisung von Deutsch-Ostafrika* (Berlin, 1897), pp.77–9.
30 Cf. J.-P. Chrétien, 'Le commerce du sel de l'Uvinza au XIXe siècle: de la cueillette au monopole capitaliste', *Revue Française d'Histoire d'Outre-mer*, 3 (1978), pp.401–22.
31 Archives Africaines de Bruxelles, EIC 226.
32 Deutsches Zentralarchiv, *Reichskolonialamt*, 622, f. 107-108 (correspondence dating from 11 Aug. 1897).
33 Archives Africaines de Bruxelles, dossier de l'EIC, 9, Boma, 28 Sept. and 24 Dec. 1897.
34 Archives des Pères Blancs, Rome, Diaire de St-Antoine (written by Van der Burgt),

35 R. Kandt, *Caput Nili.* 2nd edn (Berlin, 1919), Vol. II, pp.83–97.
36 Archives des Pères Blancs, Diaire de Mugera, 15 Feb., 24–25 Mar. and 3–4 Apr. 1899.
37 H. Meyer, *Les Barundi* (trans. Paris, 1984), pp.129–30 (translation of *Die Barundi* (Leipzig, 1916)).
38 Cf. L. Kavakure, *Famines et disettes au Burundi (Fin du XIXe siècle - 1ère moitié du XXe siecle)*, (Mémoire, Université du Burundi, Bujumbura, 1982).
39 Interview with Bernard Bugombe, Mushubi (Hutu), born around 1895, Vyuya, 15 May 1983.
40 Interview with Daniel Kiramvu; Interview with Abraham Mugaye, Musapfu (Tutsi), Matana, 10 Sept. 1971.
41 Interview with D. Kiramvu, Mujiji (Hutu), born around 1885, Gitaza, 7 Feb. 1983.
42 Interview with Paul Bwandondeye, Mushoma, Munyinya, 25 May 1988.

Ten

Bunyoro
& the Demography of Slavery Debate
Fertility, kinship & assimilation

SHANE DOYLE*

Introduction

Bunyoro is one of the oldest kingdoms in East Africa. It is reputed to have been the most powerful state in the interlacustrine region many centuries ago, but its strength dissipated in the first half of the nineteenth century and, after a brief resurgence in the 1870s and 1880s, it became one of the poorest and least significant parts of Uganda (see Map 4). At the heart of this story is a process of dramatic demographic change that saw Bunyoro decline from being one of the most densely populated states in East Africa to becoming the district with the second lowest population density in colonial Uganda. Bunyoro's demographic problems developed in the nineteenth century and appear to have provided the primary stimulus for the kingdom's rapidly increasing involvement in raiding and trading for slaves. As a number of chapters in this volume have illustrated, demography lies at the heart of slavery, which typically relies on forced migration, interferes with the marriage market and reduces life expectancy. In Africa the development of slavery should perhaps always be viewed, in part at least, as a function of the continent's low population density and consequent competitive struggle for followers and labour.[1] In a society where childlessness was becoming epidemic, the forceful acquisition of wives and workers took on a new significance.

What is ironic about Bunyoro's history, however, is that its very success in adapting rapidly to the new long-distance commerce of the late nineteenth century ultimately resulted in demographic disaster. Bunyoro became a powerful middleman in the commercial networks of the interlacustrine region, mastering the art of warfare with firearms, and profiting hugely from the exchange of coastal imports for northern Uganda's ivory and slaves. Bunyoro's new strength, its resistance to Egyptian imperialism, its aggressive territorial expansion and support for the Muslim faction in Buganda's civil wars, all tended to identify it as an opponent of Western civilisation and legitimate commerce. When Britain decided to secure its interests in the Nile basin in the early 1890s, Bunyoro, with its reputation as an unreformable bastion of the slave trade, was targeted as a threat that had to be destroyed.[2] By 1899 Bunyoro was almost entirely depopulated and its slave population had dispersed. Slavery, which had appeared to be the solution to Bunyoro's emerging demographic crisis, ultimately brought on the catastrophe that was prolonged imperial conquest.

The Debate About Slave Demography

The most influential modern theories about the demography of slavery within Africa are those of Claude Meillassoux. Meillassoux accepts that the acquisition of slaves was a route to demographic expansion, but he maintains that the additional reproductive capacity of these imported individuals was not demographically significant, nor was it a major motive for their acquisition. He argues that 'the hypothesis that [female slaves] were preferred because of their potential for reproduction is not supported by objective data', because 'neither statistics nor any other kind of evidence demonstrates the maintenance or growth of slave populations by the reproduction of slave populations among themselves'.[3] Meillassoux points out that female slaves were constantly imported into African slave-owning societies, demonstrating that enslaved women were not reproducing themselves. The few contemporary accounts of the attitudes of slave owners suggested to Meillassoux that they were uninterested in their slaves' reproduction or child-rearing responsibilities. Female slave life histories emphasised their vulnerability, poor living conditions, unstable relationships, and their children's high death rates. The demographic data that Meillassoux refers to seem to indicate serious sub-fertility or low child survival rates in slave societies, due to the use of contraception, abortion and infanticide, as well as high rates of sexually transmitted infections.[4]

It is important to note, however, that the few case studies that Meillassoux utilises form a rather narrow foundation on which to base a theory about the nature of African slavery as a whole. Moreover, the data Meillassoux refers to in Africa are problematic. Some of the sample sizes are very small, so their reliability is questionable. In addition, the sources do not make it clear at what age the women examined were enslaved. Females who had been enslaved after they had reached puberty would inevitably be likely to appear less fertile than the free women of the host society. Equally, the results of investigations into slave fertility which asked women how many live births they had had should be regarded with some caution. Similar research in contemporary Africa has been plagued by under-reporting, as children who died when very young are often forgotten and therefore not recorded. Finally, no information is provided about the background fertility of the local non-slave population, so it is impossible to say whether the slave population was indeed sub-fertile.

It is worth considering five points. First, some historians of African historical demography have argued that women tended to experience *higher* fertility when their status declined, as they became less capable of controlling their own fertility.[5] Secondly, in many societies the best strategy for a slave woman who wanted to enhance her status would have been for her to have her master's baby. Thirdly, North American evidence shows that, while masters were unwilling to allocate resources to the upbringing of unproductive slave children, they definitely did want their slaves to produce children.[6] The particular attraction of female slaves was not simply their wide-ranging skills and their reduced capacity for violence or escape.[7] Female slaves' reproductive potential certainly *was* an added value, perhaps not a quality that owners always nurtured but one that was useful. Fourthly, in some contexts, men preferred to purchase and marry slave women rather than pay bridewealth for free wives, because slaves were often cheaper and had the major benefit of being kinless. The slave-owner had no in-laws pressuring him, and as 'slaves were by definition kinless people, marriage to a slave wife gave a man total control over his offspring'. The disadvantage, of course, was that marriage to a slave brought no opportunities for affinal alliances.[8]

Fifthly, and most importantly, it is now very clear that some slave populations, most famously that of late eighteenth- and early nineteenth-century North America, did grow extremely fast by natural increase. North American slaves had an early age at first birth, because there was no material reason to delay marriage. Owners tended to avoid breaking up slave marriages because the disruption reduced productivity and social stability. Adult slaves, moreover, had relatively low death rates. This meant that slave fertility was extremely high, higher than that of free blacks. Undoubtedly infant and child mortality rates were high, because unproductive slave children were poorly fed, while mothers were overworked and forced to limit the duration of breastfeeding. Nonetheless, the case of North America disproves the assumption that slave populations cannot grow by natural increase. What the North American research has done is to refocus demographic attention on key social and environmental factors, away from the psychological trauma and insecurity that seemed to Meillassoux to have had such a major impact on slave demography.[9] The point of this argument is not to suggest that the institution of slavery in Bunyoro was similar to the system which operated in North America. Rather, it is to suggest that the demography of slavery across Africa might have varied as much as that of the Americas, and to focus attention on the actual conditions under which slaves lived.

The Sources

The recent dramatic developments in the demographic history of North American slaves are, however, unlikely to be matched in the study of African societies. Interlacustrine East African societies in the age of slavery simply did not produce the kind of sources that have been exploited so skilfully by Americanists, such as parish registers of baptism, marriage and death, censuses, tax registers, probate inventories, and estate records of expenditure. Even archaeological investigations which might shed some light on factors such as slave malnutrition, workloads, or average age at death would be impossible in Bunyoro because slaves were not buried in separate cemeteries.[10]

Nonetheless, the sources that are available for a demographic study of Nyoro slavery are quite varied, including the precolonial writings of European travellers and officials of the Egyptian Equatoria empire, nineteenth-century missionary records, twentieth-century ethnographies and histories, colonial archival material, and oral histories. Unfortunately these sources have a number of problems. They are typically more qualitative than quantitative. Precolonial European writings rarely provided eye-witness descriptions of Nyoro slaves' status and living conditions. This was primarily because few Europeans spent substantial periods of time in Bunyoro before the 1890s. Short-term European visitors would have struggled to distinguish a slave from a servant, dependant or wife without inquiring directly about such an individual's status, a rather unlikely scenario given Europeans' elitist focus at the time. Missionaries, whose correspondence and diaries provide such a wealth of information on precolonial slavery in Buganda, decided against establishing a mission station in Bunyoro before the colonial conquest. Buganda's missionaries do at least provide valuable information on the numbers of Banyoro enslaved by Ganda raiding parties, and less reliable second-hand accounts of the numbers of Ganda slaves taken or bought by the Banyoro. It is surprising, meanwhile, that slavery and its abolition are barely mentioned in the colonial documentary record, as the archival sources on the first decade of colonial administration in Bunyoro are extremely rich, as befitted Uganda's second most important district of the time. It seems likely that this was because slavery had effectively come to an end during the 1890s war of conquest.

The attempt to construct a coherent image of Nyoro slavery therefore relies heavily on retrospective accounts. Fortunately colonial Bunyoro received the attention of a succession of amateur and professional ethnographers, some of whom did enquire about the history of pre-colonial slavery. These sources suffer from a number of defects, however. Ethnographies written by Europeans typically repeated the official colonial stereotype of Kabaleega's reign as one dominated by endless involvement in raiding and trading slaves. Many accounts of slavery in the literature are excessively normative or rather confused. Moreover, many ethnographers tended to derive their information from elite sources within Nyoro society. It is perhaps unsurprising therefore that the resultant ethnographies appear to have exaggerated the dependent status of agriculturalists in precolonial Bunyoro, prioritised the role of royal and chiefly patronage in the distribution of slaves throughout Nyoro society, and suggested that the acquisition by members of the elite of vulnerable Banyoro as slaves was simply a matter of charity.

Some of these defects have been corrected through the collection of oral information from elderly Banyoro. These sources emphasised, among other things, the ability of individuals to acquire slaves through trade, primarily it seems to become wives, and the violent acquisition of slaves within Bunyoro by Nyoro armies in the late nineteenth century. Equally importantly, oral interviewees provided crucial information about Bunyoro's growing demographic crisis in the late nineteenth century, which provided much of the pressure encouraging Bunyoro's increasing involvement in the acquisition of slaves in this period.

The Context: the Demography of Nineteenth-Century Bunyoro

European visitors in the late nineteenth century consistently observed that Bunyoro was one of the most densely populated parts of East Africa.[11] Wilhelm Junker, who had explored much of the Nile Valley before travelling through the heart of Bunyoro in 1886, wrote that 'of all the Negro regions visited by me, Bunyoro and Buganda were by far the most densely populated.'[12] Interestingly, in 1893 Henry Colvile, the leader of the British invading army, found Bunyoro as a whole to be 'far more thickly populated and highly cultivated' than Buganda, though it is important to note that Buganda had suffered heavy mortality and emigration during its recent civil wars.[13]

Commentators who stayed in Bunyoro for any period, however, emphasised that the kingdom's considerable population was beginning to experience significant problems of sub-fertility and high mortality. King Kamurasi [1852-69] told the explorers John Speke and James Grant in 1862 that 'it is a common infirmity in this country with some women, that all their children die before they are able to walk'.[14] Emin noted that many Banyoro women were barren, while, of those with children, 'most of them have only two or three ... whereas the Waganda and Wakidi are often blessed with ten to twelve.'[15] Many Banyoro interviewees agreed that nineteenth-century Bunyoro experienced a demographic crisis.[16] This largely resulted from the impact of new epidemic diseases such as cholera and smallpox and new levels of civil war and slave raiding by Buganda. In Bukerebe, a society to the south of Lake Victoria, similar problems of demographic decline resulted in an increase in the demand for slaves during the nineteenth century. According to Hartwig, 'manpower was at a premium' and this 'increased the desire to acquire labour for agricultural work'.[17] It seems that in Bunyoro the nature and scale of slavery also changed during the course of the nineteenth century, in response to declining fertility and rising mortality.

The Nature of Indigenous Slavery in Bunyoro

In Bunyoro, as was typical of Africa, there existed a continuum of dependence and servitude. Even Bunyoro's future elite learned how to be a chief through serving as a page at a royal or chiefly court.[18] This was a strongly differentiated society. What is particularly interesting about Bunyoro in the nineteenth century is the way in which the nature of social differentiation appears to have changed. Historically it seems that this kingdom was characterised by a relatively rigid separation between the ruling elite, consisting of the royal Babito clan and Bahuma pastoralists, and the agriculturalist majority, who were referred to by the elite as Bairu. This was a very similar social system to that found in other interlacustrine kingdoms such as Nkore, Karagwe, Rwanda and Burundi. Before the late nineteenth century senior chiefships were typically held by royal princes or members of powerful pastoralist families, and agriculturalists were required to provide labour and tribute to their chiefs and patrons, who used access to cattle as one means of securing their dominance over the cultivators.

Early European depictions of the relationship between the pastoralists and agriculturalists were influenced by their conviction that 'Hamitic' pastoralists had long before 'conquered' the inferior race of Bantu Bairu 'aborigines', an understanding of the past that it seems Babito and Bahuma informants did nothing to dispel. According to the missionary ethnographer John Roscoe, the 'Bairu' agriculturalists were 'of a much lower type than the invaders' and 'were despised by the pastoral people, not because of their poverty, but because of their mode of life'. Roscoe's comment that the agriculturalist 'serfs were looked upon as slaves by the pastoral people' indicates how difficult it is to come to a clear definition of slavery in Bunyoro. Elite Banyoro were hardly disinterested sources, often trying to blur the difference between subject and slave. The value of early European writings was further lessened by the authors' understanding of historical process in racial terms and occasional vagueness of definition.[19] Unsurprisingly, this tendency towards confusion was reinforced by the use of the same word, Bairu, as a generic term for slaves, and as the term for free agriculturalists. Bairu was a term denoting poverty, low status and, to the elite at least, service. It seems reasonable to assume that referring to both slave and subject by the same name served to reinforce Bunyoro's elite's claim to superiority.

Bunyoro's agriculturalists, however, were neither slaves nor serfs, since legally they were entitled to move from one patron to another. In theory a free agriculturalist could settle and farm wherever he could find unused land, though in practice total independence was a near impossibility.[20] This relative freedom of movement would potentially have limited the extent to which the wealthy and powerful could have extracted labour and tribute from their clients and subjects, which presumably helps explain why Bunyoro's elite chose to possess slaves. Interestingly, it seems that the number of slaves in Nyoro society increased significantly during the course of the nineteenth century, at the same time as Bunyoro's rigid social system experienced significant change. By the mid-nineteenth century decades of princely secession and civil war had proved the danger of appointing princes to regional chiefships. Chiefs began to be appointed according to ability, irrespective of their social status. Meanwhile, Bunyoro's livestock economy experienced serious decline due to disease and losses to invading raiders. Bunyoro was on its way to becoming a cattle kingdom in ritual more than reality. When the Bahuma, as well as many branches of the ruling Babito clan, supported the losing candidate in the bitter succession war of 1869–71 their political fortunes declined in parallel with their economic significance.[21] A number of Bahuma left the kingdom, while many of those who remained lost their previous social dominance.[22]

Having overcome the opposition of Bunyoro's great provincial families, Bunyoro's new king Kabaleega [1871–99] set about instituting political reforms aimed at reducing their power and countering their centrifugal tendencies. Royal political control and directionism increased under Kabaleega, as he appointed men of proven ability to an increasingly centralised administration dominated by a new kind of military chiefship. When Kabaleega came to the throne only one of Bunyoro's county chiefs was an agriculturalist by origin. Nyakamatura was not only a commoner but a slave, whose abilities caused Kabaleega's father, Kamurasi [1852–69], to free him, give him a new name and make him a chief. Personal friendship and proven loyalty to Kabaleega hastened Nyakamatura's rise to power, which saw him become first minister in 1887. Kabaleega is remembered as having promoted many people of lowly birth because their ability 'brought honour or profit to the kingdom'. Kabaleega's most powerful chiefs were men such as Rwabudongo, a commoner who was remarkably successful in both warfare and the new long-distance commerce. Merit also saw the rapid promotion of a number of foreigners, such as the war captive Ireeta, who was freed to ultimately become Bunyoro's leading general.[23]

In many ways Bunyoro was becoming a more open society, but, as in so many African communities, the arrival of firearms and long-distance trading opportunities brought not only new opportunities but also new threats and vulnerability for the poor. The new commerce of the nineteenth century gave wealth and military force new significance as sources of authority.[24] Kabaleega is remembered as 'emphasising wealth above all other things'. 'His strong social control was resented by the people.' Trade and government authoritarianism are associated in historical memory in part because a new avidity provoked a change in political values.[25] Under Kabaleega the relationship between ruler and ruled swung more towards exploitation than reciprocity. The new commerce provided rulers with both reason and means for revising the norms of government, which became increasingly about extraction, accumulation and control.[26] Taxation became 'more or less a regulation', and in some cases even became monetised.[27] Guns meanwhile immensely increased the government's physical power relative to that possessed by the rest of Nyoro society, becoming the resource in which Kabaleega 'put his faith as the only reliable source of power'.[28] Kabaleega's well-armed regiments are remembered with a great deal of bitterness by ordinary Banyoro because of their reputation for uncontrolled plundering, violence and abduction.[29]

The most detailed descriptions of slavery in Bunyoro give little sense of how the institution changed in response to these developments. According to the leading Nyoro historian, John Nyakatura, the 'institution of slave ownership seems to have been long established in Bunyoro'. Nyakatura described three main 'traditional' categories of slaves. *Embomboza* slaves were 'men and women acquired by a master who had found them roaming, destitute, without kin or friend. Such persons might have lost their families through death or some other calamity.' 'The new master offered them patronage and a sense of belonging.' The second category were young war captives.

> When they grew up, their masters helped them to marry. Their children were accepted in the clan of their masters. Even if their kin came later to claim them, their children would never be given back. They were now part of the clan, as the slaves born in the clan. Sometimes if a man did not have any children of his own and no close kin, he could make a trusted slave his heir. At his death, the slave would take over the household, as well as his master's wives and his clan affiliations. His children were granted full recognition as members of the clan.

Thirdly, there were 'other slaves who were purchased from the countries neighbouring Bunyoro'. This is a very benign depiction of a slave system, where enslavement served partly as a form of welfare, and was a route to inclusion and ultimately citizenship and freedom. Nyakatura's description, however, leaves some questions unanswered. Who were war captive slaves allowed to marry: other slaves, or friends or clients of the owner? Was slave status inherited only by the children of the original war captive, or could it be permanently hereditary? Nevertheless, this account emphasises three key aspects of Nyoro slavery: the role of the slave in patron-client networks, the value of slaves as potential heirs in a society where childlessness was relatively common, and finally the importance of female slaves as potential wives. 'Only a slave could be married free without any exchange of bridewealth' in precolonial Bunyoro, which made them extremely attractive.[30]

The early colonial ethnographer, Roscoe, adds further valuable detail on the nature of slavery in Bunyoro. Slaves were property which could be inherited and traded 'like cattle', though domestic slaves who had been inherited 'were regarded almost as members of his [the heir's] family and were not sold'. If an owner married a slave woman and she bore him a child, then both woman and child were free and absorbed into the man's clan, 'though her children might only inherit his property if he had no child by any other wife'. Slaves then could be well treated, and could be freed. Liberty, however, might not mean equality, and it is likely the stigma of slave origins was felt strongly, for the first generation at least. Bunyoro was not unusual in having a hierarchy within the institution of slavery, with slave wives and inherited and domestic slaves at the top. The lowest status slaves were labourers and those who had been captured in war. Legally an owner 'might kill a slave just as he might kill one of his cows and no one would question his action'. Slaves had the poorest living conditions in Bunyoro, and as the quality of a person's diet matched their status within the household, it is likely slaves suffered the poorest nutrition in Nyoro society.[31]

While slaves were legally extremely vulnerable to harsh treatment, they were not it seems dehumanised. Slaves, typically being kinless, could be regarded as being particularly trustworthy and therefore useful by their masters, acting as their agents. Slaves' ghosts, moreover, were particularly feared, presumably because they were at the same time removed from the family, but also intimate. Informants suggested that this fear discouraged owners from mistreating their slaves overmuch. 'If you ever mistreated a slave ... his ghost would always disturb the family ... And that one is very, very dangerous, even more dangerous than the ghost of a relative.'[32] Yet slavery is still best understood as the exploitation of the weak by the powerful. An *embomboza* slave, according to one elite informant, was a poor cultivator who 'couldn't stand up for himself ... without joining other families. At that time if a person refused to obey, they would take him by force.' Such a person was 'compared to a rich man's dog'. Poverty and vulnerability also caused the pawning of children to be frequent in precolonial Bunyoro. According to one informant, the poor used to tell their children 'I will not be able to look after you, so go and ... grow up from the family of the rich.' In the time of Kabaleega, when abduction by royal soldiers was common, people 'would choose to take their children to live with ... someone close to the king who could protect them'. Such children were then forced by their new protectors to 'do all the work [they] wanted'. Pawns could theoretically be redeemed at any time, but in reality it is likely that most pawns' dependence on their masters was near-permanent. Daughters were pawned 'on the understanding that they would be legally married when they grew up', their masters effectively acquiring the rights of the parent.[33]

Recent writing on the definition of servitude in Africa has caused slavery to be regarded less as an institution focused on the securing of labour, and more as one which revolved around the denial of legal and social status. Slaves have been categorised as the effectively kinless, who were not full members of societies that were founded on the family, lineage and clan. Lacking the basic rights of citizenship, they could expect to be protected by neither law nor blood relationship. They were excluded and marginal.[34] Modern-day Banyoro would not argue with this discourse of vulnerability, their discussions frequently associating slavery with poverty, the absence of family ties and mistreatment that a free person would not have to endure. But informants emphasised three aspects of slavery in Bunyoro that seem rather unusual.

First, the association of kinlessness with slavery was not absolute in the historical memory of this society. To give one example, one category of slavery which has not featured in the literature on Bunyoro is that of the male slave whose family agreed to his being given away while he was still in the womb. 'In the past people used to book women for marriage before they were even born. If it happened that the child born was a girl she would be taken as a wife and if a boy he would be taken as a slave. He would become a slave in the clan that booked the pregnancy because they had already paid bride price.'[35] Moreover, informants' testimonies also differed from the current academic orthodoxy in that their definitions of slavery always began with a statement that a slave was someone whose work was unpaid, despite their coming from outside the household: 'Omwiru is a person who works for free.'[36] They emphasised the diverse and unremitting nature of the labour demands placed upon slaves to distinguish them from other dependants: 'he would work without resting. For example from the well he would go to fetch firewood and from firewood to slaughtering a goat or chicken.'[37] Yet Banyoro did not define the slave as worker only in a narrowly economic, productive sense. They also valued slaves as a route to a more leisurely life. Thus, while the household's slaves were busy cultivating, its head 'would still be smoking his pipe seated at the fireplace ... [or] lying in bed'. Saying that slave-owners 'were like kings' was a statement about their quality of life as much as their status.[38]

Thirdly, informants suggested that late precolonial Bunyoro was exceptionally open to the rapid assimilation of slaves. As in many societies, if a female slave's children were fathered by her master, they would be free. But even within a slave's lifetime, the shedding of slave status was possible. For women, getting married and having children was the obvious route to the achievement of relative freedom. 'Once she had a child she would cease being a slave woman', as one informant put it.[39] For men, long and devoted service could enable slaves to be considered part of the owner's family, so that they were allowed to take on their owner's clan identity. Owners would pay bridewealth and even provide land for the most favoured slaves, thus granting them the status of a household head. Informants typically described such assimilation in the language of kinship: 'It was also possible for a slave to marry your daughter ... you would no longer refer and treat that person as a slave. He would have become your son.'[40] Of course, not all slaves enjoyed such generosity, and it is likely that assimilation was easier for Batooro and Baganda slaves than for those from more distant ethnic groups.⁴¹ Nonetheless, the oral evidence clearly suggests that slaves were assimilated into Nyoro society relatively easily. One possible explanation for this was the demand for kin which arose from the kingdom's demographic crisis.⁴²

War, commerce and the demographic balance sheet

For most of the nineteenth century Bunyoro suffered regular invasions by Ganda slave raiders. The Baganda are remembered for their brutality, their kingdom being referred to as Mhwahwa, 'land of the wild dogs'. In the 1880s a missionary based in Buganda observed that '[v]ast numbers of slaves of both sexes are introduced from Bunyoro'. The demographic loss to Bunyoro of these slave raids was greater than the total number of individuals removed, for the raiders had no interest in adult males as potential slaves. As the explorer John Hanning Speke reported in 1862, the Baganda army returned from Bunyoro with 'immense numbers of cows, women and children, but not men', for they were killed.⁴³ One British visitor believed that central Buganda had a sex ratio of 3.5:1 because so many women captives were brought in to that kingdom.⁴⁴ Bunyoro lost population in other directions as well. The historian John Tosh was informed that Langi raiders took significant numbers of Banyoro women and children as slaves from the 1850s.⁴⁵ In addition, Sudanese and coastal traders and soldiers of the Egyptian Equatorial empire are said to have also acquired slaves in Bunyoro between the 1860s and 1880s, but in relatively limited numbers.⁴⁶

Contemporary accounts and oral informants, however, indicate that the new long-distance commerce of the mid-nineteenth century gave Bunyoro the opportunity to reverse the kingdom's demographic decline. It seems that Banyoro had been exchanging slaves for livestock at border markets for some time before the arrival of long-distance traders around 1860.⁴⁷ Initially the new trade accelerated this outflow of population, as lust for the new trade goods tempted some owners to sell off their slaves. The growth of this lucrative commerce also encouraged rulers to order enslavement and sale as a punishment for a variety of offences. Over time, however, Bunyoro's role in the developing networks of long-distance trade changed. Bunyoro became a very successful middleman in every aspect of the new long-distance commerce, including the slave trade. Slaves and ivory were obtained by Banyoro from the Acholi, the Alur and other peoples to the north in exchange for cloth, beads and guns. Some of these slaves were then sold on to the coastal traders, although the sources do not indicate that the export of slaves from Bunyoro was on a very large scale.⁴⁸ Bunyoro's access to immense resources of ivory became its strongest advantage over Buganda, where ivory supplies were fast declining.⁴⁹ By the 1880s it had developed the most advanced armies in the region, and was beginning to challenge Buganda for military and commercial supremacy in the northern interlacustrine region. By 1890 Bunyoro was able to raid at will into Buganda, and had involved itself in Buganda's succession wars. More importantly, Bunyoro's new power enabled its armies to raid for slaves to the south and west of its advancing borders.[50]

It is possible that through the large-scale acquisition of slaves Kabaleega managed to halt Bunyoro's demographic decline. Many of these slaves were acquired as individuals, and redistributed through the normal networks of patronage. Roscoe was informed that the possession of slaves was 'universal throughout the country' in the late nineteenth century.[51] It is likely that there was some exaggeration involved in this statement, though it may not be far from the truth, if the Ganda Muslims' claim to have sold 20,000 slaves to Kabaleega between 1890 and 1892 is an accurate indication of the scale of the regional trade.[52] What is particularly unusual about Bunyoro is that Kabaleega's armies relocated entire families of captives into the core of the kingdom, presumably to work on state plantations producing food, or perhaps being used for targeted environmental management through bush clearance and resettlement.[53] In 1877 Emin Pasha found that Kabaleega had repopulated the Masindi-Londu area of central Bunyoro with slaves brought from Alur.[54] When Tooro and Busongora were re-conquered, Kabaleega 'moved a large number of Bahuma from those areas and brought them here'. An official of the Egyptian empire, Gaetano Casati, referred to one of many raids into that region, in which 10,000 cattle were captured: '[t]he Wahuma shepherds voluntarily followed their victors with their families, preferring to serve them in their capacity as cow-keepers, rather than to be separated from their flocks.'[55] The missionary Albert Achte also referred to Kabaleega's policy of transporting conquered peoples into central Bunyoro; entire Bakonzo families were moved there in the 1870s, and had almost been entirely absorbed into Nyoro society by 1900. Achte considered that 'the Munyoro has a genius for assimilating conquered people'.[56]

It is an interesting question whether these latter groups of captives should be defined as slaves. They were forcibly removed from their homes and required to work for Nyoro masters, but they were not kinless in the obvious sense that entire families were moved en bloc. Perhaps existing family ties were ignored, so that they were legally kinless, though Achte certainly implies that within a generation Nyoro society had assimilated the Bakonzo as families rather than through the destruction of their family groups. It might be better to categorise such resettled groups as subject peoples or perhaps even prisoners of war. If they are to be regarded as slaves, then the equation of slavery with kinlessness should not be held to be absolute.

Perhaps what is most interesting of all is that in popular memory the female slaves who were brought into Bunyoro and re-distributed by Kabaleega were noticeably more fecund than local women. 'Most women who produced very much, were being got from far ... the Batoro and others like that.'[57] Banyoro have a strong sense that their ancestors, due to high rates of sterility and miscarriages, were much less fertile than neighbouring ethnic groups.[58] If true, this information requires a reconsideration of the common assumption, derived from the work of Meillassoux and Harms, that slave wives had fewer babies than free wives, mainly due to psychological factors. The benefits gained by producing a child for one's master in a demographically troubled society such as Bunyoro may well have outweighed any psychological drawbacks. The disincentives towards household slave reproduction in Bunyoro were in any case less severe than in many other African societies, according to informants. An unmarried female slave who had a child by her master would not automatically shed her servile status. 'She would continue carrying out her jobs as she used to. If it meant going for firewood she would have to go with her child on the back. In case of digging she would carry the child to the garden.' Her offspring might be referred to as '"Omwana w'Omuzaana": child of the slave woman'. But such a child would be free, 'would be treated like any other child', and 'was not discriminated against'. There was no sense that the children of slave mothers suffered higher mortality than those whose mothers were free.[59] Marriage, moreover, gave a female slave a status and quality of life which at least approximated to that enjoyed by her master's other, free wives. 'Once the slave woman was married she would not be treated like a slave to the extent of being overworked.'[60] But the advantage to be gained by motherhood varied according to the context. A female slave who had a baby by one of her master's male slaves would find that 'the child would also be taken over as Omwiru or Omuzaana' (a male or female slave).[61] Slaves at court, moreover, were regarded as a resource to be utilised in the politics of patronage. If a war captive had a child at court, it 'would be given away to other people for free'.[62]

While the attractions of reproduction may have varied from one female slave to another, there is no doubt that the acquisition of servile women was driven by their sexual and reproductive potential. As one male informant put it: 'Slaves are not captured without aim but for a reason either because the master wants to marry them, or he wants them to be married by his sons, or he wants them to stay home and work for him. For slaves it is clear that they were brought purposely for work whereas women were mostly brought for marriage.'[63] Raiding parties specifically selected girls or young women, rejecting or even killing older women, presumably partly because they were more marriageable and had greater reproductive potential. Female slaves who were not married within the owner's family could be given away at a profit 'if there was a man who picked interest in her; and the brideprice would go to the master'.[64] It is interesting that when asked whether Banyoro in the past preferred to acquire males or females as slaves, male informants stated that men were preferred because they could do heavier work, while female informants emphasised that women were favoured because they could be married.[65] This unsurprisingly gendered response suggests at least that Meillassoux's absolute discounting of a female slave's reproductive value should be regarded with some suspicion.

Non-Banyoro slave wives would very probably have been sub-fertile compared with their free counterparts in their home areas. But it seems that foreign slaves were not so severely sub-fertile as free Banyoro women were believed to be. Banyoro women during the colonial period were characterised by extremely low fertility due to a combination of factors such as STDs, other infectious diseases and malnutrition, particularly during adolescence.[66] It is likely that these factors were also significant during the nineteenth century, and gave foreign women a reproductive advantage. If slave women were indeed believed to be more fertile than their Nyoro equivalents, it is hardly surprising that Banyoro men were so keen to secure female slaves in the late nineteenth century.

This issue leads on to the broader question of the impact of slavery on female status in Nyoro society. It could be argued that if the adult slave population was predominantly female in character, as female informants suggest, then this would have lowered free women's standing by association. On the other hand, one could equally hypothesise that the requirement for male slaves to perform a range of tasks that were normally reserved for women undermined male superiority. Such arguments seem too general to be of value. Three more specific aspects of female slavery can be identified, however, as having been especially likely to reduce women's status. Firstly, there existed a particular class of servile women, the *Baranga* or royal courtesans, whom some sources suggest were supposedly available for commercial sex with wealthy Banyoro. Secondly, it seems that the king's representatives frequently required attractive young women to leave their families and come to court to be disposed of at the king's pleasure. Most were reallocated to loyal servants. As one informant remembered, the king used 'to give away all the women in the palace'. Thirdly, the expansion of the slave trade supposedly resulted in some 'rebellious' women being 'taken by their husbands to be sold'.[67] All these factors would have encouraged a sense of women as a commodity with limited rights. The belief, moreover, that Nyoro women were sub-fertile compared with foreign slaves may have strengthened their negative characterisation by Nyoro men. Might this have resulted in worsening marital tensions and so declining fertility within free marriage? Or might the importation of servile labour, by relieving free wives of some of their chores, have reduced female resentment of their husbands' relative idleness (a major complaint of Nyoro women during the colonial period)?[68] Such questions are unlikely now to pass beyond the realms of speculation, but they at least remind us that slavery affected masculinity as well as femininity.

Slavery had complex consequences for Bunyoro's demography. In the late nineteenth century it enlarged and enriched Bunyoro's population, bringing various beneficial side-effects, such as a major increase in food security through the development of large, slave-owning food producers and traders.[69] Slavery, however, also increased problems of ill-health. Contemporary sources indicate that many slave-raiding parties from

Buganda introduced smallpox and other epidemic diseases causing significant mortality in Bunyoro.[70] Recurrent slave raids contributed to the abandonment of Bunyoro's periphery, as people moved away from such dangerous territory. This localised depopulation would have permitted the expansion of bushland, creating ideal conditions for the spread of disease-bearing game and insects, such as the tsetse fly. Finally, the commercialised sex associated with the *Baranga* and the circulation of women through networks of patronage would have meant that the institution of slavery hastened the spread of sexually transmitted diseases throughout Nyoro society, worsening already severe problems of low fertility and life expectancy. Slavery was a far from ideal method of achieving long-term population growth.

A Bastion of the Slave Trade, Conquest and Abolition

Slavery shaped Bunyoro's demography most profoundly in an indirect manner. From the 1870s Bunyoro was identified as a cornerstone of the East African slave trade. With time, as the Banyoro successfully resisted Egyptian imperialism and allied themselves with Buganda's Muslim faction, the kingdom's continued association with slavery in the European mind condemned Bunyoro as a resolute opponent of free, legitimate commerce and a fanatical ally of militant Islam. By the 1890s Bunyoro's success in slave raiding and trading identified it in British imperial eyes as a state that had to be dismantled in the name of civilisation and progress.[71] British forces invaded Bunyoro in 1893. By 1899 when the war was over, more than half the kingdom had been ceded to Bunyoro's neighbours, the economy had been completely destroyed, and the remnant was almost entirely depopulated. Bunyoro's demographic experience under colonial rule was the most disastrous in Uganda, and probably East Africa. It was fifty years before Bunyoro's population began to show signs of recovery from the demographic disaster that was conquest.[72]

There is no doubt that Bunyoro was indeed heavily involved in the acquisition and trade of slaves. But so were a number of other East African societies, not least Buganda. It is necessary to consider the evolution of the stereotype of Kabaleega as 'a brutal savage', whose 'reputation for treachery' and 'setting all white men at defiance' required the destruction of his kingdom. By the 1890s one British source considered that Kabaleega was 'more familiar to the public than perhaps ... any other African chief, except, indeed, his bloody majesty of Benin, and has from the first been a troublesome person to every European who has come in contact with him'.[73] The story begins in 1872 with the appointment by the Khedive of Egypt of Samuel Baker as the leader of a campaign to abolish the slave trade along the river Nile. Baker, through poor planning, ended up having to employ Sudanese slave raiders operating in northern Uganda in his effort to stamp out the slave trade there. His project failed when he unsuccessfully used these slavers to try to depose Kabaleega, whom he believed to be the ultimate source of the slaves flowing north.[74] He then began his attempt to salvage his reputation by convincing the world that the Banyoro were inherently treacherous and antagonistic to Europeans and civilisation.[75] Through his publications, which unsurprisingly differ dramatically from what he recorded in his daily diary, and his role as a foreign office adviser, Baker turned British opinion against Bunyoro.

Bunyoro's reputation as an obstacle to the forces of civilisation and legitimate commerce was further strengthened by Kabaleega's refusal to allow Egyptian troops, officials, correspondence and trade goods to travel freely across Bunyoro's territory in 1886 and his alliance with the Muslim Baganda in 1888. When Frederick Lugard of the Imperial British East Africa Company arrived in Uganda in 1890 charged with establishing British interests and legitimate trade in the region, he had already decided that Bunyoro was a bastion of the slave trade and Islam, noting that with Kabaleega 'alone I don't desire peace', 'the inhuman fiend'.[76] When Lugard learned that largely as a result of his personal ambition and disregard for commercial realities his employer faced bankruptcy, he saved his career by a masterly campaign of imperialist propaganda, in which all that had to be destroyed in Africa was combined in the representation of Kabaleega as a protector of the slave trade and militant Islam, and an obstacle to the efficient exploitation of the natural wealth of the lakes region.[77]

Therefore, when Britain determined to secure the sources of the Nile in 1893, Bunyoro was offered no reasonable conditions for peaceful incorporation into the British empire. Henry Colvile, the man charged with extending British control over Uganda, announced his plans for Bunyoro's conquest on the day he arrived in Kampala.[78] Within weeks Bunyoro's capital was occupied by an enormous force of British and Ganda troops, Buganda having enthusiastically contributed to Bunyoro's demonisation. A series of epidemics and famines followed from the deployment of large armies and the use of scorched earth policies. It is impossible to know how many Banyoro were killed during the five and a half years of war. But one British military source noted in 1898 that as a result of the combination of direct and indirect casualties and forced and voluntary emigration '[t]he whole of Unyoro has become for many years gradually depopulated, most having followed Kabarega north of the Nile'.[79]

Conquest was so demographically disastrous for Bunyoro partly because the kingdom appears to have experienced an outflow of freed slaves on a much larger scale than was common in the region. There are only a handful of references to former slaves in the abundant archival records from the early decades of colonial rule in Bunyoro.[80] What seems likely is that those parts of Bunyoro that were depopulated during the war lost their slave populations most rapidly. Masters would have struggled to sustain their households in exile, and the opportunities, and reason, for escape must have increased dramatically. The decline in Bunyoro's slave population also occurred because of the relative freedom to 'liberate' slaves that was enjoyed by Britain's local allies. The attitude of a typical British officer was that Bunyoro's slaves 'were really not far from the status of cattle and equally indifferent to a change of ownership'.[81] It seems likely therefore that, through escape or acquisition, abolition of slavery in Bunyoro was unusually thorough and rapid, and typically resulted in emigration rather than incorporation. Bunyoro may well have suffered population loss through the end of slavery on a scale to match some West African societies, such as Sokoto.[82] Given the context of Bunyoro's other demographic problems, this was a particularly painful blow, and one that must have made the recovery from conquest even harder.

Conclusion

This study has focused on the demography of slavery in nineteenth-century Bunyoro. It leaves many questions unanswered or only half answered. It is unlikely, for example, that it will ever be known how poor slave nutrition was relative to that of the free population of Bunyoro. The number of slaves in Bunyoro will similarly never be known, nor their exact age and sex profile. But recent research on slavery in North America, where sources exist that do permit such fascinating questions to be fully answered, shows that it is dangerous to rely on preconceptions about slave psychology and demographic decision-making. The relationship between status, autonomy and reproductive choices is a complex one. For a female slave child-bearing carried great risks for her personal health, a relatively poor chance of her child surviving to adolescence, and in many ways a more arduous life. Yet providing her master with a child was the best strategy available for improving a female slave's status and conditions. Slavery in Bunyoro was not a benign institution, but it did not necessarily condemn people to a permanent servile status. It is likely that it was Bunyoro's demographic problems that made assimilation so rapid and the opportunities for freedom and even wealth and power so great. The enslavement of foreigners was the logical solution to Bunyoro's demographic difficulty in the nineteenth century. It took half a century of cash cropping, labour migration, and political stability, the imperial alternative to the slave trade, for Bunyoro to begin to recover demographically from its abolition.

This book has shown that the nature of slavery in this region varied significantly over time and space. The next generation of research will no doubt expand on some of the well-established themes that have been further explored within this volume, such as slavery's complex connections with evolving concepts of clanship, gender, clientage and political power.

New sources and methodologies might permit fresh insights into slavery's impact on changing ideas about the nature of childhood, the family and the individual. Of all such intimate histories surely one of the most fascinating will be the contribution of slavery and the slave trade to the dramatic diversity in population growth rates that have characterised the Great Lakes region over the past century and a half, if not longer.

Notes

* The research for this paper was funded by an ESRC doctoral scholarship grant. Thanks are due to Emma Coombs, John Iliffe, John Lonsdale, Gerald Lubega, Musinguzi Mark, Henri Médard and Ed Steinhart.
1 Even if African slavery is regarded as emerging through the absence of landed property, it could in turn be argued that the lack of a market in land may have rested on low population density.
2 The reasons why Britain chose to ignore Buganda's expansionism, involvement in the arms and slave trades, and links with Islam are widely accepted. The most significant factors were Buganda's apparent openness, its distance from Egyptian Equatoria, the presence of mediating missionaries (particularly those of the Anglican Church Missionary Society), the opportunities provided by its competing politico-religious factions, and the weakness of Mwanga, on the one hand, and Britain's need for local allies, on the other.
3 C. Meillassoux, 'Female slavery' in C. Robertson and M. Klein (eds), *Women and Slavery in Africa* (Madison, WI, 1983), p.51. Meillassoux's focus on 'slave populations' makes his argument largely irrelevant to most of the contexts discussed in this volume.
4 C. Meillassoux, *The Anthropology of Slavery: The Womb of Iron and Gold* (Chicago, 1991), pp.78–82.
5 D. Cordell and J. Gregory, *African Population and Capitalism: Historical Perspectives* (London, 1987).
6 R. Steckel, 'The African American population of the United States, 1790–1920', in M. Haines and R. Steckel, *A Population History of North America* (Cambridge, 2000), pp.433–51.
7 Meillassoux, *Anthropology*, pp.110–11.
8 R. Harms, 'Sustaining the system: Trading towns along Middle Zaire', in C. C. Robertson and M. Klein (eds), *Women and Slavery in Africa* (Portsmouth, NH, 1997), pp.103–4; M. Twaddle, 'The ending of slavery in Buganda', in S. Miers and R. Roberts (eds), *The End of Slavery in Africa* (Madison, WI, 1988) p.140.
9 Steckel, 'The African American Population'; L. Walsh, 'The African American population of the colonial United States', in Haines and Steckel (eds), *A Population History of North America*, pp.197–208; S. Engerman, 'A population history of the Caribbean', in *Ibid.*, p.490. North American slave life expectancy was higher than elsewhere in the Americas for a number of reasons. The incidence of disease was lower, many slaves arrived in North America having already been seasoned in the Caribbean, the region enjoyed superior food security, and the high price of slaves may have encouraged a greater concern for their survival. For isolated examples of the natural increase of 'slave populations' in the Caribbean, see B. Higman, *Slave Populations of the British Caribbean, 1807–1834* (Baltimore, 1984), pp. 308–10. Thanks to Robin Law for this information.
10 Walsh, 'African American population', pp.205, 208.
11 G. Schweinfurth et al., *Emin Pasha in Central Africa: Being a Collection of His Letters and Journals* (London, 1888), p.59; R. Felkin, 'Notes on the Wanyoro tribe of Central

Africa', *Proceedings of the Royal Society of Edinburgh*, 19 (1891-2), p.138.
12   W. Junker, *Travels in Africa 1882-6* (London, 1982), pp.537-8.
13   H. Colvile, *The Land of the Nile Springs: Being an Account of How we Fought Kabarega* (London, 1895), p.115.
14   J. Speke, *Journal of the Discovery of the Source of the Nile* (London, 1863), p.556.
15   Schweinfurth et al., *Emin*, pp.16, 84-5; J. Gray (ed.), 'The diaries of Emin Pasha - extracts II', *Uganda Journal*, 25, 2 (Sept. 1961), p.167.
16   Interview 10b; see also Ints. 1b, 10a, 39, 41, 42, 44, 15, and 16. Interviews were conducted in 1996, focus group discussions in 2006; transcripts are in the possession of the author.
17   G. Hartwig, 'Changing forms of servitude among the Kerebe of Tanzania', in S. Miers and I. Kopytoff (eds), *Slavery in Africa* (Madison, WI, 1977), pp.276, 281.
18   J. Roscoe, *The Bakitara or Banyoro: the First Part of the Report of the Mackie Ethnological Expedition to Central Africa* (Cambridge, 1923), p.83.
19   *Ibid.*, pp.9-11.
20   *Ibid.*
21   J. Nyakatura, *Anatomy of an African kingdom: a History of Bunyoro-Kitara* (edited by G. N. Uzoigwe, New York, 1973), pp.98, 108-9.
22   Ints. 44 and 45.
23   Nyakatura, *Anatomy*, pp.100-1, 124-7, 138; Ints. 6 and 42; G. Casati, *Ten Years in Equatoria and the Return with Emin Pasha* 2 vols. (London, 1891), II, p.83; G. Uzoigwe, 'Kabaleega and the making of a new Kitara', *Tarikh*, 3, 2 (1970), pp.13-14; J. Nyakatura, *The Customs of the Banyoro* (Nairobi, 1970), p.112; A. Kamese, 27 Oct. 1968, E. Steinhart's interviews, (Kampala, MISR). See S. Doyle, *Crisis and Decline in Bunyoro: Environment and Population in Western Uganda, 1860-1955* (Oxford, 2006), chapter 2 for a fuller discussion of these developments.
24   J. Iliffe, *Africans: the History of a Continent* (Cambridge, 1995), p.182; Int. 3.
25   E. Kakangoro, 'Kibiro salt' (unpublished Diploma in Fine Arts dissertation, Makerere University Kampala, 1968), p.96.
26   Report of the Land Commission, Bunyoro, 1931, pp.3-4, Public Record Office, C.O./536/171; Ints. 54 and 14.
27   Ints. 38 and 62.
28   T. Parke, *Journals* 4 vols. (Royal College of Surgeons of Ireland archive, Dublin), III, 16 Feb. 1889; E. Khunyirano, E. Steinhart's interviews (Kampala MISR); Junker, *Travels*, p.483.
29   Ints. 11, 40, 28, 38, 26 and 27; G. Uzoigwe, *Revolution and Revolt in Bunyoro-Kitara* (Kampala, 1971), p.14.
30   Nyakatura, *Customs*, pp.37-8.
31   Roscoe, *Bakitara*, pp.11, 75. Certainly female slaves would have experienced a high risk of poor nutrition, as all women in Bunyoro were ritually forbidden from eating a range of high-quality foods such as chicken, eggs and fish.
32   Meillassoux, 'Female slavery', p.50; Roscoe, *Bakitara*, pp.286, 302; J. Beattie, 'The ghost cult in Bunyoro', *Ethnology*, 3 (1964), pp.132-4, 148; Male Focus Group Discussion [FGD], Kyesiga, 6 Aug. 2006; Female FGD, Bucunga, 5 Aug. 2006.
33   J. Willis Ints. 9b and c (University of Essex Digital Archive); Schweinfurth et al., *Emin Pasha*, p.117; G. Uzoigwe, 'Pre-colonial markets in Bunyoro-Kitara', *Comparative Studies in Society and History*, 14, 4 (Sept. 1972), p.52.
34   See, for example, I. Kopytoff and S. Miers, 'African 'slavery' as an institution of marginality', in Miers and Kopytoff, *Slavery*, pp.1-81.
35   Male FGD, Bucunga, 4 Aug. 2006. See also Female FGD, Kyesiga, 6 Aug. 2006; Female FGD, Buswekera, 7 Aug. 2006; Male FGD, Kyesiga, 6 Aug. 2006.
36   Male FGD, Kyesiga, 6 Aug. 2006; Female FGD, Kyesiga, 6 Aug. 2006; Female FGD, Buswekera, 7 Aug. 2006; Male FGD, Bucunga, 4 Aug. 2006.
37   *Ibid.* It is worth noting that it would have been shameful for a man to have to perform these tasks, which are typically gendered as female.
38   Female FGD, Buswekera, 7 Aug. 2006. See also P. Manning, *Slavery and African Life*

(Cambridge, 1990), pp.106, 121, 143 which analysed the role of slavery in the creation of a profit-minded leisure class in West Africa. An increase in the scale of slave ownership also appears to have accompanied the rise of the new commercially oriented chiefly elite of late nineteenth-century Bunyoro, but the focus of my informants' discussion was on the aspirations of all household heads to a life of rest in a rural system of 'subsistence servitude'. Cf. W.G. Clarence-Smith, *The Economics of the Indian Ocean Slave Trade in the Nineteenth Century* (London, 1989), p.4.

39 Male FGD, Bucunga, 4 Aug. 2006.
40 *Ibid.*
41 Male FGD, Kyesiga, 6 Aug. 2006.
42 See, for example, Female FGD, Kyesiga, 6 Aug. 2006; Female FGD, Buswekera, 7 Aug. 2006. Assimilation might also have been facilitated by Bunyoro's political ideology of relative ethnic inclusiveness. See S. Doyle, 'From Kitara to the Lost Counties: Genealogy, land and legitimacy in the kingdom of Bunyoro, Western Uganda', *Social Identities*, 12, 4 (2006), pp.457–70.
43 R. Ashe, *Two Kings of Uganda, or, Life by the Shores of Victoria Nyanza* (London, 1889), p.321; Speke, *Journal*, p.387, 20 April 1862.
44 R. Felkin, 'Notes on the Waganda tribe of central Africa', *Proceedings of the Royal Society of Edinburgh*, 13 (1885–6), p.744
45 J. Tosh, *Clan Leaders and Colonial Chiefs in Lango: the Political History of an East African Stateless Society c. 1800–1939* (Oxford, 1978), p.86.
46 Int. 1b; Uzoigwe, 'Kabaleega', p.11.
47 Nyakatura, *Anatomy*, p.130.
48 Ints. 8, 27, 44, 54 and 55; Schweinfurth et al., *Emin*, pp.113, 118. The willing export of any slaves from Bunyoro might seem to undermine the argument that demographic concerns contributed heavily to the demand for slaves in Bunyoro. But chiefs also needed cattle and trade goods, which were in even shorter supply than slaves, labourers and followers. In any case, the context of chiefly slave ownership would have been rather different from that of ordinary household heads.
49 C.T. Wilson and R. W. Felkin, *Uganda and the Egyptian Soudan* (London, 1882), p.190.
50 Junker, *Travels*, pp.551–2.
51 Roscoe, *Bakitara*, p.11.
52 H. Médard, 'Croissance et crises de la royauté du Buganda au XIX siècle' (unpublished Ph.D. dissertation, University of Paris I, 2001), p.91; Nyakatura, *Anatomy*, p.144.
53 See Holly Hanson's chapter in this volume.
54 J. Gray (ed.), 'The diaries of Emin Pasha – extracts II', *Uganda Journal*, 25, 2 (Sept. 1961), p.163.
55 Int. 44; Casati, *Ten Years*, I, p.261.
56 A. Achte, 'Quelques notes ethnographiques sur les peuples des grands lacs' (unpublished MS, Rome, White Fathers Archive, 1900), p.5.
57 J. Willis Ints. 8b.
58 Ints. 39, 16, 15, 41,10a and 10b; Male FGD, Kyesiga, 6 Aug. 2006.
59 Male FGD, Kyesiga, 6 Aug. 2006; Female FGD, Kyesiga, 6 Aug. 2006; see also Male FGD, Bucunga, 4 Aug. 2006.
60 Male FGD, Bucunga, 4 Aug. 2006.
61 Male FGD, Kyesiga, 6 Aug. 2006.
62 Female FGD, Buswekera, 7 Aug. 2006.
63 Male FGD, Bucunga, 4 Aug. 2006.
64 Male FGD, Kyesiga, 6 Aug. 2006.
65 Male FGD, Bucunga, 4 Aug. 2006; Male FGD, Kyesiga, 6 Aug. 2006; Female FGD, Kyesiga, 6 Aug. 2006; Female FGD, Buswekera, 7 Aug. 2006.
66 Bakiga women, for example, were more than 60% more fertile than Banyoro women during the colonial period.
67 Schweinfurth et al., *Emin*, pp.87, 117; J. Willis Ints. 16a; Uzoigwe, 'Pre-colonial markets', p.52.
68 Female FGD, Kyesiga, 6 Aug. 2006. 'Each wife was allocated a slave to help her with

work, e.g. collecting firewood or fetching water.'
69 *Ibid.*; Ints. 11 and 25.
70 Schweinfurth et al., *Emin*, pp.94, 180; Nyakatura, *Customs*, pp.66–7.
71 Similar perceptions and consequences can be identified in the conquest of Asante and Dahomé.
72 Doyle, *Crisis and Decline*, chapters 3, 6 and 9.
73 A. Thruston, *African Incidents* (London, 1900), pp.126, 83; H. Colvile, Uganda Diary (Matlock, Derbyshire County Records Office), 11 Feb. 1894, 19 May 1894, 7 Nov. 1893.
74 S. Baker, Diaries MS, 4 vols. (London, R.G.S.), IV, 23 Mar.–27 July 1872.
75 S. Baker, *Ismailia: a Narrative of the Expedition to Central Africa for the Suppression of the Slave Trade* 2 vols (London, 1874), II.
76 M. Perham and M. Bull, *The Diaries of Lord Lugard* 4 vols (London, 1959), II, pp.85–8, 121; III, p.120.
77 J. Galbraith, *Mackinnon and East Africa, 1878–1895: a Study in the 'New Imperialism'* (Cambridge, 1972), pp.165, 192–8, 207.
78 H. Colvile, Uganda Diary, (MDCRO) 7 Nov. 1893.
79 Martyr to commissioner, 12 Aug. 1898, E.S.A., A4/12; C. Sykes, *Service and Sport on the Tropical Nile* (London, 1903), pp.76–9; Broome to commissioner, 17 Oct. 1898, Entebbe Secretariat Archives, A4/13.
80 Ints. 26 and 27.
81 Colvile, Uganda Diary, 10 Jan. 1894, I; Cunningham to commissioner, 17 May 1895, E.S.A., A4/1; T. Ternan, Diaries, R.H.O., MSS Afr. r. 128, 23–25 May 1895, 25 Sept. 1895, 13 Nov. 1896.
82 S. Miers and M. Klein, 'Introduction', in S. Miers and M. Klein (eds), *Slavery and Colonial Rule in Africa* (London, 1999), p. 7.

References

Abrahams, R. G., *The Peoples of Greater Unyamwezi, Tanzania: Nyamwezi, Sukuma, Sumbwa, Kimbu, Konongo* (London, 1967)
Abrahams, R. G., *The Political Organization of Unyamwezi* (Cambridge, 1967)
Achte, A., 'Quelques notes ethnographiques sur les peuples des grands lacs' (unpublished MS, Rome, White Fathers Archive, 1900)
Allen, T., 'A flight from refuge, the return of refugees from Southern Sudan to Northwest Uganda in the late 1980s', in T. Allen (ed.) *In Search of Cool Ground: War, Flight and Homecoming in Northeast Africa* (London, 1996)
Alpers, E. A., *Ivory and Slaves: Changing Patterns of International Trade in East Central Africa to the later Nineteenth Century* (Berkeley, CA, 1975)
Alpers, E. A., 'The story of Swema: female vulnerability in nineteenth-century East Africa', in Claire C. Robertson and Martin A. Klein (eds), *Women and Slavery in Africa* (Portsmouth, NH, 1997), pp.185-219
Amaza, O. O., *Museveni's Long March from Guerrilla to Statesman* (Kampala, 1998)
Anon., 'St Joseph de Kipalapala', *Chronique trimestrielle*, 35 (July 1887), pp.433-5
Anttila, R., *Historical and Comparative Linguistics* (Amsterdam, 1989)
Ashe, R., *Chronicles of Uganda* (New York, 1895)
Ashe, R., *Two Kings of Uganda, or, Life by the Shores of Victoria Nyanza* (London, 1889)
Baker, S., *Ismailia: a Narrative of the Expedition to Central Africa for the Suppression of the Slave Trade* 2 vols. (London, 1874)
Barrett-Gaines, K., 'Katwe salt in the African Great Lakes regional economy, 1750s-1950s' (unpublished PhD dissertation, Stanford University, 2001)
Batala-Nayenga, F. P., 'An economic history of the lacustrine states of Busoga, Uganda, 1750-1930' (unpublished PhD dissertation, University of Michigan, 1976)
Baumann, O., *Der Sansibar-Archipel* (Leipzig, 1897)
Baumann, O., *Durch Massailand zur Nilquelle* (Berlin, 1894)
Baur, E. and A. Le Roy, *À travers le Zanguebar. Voyage dans l'Oudoé, l'Ouzigoua, l'Oukwèrè, l'Oukami et l'Ousagara* (Tours, 1886)
Bazin, J. and E. Terray (eds), *Guerres de lignages et guerres d'états en Afrique* (Paris, 1982)
Beachey, R. W., 'The arms trade in East Africa in the late nineteenth century', *Journal of African History*, 3 (1962), pp.451-67
Beachey, R., 'The East African ivory trade in the nineteenth century', *Journal of African History*, 8, 2 (1967), pp.269-90
Beattie, J., 'The ghost cult in Bunyoro', *Ethnology*, 3 (1964), pp.127-51

References

Beattie, J., *The Nyoro State* (Oxford, 1971)
Becker, J., *La vie en Afrique, ou trois ans dans l'Afrique Centrale* 2 vols. (Paris, 1887)
Behrend, H., *Alice Lakwena and the Holy Spirits: War in Northern Uganda 1986-87* (Oxford, 1999)
Bennett, N. R., *A History of the Arab State of Zanzibar* (London, 1978)
Bennett, N. R., *Arab versus European. Diplomacy and War in Nineteenth-Century East Central Africa* (New York, 1986)
Bennett, N. R., *Mirambo of Tanzania, 1840?-1884* (New York, 1971)
Bennett, N. R. (ed.), *Stanley's Despatches to the New York Herald, 1871-1872, 1874-1877* (Boston, MA, 1970)
Birmingham, D. B. and P. M. Martin (eds), *History of Central Africa* 2 vols. (London, 1983)
Blackburn, R., *The Making of New World Slavery* (London, 1997)
Blohm, W., *Die Nyamwezi* 2 vols. (Hamburg, 1931-1933)
Bontinck, F., *L'autobiographie de Hamed ben Mohammed el-Murjebi, Tippo Tip (ca. 1840-1905)* (Brussels, 1974)
Bösch, F., *Les Banyamwezi. Peuple de l'Afrique Orientale* (Münster, 1930)
Botte, R., 'Processus de formation d'une classe sociale dans une société africaine précapitaliste', *Cahiers d'études africaines*, 4, 14 (1974), pp.605-26
Botte, R., 'Ruanda and Burundi, 1889-1930: chronology of a slow assassination', *International Journal of African Historical Studies*, 18, 1 (1985), pp.53-91 and 18, 2 (1985), pp.289-314
Bourdieu, P., [P. Sherrard, trans.] 'The sentiment of honour in Kabyle society', in J. G. Peristiany (ed.), *Honour and Shame: The Values of Mediterranean Society* (London, 1965), pp.191-241
Brass, T. and M. van der Linden (eds), *Free and Unfree Labour: The Debate Continues* (Bern, 1997)
Brown, B., 'Muslim influence in trade and politics in the Lake Tanganyika region', *International Journal of African Historical Studies*, 4, 3 (1971) pp.617-29
Burton, R. F., *The Lake Regions of Central Africa, a Picture of Exploration* (London, 1860)
Cameron, V. L., *Across Africa* 2 vols. (London, 1877)
Casati, G., *Ten Years in Equatoria and the Return with Emin Pasha* 2 vols. (London, 1891)
Ceulemans, P., *La question arabe et le Congo (1883-1892)* (Brussels, 1959)
Chaillé Long, C., *Central Africa* (London, 1876)
Chrétien, J.-P., 'Exchanges and hierarchies in the East African interlacustrine kingdoms', *Research in Economic Anthropology*, 4 (1981), pp.19-30
Chrétien, J.-P., *L'Afrique des Grands Lacs* (Paris, 2000)
Chrétien, J.-P., 'Le commerce du sel de l'Uvinza au XIXe siècle: de la cueillette au monopole capitaliste', *Revue Française d'Histoire d'Outre-mer*, 3 (1978), pp.401-22
Chretien, J.-P., 'Mirambo. L'unificateur des Banyamwezi (Tanzanie)', in C.-A. Julien et al. (eds), *Les Africains* vol. 6 (Paris, 1977), pp.127-57
Chrétien, J.-P., *The Great Lakes of Africa, Two Thousand Years of History* (New York, 2003)
Clarence-Smith, W. G., *The Economics of the Indian Ocean Slave Trade in the Nineteenth Century* (London, 1989)
Claus, H., *Die Wagogo. Ethnographische Skizze eines ostafrikanischen Bantustammes* (Leipzig, 1911)
Cohen, D. W., 'Food production and food exchange in the precolonial Lakes Plateau Region', in R. I. Rotberg (ed.), *Imperialism, Colonialism, and Hunger in East and Central Africa* (Lexington, MA, 1983), pp.1-18
Cohen, D. W., *Womunafu's Bunafu: A Study of Authority in a Nineteenth-Century African Community* (Princeton, NJ, 1977)
Collins, R. O., 'Anglo-Congolese negotiations, 1900-1906', *Zaire*, 12, 6 (1958), pp.479-512

References

Collins, R. O., 'Ivory poaching in the Lado Enclave', *Uganda Journal*, 24, 2 (1960), pp.217-28
Collins, R. O., *The Southern Sudan 1883-1898; a Struggle for Control* (New Haven, CT, and London, 1962)
Colomb, Captain, *Slave Catching in the Indian Ocean. A Record of Naval Experiences* (London, 1873)
Colvile, H., *The Land of the Nile Springs: Being an Account of How We Fought Kabarega* (London, 1895)
Comaroff, J., 'Sui generis. Feminism, kinship theory and "structural" domains', in J. F. Collier and S. J. Yanagisako (eds), *Gender and Kinship. Essays towards a Unified Analysis* (Stanford, CA, 1987), pp.53-85
Cooper, F., *Colonialism in Question, Theory, Knowledge, History* (Berkeley and Los Angeles, 2005)
Cooper, F., *From Slaves to Squatters. Plantation Labour and Agriculture in Zanzibar and Coastal Kenya (1890-1925)* (New Haven, CT, 1980; Nairobi, 1981)
Cooper, F., *Plantation Slavery on the East Coast of Africa* (New Haven, CT, 1977)
Cooper, F., 'The problem of slavery in African studies', *Journal of African History*, 20, 1 (1979), pp.103-25
Coquilhat, C., *Sur le Haut-Congo* (Paris, 1888)
Cordell, D. and J. Gregory, *African Population and Capitalism: Historical Perspectives* (London, 1987)
Coulbois, F., *Dix Années au Tanganyika* (Limoges, 1901)
Crisp, J., 'Ugandan refugees in Sudan and Zaire: the problem of repatriation', *African Affairs*, 85, 1 (1986), pp.163-80
Cunningham, J. F., *Uganda and its Peoples* (New York, 1969 [1905])
Curtin, P. D. *The World and the West, The European Challenge and the Overseas Response in the Age of Empire* (Cambridge, 2000)
Czekanowski, J., *Forschungen im Nil-Kongo-Zwischengebiet, vol. I, Ethnographie Zwischenseengebiet Mpororo-Ruanda* (Leipzig, 1917)
Dauber, H. (ed.), *"Nicht als Abentheurer bin ich hierhergekommen..." 100 Jahre Entwicklungs-"Hilfe". Tagebücher und Briefe aus Deutsch-Ostafrika 1896-1902* (Frankfurt/Main, 1991)
Davis, D. B., *The Problem of Slavery in Western Culture* (Ithaca, NY, 1966)
De Bauw, G., 'La zone Uere-Bomu', *Belgique Coloniale*, 17 February 1901, pp.73-4
De Jonghe, E., *Les formes d'asservissement dans les sociétés indigenes du Congo belge* (Brussels, 1949)
de Maret, P., 'L'évolution monétaire du Shaba Central entre le 7e et le 18e siècle', *African Economic History*, 10 (1981), pp.117-49
de St.-Marcq, Le Clément, *Mouvement Géographique*, 25 May 1890, p.42
Delhaise, C., *Les Warega (Congo Belge)* (Brussels, 1909)
Dernburg, B., *Zielpunkte des Deutschen Kolonialwesens. Zwei Vorträge* (Berlin, 1907)
Deutsch, J.-G., *Emancipation without Abolition in German East Africa, c. 1884-1914* (Oxford, 2006)
Devereux, W. C., *A Cruise in the 'Gorgon'* (London, 1869)
Doornbos, M., *The Ankole Kingship Controversy: Regalia Galore Revisited* (Kampala, 2001)
Doyle, S. D., 'An environmental history of the kingdom of Bunyoro in western Uganda, from c.1860 to 1940', (unpublished PhD thesis, University of Cambridge, 1998)
Doyle, S. D., *Crisis and Decline in Bunyoro: Environment and Population in Western Uganda, 1860-1955* (Oxford, 2006)
Doyle, S., 'From Kitara to the Lost Counties: Genealogy, land and legitimacy in the kingdom of Bunyoro, Western Uganda', *Social Identities*, 12, 4 (2006), pp.457-70
Eberstein, F. von, 'Rechtsanschauungen der Eingeborenen von Kilwa', *Mitteilungen von Forschungsreisenden und Gelehrten aus den deutschen Schutzgebieten*, 9 (1896), pp.170-83

References

Ehret, C., 'Bantu expansions, re-envisioning a central problem in early African history', *International Journal of African Historical Studies*, 34, 1 (2001), pp.5-40

Ehret, C., 'Subclassifying Bantu: the evidence of stem morpheme innovation', in J.-M. Hombert and L. M. Hyman (eds), *Bantu Historical Linguistics: Theoretical and Empirical Perspectives* (Stanford, CA, 1999), pp.43-147

Ehret, C., *An African Classical Age: Eastern and Southern Africa in World Prehistory History, 1000BC to AD400* (Charlottesville, VA, 1998)

Elkins, S., *Slavery, A Problem in American Institutional Life* (Chicago, IL, 1965)

Eltis, D. (ed.), *Coerced and Free Labour: Global Perspectives* (Stanford, CA, 2002)

Elton, J. F., 'On the coast country of East Africa, south of Zanzibar', *Royal Geographical Society Journal*, 44 (1874), pp.227-52

Elton, J. F., *Travels and Researches among the Lakes and Mountains of Eastern and Central Africa*, ed. by H. B. Cotterill (London, 1879)

Engerman, S., 'A population history of the Caribbean', in M. Haines and R. Steckel (eds), *A Population History of North America* (Cambridge, 2000), pp.483-528

Engerman, S. (ed.), *Terms of Labour: Slavery, Serfdom, and Free Labour* (Stanford, CA, 1999)

Erlich, H. and I. Gershoni, *The Nile: Histories, Cultures, Myths* (New York and London, 2000)

Evangelischer Afrikaverein, *Das Deutsche Reich und die Sklaverei in Afrika!, Stenographischer Bericht der am 18. Januar 1895 in der Tonhalle zu Berlin auf Veranlassung des ev. Afrikavereins abgehaltenen Versammlung* (Leipzig, 1895)

Ewald, J. J., *Soldiers, Traders and Slaves: State Formation and Economic Transformation in the Greater Nile Valley, 1700-1885* (Madison, WI, and London, 1990)

Fair, L., 'Dressing up: clothing, class and gender in post-abolition Zanzibar', *Journal of African History*, 39, 1 (1998), pp.67-74

Fallers, L., *Bantu Bureaucracy. A Century of Political Evolution among the Basoga of Uganda* (Chicago, IL, 1956)

Fallers, L., 'Despotism, status culture and social mobility in an African kingdom', *Comparative Studies in Society and History*, 2 (1959), pp.4-32

Fallers, L., 'Social stratification in traditional Buganda', in Lloyd Fallers (ed.), *The King's Men* (London, 1964), pp.64-113

Fallers, L. (ed.), *The King's Men* (London, 1964)

Falola, T. and P. E. Lovejoy, 'Pawnship in historical perspective', in T. Falola and P. E. Lovejoy (eds), *Pawnship in Africa. Debt Bondage in Historical Perspective* (Boulder, CO, 1994), pp.1-26

Faupel, Rev. J. F. *African Holocaust: the Story of the Uganda Martyrs* (London, 1962)

Feierman, S., 'A century of ironies in East Africa (c.1780-1890)', in P. Curtin, S. Feierman, L. Thompson and J. Vansina (eds), *African History* (London, 1978), pp.391-418

Feierman, S., *Peasant Intellectuals: Anthropology and History in Tanzania* (Madison, WI, 1990)

Feierman, S., *The Shambaa Kingdom. A History* (Madison, WI, 1974)

Felkin, R., 'Notes on the Waganda tribe of central Africa', *Proceedings of the Royal Society of Edinburgh*, 13 (1885-6), pp.699-770

Felkin, R., 'Notes on the Wanyoro tribe of Central Africa', *Proceedings of the Royal Society of Edinburgh*, 19 (1891-2), pp.136-92

Finley, M. I., *Ancient Slavery and Modern Ideology* ed. by B. D. Shaw (Princeton, NJ, 1998)

Finley, M. I., *Esclavage antique et idéologie moderne* (Paris, 1981)

Fischer, G. A. 'Am Ostufer des Victoria-Njanza', *Petermanns Mittheilungen*, 41 (1895) pp.1-6, 42-6, 66-72

Fisher, H. J., *Slavery in the History of Muslim East Africa* (London, 2001)

Fisher, R. H., *Twilight Tales of the Black Baganda* (London, 1912)

Fleisher, J., 'Behind the Sultan of Kilwa's "Rebellious Conduct"', in A. M. Reid and

References

P. J. Lane (eds), *African Historical Archaeologies* (New York, 2004), pp.101-10

Fortt, J. M. 'The distribution of the immigrant and Ganda population within Buganda', in A. I. Richards (ed.), *Economic Development and Tribal Change* (Cambridge, 1954), pp.77-118

Fortt, J. M. and D. A. Hougham, 'Environment, population and economic history', in A. I. Richards, F. Sturrock, and J. M. Fortt (eds), *Subsistence to Commercial Farming in Present-Day Buganda* (Cambridge, 1973), pp.17-46

Fosbrooke, K., 'The defensive measures of certain tribes in North-Eastern Tanganyika, Part 2', *Tanganyika Notes and Records*, (1954) pp.36-57

Fourshey, Catherine Cymone, *Agriculture, Ecology, Kinship and Gender: A Social and Economic History of Tanzania's Corridor 500 BC to 1900 AD* (Ann Arbor, MI, University Microfilms International, 2002)

Fraas, P., *A Nande-English and English-Nande Dictionary* (Washington, DC, 1961)

Furley, O. W., 'The Sudanese troops in Uganda', *African Affairs*, 58, 233 (1959), pp.311-28

Gahama, J., *Le Burundi sous l'administration Belge* (Paris, 2001)

Galbraith, J., *Mackinnon and East Africa, 1878-1895: a Study in the 'New Imperialism'* (Cambridge, 1972)

Genovese, E., *Roll, Jordan, Roll* (New York, 1974)

Giblin, J. L., 'Pawning, politics and matriliny in Northeastern Tanzania', in T. Falola and P. E. Lovejoy (eds), *Pawnship in Africa. Debt Bondage in Historical Perspective* (Boulder, CO, 1994), pp.43-53

Gitta, C., 'International human rights: An imperial imposition? (A case study of Buganda, 1856-1955)' (unpublished PhD dissertation, Columbia University, 1998)

Glassman, J., *Feasts and Riot. Revelry, Rebellion, and Popular Consciousness on the Swahili Coast, 1856-1888* (Portsmouth, NH, 1995)

Glassman, J., 'No words of their own', *Slavery and Abolition*, 16, 1 (1995), pp.131-45

Glassman, J., 'The bondsman's new clothes. The contradictory consciousness of slave resistance on the Swahili coast', *Journal of African History*, 32, 2 (1991), pp.277-312

Godelier, M., T. R. Trautmann and F. E. Tjon Sie Fat, 'Introduction', in M. Godelier, T. R. Trautman and F. E. Tjon Sie Fat (eds), *Transformations of Kinship* (Washington, DC, 1998), pp.1-18

Goody, J., *Technology, Tradition, and the State in Africa* (Cambridge, 1971)

Gorju, J., *Entre le Victoria, l'Albert et l'Edouard* (Rennes, 1920)

Gottberg, A., *Unyamwesi. Quellensammlung und Geschichte* (Berlin, 1971)

Grahame, I., *Amin and Uganda; a Personal Memoir* (London, 1980)

Grant, J. A., *A Walk Across Africa or Domestic Scenes from my Nile Journal* (Edinburgh and London, 1864)

Gray, J. M., 'Arabs on Lake Victoria', *Uganda Journal*, 22, 1 (Mar. 1958), pp.76-81

Gray, J. M., 'Livingstone's Muganda servant', *Uganda Journal*, 2, 13 (September 1949), pp.119-29

Gray, J. M. (ed.), 'The diaries of Emin Pasha - extracts II', *Uganda Journal*, 25, 2 (Sept. 1961), pp.149-70

Gray, R., *A History of Southern Sudan 1839-1889* (London, 1961)

Green, R. H., 'Magendo in the political economy of Uganda: Pathology, parallel system or dominant sub-mode of production' (IDS Discussion Paper, Institute of Development Studies, University of Sussex, 1981)

Greene, S. E., *Gender, Ethnicity and Social Change on the Upper Slave Coast: A History of the Anlo-Ewe* (Portsmouth, NH, 1996)

Gustin, Lieutenant, 'Vers le Nil', *Mouvement Géographique* (1898), col. 229

Guthrie, M. *Comparative Bantu* 4 vols (Farnborough, 1967-71)

Guy, J., *The Destruction of the Zulu Kingdom* (Pietermaritzburg, 1994)

Guyer, J. I., 'Household and community in African Studies', *African Studies Review*, 24

References

(1981), pp.87-137
Guyer, J. I., *Marginal Gains: Monetary Transaction in Atlantic Africa* (Chicago, IL, 2004)
Guyer, J. I. and S. M. Eno Belinga, 'Wealth in people as wealth in knowledge: accumulation and composition in Equatorial Africa', *Journal of African History*, 36, 1 (1995), pp.91-129
Hahner-Herzog, I., *Tippu Tip und der Elfenbeinhandel in Ost- und Zentralafrika im 19. Jahrhundert* (München, 1990)
Hansen, H. B., 'Pre-colonial immigrants and colonial servants. The Nubians in Uganda revisited', *African Affairs*, 90 (1991), pp.559-80
Hansen, H. B. and M. Twaddle (eds), *Changing Uganda* (London, 1991)
Hansen, H. B. and M. Twaddle (eds), *Developing Uganda* (Oxford, 1998)
Hansen, H. B. and M. Twaddle (eds), *From Chaos to Order, the Politics of Constitution-making in Uganda* (London, 1995)
Hansen, H. B. and M. Twaddle (eds), *Uganda Now* (London, 1988)
Hanson, H. E., *Landed Obligation: The Practice of Power in Buganda* (Portsmouth, NH, 2003)
Harms, R., 'Sustaining the system: Trading towns along Middle Zaire', in C. C. Robertson and M. Klein (eds), *Women and Slavery in Africa* (Portsmouth, NH, 1997), pp.95-110
Harrell-Bond, B. E., *Imposing Aid* (Oxford, 1986)
Hartwig, G. W. 'Changing forms of servitude among the Kerebe of Tanzania', in S. Miers and I. Kopytoff (eds), *Slavery in Africa* (Madison, WI, 1977), pp.261-85
Hartwig, G. W., *The Art of Survival in East Africa: The Kerebe and Long-Distance Trade, 1800-1895* (New York, 1976)
Hartwig, G. W., 'The Victoria Nyanza as a trade route in the nineteenth century', *Journal of African History*, 11, 4 (1970), pp.535-52
Hattersley, C. W. *The Baganda at Home* (London, 1968 [1908])
Hermann, A., 'Ugogo - Das Land und seine Bewohner', *Mitteilungen aus den deutschen Schutzgebieten*, 5 (1892), pp.191-203
Hermann, R., 'Statistik der farbigen Bevölkerung von Deutsch Afrika, III. Ostafrika', *Koloniale Monatsblätter*, 16, 4 (1914), pp.172-6
Higman, B., *Slave Populations of the British Caribbean, 1807-1834* (Baltimore, 1984)
Hinde, S. L., *The Fall of the Congo Arabs* (London, 1897)
Hochschild, A., *King Leopold's Ghost: A Story of Greed, Terror, and Heroism in Colonial Africa* (Boston, MA, 1998)
Holmes, C. F., 'Zanzibari influence at the southern end of Lake Victoria. The lake route', *International Journal of African Historical Studies*, 4, 3 (1971), pp.477-503
Holt, P. M. and M. W. Daly, *A History of the Sudan* 5th edn (London, 2000)
Hore, E. C., *Missionary to Tanganyika, 1877-1888*, ed. J. B. Wolf (London, 1971)
Iliffe, J., *A Modern History of Tanganyika* (Cambridge, 1979)
Iliffe, J., *Africans: the History of a Continent* (Cambridge, 1995)
Iliffe, J., *Honour in African History* (Cambridge, 2005)
Iliffe, J., *The African Poor* (Cambridge, 1987)
James, W., 'Perceptions from an African slaving frontier', in L. Archer (ed.), *Slavery and other Forms of Unfree Labour* (London, 1988), pp.133-41
Jamison, M., *Amin and Uganda: an Annotated bibliography* (Westport, CT, and London, 1992)
Jensen, J., 'Die Erweiterung des Lungenfischs-clan in Buganda (Uganda) durch den Anschluss von Bavuma Gruppen', *Sociologus*, 2, 19 (1969) pp.153-66
Joachim, M., 'Sizia oder Schicksale einer Negersklavin. Von ihr selbst erzählt', *Afrika-Bote*, 1905/6, pp.109-15
Johnson, D. H., 'Recruitment and entrapment in private slave armies: the structure of the Zariba in the Southern Sudan' *Slavery and Abolition*, 13, 1 (1992), pp.162-173

References

Johnson, D. H., 'Sudanese military slavery from the eighteenth to the twentieth century', in L. Archer (ed.), *Slavery and Other Forms of Unfree Labour* (London and New York, 1988)

Johnson, D. H., 'The structure of a legacy: Military slavery in Northeast Africa' *Ethnohistory*, 36, 1, (Winter 1989), pp.72-88

Johnston, H., *A Comparative Study of the Bantu and Semi-Bantu Languages* (Oxford, 1919)

Johnston, H., *The Uganda Protectorate* (London, 1902)

Jones-Bateman, P. L. (ed.), *The Autobiography of an African Slave Boy (Martin Furahani)* (London, 1891)

Junker, W. [tr. A. H. Keane], *Travels in Africa during the Years 1882-1886* (London, 1892)

Kabemba, A., 'Les rapports entre Arabes et Manyema dans l'histoire du XIXe siècle', *Cahiers du CERUKI*, séries C2 (Sciences Humaines), 1979

Kaggwa, A. [ed. M. M. Edel, tr. E. B. Kalibala], *Customs of the Baganda* (New York, 1934)

Kaggwa, Sir A., *Basekabaka be Buganda* (typescript of English translation by Simon Musoke, Africana Collection, Makerere University Library)

Kaggwa, Sir A., *The Kings of Buganda*. M. S. M. Kiwanuka, translator and editor (Nairobi, 1971)

Kaji, S., *Vocabulaire Hunde* (Tokyo, 1992)

Kakangoro, E., 'Kibiro salt' (unpublished Diploma in Fine Arts dissertation, Makerere University, Kampala, 1968),

Kamuhangire, E., 'The pre-colonial economic and social history of East Africa, with special reference to south-western Uganda salt lakes region', *Hadith*, 5 (1976), pp.67-91

Kamuhangire, E., 'The pre-colonial history of south western Uganda' (unpublished PhD thesis, Makerere University, Kampala, 1996)

Kandt, R., *Caput Nili*, 2nd edn (Berlin, 1919)

Karlström, M., 'Modernity and its aspirants: moral community and developmental eutopianism', *Current Anthropology*, 45, 5 (2005), pp.595-619

Karugire, S., *A History of the Kingdom of Nkore* (Oxford, 1971)

Karugire, S., 'Relations between Bairu and Bahima in nineteenth-century Nkore', *Tarikh*, 3, 2 (1970), pp.22-33

Katamba, F., 'Bantu Nominal Morphology', in D. Nurse and G. Philippson (eds), *The Bantu Languages* (London, 2003), pp.103-20

Katate, A. and L. Kamugungunu, *Abagabe b'Ankole* (Kampala, 1955)

Katende, A. B., A. Birnie and B. Tengnas (eds), *Useful Trees and Shrubs of Uganda* (Nairobi, 1995)

Katoke, I., *The Karagwe Kingdom: A History of the Abanyambo of North-West Tanzania* (Nairobi, 1975)

Kavakure, L., *Famines et disettes au Burundi (fin du xixe siècle - 1ere moitie du xxe siecle)*, (Mémoire, Université du Burundi, Bujumbura, 1982)

Keim, C., 'Long distance trade and the Mangbetu', *Journal of African History*, 24 (1983), pp.1-22

Keim, C., 'Women in slavery among the Mangbetu c. 1800-1910', in C. C. Robertson and M. A. Klein (eds), *Women and Slavery in Africa* (Portsmouth, NH, 1997 [first published 1983]), pp.144-59

Keltie, J. S. (ed.), *The Story of Emin's Rescue as told in Stanley's Letters* (New York, 1969 [1890])

Kenny, M. G., 'Pre-colonial trade in Eastern Lake Victoria', *Azania*, 14 (1979), pp.97-107

Kiwanuka, M. S. M., *A History of Buganda from the Foundation of the Kingdom to 1900* (New York, 1972)

Kjekshus, H., *Ecology Control and Economic Development in East African History. The Case of*

References

Tanganyika 1850-1950 (London, 1996 [first published 1977])

Klieman, K., *'Pygmies were our compass': Bantu and Batwa in the history of West Central Africa, early times to c. 1900 C.E.* (Portsmouth, NH, 2003)

Kokole, O. H. 'Idi Amin, "the Nubi" and Islam in Ugandan Politics, 1970-1979', in H. B. Hansen and M. Twaddle (eds), *Religion and Politics in East Africa* (London/Nairobi/Kampala/Athens, OH, 1995)

Koponen, J., *Development for Exploitation: German Colonial Policies in Mainland Tanzania, 1884-1914* (Helsinki, 1994)

Koponen, J., *People and Production in Late Precolonial Tanzania: History and Structures* (Uppsala, 1988)

Kopytoff, I., 'The cultural context of African abolition', in S. Miers and R. Roberts (eds), *The End of Slavery in Africa* (Madison, WI, 1988), pp.485-503

Kopytoff, I. and S. Miers, 'Introduction. African "slavery" as an institution of marginality', in S. Miers and I. Kopytoff (eds), *Slavery in Africa. Historical and Anthropological Perspectives* (Madison, WI, 1977), pp.3-81

Krapf, J. L., *Reisen in Ostafrika ausgeführt in den Jahren 1837 bis 1855* 2 vols (Kornthal/Stuttgart, 1964 [first published 1858])

Krelle, H., *Anton und seine Anna* (Berlin, 1929)

Krenzler, E., 'Sklaverei und Sklavenhandel in Ostafrika', *Jahresberichte des Württembergischen Vereins für Handelsgeographie*, 5-6 (1886-88), pp.69-79

Kwamena-Poh, M. et al., *African History in Maps* (Harlow, 1992)

Lagae, C. R., *Les Azande ou Niam-Niam. L'organisation zande. Croyances religieuses et magiques, coutumes familiales* (Brussels, 1926)

Lamp, F., *The Art of the Baga: A Drama of Cultural Reinvention* (New York and Munich, 1996),

Lanning, E. C., 'Sultan Fademulla Murjan of Aringa', *Uganda Journal*, 18, 2 (1954), pp.178-80

Larson, P. M., *History and Memory in the Age of Enslavement. Becoming Merina in Highland Madagascar 1770-1822* (Portsmouth, NH, 2000)

Law, R. C. C., 'Human sacrifice in pre-colonial West Africa', *African Affairs*, 84 (1985), pp.53-87

Le Roy, A., *Mehr Licht in die Zustände des dunklen Weltteils. Die Sklaverei und ihre Bekämpfung* (Münster, 1890)

Leopold, M., *Inside West Nile: Violence, History and Representation on an African Frontier* (Oxford, 2005)

Leopold, M., 'Slavery in Sudan, past and present', *African Affairs*, 102 (2003), pp.653-61

Leopold, M., 'The roots of violence and the reconstruction of society in North Western Uganda' (unpublished DPhil thesis, Division of Life Sciences, University of Oxford, 2001)

Leopold, M., '"The War in the North": Ethnicity in Ugandan press explanations of conflict 1996-97', in T. Allen and J. Seaton (eds), *The Media of Conflict: War Reporting and Representations of Ethnic Violence* (London and New York,1999), pp.219-43

Leopold, M., '"Trying to hold things together": International NGOs caught up in an emergency in North Western Uganda', in O. Barrow and M. Jennings (eds), *The Charitable Impulse: NGOs and Development in East and North East Africa* (Oxford, 2001)

Linden, I., *Christianisme et pouvoir au Rwanda 1900-1990* (Paris, 1999)

Livingstone, D., *The Last Journals of David Livingstone, in Central Africa from Eighteen Hundred and Sixty-five to his Death*, Horace Waller ed. (New York, 1875)

Lonsdale, J. M., 'The conquest state of Kenya, 1895-1905', in B. Berman and J. M. Lonsdale, *Unhappy Valley. Conflict in Kenya and Africa* 2 vols (London, 1992), vol. 1, pp.13-44

Lovejoy, P. E., *Transformations in Slavery: A History of Slavery in Africa* 2nd edn (Cambridge, 2000)

References

Lüdtke, A., 'Einleitung. Herrschaft als soziale Praxis', in A. Lüdtke (ed.), *Herrschaft als soziale Praxis* (Göttingen, 1991), pp.9-63

Lugan, B., 'Les réseaux commerciaux au Rwanda dans le dernier quart du XIXe siècle', *Etudes d'Histoire Africaine*, 9-10 (1977-78), pp.183-212

Lugard, F. D. *The Rise of Our East African Empire: Early efforts in Nyasaland and Uganda* (Edinburgh and London, 1893)

Lukyn Williams, F., 'Early explorers in Ankole', *Uganda Journal*, 2, 1 (1935), pp.196-208

Macdonald, J. R., *Soldiering and Surveying in British East Africa* (London, 1897)

MacGaffey, W., 'Changing representations in Central African History', *Journal of African History*, 46, 2 (2005), pp.195-201

MacGaffey, W., *Religion and Society in Central Africa* (Chicago, IL, 1986)

Mackay, A. M. (ed. by his sister), *A.M. Mackay: Pioneer Missionary to Uganda* (London, 1890)

MacKenzie, J. M., *The Empire of Nature; Hunting, Conservation and British Imperialism* (Manchester, 1988)

Mair, L., *An African People in the Twentieth Century* (London, 1934)

Mair, L., *Native Marriage in Uganda* (London, 1940)

Manning, P., *Slavery and African Life: Occidental, Oriental, and African Slave Trades* (Cambridge, 1990)

Maquet, J. J., *The Premise of Inequality in Ruanda* (London, 1970)

Marissal, J., 'Le commerce zanzibarite dans l'Afrique des Grands Lacs au XIXe siècle', *Revue Française d'Histoire d'Outre-Mer*, 65, 239 (1978), pp.212-55

Marissal, J., 'Mohammed bin Khalfan', in C. A. Julien (ed.), *Les Africains* (Paris, 1978), vol. 11, pp.49-71

Mazrui, A. A., 'Religious strangers in Uganda: from Emin Pasha to Amin Dada', *African Affairs*, 76, 302 (1977), pp.21-38

Mazrui, A. A. 'The resurrection of the warrior tradition in African political culture', *Journal of Modern African Studies*, 13, 1 (1975), pp.67-84

Mazrui, A. A. (ed.), *The Warrior Tradition in Modern Africa* (Leiden, 1977)

McConnell, R. E., 'Notes on the Lugwari tribe of Central Africa', *Journal of the Royal Anthropological Institute of Great Britain and Ireland*, 65 (July to December 1925), pp.439-67

McLynn, F., *Stanley, Sorcerer's Apprentice* (London, 1991)

Meagher, K., 'The hidden economy: informal and parallel trade in Northwestern Uganda', *Review of African Political Economy*, 47 (1990), pp.64-83

Médard, H., 'Croissance et crises de la royauté du Buganda au XIXe siècle' (unpublished PhD dissertation, Université Paris I Pantheon Sorbonne, U.F.R. d'Histoire, 2001)

Médard, H., *Le royaume du Buganda au XIXe siècle: mutations politiques et religieuses d'un grand état d'Afrique de l'est* (Paris, 2007)

Meeussen, A. E., *Bantu Lexical Reconstructions* (Tervuren, 1980)

Meillassoux, C., *Anthropologie de l'esclavage. Le ventre de fer et d'argent* (Paris, 1986)

Meillassoux, C., 'Female slavery' in C. Robertson and M. Klein (eds), *Women and Slavery in Africa* (Madison, WI, 1983), pp.49-66

Meillassoux, C., *L'esclavage en Afrique precoloniale* (Paris, 1975)

Meillassoux, C., *The Anthropology of Slavery: The Womb of Iron and Gold* (Chicago, IL, 1991)

Meldon, J., 'Notes on the Bahima of Ankole', *Journal of the Africa Society*, 6 (1907), pp.136-53 and 234-49

Meyer, H., *Les Barundi* (trans. Paris, 1984 of *Die Barundi* (Leipzig, 1916))

Middleton, J. F. M., *The Lugbara of Uganda* 2nd edn (Fort Worth, TX, and London, 1992)

Middleton, J. F. M., 'Some effects of colonial rule among the Lugbara', in V. Turner (ed.), *Colonialism in Africa, 1870-1960* (Cambridge, 1971), pp.6-48

References

Middleton, J. F. M., 'Trade and markets among the Lugbara of Uganda', in P. Bohannon and G. Dalton (eds), *Markets in Africa* (Chicago, IL, 1962), pp.561-78
Miers, S. and I. Kopytoff (eds), *Slavery in Africa* (Madison, WI, 1977)
Miers, S. and M. Klein, 'Introduction', in S. Miers and M. Klein (eds), *Slavery and Colonial Rule in Africa* (London, 1999), pp.1-15
Miers, S. and M. Klein (eds), *Slavery and Colonial Rule in Africa* (London, 1999)
Miers, S. and R. Roberts (eds), *The End of Slavery in Africa* (Madison, WI, 1988)
Miller, J. C. 'Imbangala lineage slavery (Angola)', in S. Miers and I. Kopytoff (eds), *Slavery in Africa* (Madison, WI, 1977), pp.205-33
Mitchell, T., *Colonising Egypt* (Cambridge, 1988)
Moore, E. D., *Ivory, Scourge of Africa* (New York and London, 1931)
Morton, F., 'Pawnship and slavery on the Kenya coast. The Miji Kenda case', in T. Falola and P. E. Lovejoy (eds), *Pawnship in Africa. Debt Bondage in Historical Perspective* (Boulder, CO, 1994), pp.27-42
Moyse-Bartlett, H., *The Kings African Rifles: A Study in the Military History of East and Central Africa, 1890-1945* (Aldershot, 1956)
Muhoozi, C., 'Migration and socio economic change in Uganda' (unpublished MA thesis, History Department, Makerere University)
Mujawimana, E., 'Le Commerce des esclaves au Rwanda' (unpublished History BA thesis, Université National du Rwanda, Ruhengeri, 1983)
Mukasa, H., *Simuda Nyuma part III* (English translation by John Rowe, microfilmed manuscript, Center for Research Libraries, University of Chicago)
Müller, F.-F., *Deutschland, Zanzibar, Ostafrika. Geschichte einer Deutschen Kolonialeroberung, 1884-1890* (Berlin, 1959)
Murphy, J. D., *Luganda-English Dictionary* (Washington, DC, 1972)
Mushanga, T. M., 'The clan system among the Banyankole', *Uganda Journal*, 34 (1970), pp.29-34
Mushanga, T. M., 'The end of racial inequality in Ankole' (unpublished ms., 1994)
Musisi, N. B. 'Women, "elite polygyny", and Buganda state formation', *Signs: Journal of Women in Culture and Society* 16, 4 (1991), pp.757-86
Muvumba, J., 'The politics of stratification and transformation in the kingdom of Ankole, Uganda' (unpublished Ph.D. thesis, Department of Government, Harvard University, 1982)
Newbury, D., '"Bunyabungo": the Western Rwandan frontier, 1750-1850', in I. Kopytoff (ed.), *The Internal African Frontier: The Reproduction of Traditional African Societies* (Bloomington, IN, 1987), pp.164-92
Newbury, D., *Kings and Clans, Ijwi Island and the Lake Kivu Rift, 1780-1840* (Madison, WI, 1991)
Newbury, D., 'Lake Kivu regional trade in the nineteenth century', *Journal des Africanistes*, 50, 2 (1980), pp.6-30
Newbury, D., 'The clans of Rwanda: an historical hypothesis', *Africa*, 4, 50 (1980) pp.389-403
Njiga, B., 'La principauté de Nyangezi: essai d'histoire socio-économique (1850-1960)', (mémoire de licence en histoire, Institut Supérieur Pédagogique, Bukavu, 1978)
Nolan, F. P., 'Christianity in Unyamwezi, 1878-1928' (unpublished PhD dissertation, University of Cambridge, 1977)
Northrup, D., 'A church in search of a state: Catholic missions in Zaïre, 1879-1930', *Journal of Church and State*, 30 (1988), pp.313-19
Northrup, D., *Beyond the Bend in the River: African Labour in Eastern Zaire, 1865-1940* (Athens, OH, 1988)
Northrup, D., 'The ending of slavery in the eastern Belgian Congo', in S. Miers and R. Roberts (eds), *The End of Slavery in Africa* (Madison, WI, 1988), pp. 462-82

References

Nsanze, A., *Le Burundi ancien. L'économie du pouvoir de 1875-1920* (Paris, 2001)
Nurse, D., 'Towards an historical classification of East African Bantu languages', in J.-M. Hombert and L. M. Hyman (eds), *Bantu Historical Linguistics: Theoretical and Empirical Perspectives* (Stanford, CA, 1999), pp.1-41
Nurse, D. and H. R. T. Muzale, 'Tense and aspect in Great Lakes Bantu languages', in J.-M. Hombert and L. Hyman (eds), *Bantu Historical Linguistics: Theoretical and Empirical Perspectives* (Stanford, CA, 1999), pp.517-44
Nurse, D. and T. Hinnebusch, *Swahili and Sabaki: A Linguistic History* (Berkeley and Los Angeles, CA, 1993)
Nyakatura, J., *Anatomy of an African kingdom: a History of Bunyoro-Kitara*, edited by G. N. Uzoigwe (New York, 1973)
Nyakatura, J., *The Customs of the Banyoro* (Nairobi, 1970)
O'Fahey, R. S., 'Slavery and the slave trade in Dar Fur', *Journal of African History*, 14, 1 (1973), pp.29-43
Obbo, C., 'Village strangers in Buganda society', in W. A. Shack and E. P. Skinner (eds), *Strangers in African Societies* (Berkeley, CA, 1979), pp.227-242
Oberg, K., 'The kingdom of Ankole in Uganda', in M. Fortes and E. E. Evans-Pritchard (eds), *African Political Systems* (London, 1940), pp.128-50
Ogot, B. A. (ed.), *War and Society in Africa* (London, 1972)
Oliver, R., *The Missionary Factor in East Africa* (London, 1965)
Omer-Cooper, J. D., *History of Southern Africa* (London, 1987)
Ongala, S., 'Les arabisés Kusu et la création et l'évolution du poste de Walikale (1901-1954)', (Travail de fin d'études, ISP, Bukavu, 1978)
Packard, R. M., *Chiefship and Cosmology: An Historical Study of Political Competition* (Bloomington, IN, 1981)
Page, M. E., 'The Manyema hordes of Tippu Tip. A case study in social stratification and the slave trade in Eastern Africa', *International Journal of African Historical Studies*, 7, 1 (1974) pp.69-84
Page, M. E., 'Tippu Tip and the Arab "defense" of the East African slave trade', *Études d'histoire africaine*, 6 (1974), pp.105-17
Pain, D., 'The Nubians, their perceived stratification system and its relation to the Asian Issue', in M. Twaddle (ed.), *Expulsion of a Minority* (London, 1975)
Patterson, O., *Slavery and Social Death* (Cambridge, MA, 1982)
Penningroth, D., *The Claims of Kinfolk* (Chapel Hill, NC, 2003)
Perham, M. and M. Bull, *The Diaries of Lord Lugard* 4 vols (London, 1959)
Perham, M., *Lugard: The Years of Adventure, 1858-1898* (Hamden, CT, 1968)
Perlman, M. L. 'The traditional systems of stratification among the Ganda and Nyoro of Uganda', in A. Tuden and L. Plotnicov (eds), *Social Stratification in Africa* (New York, 1970), pp.125-161
Peters, C. [tr. H. W. Dulcken], *New Light on Dark Africa* (London, 1891)
Pirouet, M. L., *Black Evangelists: The Spread of Christianity in Uganda 1890-1914* (London, 1978)
Pitt-Rivers, J., 'Postscript: the place of grace in anthropology', in J. G. Peristiany and J. Pitt-Rivers (eds), *Honor and Grace in Anthropology* (Cambridge, 1992), pp.215-46
Pouwels, R., 'Eastern Africa and the Indian Ocean to 1800: reviewing relations in historical perspective', *International Journal of African Historical Studies*, 35, 2/3 (2002), pp.385-425
Pouwels, R. L., *Horn and Crescent. Cultural Change and Traditional Islam on the East African Coast, 800-1900* (Cambridge, 1987)
Presley, C., *Kikuyu Women, the Mau Mau Rebellion and Social Change in Kenya* (Boulder, CO, 1992)
Prestholdt, J., 'On the global repercussions of East African consumerism', *American Historical Review*, 109, 3 (2004), pp.755-82

References

Pruen, S. T., 'Slavery in East Africa. Letter from Dr. Pruen, Mpwapwa', *Church Missionary Intelligencer*, 13 (1888), pp.661-5

Pruen, S. T., *The Arab and the African. Experiences in Eastern Equatorial Africa during a Residence of Three Years* (London, 1891)

Prunier, G., 'Le magendo', *Politique Africaine*, 9 (1983), pp.53-62

Prunier, G., 'Military slavery in the Sudan during the Turkiyya', *Slavery and Abolition*, 13, 1 (April 1992), pp.129-39

Ramsay, H., 'Uha, Urundi, Ruanda', *Mitteilungen aus den deutschen Schutzgebieten*, 3 (1897), pp.177-182.

Raum, O. F., 'German East Africa - changes in African tribal life under German administration, 1892-1914', in V. Harlow and E. M. Chilver (eds), *History of East Africa* (Oxford, 1965), vol. 2, pp.163-207

Rehse, H., *Land und Leute* (Stuttgart, 1910)

Reichard, P., *Deutsch-Ostafrika. Das Land und seine Bewohner, seine politische und wirtschaftliche Entwicklung* (Leipzig, 1892)

Reichard, P., 'Die Wanyamwezi', *Deutsche Kolonialzeitung*, 3 (1890), pp.228-78

Reid, A. and D. Schoenbrun, 'The emergence of social formations and inequality in the Great Lakes Region', *Archaeological Review from Cambridge*, 13, 1 (1994), pp.51-60

Reid, R., *Political Power in Pre-Colonial Buganda: Economy, Society and Warfare in the Nineteenth Century* (Oxford, 2002)

Reid, R., 'The Ganda on Lake Victoria: a nineteenth-century East African imperialism', *Journal of African History*, 39, 3 (1998), pp.349-63

Reid, R., 'War and militarism in pre-colonial Buganda', *Azania*, 34 (1999) pp.45-60

Renault, F., *Lavigerie, l'Esclavage Africain et l'Europe* (Paris, 1971)

Renault, F., *Tippo-Tip. Un Potentat Arabe en Afrique Centrale au XIXème siècle* (Paris, 1987)

Reyna, S. P., *Wars Without End, The Political Economy of a Precolonial African State* (Hanover, NH, 1990)

Richards, A. I., *Economic Development and Tribal Change* (Cambridge, 1954)

Roberts, A. D., 'Firearms in North-Eastern Zambia before 1900', *Transafrican Journal of History*, 1, 2 (1971), pp.3-21

Roberts, A. D., 'Nyamwezi trade', in R. Gray and D. Birmingham (eds), *Pre-Colonial African Trade in Central and Eastern Africa before 1900* (London, 1970), pp.39-74

Roberts, A. D., 'The Nyamwezi', in A. D. Roberts (ed.), *Tanzania before 1900* (Nairobi, 1968), pp.117-50

Roberts, R. and S. Miers, 'Introduction', in S. Miers and R. Roberts (eds), *The End of Slavery in Africa* (Madison, WI, 1988), pp.3-70

Robertshaw, P., 'The age and function of earthworks sites in Western Uganda', *Uganda Journal*, 47 (2001), pp.20-33

Robertshaw, P., 'The ancient earthworks of western Uganda: capital sites of a Cwezi Empire?', *Uganda Journal*, 48 (2002), pp.17-32

Robertshaw, P., 'Women, labor, and state formation in Western Uganda', in E. A. Bacus and L. J. Lucero (eds), *Complex Polities in the Ancient Tropical World* (Washington, DC, 1999), pp.51-65

Robertshaw, P. and D. Taylor, 'Climate change and the rise of political complexity in Western Uganda', *Journal of African History*, 41, 1 (2000), pp.1-28

Robertson, C. C. and M. Klein (eds), *Women and Slavery in Africa* (Portsmouth, NH, 1997 [first published Madison, WI, 1983])

Robertson, C. C. and M. Klein, 'Women's importance in African slave systems', in C. C. Robertson and M. Klein (eds) *Women and Slavery in Africa* (Madison, WI, 1983), pp.3-17

Robinson, R. and J. Gallagher, *Africa and the Victorians* (New York, 1961)

Rockel, S. J., '"A nation of porters". The Nyamwezi and the labour market in mid-nineteenth-century Tanzania', *Journal of African History*, 41, 2 (2000), pp.173-95

References

Rockel, S. J., 'Caravan porters of the *Nyika*. Labour, culture, and society in nineteenth-century Tanzania' (unpublished PhD dissertation, University of Toronto, 1997)

Rockel, S. J., 'Relocating labor. Sources from the nineteenth century', *History in Africa*, 22 (1995), pp.447-54

Rockel, S. J., 'The roots of a nation. Integration in nineteenth-century Tanzania', *History and African Studies Series*, University of Natal, Pietermaritzburg (30 September 1998), pp.1-18

Rockel, S. J., 'Wage labor and the culture of porterage in nineteenth-century Tanzania. The central caravan route', *Comparative Studies of South Asia, Africa and the Middle East*, 15 (1995), pp.14-24

Roscoe, J., *The Baganda: an Account of their Native Customs and Beliefs* (London, 1911) and 2nd edn (London, 1965)

Roscoe, J., *The Banyankole* (London, 1911)

Roscoe, J., *Twenty Five Years in Uganda* (Cambridge, 1923)

Rowe, J., 'Islam Under Idi Amin: a case of déjà vu?', in H. Hansen and M. Twaddle (eds), *Uganda Now* (London, 1988), pp.267-79

Rowe, J., 'Revolution in Buganda 1856-1900. Part One: The reign of Mukabya Mutesa, 1856-1884' (unpublished PhD dissertation, University of Wisconsin, 1966)

Rusch, W., *Klassen und Staat in Buganda vor der Kolonialzeit* (Berlin, 1975)

Schoenbrun, D., *A Green Place, A Good Place: A Social History of the Great Lakes Region, Earliest Times to the 15th Century* (Portsmouth, NH, 1998)

Schoenbrun, D., *Comparative Vocabularies for Slavery, Vulnerability, Violence, and Social Standing in Great Lakes Bantu: Etymologies, Semantics, and Distributions* (Köln, in preparation)

Schoenbrun, D., 'Gendered histories between the Great Lakes: varieties and limits', *International Journal of African Historical Studies*, 29, 3 (1996), pp.461-92

Schoenbrun, D., 'Great Lakes Bantu: classification and settlement chronology', *Sprache und Geschichte in Afrika*, 15 (1994), pp.91-152

Schoenbrun, D., *The Historical Reconstruction of Great Lake Bantu Cultural Vocabulary: Etymologies and Distributions* (Köln, 1997)

Schweinfurth, G. et al., *Emin Pasha in Central Africa: Being A Collection of His Letters and Journals* (London, 1888)

Schweinitz, Graf H. von, *Deutsch-Ostafrika in Krieg und Frieden* (Berlin, 1894)

Seftel, A. (ed.), *Uganda: The rise and fall of Idi Amin* (Baileys African Photo Archives, Lanseria, South Africa, 1994)

Shaw, R., 'The production of witchcraft/witchcraft as production', *American Ethnologist*, 24, 4 (1997), pp.856-76

Sheriff, A. M. H., *Slaves, Spices and Ivory in Zanzibar. Integration of an East African Commercial Empire into the World Economy, 1770-1873* (London, 1987)

Shorter, A., 'Nyungu ya Mawe and the Empire of the Ruga-Ruga', *Journal of African History*, 9 (1968), pp.235-59

Sikainga, A. A., 'Military slavery and the emergence of a Southern Sudanese diaspora in the Northern Sudan, 1884-1954', in J. Spaulding and S. Beswick (eds), *White Nile, Black Blood; War, Leadership and Ethnicity from Kampala to Khartoum* (Asmara, Eritrea, and Lawrenceville, NJ, 2000).

Simpson, D. H. (ed.) 'A bibliography of Emin Pasha', *Uganda Journal*, 24 2, (1960), pp.138-65

Smalldone, J., *Warfare in the Sokoto Caliphate* (Cambridge, 1975)

Smith, C. S., *Explorations in the Zanzibar Dominions* (London, 1887)

Smith, I. R., *The Emin Pasha Relief Expedition, 1886-1890* (Oxford, 1972)

Smith, R. S., *Warfare and Diplomacy in Precolonial West Africa* (London, 1989)

Smith, R. S. and J. F. Ade Ajayi, *Yoruba Warfare in the Nineteenth Century* (Ibadan and Cambridge, 1971)

References

Soghayroun, I., *The Sudanese Muslim Factor in Uganda* (Khartoum, 1981)
Southall, A., 'General Amin and the coup: Great man or historical inevitability?' *Journal of Modern African Studies*, 13, 1, (1975), pp.83-105
Southall, A., 'Social disorganisation in Uganda before, during and after Amin', *Journal of Modern African Studies*, 18, 4, (1980), pp.627-36
Southwold, M., *Bureaucracy and Chiefship in Buganda: The Development of Appointive Office in the History of Buganda* (East African Studies No. 14. Kampala, n.d)
Southwold, M., 'Leadership, authority, and the village community,' in L. Fallers (ed.), *The King's Men* (New York, 1964), pp.211-55
Spear, T., 'Early Swahili history reconsidered', *International Journal of African Historical Studies*, 33, 2 (2000), pp.279-83
Speke, J., *Journal of the Discovery of the Source of the Nile* (London, 1863)
Spellig, F., 'Die Wanjamwezi. Ein Beitrag zur Völkerkunde Ostafrikas', *Zeitschrift für Ethnologie*, (1927/28), pp.201-41
Stampp, K., *The Peculiar Institution* (New York, 1956)
Stanley, H. M., *In Darkest Africa, or the Quest, Rescue, and Retreat of Emin, Governor of Equatoria* (London, 1890)
Stanley, H. M., *Through the Dark Continent* (London, 1878)
Stanley, R. and A. Neame (eds.), *The Exploration Diaries of H.M. Stanley* (New York, 1961)
Steckel, R., 'The African American population of the United States, 1790-1920', in M. Haines and R. Steckel (eds), *A Population History of North America* (Cambridge, 2000), pp.433-51
Steere, E., *Collections for a Handbook of the Nyamwezi Language as Spoken in Unyanyembe* (London, 1871)
Steinfeld, R. J., *The Invention of Free Labour: The Employment Relation in English and American Law and Culture* (Chapel Hill, NC, 1991)
Steinhart, E., *Conflict and Collaboration* (Princeton, NJ, 1977)
Steinhart, E., 'The kingdoms of the March', in J. B. Webster (ed.), *Chronology, Migration and Drought in Interlacuastrine Africa* (Halifax, 1979), pp.189-213
Stephens, R., 'Motherhood in Interlacustrine Africa, ca. 500-ca. 1500 CE: infertility, adoption, gender and marriage' (unpublished Seminar Paper, Northwestern University, 2003)
Steudel, E., 'Die ansteckenden Krankheiten der Karawanen Deutsch-Ostafrikas, ihre Verbreitung unter der übrigen Bevölkerung und ihre Bekämpfung', *Koloniales Jahrbuch 1894* (Berlin, 1895), pp.171-202
Stewart, F., *Honor* (Chicago, IL, 1994)
Stigand, Major C. H., *Equatoria, the Lado Enclave* (London, Bombay, Sydney, 1923)
Stuhlmann, F., *Mit Emin Pascha ins Herz von Afrika. Ein Reisebericht* (Berlin, 1894)
Sunseri, T., *Vilimani: Labor Migration and Rural Change in Early Colonial Tanzania* (Portsmouth, NH, 2002)
Swann, A. J., *Fighting the Slave Hunters in Central Africa. A Record of Twenty Six Years of Travel and Adventure round the Great Lakes and of the Overthrow of Tip-Pu-Tip, Rumaliza and Other Great Slave-Traders* (London, 1969 [first published 1910])
Sykes, C., *Service and Sport on the Tropical Nile* (London, 1903)
Tantala, R., 'The early history of Kitara in Western Uganda, process models of religious and political change' (unpublished PhD Dissertation, University of Wisconsin, Madison, 1989)
Taylor, C., *A Simplified Runyankore-Rikiga-English Dictionary* (Kampala, 1998)
Terray, E., 'Contribution à une étude de l'armée asante', *Cahiers d'Études Africaines* 16, 1-2 (1976), pp.297-356
Testart, A., *L'esclave, la dette et le pouvoir* (Paris, 2001)
Thomson, J., *Through Masai Land. A Journey of Exploration among the Snowclad Volcanic*

References

Mountains and Strange Tribes of Eastern Equatorial Africa. Being a Narrative of the Royal Geographical Society's Expedition, to Mount Kenia and Lake Victoria Nyanza, 1883-188 (London, 1885)

Thornton, J. K. *Africa and Africans in the Making of the Atlantic World, 1400-1800* (Cambridge, 1998)

Thornton, J. K., *Warfare in Atlantic Africa, 1500-1800* (London, 1999)

Thruston, A., *African Incidents* (London, 1900)

Tippu Tip (ed. and tr. by H. Brode), 'Autobiographie des Arabers Schech Hamed bin Muhammed el Murjebi, genannt Tippu Tip', *Mitteilungen des Seminars für orientalische Sprachen* (1902), pp.175-277

Tippu Tip, *Maisha ya Hamed bin Muhammed el Murjebi yaani Tippu Tip* (Nairobi, 1966)

Toeppen, K., 'Handel und Handelsverbindungen in Ostafrika', *Mitteilungen der Geographischen Gesellschaft in Hamburg*, (1885-86), pp.222-35

Tominaga, C., 'Indian immigrants and the East African slave trade', *Seri Ethnological Studies Osaka*, 43 (1996), pp.295-317

Tosh, J., *Clan Leaders and Colonial Chiefs in Lango: the Political History of an East African Stateless Society c. 1800-1939* (Oxford, 1978)

Traite des esclaves en Afrique. Renseignements et documents recueillis pour la Conférence de Bruxelles (1840-1890) (Brussels, 1890)

Tucker, A. R., *Eighteen Years in Uganda and East Africa* (Westport, CT, 1970 [1911])

Tuden, A. and L. Plotnicov, *Social Stratification in Africa* (New York, 1970)

Turney-High, H. H., *Primitive War* (New York, 1949)

Twaddle, M., *Kakungulu and the Creation of Uganda 1868-1928* (Athens, OH, 1993)

Twaddle, M., 'Muslim revolution in Buganda' *African Affairs*, 71 (1972), pp.54-72

Twaddle, M., 'Slaves and peasants in Buganda', in L. J. Archer (ed.), *Slavery and Other Forms of Unfree Labour* (London, 1988), pp.118-29

Twaddle, M., 'The emergence of politico-religious groupings in late nineteenth-century Buganda', *Journal of African History*, 29, 1 (1988), pp.81-92

Twaddle, M., 'The ending of slavery in Buganda', in S. Miers and R. Roberts (eds), *The End of Slavery in Africa* (Madison, WI, 1988), pp.119-49

Ullman, S., *Semantics: An Introduction to the Science of Meaning* (New York, 1979)

Unomah, A. C. and J. B. Webster, 'East Africa. The expansion of commerce', in J. E. Flint (ed.), *Cambridge History of Africa*, Vol. 5 (Cambridge, 1976), pp.270-318

Unomah, A. C., 'Economic expansion and political change in Unyanyembe, (1840 to 1900)', (unpublished PhD dissertation, University of Ibadan, 1972)

Uzoigwe, G., 'Kabaleega and the making of a new Kitara', *Tarikh*, 3, 2 (1970), pp.5-21

Uzoigwe, G. 'Precolonial markets in Bunyoro Kitara', *Comparative Studies in Society and History*, 14 (1972) pp.422-55

Uzoigwe, G., *Revolution and Revolt in Bunyoro-Kitara* (Kampala, 1971)

van Binsbergen, W., '"Then give him to the crocodiles", violence, state formation, and cultural discontinuity in west central Zambia, 1600-2000', in W. van Binsbergen (ed.), *The Dynamics of Power and the Rule of Law* (Leiden, 2003), pp.197-219

Van der Burgt, J.-M., *Dictionnaire français-kirundi* (Bois-le Duc, 1903)

Van Eetvelde, 'Rapport au roi, 25 January 1897', *Bulletin Officiel de l'Etat Indépendant du Congo* (1897), pp.47-9

Van Gennep, A., *The Rites of Passage* (transl. by M. B. Vizecom and G. L. Caffee, Chicago, IL, 1960)

Vandewoude, E. J. (ed.), *Documents relatifs à l'ancien district du Kivu* (Léopoldville, Section Documentation, Bureau Archives, 1959, N° 1 Instructions concernant territoires litigieux, 1900)

Vannutelli, V., *Beatificationis seu declarationis martyrii ven. servorum dei Caroli Lwanga, Matthiae Mulumba et sociorum vulgo "de Ouganda". In odium fidei, uti fertur, interfectorum. Positio super martyrio et signis* (Rome, 1918)

References

Vansina, J., *Antecedents to Modern Rwanda: The Nyiginya Kingdom* (Madison,WI, 2004)
Vansina, J., *Le Rwanda ancien. Le royaume nyinginya* (Paris, 2001)
Velten, C. (ed.), *Desturi za Wasuaheli na Khabari za Desturi za Sheri'a za Wasuaheli* (Göttingen, 1903)
Velten, C., 'Sitten und Gebräche der Suaheli', *Mitteilungen des Seminars für orientalische Sprachen. Afrikanische Studien I* (Berlin, 1898), pp.9-83
Vernet, T., 'Le commerce des esclaves sur la côte swahili, 1500-1750', *Azania*, 38 (2003), pp.69-97
Vernet, T., 'Les cités-états swahili de l'archipel de Lamu, 1585-1810' (unpublished PhD dissertation, Université Paris I, 2005)
Virmani, A. M., 'The resettlement of Ugandan refugees in Southern Sudan, 1919-86', (unpublished PhD dissertation, Field of Political Science, Northwestern University, Evanston, IL, 1996)
Von Trotha, L., *Meine Bereisung von Deutsch-Ostafrika* (Berlin, 1897)
Waller, R., 'The traditional economy of Buganda' (unpublished MA dissertation, University of London, School of Oriental and African Studies, 1971)
Walsh, L., 'The African American population of the colonial United States', in M. Haines and R. Steckel (eds), *A Population History of North America* (Cambridge, 2000), pp.197-208
Wikan, U., 'Shame and honour, a contestable pair', *Man*, New Series 19 (1984), pp.635-52
Willis, J., 'Clan and history in Western Uganda: a new perspective on the origins of the pastoral dominance', *The International Journal of African Historical Studies*, 3, 30 (1997), pp.583-600
Willis, J., 'Kinyoni and Kateizi, the contested origins of pastoral dominance in south-western Uganda', in J-P Chrétien and J-L Triaud (eds), *Histoire d'Afrique, les enjeux de memoire* (Paris, 1999), pp.119-36
Willis, J., 'The administration of Bonde 1920-60. A study of the implementation of indirect rule in Tanganyika', *African Affairs*, 92 (1993), pp.53-67
Willis, J., *Mombasa, the Swahili and the Making of the Mijikenda* (Oxford, 1993)
Willis, J. and S. Miers, 'Becoming a child of the house. Incorporation, authority and resistance in Giryama Society', *Journal of African History*, 38, 3 (1997), pp.479-95
Wilson, C. T. and R. W. Felkin, *Uganda and the Egyptian Soudan* (London, 1882)
Wissmann, H. von, 'Araberfrage und Sklavenhandel. Ein Vortrag', *Deutsche Kolonial-zeitung*, 1 (1888), p.352
Wood, L. J. and C. Ehret, 'The origins and diffusions of the market institution in East Africa', *Journal of African Studies*, 7 (1980), pp.1-17
Woodward, P. 'Uganda and Southern Sudan', in H. Hansen and M. Twaddle (eds), *Uganda Now* (London, 1988), pp.224-38
Wright, M., 'Women in peril: A commentary on the life stories of captives in nineteenth-century East-Central Africa', *African Social Research*, 20 (Dec. 1975), pp.800-19
Wright, M., *Strategies of Slaves and Women. Life-Stories from East/Central Africa* (New York, 1993)
Wright, M., *Buganda in the Heroic Age* (Nairobi, 1971)
Wrigley, C., *Crops and Wealth in Uganda: A Short Agrarian History* (Kampala, 1959)
Wrigley, C., *Kingship and State, the Buganda Dynasty* (Cambridge, 1996)
Zimbe, B. M., *Buganda ne Kabaka* (Mengo, 1939, typescript translation, 'Buganda and the King', Cambridge University Library)

Index

abolition (see also emancipation): 7, 19, 20, 234, 245, 247
Abyssinia (Ethiopia): 8, 10, 11, 50, 126, 148
Acholi: 19, 139, 241
adultery: 89
Alpers, E.: 2, 15
America: 20, 24, 79, 84, 116, 130, 192, 233, 234, 247
Ankole (see also Nkore):27, 189-209
Anttila, R.: 41
Arabs: 2, 3, 8, 12, 23, 84, 90, 112, 113, 115, 116, 117, 126, 127, 128, 129, 130, 131, 136, 140, 191, 198, 199, 204, 210, 212, 213, 215, 216, 217, 219, 222, 223, 225, 226, 227
Atlantic slavery: 15, 33, 56

Bagamoyo: 55, 82, 210, 217, 218
Baganda: see Buganda
Baha: see Buha
Bahaya: see Buhaya
Bairu: see Iru
bananas: 39, 83, 112, 162, 228
Banyoro: see Bunyoro
bashumba: 4, 12, 66, 192, 193, 194, 195, 196, 197, 204, 228
Basoga: see Soga
bazaana: 16, 43, 44, 45, 46, 49, 54, 67, 106, 147, 176, 195, 196, 197, 198, 199, 204, 205, 243
Baziba: see Kiziba
Bazinza: see Zinza
beads: 8, 53, 79, 80, 119, 222, 225, 226, 227, 241

Belgian Congo: 80, 119
Belgium: 111, 115, 118
Berlin Conference (1885): 114, 212
bridewealth: 16, 31, 65, 79, 85, 93, 94, 101, 112, 182, 194, 195, 197, 228, 233, 238, 240
Britain: 2, 3, 7, 11, 19, 23, 26, 84 98, 115, 117, 118, 119, 120, 124, 125, 126, 127, 131, 132, 133, 134, 135, 137, 178, 200, 212, 218, 232, 235, 241, 245, 246, 247, 248
Buganda: 1-37, 47, 48, 52, 55, 56, 59, 60, 61, 62, 63, 64, 65, 66, 67, 79, 81, 84, 143, 135, 137, 145-88, 191, 192, 198, 199, 200, 201, 202, 204, 218, 227, 231, 234, 235, 240, 241, 242, 245, 246
Buha: 3, 21, 60, 61, 63, 64, 65, 66, 83, 226, 228
Buhavu: 224
Buhaya: 11, 13, 14, 15, 16, 18, 19, 20, 21, 60, 63, 64, 65, 66, 67, 223, 225
Bukerebe: see Ukerewe
Bunyoro: 13, 19, 27, 52, 59, 60, 61, 62, 63, 64, 65, 66, 67, 155, 156, 159, 168, 231-51
Burton, R.: 78, 84, 85, 92, 95
Burundi: 2, 4, 5, 8, 11, 12, 14, 15, 17, 21, 22, 28, 30, 31, 32, 60, 61, 62, 63, 64, 66, 79, 83, 113, 189, 210-30
Bushi: see Shi
Bushiri: 126, 210
Busoga: see Soga
Busongora: 200, 242
Buvuma: 21, 155, 177

269

Index

Buzinza: see Zinza

caravans: 11, 12, 41, 63, 67, 77, 79, 80, 81, 82, 83, 84, 86, 87, 90, 95, 113, 114, 116, 167, 191, 199, 210, 214, 215, 216, 217, 218, 219, 220, 224, 225
Catholic Church and missions (see White Fathers and Mill Hill Fathers): 6, 7, 22, 23, 31, 116, 174, 210, 213, 214, 215, 216, 217, 218, 219, 221, 223, 227, 242
cattle: 4, 21, 25, 30, 39, 50, 63, 66, 78, 79, 80, 85, 86, 87, 97, 98, 112, 128, 129, 130, 133, 163, 178, 193, 194, 195, 197, 199, 200, 203, 204, 205, 216, 218, 222, 223, 224, 225, 228, 236, 237, 238, 239, 241, 242, 247
Christian missions: (see also Catholic missions and Protestant missions): 3, 6, 18, 50, 78, 85, 89, 114, 115, 131, 168, 191, 200, 201, 203, 204, 210, 234, 241
clientage: 15, 16, 17, 24, 25, 26, 27, 28, 29, 32, 41, 43, 44, 47, 49, 50, 52, 54, 55, 60, 62, 63, 66, 95, 96, 98, 99, 147, 175, 178, 179, 183, 186, 195, 196, 197, 205, 221, 222, 234, 236, 237, 238, 242, 243, 245, 247
cloth: 19, 53, 79, 80, 81, 90, 91, 112, 152, 169, 199, 216, 220, 222, 223, 224, 225, 226, 241
concubines: 15, 31, 131, 157, 166, 176, 179, 181
Congo basin: 114, 212, 213, 226
Congo Free State: 19, 111, 114, 124, 127, 131, 132, 210, 215, 226
Congo: 2, 10, 23, 32, 114, 117, 124, 136, 212, 213, 217, 218, 220, 226, 227
Cooper, F.: 7, 24
copper and brass: 8, 79, 80, 81, 159, 225
cowries: 112, 178, 199
credit: 41, 53, 54, 73, 81, 82, 88, 89, 94, 107, 132, 175, 176, 179, 183, 193, 196

day labourers: 12
dependent labour: 189, 191, 192, 198

Eastern Congo: 23, 82, 111-23
Egypt: 10, 26, 126, 127, 130, 131, 133, 231, 234, 241, 242, 245, 246
emancipation (see also abolition): 16, 30, 31, 68, 93, 108, 201, 220, 237, 238, 239, 243, 246, 247
Emin Pasha: 124, 130, 133, 135, 136, 200, 235, 242
Equatoria: 127, 128, 130, 234, 241
Europe: 3, 4, 5, 10, 11, 12, 16, 22, 24, 40, 59, 78, 79, 98, 111, 112, 114, 116, 117, 126, 132, 137, 151, 152, 185, 191, 200, 204, 210, 212, 214, 215, 216, 216, 217, 218, 219, 222, 234, 235, 236, 245, 246
execution: 16, 95, 133, 119, 148, 149, 151, 169, 197, 239

famine: 12, 18, 19, 56, 62, 77, 82, 88, 89, 94, 96, 216, 217, 221, 223, 224, 228, 246
fines: 28, 30, 41, 96, 118, 132
Finley, M.: 24, 25
Fipa: 63, 78, 79, 80, 81, 84
firearms: 19, 40, 79, 80, 53, 81, 85, 87, 88, 101, 104, 113, 126, 127, 128, 129, 132, 140, 142, 152, 157, 170, 178, 191, 199, 200, 212, 223, 231, 237, 238, 241, 248
followers: 18, 22, 54, 55, 56, 86, 87, 88, 90, 112, 127, 131, 139, 161-73, 177, 179, 180, 182, 183, 226, 231
food: 8, 12, 19, 53, 54, 66, 79, 80, 82, 83, 86, 91, 112, 116, 118, 119, 128, 129, 134, 139, 167, 181, 182, 192, 217, 221, 223, 224, 228, 242, 244
forced labour: 20, 25, 63, 111-23, 125, 132, 152, 195, 196, 201, 202, 203, 204

gendered labour: 47, 50, 193, 197, 227
Germany: 2, 3, 4, 7, 16, 19, 22, 23, 31, 60, 76, 78, 87, 94, 124, 126, 129, 130, 210-28
gift: 41, 45, 49, 60, 162, 168, 176, 179, 181, 183, 185, 192, 193, 194, 196, 228
Gisaka: 214, 216, 217, 222, 223, 224, 225
Glassmann, J.: 15, 55
goats: 8, 181, 232, 225, 240
grain: 39, 43, 50, 78, 79, 83

Harms, R.: 233
Hartwig, G.: 4, 7, 12, 13, 15, 17, 21, 24, 56, 235
Haya: 11, 13, 14, 15, 16, 18, 19, 20, 21,

Index

60, 63, 64, 65, 66, 223, 225
Hima: 23, 25, 32, 59, 157, 189, 191, 193, 194, 195, 196, 197, 198, 200, 201, 202, 203, 204, 205, 219, 236, 237, 242
hippopotamus teeth: 79
Hirth, J. J.: 213, 214, 215, 217, 218, 219, 220, 221, 225, 227
hoe: 8, 79, 80, 91, 92, 129, 223, 227
Hugo, V.: 41
Huma: see Hima
human sacrifice: 28, 152, 165
Hutu: 5, 12, 23, 32, 44, 59, 225, 227

Iliffe, J.: 4, 36, 48, 54
Imperial British East African Company: 124, 130, 131, 246
indenture: 50, 65, 147, 192, 194, 195
indentured labour: 50, 192, 194, 195
India: 79, 81, 82, 84, 102, 113, 210, 219
inheritance: 15, 23, 25, 27, 28, 40, 41, 53, 90, 93, 94, 119, 154, 175, 176, 179, 183, 184, 238, 239
Iru: 23, 32, 43, 44, 46, 59, 62, 70, 189, 191, 194, 195, 197, 198, 200, 201, 203, 204, 205, 207, 236, 240, 243
Islam: 3, 18, 19, 23, 24, 80, 82, 117, 124, 125, 126, 127, 130, 131, 133, 134, 135, 136, 137, 139, 140, 213, 214, 219, 226, 227, 229, 231, 242, 245, 246, 248
ivory: 8, 10, 11, 17, 79, 80, 81, 82, 85, 86, 87, 88, 90, 97, 113, 114, 116, 117, 118, 126, 127, 129, 132, 140, 161, 163, 166, 167, 172, 191, 199, 213, 218, 219, 223, 224, 231, 241

Kaggwa, A.: 28, 163, 164, 168
Kamba: 10, 13
Karagwe: 10, 11, 17, 21, 81, 214, 215, 217, 219, 236
Katanga: 8, 63, 80, 82, 84
Katoke: 222
Kazeh: see Tabora
Kenya: 2, 8, 10, 23, 131
kidnapping: 12, 14, 23, 64, 85, 88, 139, 160, 176, 177, 178, 139, 227, 238, 239
Kimbu: 78
Kiswahili: 63, 65, 67, 79, 80, 81, 86, 134, 213
Kiwanuka, M.S.M.: 161, 167
Kiziba: 11, 60, 63, 66, 67
Kooki: 18, 19, 61

Kopytoff, I.: 24, 26, 27, 41, 51, 57

labour: 4, 25, 39, 49, 50, 58, 63, 65, 76, 82, 83, 84, 89, 92, 98, 125, 135, 147, 150, 162, 164, 166, 167, 171, 186, 191, 194, 199, 201, 202, 204, 228, 231, 235, 236, 247
Lake Albert: 2, 20, 26, 117, 124, 126, 130, 132, 133
Lake Edward: 2
Lake Kivu: 2, 60, 117, 210, 212, 213, 215, 216, 222, 224, 225
Lake Kyoga: 2
Lake Tanganyika: 2, 6, 10, 21, 78, 79, 80, 81, 82, 84, 87, 113, 114, 117, 118, 199, 210, 212, 213, 218, 222, 226, 227, 228
Lake Victoria: 2, 4, 6, 10, 21, 22, 39, 43, 46, 50, 78, 79, 81, 87, 162, 212, 216, 235
Lango: 19, 241
Lendu: 26, 131
Léopold II: 111, 114, 115, 117, 124, 132, 210, 212, 213
Livingstone, D.: 5, 91, 112
Lovejoy, P.: 7, 15, 16, 32, 56, 57, 175, 179, 185
Lugard, F.: 131, 133, 200, 246
Lunyoro: see Bunyoro
Lusoga: see Soga

Makerere: 128, 137, 138
Manning, P.: 14
Manyema: 11, 31, 82, 84, 199
marriage: 6, 16, 27, 30, 31, 48, 53, 55, 78, 86, 93, 94, 98, 127, 174, 177, 179, 180, 181, 182, 185, 195, 200, 231, 233, 234, 240, 243, 244
Meillassoux, C.: 4, 58, 232, 233, 243
Miers S.: 14, 24, 27, 41, 51, 57, 98
migration: 2, 78, 218, 231, 235, 246, 247
Mill Hill Fathers: 6, 174, 176, 177, 180, 181
Mount Elgon: 10
Mrima: 12, 15, 55
Muganda: see Buganda
Muiru: see Iru
Mulira, E.M.K.: 8, 175, 176, 185
Mumia: 10
Musoga: see Soga
muzaana: see *bazaana*

Ngoni: 22, 85

271

Index

Nile: 8, 10, 11, 13, 32, 112, 113, 118, 124, 128, 130, 131, 132, 134, 232, 235, 245, 246
Nkore: 3, 4, 11, 12, 13, 14, 15, 18, 19, 21, 22, 25, 31, 51, 52, 60, 61, 62, 63, 64, 65, 66, 67, 189-209, 236
Nyamwezi: 7, 8, 10, 11, 12, 14, 15, 19, 21, 25, 31, 32, 44, 50, 63, 76-110, 113, 212, 214, 218, 225, 226, 227

Oberg, K.: 189, 191

patronage: (see clientage)
Patterson O.: 48, 193, 204, 205
pawnship: 29, 52, 53, 54, 61, 74, 89, 90, 98, 175, 176, 179, 183, 196, 239
plantation slavery: 8, 20, 24, 82, 84, 114, 116, 117, 233, 242
porterage: 79, 80, 81, 82, 83, 85, 93, 94, 95, 114, 117, 118, 119, 120, 126, 127, 129, 155, 176, 201, 202, 218, 219, 225
Protestant Church and missions: 4, 5, 6, 19, 22, 23, 90, 164, 201, 210, 212, 213, 236

railway: 82, 136
Renault, F.: 5, 7, 8, 12
rice: 63, 73, 83, 116, 117
Richards, A.: 3
Roscoe J.: 4, 155, 179, 181, 236, 238, 242
Rowe, J.: 161
rubber: 115, 116, 117, 118, 120, 224
runaway slaves: 15, 29, 30; 89, 92, 95, 97, 98
Rusubi: see Ussuwi
Rwanda: 2, 3, 5, 6, 8, 10, 11, 12, 13, 14, 15, 17, 19, 21, 22, 27, 28, 30, 31, 44, 47, 59, 60, 61, 62, 63, 64, 65, 66, 67, 79, 113, 189, 199, 210-30, 236
Rwenzori: 44, 64

Sabaki: 45, 63, 64, 67
salt: 8, 79, 80, 81, 181, 226, 227
serfs: 24, 66, 191, 236
servile labour: 191, 193, 205, 244
sesame: 167
sheep: 130
Shi (Bushi): 59, 60, 62, 63, 64, 216, 217, 222, 224, 226
slave children: 15, 16, 21, 23, 28, 84, 85, 86, 88, 92, 93, 94, 96, 116, 127, 128, 129, 130, 131, 132, 139, 157, 175, 179, 181,182, 197, 215, 219, 220, 221, 223, 224, 225, 226, 227, 228, 232, 233, 238, 241; (boys: 23, 29, 30, 90, 91, 94, 133, 200, 216, 219, 221, 226, 228, 240); (girls: 28, 93, 178, 183, 184, 197, 215, 216, 219, 221, 223, 226, 227, 240, 243)
slave labour: 8, 25, 57, 97, 111-23, 176, 179, 233, 234, 239, 240, 243
slave mortality: 89, 129, 88, 89, 112, 118, 128, 133, 199, 241, 243
slave prices and exchange commodities: 8, 30, 53, 79, 84, 85, 86, 90, 91, 92, 98, 112, 126, 157, 178, 221, 216, 219, 221, 222, 223, 224, 227, 228, 241, 248
slave wives (see also concubines): 23, 31, 84, 93, 94, 95, 96, 98, 112, 120, 133, 166, 168, 176, 180, 181, 182, 184, 224, 231, 233, 235, 238, 239, 243, 243, 244
Smith, R.: 148, 149, 150
social death: 39, 48, 91, 193, 205, 220
Soga: 10, 13, 14, 17, 18, 19, 20, 21, 25, 29, 48, 61, 63, 66, 155, 165, 168, 177, 179, 181, 183, 184
Somali: 11, 126, 133
Southall, A.: 136, 137
Speke, J.H.: 10, 235, 241
Stanley H.M.: 5, 114, 130, 155, 200, 212
Stanleyville/Kisangani: 112, 113, 114, 116, 117
Sudan/Egyptian Sudan: 2, 5, 6, 8, 10, 11, 12, 13, 22, 31, 32, 117, 124, 125, 126, 127, 128, 129, 130, 131, 132, 133, 136, 137, 138, 139, 241
Sudanese slave soldiers/community: 3, 11, 19, 20, 21, 23, 24, 26, 124-44, 241, 246
sugar cane plantation: 125
Sukuma: 22, 65, 70, 78, 87, 218
Sumbwa: 11, 63, 65, 78, 199, 214, 217, 222, 223, 225, 226, 227
Swahili coast/Indian ocean coast: 5, 6, 7, 8, 10, 12, 13, 15, 22, 23, 32, 39, 45, 46, 49, 50, 52, 54, 55,56, 57, 58, 59, 61, 67, 78, 79, 80, 81, 83, 84, 85, 86, 87, 90, 92, 93, 94, 95, 114, 130, 186, 191, 199, 210, 212, 213, 214, 217, 218, 231
Swahili trade and traders: 5, 7, 10, 11, 12, 13, 14, 15, 19, 21, 22, 23, 31, 32,

Index

50, 85, 111, 112, 113, 115, 116, 117, 119, 127, 157, 190, 198, 199, 204, 210, 213, 216, 217, 219, 222, 225, 227, 241

Tabora: 5, 12, 16, 63, 76, 77, 78, 81, 82, 83, 84, 86, 87, 90, 93, 95, 102, 212, 215, 217, 218, 220, 226
Tanganyika: 2, 7, 78, 80, 82, 126, 131, 219
Tanzania: 2, 5, 6, 8, 10, 12, 22, 55, 138
taxes: 20, 80, 81, 86, 94, 118, 120, 125, 132, 135, 165, 201, 202, 203, 204, 212, 225, 234, 239
Thornton, J.: 7, 15, 32, 56, 57
Tippu Tip: 82, 111, 113, 114, 116
tobacco: 78, 80, 98, 223
Toro/Tooro: 14, 17, 19, 20, 21, 240 242
tribute labour: 168
tribute: 17, 49, 60, 86, 119, 162, 163, 164, 168, 201, 236, 237
Tutsi (Tuutsi): 5, 12, 23, 32, 44, 59, 78, 219, 221, 227, 229
Twaddle, M.: 1, 6, 7, 16, 31, 151, 161, 167, 175, 176, 177, 179, 180, 201

Ugogo: 80, 85
Ujiji: 12, 79, 81, 82, 83, 84, 95, 113, 114, 212, 213, 226
Ukerewe: 4, 7, 10, 11, 12, 13, 14, 15, 17, 20, 21, 22, 24, 25, 30, 32, 46, 56, 60, 61, 63, 64, 66, 67
unfree labour: 4, 12, 63, 111-23, 125, 161, 166, 167, 168, 170, 239, 242
unpaid labour: 192, 193, 195, 196, 201, 202, 204, 240
Unyanyembe: 50, 78, 96, 97, 98, 114, 212, 213
Upper Congo: 112, 113, 126, 216
Ushirombo: 212, 222
Ussuwi: 11, 14, 17, 21, 22, 214, 215, 217, 222, 223, 225

Vansina, J.: 14, 21, 65

wage labour: 50, 82, 83, 119, 120, 127, 162, 202
warlord: 18, 19, 32, 82, 87, 97
West Africa: 16, 23, 24, 148, 149, 183, 185, 247
White Fathers (see also Catholic Church and missions): 5, 6, 12, 16, 22, 29, 31, 210, 212, 213, 218, 219, 222, 223, 225, 226
Willis, J.: 14, 98,
witchcraft: 17, 89
Wright, Marcia: 15, 55
Wright, Michael: 169, 171
Wrigley, C.:14

Zaire: 124, 129, 136, 137, 138
Zanzibar: 2, 8, 10, 12, 21, 38, 51, 77, 79, 81, 84, 95, 111, 112, 113, 114, 212, 220, 226
Zinza: 11, 15, 17, 20, 22, 50, 66, 67, 78, 223, 224, 225

www.ingramcontent.com/pod-product-compliance
Lightning Source LLC
Chambersburg PA
CBHW031237290426
44109CB00012B/327